SOCIAL CHANGE AND INNOVATION
IN THE LABOUR MARKET

Social Change and Innovation in the Labour Market

*Evidence from the Census SARs on Occupational Segregation
and Labour Mobility, Part-Time Work and Student Jobs,
Homework and Self-Employment*

CATHERINE HAKIM

OXFORD UNIVERSITY PRESS
1998

Oxford University Press, Great Clarendon Street, Oxford OX2 6DP

Oxford New York

Athens Auckland Bangkok Bogota Bombay
Buenos Aires Calcutta Cape Town Dar es Salaam
Delhi Florence Hong Kong Istanbul Karachi
Kuala Lumpur Madras Madrid Melbourne
Mexico City Nairobi Paris Singapore
Taipei Tokyo Toronto Warsaw

and associated companies in
Berlin Ibadan

Oxford is a trade mark of Oxford University Press

Published in the United States
by Oxford University Press Inc., New York

British Library Cataloguing in Publication Data
Data available

Library of Congress Cataloging in Publication Data
Hakim, Catherine.
Social change and innovation in the labour market:
evidence from the census SARs on occupational segregation
and labour mobility, part-time work and student jobs, homework
and self-employment / Catherine Hakim.
Includes bibliographical references.
1. Labor market—Great Britain.   I. Title.
HD5765.A6H33   1998   331.12'0941—dc21   97–44853
ISBN 0–19–829381–X

1 3 5 7 9 10 8 6 4 2

Typeset by Hope Services (Abingdon) Ltd.
Printed in Great Britain
on acid-free paper by
Biddles Ltd.,
Guildford & King's Lynn

For WRH

ACKNOWLEDGEMENTS

The SARs research project on which this book is based was funded by ESRC research grant No. 235974. Access to the SARs files was provided by courtesy of the ESRC/JISC/DENI programme which arranged for the creation of these valuable research datasets, which remain Crown Copyright. I am indebted to the Census Microdata Unit at Manchester University for help with accessing the SARs and for providing documentation on the files. I thank the Computing Service staff both at Manchester and at the LSE for assistance with processing these enormous datasets. I thank the OECD for supplying unpublished comparative analyses on part-time work used in Fig. 2.

The following appear in this book by permission:

Fig. 1 reprinted from *Employment in Europe 1995* (1995), by permission of the European Commission.

Tables 1.3, 1.5, 1.6, and 1.7 reprinted from Hakim, 'Segregated and integrated occupations: a new approach to analysing social change', *European Sociological Review* (December 1993), by permission of Oxford University Press.

Table 2.12 reprinted from Hakim, 'A century of change in occupational segregation 1891–1991', *Journal of Historical Sociology* (December 1994), by permission of Blackwell.

CONTENTS

LIST OF FIGURES

LIST OF TABLES

LIST OF CASES

ABBREVIATIONS

BHPS	British Household Panel Study
BSAS	British Social Attitudes Survey
CPS	Current Population Survey (of the USA)
DI	Dissimilarity Index
EC	European Commission
ECJ	European Court of Justice
EOC	Equal Opportunities Commission
ESRC	Economic and Social Research Council
EU	European Union
EUROSTAT	Statistical Office of the European Communities
FES	Family Expenditure Survey
GHS	General Household Survey
GROS	General Register Office Scotland
ILO	International Labour Office (of the United Nations)
ISCO	International Standard Classification of Occupations (of the ILO)
ISEI	International Socio-Economic Index (of occupational status)
LFS	Labour Force Survey
NCDS	National Child Development Study (1958 cohort study)
nec	not elsewhere classified (in the occupational classification)
NES	New Earnings Survey
NLS	National Longitudinal Surveys (of Labour Market Behaviour)
NTS	National Travel Survey
NUS	National Union of Students
OECD	Organisation for Economic Co-operation and Development
ONS	Office for National Statistics
OOPEC	Office for Official Publications of the European Communities
OPCS	Office of Population Censuses and Surveys (England and Wales)
PSID	Panel Study of Income Dynamics
PUMF	Public Use Microdata Files (of the Canadian Population Census)
PUS	Public Use Sample (of the USA Population Census)
RG	Registrar-General (of England and Wales)
SAR	Sample of Anonymised Records

SCELI	Social Change and Economic Life Initiative (ESRC research programme)
SEG	Socio-Economic Group
SIOPS	Standard International Occupational Prestige Scale
SOC	Standard Occupational Classification (of Great Britain)
TTWA	Travel To Work Area
UK	United Kingdom (Great Britain plus Northern Ireland)
USA	United States of America
WES	Women and Employment Survey

Abbreviations used in tables

—	no cases in this cell
..	data not available/not collected
~	too few cases for calculation to be made
*	less than 0.5%
FT	full-time
PT	part-time
M	males, men
F	females, women
T	total/all persons
S/E	self-employed

1

Introduction

Nothing stands still. We are aware that the labour market is in constant flux, expanding and contracting with the economic cycle. But like other institutions it is also in a continual process of change and renewal, adapting to new technology and other social and economic innovations, so that the composition and character of jobs and workers do not stand still. These changes are concealed by the highly standardized way in which national statistics are collected and published, and by the fixed concepts, of employment and a job, on which they rest. Labour market statistics have their rigidities too. It is only when researchers gain access to microdata from the large national datasets that we can begin to discover the changes and innovations hidden behind the smooth continuities of official statistics. The release of the 1% and 2% Samples of Anonymised Records from the British 1991 Census provided a golden opportunity to do just this. This book presents the results. As expected, it offers many surprises.

LABOUR MARKET RESTRUCTURING AND SOCIAL CHANGE

While the dataset is British, the labour market issues addressed in the analysis pertain to all advanced industrial societies. They include some of the most topical questions that are currently the focus of research in Europe, the USA, and other countries. Changing patterns of work commitment, the redistribution of employment between full-time and part-time workers, changes in the sexual division of labour, innovations in the organization of working time, and changes in work organization are contributing to substantial changes in the nature of work and employment in the 1990s and beyond that into the 21st century (Gladstone, 1992; Howard, 1995; Hakim, 1996a; Crompton, Gallie, and Purcell, 1996). Some argue that employment itself and the standard job offering lifetime employment are disappearing, to be replaced by the 'portfolio' job combining self-employment, fixed-term contracts, multiple part-time jobs, and home-based work (Handy, 1984, 1994). Others believe that the current disruption of well-established structures and labour market processes are a temporary aberration, brought about by repeated recessions and decades of high unemployment, and look forward to a return to the status quo ante as soon as the economy starts to grow again.

While opinion is divided over the longevity of current turbulence, there is greater agreement on the significance of certain developments. This study addresses several innovations in the labour market resulting from wider social change:

- the social and economic consequences of the feminization of the workforce, including changes in patterns of employment and labour mobility and changes in occupational segregation, in particular the growth of integrated occupations employing both men and women;
- the growth of part-time work and its consequential diversification into several types of job, recruiting not only female prime-age workers but also other new groups on the margins of the workforce, and permitting a gradual process of labour market entry and labour market exit among young people and older workers;
- the emergence of a new pattern of part-time work combined with education as the norm among the majority of full-time students from the age of 16 onwards, as a result of the transition to a mass education system;
- the sudden renewal and resurgence of two forms of 'non-standard' work that, not long ago, many believed to be almost extinct in northern Europe and the USA—homework and self-employment;
- and the polarization of the female workforce in rich modern societies.

Finally, we explore the connections between these changes in the labour market.

BRITAIN AS A CASE STUDY

In many respects Britain provides the ideal strategic case study, as the relatively unregulated labour market permits a rapid pace of change and presents fewer barriers to innovations in work organization (both good and bad). Compared to other European countries, there is a remarkable absence of statute law controlling and regulating the labour market. For example, there have never been any general laws forbidding Sunday work, specifying annual holiday entitlement, or maximum daily work hours. A hairdresser and a carpenter are not obliged to hold qualifications or a licence before starting work. Britain often appears to be a case of unregulated chaos and anarchy in the eyes of the European Commission. In reality, common law, collective bargaining, and the social conventions called 'custom and practice' combine to produce much the same pattern of order and regulation of the labour market as found elsewhere in Europe (Gladstone, 1992; Hepple and Hakim, 1997), but on a much more flexible basis than with statute law in other European countries (Blanpain and Rojot, 1997). This is amply demonstrated by the much earlier development of part-time work in Britain than in the rest of Europe (Hakim, 1993*a*, 1997; Blossfeld and Hakim, 1997). In most European countries, statute law had to be changed first before part-time jobs could legitimately be created, and the innovation was inevitably structured and constrained by new statute law rather than developing in a haphazard and varied manner as it did in Britain from 1950 onwards, with the speed of change determined by social and economic factors, by the employers and workers most immediately involved, rather than by labour lawyers and politicians. The results of this unfettered growth are analysed in Chapter 5, which reveals a greater diversity of part-time jobs in Britain than is found elsewhere in Europe (see Fig. 5.1).

Change and innovation can happen more easily in Britain, unconstrained by regulations, whether good or bad. Britain can almost be regarded as a kind of ongoing natural experiment, a situation that was reinforced by the insistently *laissez-faire* policies of the Conservative government from 1979 to 1997. Theory attempts to formulate what happens all other things being equal, that is, in the absence of major constraints limiting choice or forcing choice in particular directions. So the British case provides a theoretically important case study of labour market processes and innovations in a period of economic restructuring.

THE 1991 CENSUS 1% AND 2% SARS

The 1991 Population Census of Great Britain represents a milestone for social scientists in that it was the first to allow researchers access to anonymous samples of microdata for 1% and 2% samples of the population, and hence for 1% and 2% samples of the labour force. Such files have long been available to researchers in the USA and Canada, where they are called Public Use Samples (PUS) and Public Use Microdata Files (PUMF) respectively. The Economic and Social Research Council (ESRC) persuaded the Office of Population Censuses and Surveys (now part of the Office of National Statistics) to create the census extract tapes and paid for the work. The ESRC also funds the Census Microdata Unit (CMU) at Manchester University to disseminate the tapes, provide documentation, and enhance the research value of the data with additions, such as earnings proxy data for employees from the New Earnings Survey (NES), the Goldthorpe class schema, occupational status and prestige scales, and socio-economic area indicators and classifications (see Annex A).

Before this, analysis of the British population census data was restricted to the aggregate statistics contained in published reports and other outputs. Admittedly, these provided the basis for a vast range of research work (Hakim, 1982). However, access to the 1% and 2% Samples of Anonymised Records (SARs) makes a qualitative difference to the types of analysis that can be undertaken. The potential for new kinds of research work is huge. At the same time, the novelty of the dataset poses its own problems, especially as there has been only limited documentation on the new census files. Features of the dataset that might be pitfalls for the unwary can also represent opportunities for the innovator who identifies their full scope and potential. Just one example is the extensive retrospective labour market data in the 1991 Census microdata, which was not clearly identified or documented by the Census Office or by the CMU, which was not analysed in the published census reports, and emerged unannounced in SAR analyses on the occupational structure (Hakim, 1995a). The census retrospective data is used extensively in this book in analyses of labour turnover. This book provides an important supplement to official census reports on the labour force.

The SARs contain microdata: individual level responses to the 1991 Census, with unique identifiers removed in order to protect the confidentiality of respondents. Names and addresses are never entered into the computer files of census results, so they are anonymous right from the start. The sampling process itself further anonymizes the SAR files. However, some items of information are deleted, or truncated, to anonymize the SARs yet further before they are released for research analysis in the academic community. The labour market data available is very limited, consisting of coded responses to eight 1991 Census questions on economic activity status; whether someone was currently doing paid work or had any paid work in the preceding ten years; occupation; industry; hours worked per week in the main job; distance to workplace; means of transport for daily journey to work; and details of any post-secondary level degrees, professional and vocational qualifications. The labour market data is of course supplemented by information on age, sex, household, and housing characteristics.

There are important differences between the two SARs, which were selected separately, with no overlapping cases, from the census 10% sample with fully coded data. The 2% SAR provides a sample of individuals in households and in communal establishments, over 1.1 million individual records in total. Because of its larger size, many of the variables are available only at an aggregated level. The 1% SAR is a hierarchical file of some 200,000 households, with full information on household characteristics and on all the members of the household, 540,000 people in total. It permits relationships between household members to be studied and includes some variables not available in the 2% SAR, in particular a number of derived variables based on occupation coding. The 1% SAR also contains the most detailed classifications of key labour market variables, such as occupation (with 358 occupational categories), industry (185 categories), and subject of higher education qualifications (88 categories). The 2% SAR contains broader classifications of occupation (73 categories), industry (60 categories), and subject of higher education qualifications (35 categories).

From the point of view of the labour market analyst, the design of the SARs is not ideal. Because its larger size makes it more useful for studies of small subgroups in the labour market, such as working students or men with part-time jobs, the 2% SAR would normally be the preferred dataset. However, many of the key variables of interest to the labour market analyst have been placed in the 1% SAR rather than in the 2% SAR. As a result both SARs have to be used throughout this study. As a general rule, the 2% SAR was chosen for its larger sample: roughly 700,000 people of working age (16–64 years) of whom half a million are in work. The 1% SAR is smaller, about 340,000 people of working age of whom one-quarter of a million are in work. Because certain variables are only available in the 1% SAR, in particular essential labour market variables, the 1% SAR is used where necessary, although its smaller size can be restrictive. The analyses in Chapters 3 and 9 rely exclusively on the 1% SAR, as the key variables are available only in that file. Other chapters generally rely on the 2% SAR. This means there is a small overlap, between Chapters 2 and 3 for example, when some analyses have to be repeated on the two files separately. Most of the analyses were in fact run twice, with both SARs, with virtually identical results on labour market topics. Where there are differences in the results, this is usually due to the fact that they employ classifications with different levels of detail, as illustrated by Table 2.1. On other topics, such as ethnicity, there may be more noticeable differences between the two SARs. Labour market specialists are in the happy position of being able to choose freely between the two datasets according to the level of detail required in the labour market variables, and even to use them interchangeably and in combination, as we do here.

The 1991 Census covered almost as restrictive a range of topics as in the 1981 Census, and far fewer than in the 1971 Census (Hakim, 1982). The ESRC's Census Microdata Unit has enhanced the value of the SARs by adding information from other sources as well as creating extra derived variables. For labour market analysts, the most important of these additions is estimated earnings for each employee in the SAR samples. Earnings estimates are taken from the 1991 New Earnings Survey (NES) and refer to average hourly earnings in pence excluding any overtime pay. Because the NES does not provide information on the earnings of self-employed people, no earnings estimates were added to the records of the self-employed in the SARs. Students with a current or previous job were also assigned NES earnings estimates, but all of these cases are classified as people not currently in work in the SAR files. Annex A provides further details.

In addition to data imported from other government sources, the SARs contain derived variables used by academic social scientists. The four most important are Goldthorpe's class schema, and three continuous measures of occupational status and occupational prestige: the Cambridge occupational status scale, the International Socio-Economic Index (ISEI) of occupational status (Ganzeboom *et al.*, 1992), and Treiman's Standard International

Occupational Prestige Scale (SIOPS) (Treiman, 1977). These variables are described further in Annex A and are employed in Chapter 3.

It can be seen that the SAR files combine the advantages of large nationally representative census samples with features that are more commonly found in academic surveys.

The 1% and 2% SARs are much smaller samples than are presented in the published census statistics, but they still offer the advantages of all census data. First, the SARs provide nationally representative statistics on the working age population and on all subgroups within it, including subgroups that are hopelessly tiny in ordinary 'national' datasets—such as working students, men with part-time jobs, the self-employed, and home-based workers—subgroups that provide the subject matter for chapters of this book. Second, tests of statistical significance become redundant with census samples: all observable differences between subgroups, however small, are reliable and easily satisfy the usual tests of statistical significance. This is very obviously the case for census 10% sample statistics, but it is also true of the 1% and 2% SARs. In several cases where group differences of only 1 percentage point were observed, tests of statistical significance invariably showed the results to be statistically significant (i.e. reliable) at the 5% level and almost always showed them to be significant at the 0.1% level or the 0.01 level or beyond that. In effect, *all* the results presented in this book are statistically significant, that is, not due to sampling variation. Discussion of the results thus focuses on the *substantive* importance of findings and on the *size* of effects rather than the adequacy of the sample. Third, the census SARs are large enough to allow us to study very small labour market subgroups in as much detail as the available variables permit. This is the key advantage exploited by the present study. For example, in Chapter 5 we are able to identify the characteristics of people working in 'marginal' jobs and how they differ from people working in the more conventional 'half-time' jobs. Chapter 9 presents a national case study of pharmacists, an occupational group that constitutes just 0.1% of the workforce in Britain.

All tables in this report based on SAR analyses present data for the resident population of working age (16–64 years) in Great Britain, or for subgroups of this population. Some analyses cover everyone who reported a current or last occupation (including student jobs); other analyses cover people in employment only, that is, current jobs excluding student jobs. Tables extracted from published census reports usually cover a wider age group: the resident population in employment aged 16 and over or 18 and over and, as noted in Chapter 6, student jobs are sometimes included and sometimes excluded from the employment count.

A NEW TYPOLOGY OF SEX-SEGREGATED AND INTEGRATED
OCCUPATIONS

The new 1% and 2% SARs provide the main dataset employed for this study, supplemented in places by data from the main government statistical surveys such as the Labour Force Survey (LFS), General Household Survey (GHS), and NES (Hakim, 1982). Published census statistics are also analysed as an essential preliminary stage to many SAR analyses. The published census statistics consist of 100% counts and 10% sample results, easily dwarfing statistics from the 1% and 2% SARs and providing far more reliable and detailed data on certain topics than the SARs could ever provide. In particular, the new classification of sex-segregated and integrated occupations employed throughout the study was based on an analysis of the published 10% sample statistics on the occupational structure that was carried out before commencing the SAR analyses.

The classification of occupations into three types: male-dominated, female-dominated, and integrated (or mixed) occupations (Table 1.1), rather than into just two groups (male and female occupations), follows a new theoretical and methodological framework for the analysis of occupational segregation presented in detail in Hakim (1993*b*) and developed further in Chapter 2. In brief, single number indices of occupational segregation, such as the popular Dissimilarity Index (Table 1.2) and the Marginal Matching Index recently espoused by the International Labour Office (Siltanen, Jarman, and Blackburn, 1995), are rejected[1] in favour of a more informative mapping of women's position in the occupational structure and the pattern of occupational segregation. The Dissimilarity Index (DI) and other single number indices only take a value of zero when there is an absolutely uniform

---

[1] Despite being adopted by the ILO, the Marginal Matching Index (Blackburn, Siltanen, and Jarman, 1995) has attracted just as much criticism (Lampard, 1994; Watts, 1994, forthcoming) as all the other single number measures of occupational segregation (James and Taeuber, 1985; Hakim, 1992*a*: 130–3; Watts, 1993). Another margin-free measure has recently been proposed by Charles and Grusky (1995) for cross-national comparisons. Because all the single number measures are related, logically and mathematically, they produce roughly the same results in practice (Rubery and Fagan, 1993: 31) and share the same substantive and methodological weaknesses. For example, they are useless in studying vertical segregation, which is far more important than horizontal segregation (Hakim, 1979: 27–9; 1996*a*: 149–52) and is slowly being recognized as the only issue for public policy (European Commission, 1994*d*: 42). Our conclusion, from extensive reviews of the literature (Hakim, 1979, 1992*a*, 1993*b*), is that all single number indices are simply not very informative as to what is happening when there is any change, are useless for studying vertical occupational segregation, and are hugely sensitive to the occupational classification used, as well as being technically flawed in one way or another. Similarly, Rubery (1988: 14) concluded that single number measures provide a poor basis for cross-national comparisons because differences between countries in the occupational and industry classifications used greatly affect scores on single number indices.

TABLE 1.1. *The pattern of occupational segregation in Britain,*
1991

No. of occupations	Type of occupation	All	Men	Women
All economically active				
371	Male	42	67	9
	Integrated	18	19	16
	Female	40	14	75
78	Male	40	63	9
	Integrated	22	23	21
	Female	38	14	70
10	Male	26	38	9
	Integrated	42	45	39
	Female	32	17	52
Full-time employees				
371	Male	48	68	11
	Integrated	17	17	17
	Female	35	15	72
78	Male	44	63	11
	Integrated	23	22	23
	Female	33	15	66
10	Male	28	37	11
	Integrated	42	44	39
	Female	30	19	50
Part-time employees				
371	Male	7	37	4
	Integrated	8	17	7
	Female	85	46	89
78	Male	8	34	5
	Integrated	10	17	9
	Female	82	49	86
10	Male	6	18	5
	Integrated	37	43	36
	Female	57	39	59
Base=100%	all economically active	2525	1440	1086
000s	full-time employees	1635	1046	589
	part-time employees	423	44	80

Note: In this table, part-time status is self-defined.

Source: 1991 Census, Great Britain, 10% sample data for residents aged 16 and over reported in table 4, *Economic Activity* report.

sex ratio in every single occupational group in the workforce.[2] This is clearly unrealistic, allowing for no element of random variation in the processes that

[2] The Dissimilarity Index is half the sum (weighted or unweighted) of the absolute differences between the male and female coefficients of representation in each occupation, as illustrated most clearly in G. Williams (1976). The DI was originally developed in the 1950s in

TABLE 1.2. *Dissimilarity Index scores, 1991*

Occupational classification with	Dissimilarity of male/female workforces			Dissimilarity of FT/PT workforces
	All	FT	PT	All
371 groups	63	60	46	54
78 groups	58	55	41	51
10 groups	38	35	23	41

Source: 1991 Census, Great Britain, 10% sample data for residents aged 16 and over reported in table 4, *Economic Activity* report.

match people to occupations, as well as excluding the possibility of some residual differences between men and women in their occupational preferences. Some degree of variation around the mean is a more realistic baseline assumption and the new classification identifies a middle group of 'integrated', 'mixed', 'desegregated', or 'gender-neutral' occupations employing representative proportions of women and men. The key theoretical advance is that this typology allows us to focus on what is 'right' about gender-neutral occupations as compared with sex-segregated occupations; it encourages a sharper focus on the labour market processes and work organization that promote integration; and it facilitates case studies in place of the long-standing concern with measuring trends over time at the national level (Hakim, 1993*b*, 1993*c*, 1996*d*).

The new typology has been used to compare trends in occupational segregation in the full-time and part-time workforces, leading to the discovery that the overall level of occupational segregation is the sum of two opposing trends: a lower and falling level of occupational segregation in the full-time workforce that is concealed and cancelled by a high and rising level of occupational segregation in the part-time workforce (Hakim, 1993*b*). In effect, the growth of the part-time workforce has hidden a genuine decline in occupational segregation among full-time workers, a result confirmed, indirectly or directly, by other studies (Watts and Rich, 1992; S. Jacobs, 1995: 167). This analysis could not have been carried out with any of the single number

the USA for studies of the residential segregation of racial or ethnic minorities, and it is still used by social geographers as well as being adopted for employment and social mobility research. The DI has the advantage of being symmetrical for men and women, with a maximum upper value of 1 or 100% when men and women never share occupations, and a lower value of zero when all occupations have a uniform sex ratio. The DI is usually described as showing the proportion of women (or men) who would have to change jobs in order to equalize the sex-ratio across occupations, but this interpretation is both wrong and unrealistic. Over the past forty years, an extensive critical methodological literature has developed on the DI and on the many alternatives to it (James and Taeuber, 1985; Hakim, 1992*a*: 130–3, 145–6; Blackburn, Siltanen, and Jarman, 1995; Charles and Grusky, 1995; Watts, forthcoming).

indices. The new typology has also been used to study movement between sex-segregated and integrated occupations over the lifecourse, revealing relative stability in European countries, in contrast with the more volatile USA labour market (S. Jacobs, 1995).

The new typology was inspired by Rytina's analyses for the USA (Rytina, 1981; Rytina and Bianchi, 1984), which also inspired Sokoloff (1992) to use a similar approach in a study of black and white female professionals in the USA. Both Rytina and Sokoloff identified a middle band of integrated occupations around the 40% average female share of the USA workforce in the 1970s. Integrated occupations in the USA were defined as those with 40% ± 20% female workers to produce the following classification:

> male occupations   <20% female
> mixed occupations   21%–59% or 20%–60% female (40% ± 20%)
> female occupations >60% female.

On this basis, one-quarter of the USA workforce was employed in integrated occupations in 1970, rising to one-third in 1980 (Table 1.3), a relatively fast pace of change. The middle band of integrated occupations was defined more narrowly in the present study, as ±15% around the average. At the time of the 1991 Census women constituted 43% of all economically active and 36% of full-time employees, a situation that persisted well into the 1990s. For example, in spring 1997 women constituted 33% of the full-time workforce and 44% of all economically active. The middle band of mixed occupations was thus defined as 40% ±15% or occupations with between 25% female workers and 55% female workers. Male-dominated and female-dominated occupations are the remaining extreme groups. The typology applied throughout the census analyses for Britain thus consists of:

> male occupations   <25% female
> mixed occupations   25%–55% female (40% ± 15%)
> female occupations >55% female.

This typology was applied to census 10% sample data on the occupational structure, that is, to data for 2.5 million economically active residents aged 16 and over, excluding student jobs, comprising 1.5 million men and 1 million women. The source is table 4 in the 1991 Census *Economic Activity* report for Great Britain, which provides 10% sample data for all three levels of the 1990 Standard Occupational Classification (SOC). These 10% statistics provide a far more reliable basis for the classification used throughout this report than the 1% and 2% SARs could provide. It follows that the classification is far more reliable than those produced within datasets from small national surveys of 1,000–2,000 respondents that attempted to identify segregated and integrated occupations on the basis of occupational sex-ratios within the survey dataset.

One frequent error in academic studies of occupational segregation is for researchers to rely exclusively on their own survey datasets, instead of data from the population census, or statistical surveys such as the LFS, to produce occupational classifications, as illustrated by Tomaskovic-Devey (1993) and Scott (1994: 7, 124). This error is prompted in part by prejudice (Hakim, 1987*a*: 169), in part by the mistaken idea that the segregation of *jobs* in individual workplaces is the key theoretical concern, rather than the segregation of *occupations* at the national level (Bielby and Baron, 1984; Hakim, 1996*a*: 149–52). The primary concern of studies of occupational segregation is whether women and men have equal access to all occupations—for example whether pharmacy as a profession is open or closed to women, and not with whether every single pharmacy shop in the country employs a female pharmacist. This important theoretical point is often overlooked as a result of research reports using the terms occupational segregation and job segregation as equal alternatives, purely for stylistic variation. In most countries, including advanced industrial societies, the vast majority of workplaces and enterprises are relatively small (Storey, 1994: 20–5; see also Chapter 8), making it very likely that particular jobs will be done by only one person, necessarily either male or female. In addition, there can be good reasons for workplaces to employ mainly men or mainly women if the service offered is not unisex. For example, most dress shops employ female assistants and most male outfitters employ male shop assistants. Job segregation at workplace level is invariably more pronounced than in national studies of occupational segregation. But this is not necessarily significant theoretically or from a policy perspective, nor even in common-sense understandings of occupational segregation.[3]

The results of our analysis of the census 10% sample statistics are presented in Annex B and in Tables 1.1 and 1.2. Annex B presents complete listings of the 1990 SOC occupational groups ranked by % female, in three versions: for 371 occupational groups, for 78 occupational groups, and for the 10 Major Groups. The listings are sufficiently detailed to permit other researchers to produce their own, slightly different, trichotomous classifications for use in their research. One alternative to the classification used in this book is to use a single unvarying midpoint of 50% female for all analyses of occupational segregation, as follows:

> male occupations   <30% female
> mixed occupations   30%–70% female (50% ± 20%)
> female occupations >70% female

---

[3] The 1986 SCELI survey in Britain showed that when asked whether 'your type of job' is done mainly by men, mainly by women, or by a mixture of men and women, most people answer with reference to the broad, national picture rather than to the situation in their particular workplace. As a result, there are very close correlations between measures of occupational segregation based on national statistics and survey results on perceived job segregation (Scott, 1994: 7).

TABLE 1.3. *The growth of integrated occupations in the
USA 1970–1980*

	Type of occupation	Distribution of workforce		
		% of all	% of men	% of women
1970	Male-dominated	59	75	9
	Integrated	23	18	16
	Female-dominated	18	7	75
1980	Male-dominated	48	53	6
	Integrated	33	39	31
	Female-dominated	19	8	63
	All occupations	100	100	100

Note: Integrated occupations are defined as ±20% around the 40% average female share of the workforce, as follows: male jobs are those with up to 20% female workers; integrated jobs are those with 21%–59% female workers; female jobs are those with 60%+ female workers.

Source: Derived from table 3 in Rytina and Bianchi (1984).

This typology has been used in recent studies of the USA, where women do in fact now constitute about 50% of the workforce and typically work full-time hours. It is used in Table 2.12 in this volume to give a precise British comparison with an earlier USA study. A typology with a 50% midpoint is frequently used in cross-national comparative studies, where there is no single common figure for the female share of the workforce to use as a benchmark. For a comparative study of occupational segregation across the European Union, Rubery and Fagan (1993: 31) adopted the following version of this typology with a more narrowly defined middle band of integrated occupations:

> male occupations   <40% female
> mixed occupations   40%–59% female (50% ± 10%)
> female occupations >60% + female

as shown in Table 1.4.

The argument against using a typology with a 50% midpoint in the present study is that women have never constituted 50% of the workforce in Britain, nor anywhere else in Western Europe, and they still constitute no more than one-third of the full-time workforce in Britain (Hakim, 1996a: 61–3) and in most Western European countries (Blossfeld and Hakim, 1997). So a 50% midpoint distorts analyses, with the distribution of the workforce frequently unbalanced around an artificial (even fictitious) midpoint, as demonstrated by Table 1.4. In practice, few occupations have a sex ratio close to the 40/60

TABLE 1.4. *The pattern of occupational segregation in the European Union, 1990*

	Type of occupation	% of men	% of women	No. of occupations
Belgium	Male	70	16	56
	Mixed	24	48	12
	Female	6	36	12
Denmark	Male	70	13	52
	Mixed	16	16	10
	Female	14	71	20
West Germany	Male	74	20	51
	Mixed	7	10	13
	Female	19	70	18
Greece	Male	61	18	57
	Mixed	35	61	13
	Female	4	21	11
Spain	Male	78	27	64
	Mixed	19	43	9
	Female	3	31	10
France	Male	73	18	54
	Mixed	15	21	13
	Female	13	60	14
Ireland	Male	81	25	56
	Mixed	9	23	10
	Female	10	52	13
Luxembourg	Male	50	11	46
	Mixed	33	45	16
	Female	17	44	11
The Netherlands	Male	71	15	56
	Mixed	24	47	12
	Female	5	38	10
Portugal	Male	37	12	52
	Mixed	43	53	19
	Female	18	35	12
UK	Male	74	18	47
	Mixed	6	6	11
	Female	20	76	19

Note: Male occupations are those with up to 40% female workers; mixed occupations are those with 40%–59% female workers (50% ±10%); female occupations are those with 60%+ female workers.

Source: 1990 LFS data from EUROSTAT, using ISCO68 2-digit classification of occupations, extracted from table 1.8 in Rubery and Fagan (1993: 31) which shows no data for Italy and no EU total.

average for the workforce, or close to a 50/50 split. This means that the results
in this book are not enormously sensitive to the midpoint chosen. Many of
the SAR analyses were run with both versions of the typology, with very similar results.[4] That is, the results are robust and not heavily dependent on the
particular definition of integrated occupations adopted, as illustrated by
Table 10.1.

One effect of using the 10% sample statistics to identify segregated and
integrated occupations is that the 1% and 2% SARs occasionally yield results
that are inconsistent with the typology. This happens most often with relatively small occupations. The SARs data may suggest than an occupation is
integrated whereas the larger 10% sample shows it to employ a majority of
men or women. Similarly, the SARs data may suggest that an occupation is
dominated by men or women whereas the 10% statistics show it to be integrated. These inconsistencies are relatively rare, but they underline the point
that even the 1% and 2% SARs are not absolutely reliable sources of information on the occupational structure as a whole. The potential for misclassi-
fications of occupation type within surveys of a few thousand respondents is
infinitely greater.

It is well established that measures of occupational segregation record
higher values with detailed occupational classifications and record lower values with highly aggregated occupational classifications, such as the 10 Major
Groups version of SOC and the 9–12 broad groups typically used in cross-
national comparative studies (Hakim, 1992*a*: 132). This is demonstrated in
Table 1.2 showing DI scores for sex segregation in the total labour market (all
economically active) and in the full-time employee and part-time employee
workforces. With an occupational classification identifying 371 separate
occupational groups, the DI score reaches 63 (on a scale of 0–100), falls
slightly to 58 at the 78 occupational group level, and then falls sharply to 38
at the level of 10 Major Groups. Table 1.1 shows why the index falls so
sharply: as occupations are grouped into broader categories, the percentage
of the workforce in integrated occupations increases—from 18% with 371
occupations to 42% when only 10 Major Groups are used. The key point
demonstrated by Tables 1.1 and 1.2 is that the reduction from 371 to 78 occupational groups has a relatively small impact on DI scores and on the percentage of workers identified as employed in integrated occupations, whereas
the reduction from 78 to 10 occupational groups has a dramatic effect on
both measures, almost halving the DI and almost doubling the percentage in
mixed occupations. For our purposes, this is convenient, as it means the
371 group and 78 group occupational classifications can be used almost

---

[4] As noted in Annex A, three versions of the occupational segregation classification have
been added to the SARs, with integrated occupations variously defined as 40% ±15%
(JobSeg1), 50% ±20% (JobSeg2), and 30% ±15% (JobSeg3).

interchangeably. In practice, we are forced to use both. The 1% SAR uses the classification with 371 groups while the 2% SAR uses the 78 group classification. The 2% SAR offers a larger sample, which is helpful for studying minority groups in the workforce, such as people in integrated occupations. However the 1% SAR offers the more detailed information on occupations. As it happens, the new typology yields a very similar distribution at the 78 and 371 group levels (Table 1.1), so we can use the two SARs fairly interchangeably without a marked effect on research results. However, the results in Tables 1.1 and 1.2 confirm yet again that analyses of occupational segregation carried out with highly aggregated data with fewer than 20 occupational groups, as is typically the case in virtually all cross-national comparative research (Hakim, 1992*a*: 132; Charles and Grusky, 1995), are of dubious value, as they conceal more than they reveal.

The definitive results for spring 1991 are of course those in Table 1.1 based on the census 10% statistics. Results from the SARs in Chapter 2 differ slightly (see Table 2.1), in part because of the smaller samples, in part due to small differences in coding and classification introduced in the SARs to preserve confidentiality (see Annex A), and also due to differences in base populations (residents aged 16 and over in Table 1.1 instead of residents aged 16–64 years in Table 2.1). Despite these differences, the results for people in work (current jobs) in Table 2.1 are almost identical to the results for all economically active (including the unemployed reporting a job in the last ten years) in Table 1.1.

RECENT TRENDS IN OCCUPATIONAL SEGREGATION

One of the weaknesses of the DI is that it requires comparisons of pairs, and only permits comparisons of pairs. It thus provides a poor basis for comparisons across the full-time and part-time workforces because there is no single common measure applied to all subgroups in the workforce. Using the DI to compare the full-time and part-time workforces shows that they are highly segregated, with a score of 54 in 1991 (Table 1.2). The equivalent DI score for 1971 was 49, so it is clear that the full-time and part-time workforces are diverging rather than converging over time (Hakim, 1993*b*: 294; S. Jacobs, 1995: 167). As the part-time workforce grows in size it is becoming more differentiated rather than integrated into the mainstream; the peculiarities of a minority sector are becoming more rather than less extreme. This is not clear from the DI scores for the part-time workforce, which imply a lower level of sex-segregation than in the full-time workforce (Table 1.2), but it is clear in Table 1.1, which reveals the part-time workforce to consist almost exclusively of female occupations. In contrast, the full-time workforce shows only a small preponderance of male-dominated occupations: 48% compared to 35%

for female-dominated occupations or 44% and 33% at the more aggregated
level of 78 occupational groups.

Integrated occupations constitute a minority group. Indeed they have frequently been identified and then ignored in earlier studies because they constituted such an insignificantly small group (Hakim, 1993*b*: 296). The 1971
Census and 1981 Census 10% sample statistics identified only 15% of people
in employment in integrated occupations (Table 1.5) compared to 18% in the
1991 Census (Table 1.1). There was little net change over the decade 1970–80
(Hakim, 1981; Rubery and Tarling, 1988: 113). The long-term trend is clearly
for integrated occupations to grow in importance as occupational segregation declines in the workforce as a whole, but growth is very slow indeed in
Britain (Hakim, 1994, 1996*a*: 173) as compared with the faster pace of
change in the USA (Tables 1.3 and 1.6). The growth of integrated occupa-

TABLE 1.5. *The pattern of occupational segregation in*
Britain, 1971–1981

Type of occupation		% of all	% of men	% of women	% of occupations
All in employment					
1971	Male	49	72	9	66
	Integrated	15	16	15	18
	Female	36	12	76	16
1981	Male	48	72	9	68
	Integrated	15	16	15	17
	Female	37	12	76	15
Full-time employees					
1971	Male	54	72	10	
	Integrated	16	16	17	
	Female	30	12	73	
1981	Male	55	75	11	
	Integrated	12	12	13	
	Female	33	13	76	
Part-time employees					
1971	Male	15	61	8	
	Integrated	12	17	11	
	Female	73	22	81	
1981	Male	8	49	5	
	Integrated	7	14	6	
	Female	85	37	89	

Note: The two censuses used different occupational classifications, with
223 occupational groups in 1971 and 547 groups in 1981. This raises the
level of segregation revealed in the 1981 data.

Source: 1971 Census and 1981 Census, Great Britain, 10% sample data
for residents aged 16 and over in employment. For 1981 only, figures for
the full-time and part-time workforces relate to employees in employment, excluding the self-employed.

tions is an exclusive feature of the full-time workforce, as occupational segregation is stable or increasing rather than declining in the part-time workforce (Hakim, 1993*b*). The 1971 Census 10% sample statistics showed 16% of full-timers and 12% of part-timers working in integrated occupations (Table 1.5) compared to 17% and 8% respectively in 1991 (Table 1.1). In the following chapters some analyses are restricted to the full-time workforce, with the part-time workforce studied separately in some detail in Chapter 5. The results confirm the validity of this approach and that the full-time and part-time workforces constitute two separate and distinctive sectors of the labour market, recruiting workers with different sex-role preferences and work orientations (Hakim and Jacobs, 1997), with conflicting trends in occupational segregation (Hakim, 1993*b*), and with different patterns of labour mobility (Hakim, 1996*c*). Thus declining occupational segregation and the increasing differentiation of full-time and part-time work constitute two fundamental, if conceptual, structural features of the labour market at the start of the 21st century. These two structural features, and the associated trends, are observed most clearly in the relatively unregulated British labour market, but are also observed, to varying degrees, in other advanced industrial economies (Rubery and Fagan, 1993; Hakim, 1996*a*; Fagan and Rubery, 1996; Blossfeld and Hakim, 1997).

Annex B provides complete listings of integrated occupations. Among the 371 occupation groups, there are 71 integrated occupations (19% of all occupations) which run from No. 730 'Collector salespersons and credit agents' with 54% female workers to No. 599 'Other craft and related occupations not elsewhere classified' with 26% female workers. The occupation numbers in Annex B refer to occupation codes in the 1990 SOC, *not* to the quite different and arbitrary codes confusingly assigned to these occupations in the SAR files. In 1971, integrated occupations included registrars, publicans (owners or managers of bars), restaurateurs, the acting profession, painters and artists, authors and journalists, personnel managers, various associate professional occupations including laboratory technicians, telegraph and radio operators, bakers and confectioners, bus conductors, caretakers, tannery workers, weavers, and a wide variety of unskilled and semi-skilled occupations in textiles, food-processing, printing, agriculture, services, and sport (Hakim, 1993*b*: 299). Most of these occupations remained integrated until 1991, by which time they were joined by an impressive list of additions: biologists, biochemists, and other natural scientists; social scientists; economists; statisticians; lawyers (solicitors) and others working in legal services; marketing managers; general administrators in national government (up to principal and grade 6); administrative and executive officers in local government; taxation experts; managers in services; public relations managers; trade union officials; school inspectors; university and other higher education teachers; pharmacists; dispensing opticians; ophthalmic opticians;

dentists; family doctors; vets; archivists; and industrial designers. A smaller number of skilled, semi-skilled, and unskilled occupations also became integrated, such as sales representatives, weighers, traffic wardens, fishmongers, shoe repairers, knitters, and petrol pump forecourt attendants. By the early 1990s integrated occupations were drawn from the complete range of the occupational distribution, including senior professional and management work as well as relatively unskilled work.

Among the 78 occupational groups of the broader classification, there are 22 integrated occupations (28% of the total) which run from No. 63 'Travel attendants and related occupations' with 55% female workers to No. 24 'Legal professionals' with 28% female workers. The effect of the broader grouping is clear. Solicitors are the largest category of legal professionals, so the legal profession as a whole (including barristers, advocates, judges, and officers of the court) is an integrated occupation. At this level, integrated occupations include health professionals; managers and administrators in national and local government; literary, artistic, and sports professionals; natural scientists; legal professionals; business and financial associate professionals; specialist managers; managers in service industries; other managers; operatives in food and drink, in textiles and tannery work, in personal and protective service.

The feminist thesis recently espoused by the European Commission (1994*d*: 42) that women's paid work utilizes feminine skills developed in women's non-market work and is thus undervalued and underpaid, just as women's non-market work itself is undervalued and unpaid, is supported by evidence for 1891, when one-third of women worked as domestic indoor servants (Hakim, 1994), but not by 1991 Census results (see Annex B). It appears that the feminist thesis is simply out of touch with recent developments in the labour market. By 1991 the most important occupations in the female-dominated sector are in fact gender-neutral rather than feminine jobs. The largest occupations, accounting for a substantial proportion of women's employment, are simply relatively low-skill jobs with no particular association with women's domestic roles. For example sales assistants and sales workers, check-out operators, clerks and cashiers, receptionists, secretaries and typists greatly outnumber nursery nurses, care assistants, nurses, midwives, primary school teachers, and child care occupations (see Annex B). The transformation of the workforce in the post-war decades means that female-dominated and male-dominated occupations have almost completely lost any connection they might have had with feminine and masculine domestic skills. Chapter 2 seeks to identify the new defining features of sex-segregated and integrated occupations at the start of the 21st century.

With a view to assisting cross-national comparative studies, Annex C presents data from the 1% SAR coded to the International Labour Office's (ILO) International Standard Classification of Occupations (ISCO88), showing the distribution of the sample of working age residents (aged 16–64 years) in employment in spring 1991 across the three types of male, mixed, and female occupations. The % female and the % working part-time are also given for each cell of the table, but as the figures are based on 1% SAR counts rather than on 10% statistics, they are somewhat less reliable than the figures in Annex B. The concentration of integrated occupations in the more skilled and highly qualified grades of white-collar work is shown clearly by ISCO88.

CROSS-NATIONAL COMPARISONS

As noted earlier, Britain provides a case study of wide interest due to its unregulated labour market, which allows change and innovation to develop without constraint. Given the special emphasis on occupational segregation as a structural feature of the labour market throughout this study, we need also to situate Britain within the broader picture of recent trends in occupational segregation. Fortunately this is simple. In all cross-national comparisons, Britain emerges as one of the most backward societies, with a highly segregated workforce that exhibits little or no change over decades. In effect, Britain provides a 'worst case' scenario on this topic.

A comparison of the USA and Britain using a common classification (Table 1.6) confirms virtually no change in the pattern of occupational segregation in the decade 1971–81 in Britain compared with a lively pace of change in the USA on two versions of the typology (Tables 1.3 and 1.6). On the other hand, occupational segregation did not increase in Britain in the 1970s, as it did in France (Table 1.7). The proportion of the workforce employed in integrated occupations actually declined in France in the decade 1969–79, from 30% to 24% for all workers, and from 32% to 27% for women in employment. The French study used an idiosyncratic definition of integrated occupations that bears no clear relationship to the average 40% female share of the workforce in the 1970s; however, it is very close to that used in Tables 1.1 and 1.5 for Britain. The comparison shows a much lower level of occupational segregation in the French workforce in 1969 and 1979 than Britain had achieved by the 1990s: 24%–30% of the French workforce was in integrated occupations compared to only 18% in Britain by 1991.

Britain's backwardness is finally confirmed by the results for European Union countries shown in Table 1.4. Admittedly, there are problems with this analysis, which does not present data for the total EU workforce and which adopts a 50% midpoint to define integrated occupations. In reality, women's share of the workforce has generally been well below 50% in all Western European countries, even on a headcount basis. In 1991 the figures were: 47% in Denmark, 44% in France and Portugal, 43% in the UK, 41% in West Germany, 40% in Belgium and the Netherlands, 37% in Italy, 36% in Greece and Luxembourg, and 35% in Spain (van Doorne-Huiskes *et al.*, 1995: 2). This explains the unbalanced distributions, especially for countries where women constitute less than 40% of the workforce so that male and mixed occupations automatically predominate. None the less, Portugal emerges as having the least segregated workforce in Western Europe, with about half of the workforce in integrated occupations, and Britain and West Germany are revealed to have the most segregated workforces, with less than 10 per cent of their workforces in integrated occupations. These results are due in part to the failure to present results separately for the full-time and part-time workforces, as is now essential (Hakim, 1993*b*: 308). Britain and West Germany both have substantial part-time workforces, whereas Portugal has almost none. Together with Finland, Portugal has the highest female full-time workrate in Europe (Hakim, 1997: 26–9; see also Table 5.1). So there is good reason to expect Portugal (and probably also Finland, omitted from Table 1.4) to have the lowest level of occupational segregation in Europe. The identification of Britain as one of the most highly segregated labour markets in Europe is perhaps surprising.

TABLE 1.6. *The growth of integrated occupations 1970–1981: the USA and Britain compared*

Type of occupation	% of jobs	Distribution of workforce		
		% of all	% of men	% of women
USA				
1970 Male-dominated	64	56	81	14
Integrated	20	16	13	21
Female-dominated	16	28	6	65
1980 Male-dominated	55	47	71	14
Integrated	29	25	23	28
Female-dominated	16	28	6	58
Great Britain				
1971 Male-dominated	70	52	76	12
Integrated	19	27	20	38
Female-dominated	11	21	4	51
1981 Male-dominated	72	50	76	10
Integrated	18	26	19	37
Female-dominated	10	24	5	52

Note: Occupation groups are based on an implicit 50% average female share of the workforce, with integrated jobs defined as 50% ±20% as follows: *male* jobs are those with up to 30% female workers in each year; *integrated* jobs are those with 30%–70% female workers in each year; *female* jobs are those with 70%+ female workers in each year.

Sources: 1970 and 1980 Census data for the USA; figures supplied by J. A. Jacobs from his own analyses of Public Use Sample tapes. 1971 and 1981 Census 10% sample data for employed workforce in Great Britain.

TABLE 1.7. *The decline of integrated occupations in France,*
1969–1979

	Type of occupation	% of jobs	Distribution of workforce		
			% of all	% of men	% of women
1969	Male-dominated	..	44	..	9
	Integrated	..	30	..	32
	Female-dominated	..	25	..	60
1979	Male-dominated	53	46	64	11
	Integrated	19	24	24	27
	Female-dominated	28	29	13	62
All occupations		100	100	100	100

Note: Male jobs are those with under 25% female workers; integrated jobs are those with 25%–50% female workers; female jobs are those with 50%+ female workers.

Source: Derived from tables 2 and 10 in Huet, Marchand, and Salais (1982), based on data for the workforce in establishments with 10 or more employees; insufficient information was provided on the 1969 results for figures for male workers, and the distribution of jobs across the three occupation groups to be calculated.

However, it is helpful for the purposes of this study. As regards the pattern of occupational segregation, Britain presents an extreme case, and hence a strategic case study. Britain provides a severe test of the thesis that integrated occupations dissolve the problems found in sex-segregated occupations. Our results on the differences between sex-segregated and integrated occupations should apply with equal or greater force to other advanced industrial societies.

STRUCTURE OF THE BOOK

The analyses in Chapters 2 to 8 address three themes: occupational segregation and its implications for earnings and labour mobility; part-time jobs and the people who take them; self-employment and the small family firms which usually start from a home base and may or may not develop into larger incorporated firms. These themes are usually studied quite separately and by different groups of social scientists who attend different conferences and read different academic journals. People who do research on the self-employed and small firms rarely look at occupational segregation and broad issues of women's employment. Research on students and the educational system is normally carried out quite independently of research on the labour market: after all, students are not in the labour market! Studies of the expanding

part-time jobs market never draw out the associations with rising self-
employment. And home-based work is almost invariably studied in isolation
from other developments in the labour market. One of the aims of this book
is to demonstrate and explore the linkages between these six apparently unrelated topics: occupational segregation, labour turnover, part-time work, student jobs, self-employment, and homework. This is made possible by the
huge size of the SARs, which allow us to study workforce minorities in some
detail and also to explore the interconnections between them. The benefits
become clear in the final, concluding chapter which draws together the key
findings from the study as a whole and demonstrates that the whole is indeed
greater than the sum of its parts. Readers may find it helpful to look at
Chapter 10 before reading chapters on the topic of particular interest to
them.

Chapters 2, 3, and 4 look at occupational segregation and the closely
related issues of the sex differential in labour mobility and in earnings. The
primary objective was to assess whether the new typology of male, female,
and mixed occupations actually means anything 'on the ground', whether it
differentiates meaningfully between substantively different groups in the
workforce. The typology was developed originally as a purely statistical exercise (Hakim, 1993b), as noted above. Analyses of the SARs were designed to
test the substantive meaning and utility of the typology. The results exceeded
expectations, and the typology was then used in subsequent chapters, prov-
ing useful in research on all the topics addressed in this book.

Single-time studies of occupational segregation, and national studies of
trends in occupational segregation give the impression of an unnatural still-
ness and stability—unnatural because it appears to contradict all we know
about the constant 'churning' in the labour market. Longitudinal data is
required to properly explore flows between segregated and integrated occupations. However, the retrospective data in the SARs can be exploited to find
out whether labour mobility patterns differ between segregated and integrated occupations or whether, as argued elsewhere (Hakim, 1996c), labour
mobility patterns are gender-specific rather than occupation-specific.
Specifically, we test J. Jacobs's 'revolving door' thesis that women are pushed
out of male-dominated occupations to a greater extent than occurs with
female-dominated or integrated occupations—in effect, that social control
mechanisms serve to exclude women from the highest status and well-
rewarded occupations.

Chapter 2 has a labour market segmentation perspective, comparing and
contrasting sex-segregated and integrated occupations to assess whether they
constitute qualitatively different sectors of the workforce rather than just statistical artefacts. In contrast, Chapter 3 adopts a social stratification perspective, and the focus is on status structures *within* the three groups of male,
female, and mixed occupations. The results confirm Goldthorpe's earlier

conclusion, reached within the perspective of social mobility research, that occupational segregation and social stratification are unrelated structural features of the labour market (Goldthorpe, 1987: 288, 295; Erikson and Goldthorpe, 1993: 276–7).

Chapter 3 also looks at the relationship between occupational segregation and the pay gap between men and women. A full analysis of the sex differential in earnings lies beyond the scope of this book, and in any event some of the key variables required for such an analysis are not available in the SARs. The more limited exercise undertaken here is to assess the evidence for the thesis that women crowded into female occupations receive a lower return on their skills than do men. Specifically, we consider whether the earnings in female occupations are less closely tied to skill levels than they are in male occupations.

Chapter 4 utilizes the retrospective employment data in the SARs to test the hypothesis that women with discontinuous work histories differ from women in continuous employment, in their personal and occupational characteristics. The results are inconclusive, largely due to data limitations in the SARs—which were in fact not designed to produce work history data as such. Furthermore, recent research has shown that women with discontinuous work histories are in the majority (Hakim, 1996a: Table 5.2). So it is in fact women in continuous employment who constitute an unusual small group.

Chapters 5 and 6 both focus on part-time jobs and part-time workers. Our first objective was to devise operational definitions for three types of part-time work: reduced hours jobs, half-time jobs, and marginal jobs. Previous studies had suggested that a classification along these lines would be more useful and meaningful in cross-national comparative studies than the simple dichotomy of full-time and part-time jobs with a weakly defined boundary line between the two (Hakim, 1991: 111, 1993b: 291). Exploratory and iterative work with the SARs eventually produced a new banding of working hours that alters the conventional distinctions between full-time and part-time jobs in Europe and identifies three substantially different types of what was previously grouped under the heading of 'part-time work' in European studies, as follows:

full-time jobs   37+ hours per week, typically 42 hours per week in Britain, with jobs requiring usual weekly hours of 46 or more separately identified as involving the unusually excessive hours normally associated with long overtime hours

reduced hours jobs   30–36 hours a week

half-time jobs   11–29 hours a week, which in practice tend to be concentrated around 20 hours a week on average

marginal jobs   up to 10 hours a week, which in practice peak at 7–8
                       hours a week, and include one-day-a-week jobs (ver-
                       tical part-time work).

The new classification is empirically based but also theoretically meaningful
in that the categories identify groups with distinctive work orientations and
labour market situations, as shown in Chapter 5. The new classification is
used throughout the book, in place of the conventional British statistical definition of part-time work as jobs involving up to and including 30 hours a
week. It has also been found useful in cross-national comparative research on
the part-time workforce (Blossfeld and Hakim, 1997) and can be regarded as
an internationally valid classification rather than a peculiarly British one.

Students in full-time education who also take paid employment are most
often doing part-time jobs. In fact most student jobs consist of marginal jobs,
illustrating the point that the new classification of part-time jobs differentiates meaningfully between types of part-time worker and types of part-time
job. Chapter 6 explores student employment and assesses its contribution to
the dramatic growth of the part-time workforce in recent years.

The SARs provide the ideal opportunity to explore the characteristics of
homeworkers and the self-employed, two minorities that are not analysed in
any detail in published census statistics. These two types of 'non-standard' or
'atypical' work are on the increase, but are still too small to be studied with
ordinary national datasets. The huge SAR samples allow us to analyse the
differences between men and women in the two groups, the connections
between the two groups, the relative concentration of the self-employed
within integrated occupations, and the relationship between homework and
occupational segregation.

Chapter 7 provides the first nationally representative study of the homework labour force since the report on the 1981 National Homeworking
Survey, updating and extending that report (Hakim, 1987*b*). It shows that
published 1991 Census statistics contain errors, and applies a new classification of homework to study trends over the decade 1981–91. Homework is
then analysed in the context of travel to work patterns. Chapter 8 examines
the characteristics of self-employed workers, an important element within
integrated occupations, as shown in Chapter 2. We seek to establish why self-
employment is so important a feature of integrated occupations. Is self-
employment a key mechanism for sidestepping the barriers present in
sex-segregated occupations within large organizations? Or does the rising
trend of self-employment simply reflect changing work orientations?

Chapters 9 and 10 synthesize the analysis and draw conclusions. Chapter
9 provides an empirical synthesis through a case study of one integrated
occupation, pharmacy. In 1991, people aged 16–64 with qualifications in
pharmacy were split exactly 50/50 between men and women. People aged

16–64 working as pharmacists were split 49/51 between women and men. Whatever definition is used, pharmacy is an integrated occupation, in Britain, and in many other European countries (Rubery and Fagan, 1993: 19; Crompton and Le Feuvre, 1996). For many years, and throughout recent recessions, the demand for pharmacists has never been fully met, with virtually no unemployment in the profession. Trained pharmacists have readily obtained work in whatever shape or form suited them, and the occupation provides a great diversity of jobs and work arrangements: full-time and part-time jobs; permanent jobs as well as temporary jobs tailored to suit workers' preferences; jobs in the public sector, in hospitals, or in the private sector, in pharmaceutical manufacturing companies or in small community chemist shops; and opportunities for self-employment and small firms as community pharmacists. Pharmacy provides an ideal strategic case study of labour market outcomes in an integrated occupation offering genuine choice in types of work and employment contracts and which has escaped all the problems of recession due to a buoyant demand for labour for some decades. The 1% SAR provides a sufficiently large sample of pharmacists to study the effects of these advantageous conditions on working hours, travel to work patterns, the incidence of self-employment and small firms, the pay gap and labour turnover, thus drawing together in a single case study all the strands of the preceding analyses.

Chapter 10 presents some wide-ranging interpretation of the findings and their theoretical and policy implications. As noted above, readers may find it helpful to read Chapter 10 first, before looking at individual chapters on specific topics, as it provides a broader context to the more focused analyses in Chapters 2 to 9.

2

Profiles of Integrated and Segregated Occupations

All modern societies have a high degree of role differentiation and specialization and have conventions for allocating roles and tasks to members on the basis of sex and age, at the minimum, along with a variety of other criteria. The sexual division of labour is sometimes reinforced by formal rules or laws permitting and restricting access to particular occupations, social and political roles. But informal rules and conventions can be equally powerful, and they have persisted long after the introduction of sex and race discrimination legislation in Europe, North America, and other modern industrialized societies in the 1960s and 1970s. Studies of occupational segregation are concerned with the degree of separation between work done mainly by men and work done mainly by women. Theories of occupational segregation claim that women lose out from this separation of male and female workforces. For example, occupational segregation is a main building block, or the sole foundation-stone of theories of patriarchy (Hartmann, 1976; Walby, 1990; Hakim, 1996a: 9–13). In the USA, race was until recently an important second factor in occupational segregation (Cunningham and Zalokar, 1992; King, 1992; Sokoloff, 1992; Tomaskovic-Devey, 1993) but it has generally been far less important in the British labour market (Mayhew and Rosewell, 1978; Stewart, 1983; Bruegel, 1994) and we do not address it here.

Policy debates commonly depict occupational segregation as a labour market imperfection or problem, as a reflection of sex discrimination in the labour market and of labour market inequality, as the main source of the sex differential in earnings and of women's disadvantaged position in the labour market. National equal opportunities agencies have an important role in abolishing overt and covert rules, regulations, and selection procedures that discriminate against women (or men) entering particular occupations. Their official reports necessarily argue against maintaining distinctions between what is regarded as men's work and what is regarded as women's work in the interests of creating a more open and competitive labour market. The Equal Opportunities Commission (EOC) in Britain has gone further, to seek the elimination of job segregation by encouraging people to enter non-traditional educational courses and jobs, and encouraging women to be economically independent throughout life, in order to 'overcome the persistent divide between men's and women's jobs'. International bodies have also identified occupational segregation as the main barrier to women's full participation in the labour market, and argued for policies that would integrate all occupations. A series of OECD reports in the 1980s drew attention to occupational segregation as a key impediment to women's integration into the economy (OECD, 1980, 1985, 1988). More recently, the OECD (1994: 24) identified occupational segregation as a major labour market rigidity inhibiting the efficient use of labour and a source of labour market inequalities in pay and other benefits. In the mid-1990s the International Labour Office (ILO) started to promote national analyses of occupational segregation as a key contribution to promoting equality of treatment for working women and eliminating gender inequality (Siltanen, Jarman, and Blackburn, 1995). The ILO argued that occupational segregation is one of the major problems faced by women workers and that a better information base was required to understand the structure of the labour market and to monitor developments within it as regards the overall level of occupational segregation.

However, the most vigorous polemics against occupational segregation are found within policy documents from the European Commission. For example, a European Commission report on Community social policy 1993–5 that is worded vigorously enough to require a disclaimer distancing it from the position of the European Commission[1] states that the Commission offers member states a new strategy 'to ensure that equal pay for men and women becomes a reality' and 'a more efficient campaign against sex discrimination on the labour market'. It claims that women 'are the victims of both pay discrimination and segregation on the labour market, primarily because of the undervaluing of their work and variations in . . . employment structures . . .

---

[1] It is conventional for reports written for the European Commission by academics, social science researchers, consultants, and other bodies independent of the EC, to carry a disclaimer stating that 'The information contained in this publication does not necessarily reflect either the position or views of the European Commission'. This procedure ensures a minimum degree of freedom of expression for people producing reports for the European Commission. In these reports, the name and institutional affiliation of the author of the report is stated on the title-page, and the routine disclaimer is placed discreetly above the publication details. Occasionally, reports of this nature are published without any disclaimer—for example, the 1996 report by the Comité des Sages, all of whom were identified by name. However, it is very unusual for reports presenting policy statements and policy reviews written by and produced *within* the European Commission by its own officials, working anonymously, to carry a disclaimer. Indeed, it is virtually unheard of for any government to publish policy statements carrying disclaimers distancing the policy proposals from the government's position. The procedure adopted for the European Commission report *Two Years of Community Social Policy: July 1993–June 1995* which announces 'a more efficient campaign against sexual discrimination in the labour market' was to state, as usual, the Directorate-General responsible for writing the report, and to place in a prominent position at the front of the report the following warning: '**Notice to readers.** The information contained in this publication does not necessarily reflect the opinion or the position of the European Commission'. It is left to readers to decide what interpretation to place on such an unusual procedure.

and pay structures' (European Commission, 1994*c*: 59–62). The European Council's fourth Community action programme on equal opportunities for women and men which runs for five years 1996–2000 pinpointed the need for sustained efforts to desegregate the labour market as the principal mechanism for promoting equality between men and women in the labour market. To this end, the EC sought, *inter alia*, to promote the diversification of vocational choices for women and men; to combat gender stereotyping of skills and jobs; and to encourage women's entrepreneurship. It welcomed new research to identify the best and most successful practices, measures, and methods to reduce labour market segregation, to promote the economic independence of women, and to promote the full and equal participation of women in social and economic life. In this document, occupational segregation is presented as an evil in its own right, independently of any links with the pay gap between men and women, which is not discussed.[2]

The European Commission's campaign to outlaw occupational segregation is all the more remarkable for refusing to take account of the conclusions of its own research reports, which argue against the desegregation of occupations as the main strategy for improving women's position in the labour market. Instead, revaluing women's caring professions and current jobs is argued to be a more effective policy (Rubery and Fagan, 1993). In effect, comparable worth policies are considered to be a more effective way forward than the unrealistic objective of desegregating the labour market.

THEORETICAL AND METHODOLOGICAL APPROACHES TO OCCUPATIONAL SEGREGATION

Occupational segregation on the basis of sex exists when men and women do different kinds of work, so that one can speak of two separate labour forces, one male and one female, which are not in competition with each other for the same jobs (Blaxall and Reagan, 1976; Hakim, 1979; Reskin, 1984; Reskin and Hartmann, 1986; Rubery and Fagan, 1993; OECD, 1994: 24). Segregation can be both horizontal and vertical and no single measure fully captures both these aspects. Most measures, in particular the popular Dissimilarity Index (DI), measure horizontal segregation, but vertical job segregation is far more important. Cross-national comparisons of the UK, USA, Canada, Sweden, Norway, Australia, and Japan suggest that vertical job segregation is largely independent of horizontal occupational segregation (Wright *et al.*, 1995). They may even display conflicting trends. A study of

---

[2] van Doorne-Huiskes *et al.* (1995: 122–50) provide an excellent description of the EC's equal opportunities policy, the legal instruments it has used, and the positive action it has promoted. However, it does not cover the Commission's fourth action programme.

trends 1901–71 in Britain showed that vertical segregation increased while horizontal segregation was falling slowly (Hakim, 1979: 27–9).

Horizontal job segregation exists when men and women are most commonly working in different types of occupation—for example, women are dressmakers and men are tailors, women are cooks and men are carpenters. Vertical job segregation exists when men dominate the higher grade and higher paid occupations and jobs, or when men are promoted further up career ladders within occupations—for example, men are heads of schools while women are teachers. Occupational classifications vary from 6–10 broad occupational groups to 400–600 specific occupations, and they generally identify some combination of vertical and horizontal segregation. For example, teachers are usually identified as a separate occupation group, which is staffed by a mixture of men and women, so it is integrated rather than segregated. More detailed classifications distinguish between primary school teachers (dominated by women in Britain and across Europe), secondary school teachers (with a mixture of men and women), and tertiary level teachers (dominated by men in Britain and across Europe). Even more detailed occupational classifications might distinguish between head teachers and directors of educational establishments at each level (who are typically male) and ordinary teachers (who are either typically female or mixed). The more detailed the occupational classification, the greater the degree of occupational segregation identified, and the greater the amount of vertical segregation that is exposed, especially with occupational classifications that seek to rank occupations by level of skill and expertise, as in ISCO88 and the British 1990 SOC classification, or by occupational status or prestige, as in Social Class and other socio-economic variables used in the SARs (see Annex A).

The wealth of information contained in occupational classifications has generally been ignored in favour of single number summary measures of the overall level of occupational segregation present in the workforce at any point in time. Statistical indices such as the DI have been seen as facilitating comparisons across time and across countries. Paradoxically, these studies have regularly produced results that are either implausible, because patriarchal societies such as Japan are found to have the lowest level of occupational segregation while a 'progressive' society pursuing egalitarian policies such as Sweden is found to have one of the highest levels of occupational segregation (OECD, 1980: 44–6, 1988; Hakim, 1992*a*: 132), or else self-defeating, because studies reveal no change at all in occupational segregation in the USA in the period 1900–70 despite dramatic changes in the labour market and occupational structure (Gross, 1968; J. Jacobs, 1989*a*; Hakim, 1993*b*: 294). Thus the meaning and validity of these indices must be in doubt. In addition, single number indices are inflexible in their application. The DI, for example, requires comparisons of pairs and only permits comparisons of pairs. It cannot provide a constant measure for comparisons across labour market subgroups, such as full-time and part-time workforces. For these and other reasons, the elegant simplicity of single number indices of occupational segregation has to be rejected in favour of a fuller mapping of the pattern of occupational segregation (Hakim, 1993*b*). The new approach identifies a separate category of integrated or mixed occupations straddling the dividing line between the two dominant categories of male and female occupations. As explained in Chapter 1, the typology is constructed from an analysis of the 1991 Census 10% sample statistics, and can be applied to any dataset employing the 1990 SOC to code and classify occupations, including the SARs, as shown in Table 2.1. (Further details are given in Annex A.)

Integrated occupations are defined statistically as those with sex ratios close to the 40%/60% average for the workforce as a whole, namely 25%–55% female workers (40% 6 15%). This chapter shows that integrated and sex-segregated occupations are also substantively different—in the types of people they employ, the types of job they contain and in workplace location. Integrated occupations are a relatively small category, employing just over one-fifth, and just under one-fifth, of men and women in the 2% and 1% SARs respectively (Table 2.1). Yet they are distinctive. In the workforce as a whole, male and female occupations are evenly balanced. However a two-thirds majority of men work in male-dominated occupations and a three-quarters majority of women work in female-dominated occupations, the usual mirror-image pattern.

TABLE 2.1. *Occupational structure in the 2% and 1% SARs*

Type of occupation	Current and last jobs	Current jobs only		
	All	All	Men	Women
2% SAR				
Male-dominated	38	39	63	9
Integrated	21	22	23	20
Female-dominated	41	39	14	71
Total	100	100	100	100
1% SAR				
Male-dominated	40	42	68	9
Integrated	17	17	19	16
Female-dominated	43	41	13	76
Total	100	100	100	100

Note: The 2% SAR uses an occupational classification with 73 groups; the 1% SAR uses a classification with 358 occupations.

Source: 2% and 1% SARs, Great Britain, data for residents aged 16–64 years.

The characteristics of sex-segregated and integrated occupations are of some importance for theories explaining the persistence of occupational segregation, and for policies seeking to eradicate occupational segregation. Edgeworth (1922) is always quoted as pointing out that women earn less than men when they are crowded into a small number of occupations, as this depresses their wages irrespective of the type of work involved. However, he went on to argue that even in the context of open access to all jobs and the same basic pay rates for men and women, male earnings would still be substantially higher than female earnings, for a host of reasons, even before male wages were uprated to provide a family wage. In effect he endorsed differential wage rates and agreed that women were about 30 per cent less productive than men in the same job, due to men's greater physical strength and motivation. In contrast, patriarchy theory argues that occupational segregation is a key mechanism used by men to limit women's power and choices, by restricting them to low-grade and low-paid work (Hartmann, 1976; Walby, 1990). It thus predicts that men will always have the major share of the higher-grade and better-paid occupations and that women will always be concentrated in the lowest-grade and worst-paid occupations. Theories developed by economists produce the same predictions, without spelling out explicitly *why* this outcome is brought about through the mechanisms they describe. Most economic 'theories' of occupational segregation do no more than *describe* the processes through which the pattern of occupational segregation is maintained, such as 'job queue' and 'labour queue' theories, which say that men (and whites) are always first in the queue and get preferential allocation (or promotion) to the best jobs (Thurow, 1969; Reskin and Roos, 1990); 'statistical discrimination theory', which states that male employers prefer not to hire (or promote) women because they believe women, on average, to be less committed, productive, stable, and reliable employees (Phelps, 1972; Arrow, 1973); or 'human capital theory', which states that men get to the top because they invest in the qualifications and work experience that are rewarded in the labour market, whereas women do not make the same investment (Becker, 1975; Blau and Ferber, 1992: 139–87). The only economic theory to explain *why* these processes occur in all societies is the variety of rational choice theory labelled the 'new home economics', which argues that some degree of division of labour is maintained within households because it is efficient and mutually beneficial, yielding productivity increases to the person who specializes in non-market work in the home as well as to the person who specializes in market work. This theory also predicts that men achieve better positions and rewards in the labour market, while most women invest their main efforts and energies in the home and family, but it points out that the roles can also be reversed, equally effectively (Becker, 1985, 1991).

Social science theories have said nothing about integrated occupations because they disappear from view in the dichotomous view of occupational

segregation promoted by single number measures of occupational segregation and their focus on 'male' and 'female' occupations. The few national
studies that identified integrated occupations in the past proceeded to
ignore them and exclude them from subsequent analyses (Hakim, 1993*b*:
296). Studies that focus on *job* segregation at workplace level have been
even more likely to set aside integrated jobs as too small to merit attention
(but see Tomaskovic-Devey, 1993: 77–83, for one exception). So there are
no theoretical predictions about the characteristics of integrated occupations and limited evidence from rare case studies (Mennerick, 1975). Most
case studies focus on men and women in non-traditional or sex-atypical
occupations (Riemer, 1982; C. Williams, 1993) rather than on integrated
occupations. Since integrated occupations are the ultimate goal of equal
opportunities policies, it seems more appropriate to focus the research
spotlight on this small group of occupations, to see what positive lessons
they might offer to policy-makers, rather than on the negative lessons of
sex-segregated occupations. A comparison of the profiles of integrated and
sex-segregated occupations is clearly of both theoretical and policy interest.

Drawing on labour market segmentation theory, we hypothesized at the
start of this project that integrated occupations would have a special role in
labour-market processes of recruitment and job-sorting. Our initial hypothesis was that integrated occupations form a kind of no man's land between
well-defined male-dominated and female-dominated occupations, a point of
entry to the workforce where people queue to get into conventional and
stable segregated and sex-labelled careers. Integrated occupations constitute
a busy crossroads, or an antechamber leading into more permanent occupational choices with their associated social and economic profiles. This
hypothesis predicted that integrated occupations would consist of gender-
neutral jobs with low entry barriers and would be 'transitional' jobs for
young people entering the labour market at one end of the life cycle, and for
older workers phasing themselves gradually out of the labour market into
full-time retirement at the other end. Integrated occupations were expected
to contrast sharply with the more stable and continuous careers offered by
sex-segregated occupations, providing a springboard into these heavily sex-
labelled occupations, and being no more than a short-term option allowing
new entrants to the labour market coming straight from full-time education,
and people (mainly women) re-entering after a long spell out of employment
to sort out their options and the opportunities for a longer-term choice of
occupation, typically in the segregated sector. Thus the integrated category
was expected to consist primarily of relatively low-grade occupations with
low entry conditions, high turnover rates, and the most pronounced degree
of labour flexibility, however defined, serving as an entry and exit route for
occupations in the segregated sector. This hypothesis was consistent with the

small size of the integrated sector, its very slow growth, and would allow some instability in the occupational content of the category.

It seemed likely that the integrated sector would also include some genuinely integrated occupations offering long-term careers to men and women, but these were expected to be in the minority, even if growing, and greatly outnumbered by the gender-neutral short-term jobs. It is to employers' advantage to give themselves the widest possible recruitment base for jobs of low skill or with high turnover. This alone suggested that jobs taken on entry to the workforce, and in the retirement years, would be the least sex-labelled of all, thus eliminating any unnecessary restrictions on sources of labour among men and women, young and old. An obvious example would be check-out operators in supermarkets, an occupation requiring limited training and where sex labelling offers no obvious advantage, given that supermarket customers encompass the full range of social characteristics. At the other extreme, personnel managers offer one example of a genuinely integrated occupation with long-term career potential. Most organizations need no more than one personnel manager, who might be of either sex, given that in most establishments the workforce includes men and women. Thus the *occupation* is open to men and women, even if most personnel manager *jobs* are segregated by virtue of there being only one or very few such posts in any organization, which might thus be filled by men only or women only.

In the event, integrated occupations did emerge as distinctive in many ways, but not along the lines hypothesized. As already indicated in Chapter 1, highly qualified and genuinely integrated occupations offering long-term careers were found to greatly outnumber low-grade gender-neutral transitional jobs. In a curious reversal of our initial hypothesis, the large group of female-dominated occupations emerged as the sector containing the largest number of sex-neutral transitional jobs. In other respects also, the three types of occupation were found to differ distinctively, but in wholly unexpected ways. The concluding section of the chapter attempts to explain the unanticipated findings from this first systematic comparison of the three occupational groups.

QUALIFICATIONS AND CAREERS

Integrated occupations were hypothesized to have the lowest entry barriers, and hence also have the lowest qualifications requirements. Data for men are taken to define the 'normal' pattern of qualifications in each occupational group; we then assess whether women are equally or better qualified than men in each type of occupation. There are good reasons for expecting women to be better qualified. It is often argued that women have to be better qualified, and have higher performance on the job, especially in male-dominated occupations, in order to overcome the sex-stereotyping and discrimination that devalues their potential suitability and actual contribution in any job. More concretely, Marshall *et al.* (1988: 80–1) found that women were systematically better qualified than men in all social classes. A cross-national comparative study of employment in the European Union also concluded that, relative to men, women tend to be better qualified for the jobs they hold, especially at professional level (Rubery and Fagan, 1993: 120, 122). In addition, working women are a self-selected group who are not representative of all women of working age whereas virtually all adult men are employed (Fiorentine, 1987; Hakim, 1996*a*, 1996*b*, 1996*c*: 19–20) and it is well established that female workrates increase with the level of educational qualifications held and hence occupational grade (Hakim, 1996*a*: 70). The one exception to this pattern might be female-dominated occupations, but here female over-qualification can again be expected, particularly in part-time jobs, as many women trade earnings and career prospects for convenience factors after childbirth, due to changing their priorities between home and work (Dex, 1987; Hakim, 1991). The lowest sex differential should be in the integrated occupations, if only because numbers are in balance in this sector.

With the increasing importance of tertiary level qualifications in the labour market, and thus qualifications inflation, and given other sources of information on secondary school qualifications (notably the LFS), the 1991 Census only collected information on higher education qualifications, classifying them into three levels as follows:

   a higher degrees of UK standard or equivalent vocational qualifications;
   b first degrees and all other qualifications of UK first degree standard, including degrees in education;
   c qualifications that are generally obtained at 18 and over, above secondary school standard and below UK first degree standard, including most nursing and teaching qualifications.

Tables 2.2 and 2.3 show the highest qualification obtained by men and women; Table 2.3 also shows whether two or more higher qualifications are held. Contrary to expectation, integrated occupations emerge as the most highly qualified group, and working women are found to be systematically *less* qualified than working men.

At first sight, there is no important sex differential in the proportion of working men and women holding higher education qualifications: 19% and 17% respectively (Table 2.2). It is analyses at this level of aggregation, in Britain and the USA, that produced the conclusion that the sex differential has disappeared (Marshall *et al.*, 1988: 80–1; Blau and Ferber, 1992: 142; Rubery and Fagan, 1993: 120, 122). The unique contribution of the 1991 Census 10% statistics is to show that men generally have higher grade qualifications than women: at degree level or above compared to women being

TABLE 2.2. *Higher education qualifications by occupation*

Occupations	Percentage of men with qualifications at each level				Percentage of women with qualifications at each level			
	Total	a	b	c	Total	a	b	c
All economically active	19	2	10	7	17	1	7	10
Managers & administrators	27	2	14	11	17	1	9	7
Professional occupations	82	13	51	18	86	7	47	33
Associate professionals	40	2	17	20	61	1	12	48
Clerical & secretarial	11	*	6	5	5	*	2	3
Craft and related	4	*	1	3	3	*	1	2
Personal & protective service	5	*	2	3	4	*	1	3
Sales occupations	11	*	5	6	3	*	1	2
Plant & machine operators	2	*	1	2	1	*	*	1
Other occupations	1	*	1	1	1	*	*	1
Inadequately described	13	1	7	5	11	1	5	5

Notes: Qualified people are those with at least one higher education qualification of the type obtained after age 18 and after completing secondary school. The qualifications include professional and vocational qualifications obtained by passing the exams of professional bodies as well as degrees awarded by universities and other higher education institutions. The qualifications are grouped into three levels:

    a higher degrees of UK standard, such as Masters degrees and Doctorates;

    b first degrees and all other qualifications of UK first degree standard, including university degrees in education;

    c post-secondary school qualifications below UK first degree level, including most nursing and many teaching qualifications.

Source: Calculated from 1991 Census 10% sample data, Great Britain, data for residents aged 18 and over who are economically active, reported in table 4 in 1991 *Census-Qualified Manpower*, Great Britain (1994).

qualified mainly below degree level. Among working men and women aged 18–64 years who had any higher qualifications, 62% of men and 44% of women had qualifications at university degree level or above. The majority of women have obtained nursing, teaching, and other vocational qualifications below university degree level; this is then reflected in their occupations, at associate professional level more often than at professional level, or teaching in primary education more often than in higher education, for example. The higher education qualifications gap between men and women is larger in older age groups and is diminishing slightly over time: 16% of men aged 50–54 and 12% of women in this age group have some type of higher qualification compared to 22% and 19% respectively among 35–39-year-olds. However, these aggregate figures for all higher education qualifications grouped together hide continuing differences in the grade of qualifications obtained and in the type of university attended. With the wholesale conversion of polytechnics and other higher education institutions into 'new' universities in the early 1990s in Britain, even greater differences will be hidden

TABLE 2.3. *Job characteristics of sex-segregated and integrated occupations*
column/cell/row percent

		Type of occupation			
		Male	Mixed	Female	Total
Higher qualifications held					
All	a higher degrees	1	2	1	1
	b first degrees	7	15	7	9
	c below degree level	6	8	11	8
	two or more	5	10	8	7
	none	86	75	80	82
Men	a higher degrees	1	3	5	2
	b first degrees	7	17	15	10
	c below degree level	6	9	10	7
	two or more	4	11	17	8
	none	87	71	70	81
Women	a higher degrees	1	1	1	1
	b first degrees	9	12	5	7
	c below degree level	5	6	11	10
	two or more	5	7	6	6
	none	85	80	83	83
Usual weekly hours (excluding overtime and meal breaks)					
All	461	15	19	4	11
	30–45	82	72	60	71
	, 30	3	9	36	18
Men	461	16	25	11	17
	30–45	83	73	82	80
	, 30	1	3	7	3
Women	461	7	10	2	4
	30–45	72	71	55	60
	, 30	21	19	43	36
Employment status (main job)					
managers		13	37	2	13
foremen		4	2	5	4
other employees		65	39	90	70
self-employed with employees		4	11	1	4
self-employed without employees		14	12	2	9
% self-employed (basic classification)					
All	with employees	4	10	1	4
	without employees	13	10	2	8
	total	17	20	3	12
Men	with employees	4	11	2	5
	without employees	13	11	4	11
	total	17	22	6	17
Women	with employees	3	7	*	2
	without employees	8	10	2	4
	total	11	17	2	6
Employees		38	15	47	100
Self-employed		57	32	11	100
solo self-employed		62	28	10	100
small firms		39	54	7	100
all men		65	31	4	100
all women		17	57	26	100
All currently in work		40	17	43	100

Source: 2% and 1% SARs, Great Britain, data for residents aged 16–64 years in employment, excluding student jobs. The table is based on the 2% SAR, apart from data on employment status in the main job from the 1% SAR. See Annex A for details of the two types of data on self-employment in the SARs.

in future censuses, so that research analyses will seem to discover sex or race discrimination when in fact employers are discriminating between different classes and types of university degree (Connor *et al.*, 1996; La Valle *et al.*, 1996). Similarly in the USA, the sex differential in qualifications increases the higher the level (Blau and Ferber, 1992: 144).

The sex differential in tertiary qualifications increases when occupation is controlled (Table 2.2). At each level of the occupational structure, working men are substantially better qualified than working women. While it remains true that women are more likely to be employed if they have higher qualifications than if they do not, working men are still generally better qualified in terms of the grade of qualifications they hold. Among managers and administrators, for example, 27% of men and 17% of women are highly qualified, but 16% of men and 10% of women are qualified at degree level or above. In professional occupations, 64% of men compared to 54% of women are qualified at degree level or above. Among associate professionals, 19% of men and 13% of women are qualified at degree level or above. The gap continues lower down the occupational ladder. In clerical and secretarial occupations, 6% of men compared to 2% of women hold a university degree or better, a factor that clearly improves chances of obtaining promotion into management and professional grade jobs. There is no evidence of female over-qualification compared to men at any level of the occupational structure, despite the highly self-selective nature of the population of working women (Fiorentine, 1987), and despite the fact that proportionally more women than men are employed in highly qualified occupations (European Commission, 1995*a*: 12).

Again contrary to expectation, integrated occupations are found to be very distinctively more qualified than the sex-segregated sector: 25% compared to 17% of workers had one or more higher education qualification, 10% compared to 6% had two or more such qualifications, 2% compared to 1% had postgraduate degrees (Table 2.3). Contrary to our initial hypothesis, women are systematically *less* well qualified than men in all three types of occupation, with the exception of male-dominated occupations, where they are slightly better qualified: 10% compared to 8% of men have degree level qualifications (Table 2.3). This pattern of men being systematically better qualified than women remains constant, with rare exceptions, across age groups and within the full-time and part-time workforces.

The thesis of the differential over-qualification of women is weakened yet further by the results for part-time workers in Chapter 5. A common feminist argument is that female part-timers are over-qualified for the work they do because employers channel women into low-grade low-paid jobs (Sokoloff, 1992: 83; Rubery, Horrell, and Burchell, 1994: 225; Fagan and Rubery, 1996: 244). In fact, male part-timers are more likely to be highly qualified than are female part-timers (see Table 5.8). Women working part-time are systematically less well qualified than male part-timers, in male, female, and integrated occupations. Indeed, the superiority of male part-timers over female part-timers, in terms of qualifications, is highest in female-dominated occupations: 20% and 3% respectively are qualified at university degree level or above.

As shown in Chapter 4 this pattern is extended and reinforced by information on labour force drop-outs: people (typically wives) who have temporarily withdrawn from the labour market, some of whom have had a job in the last ten years, and for whom information on their last occupation is therefore available. Non-working women are less well qualified even than part-time workers (see Tables 4.3 and 5.8). Female drop-outs who have not had a job for over ten years are the least qualified group in the adult population—only 3% have any higher education qualifications compared with 11% of the drop-outs who have worked in the last ten years and 17% of women in employment.

These findings offer a cautionary lesson on the value of research that focuses exclusively on women's experiences in the labour market (see for example Dex, 1987) on the grounds that women have so far been under-researched. It would be easy to interpret results for women in isolation as showing that female workers are 'over-qualified' for their jobs, hence 'under-employed', because some of them have tertiary qualifications when the job in question does not require it. The easy conclusion of discrimination fades when we discover that the same pattern is true for men, to an even greater extent. Qualifications inflation is wrongly read as evidence of discrimination. Qualifications inflation is a long-term trend, which speeds up during recessionary periods, such as the 1980s, but it seems to affect men as well as women. Similarly, some studies focus exclusively on women part-timers (due to small numbers of male part-timers in most survey datasets), find that women part-timers are substantially 'overqualified' for their jobs, and conclude that discrimination in some form is involved (Rubery *et al.*, 1994: 225). The easy accusation of discrimination is undermined by the discovery that male part-timers are also 'overqualified' for their jobs, to an even greater extent: 18% have tertiary level qualifications compared to 11% of women part-timers (see Table 5.8). Sample selection bias is one of the most important sources of incorrect research findings (Lieberson, 1985: 14–43), and unfortunately it is encouraged by the fashion for research focusing exclusively on working women (Hakim, 1996*a*: 129–30).

Among people with tertiary level qualifications, men generally have higher grade qualifications than women: they are more likely to have a university degree than sub-degree vocational qualifications, and they are more likely than women to have postgraduate degrees. It is still possible that women obtain a lower return on their educational investments than men. But even by 1991, women's investment in the qualifications needed for better jobs was still well behind men's investment in a career. In the age group 25–34 years there were signs of some catching up, but as a group men still had the edge, in terms of qualifications, in both integrated and female-dominated occupations. The hypothesis of differential female over-qualification is supported only for male-dominated occupations, which constitute some 40% of the workforce but employ only 10% of working women, who are clearly an exceptional minority.

Perhaps the most surprising finding is that women are significantly less well qualified than men working in female-dominated occupations, the field in which they might have been expected to excel, to feel most comfortable, and to invest in most heavily. One-third (30%) of men working in female occupations have some higher education qualification, compared to 17% of women (21% of women working full-time and only 12% of women working part-time); 20% of men compared to 6% of women in female occupations are qualified at degree level or above; 17% compared to 6% have two or more tertiary qualifications. The largest sex differential in qualifications is in female-dominated occupations, a factor that helps to explain women's failure to attain the higher grades of job within the sector, as shown in Chapter 3.

Overall then, integrated occupations emerge as distinctively different from segregated occupations. In this sector occupations are more likely to be labelled and stereotyped by the formal qualifications and certificated expertise involved than by the sex of the workers doing them, with the easy assumptions about informally acquired expertise this implies. The two processes are probably mutually exclusive. Occupations are more likely to avoid sex-stereotyping if access is determined by public examinations and accreditation, if the character of the work and role is defined by public bodies or membership of professional bodies with a regulating function, by formal mechanisms instead of the informal training assumed to take place within families and local communities. Other features of integrated occupations are consistent with this distinctive profile of work dominated by genuinely integrated higher grade careers rather than low-grade short-term transitional jobs.

OTHER JOB CHARACTERISTICS

Another distinctive feature of integrated occupations, equally unexpected but consistent with the highly qualified character of the group, is that they have a high proportion of self-employed workers: 20% compared to 17% of people in male occupations and only 3% of workers in female occupations (Table 2.3). Female occupations have almost no self-employment; this sector is distinctive in consisting almost entirely of dependent workers. The pattern is consistent across the full-time and part-time, male and female workforces. As a result, the employee workforce is heavily sex segregated, whereas the self-employed workforce is dominated by male and integrated occupations (bottom section of Table 2.3). It appears that self-employment offers an important route to occupational desegregation, a way of avoiding the well-entrenched sex-stereotyping and traditions of the mainstream workforce, where trade unions and employers present social barriers to change and restructuring (Cockburn, 1983, 1996; Hakim, 1997*a*: 47–52).

Half the self-employed in integrated occupations are genuine entrepreneurs or small firm owners who employ others, and half are the solo self-employed who are only marketing their own labour and services and have no employees. This is equally true of men and women. In contrast, almost all the self-employed in male occupations are solo self-employed; very few are small firm owners. This, combined with the high percentage of managers and foremen in the integrated sector (Table 2.3) means that over half of all workers in integrated occupations are in positions of authority, in large or small firms. In this respect, there is a sharp contrast with female occupations, where the vast majority (90%) of workers are dependent employees subordinate to control by others. On this dimension, integrated and female occupations form two extremes, with male occupations in between.

As regards hours worked, the contrast is again between integrated and male occupations, where long hours are typical and where there is almost no part-time work, and female occupations where part-time work (less than 30 hours a week) is common and overtime is rare, with very few people regularly working long 'overtime' hours of 46 hours a week or more (Table 2.3). The long work hours in male and integrated occupations are partly explained by the presence of the self-employed, who generally work longer hours than employees. But work hours are clearly gender-specific rather than occupation-specific, with a fair degree of consistency in hours among men, and among women, irrespective of the type of occupation they are in: only 1% of men compared to 21% of women work part-time in male occupations; 7% of men and 43% of women work part-time in female occupations (Table 2.3). The sex differential in hours worked is underlined in integrated occupations, where one-quarter of men work very long hours (46 or more a week excluding overtime) while one-fifth of women work part-time hours of less than 30 hours a week, a difference that is likely to have an impact on status attainment and earnings.

Finally the socio-economic status and occupational grade of integrated occupations also establish them firmly as career jobs more often than as low-grade transitional jobs and, beyond that, as a distinctive higher segment in the occupational and class structure (Tables 2.4 and 2.5). This is shown most clearly by the RG Social Class; results using Goldthorpe's class schema and Socio-Economic Groups (SEG) show the same pattern but in more complex detail.

Two-thirds of integrated occupations are in the Managerial and Technical

TABLE 2.4. *Job grade and earnings in sex-segregated and integrated occupations*

		Type of occupation			
		Male	Mixed	Female	Total
Socio-Economic Group (column percent)					
employers and managers—large establishments		4	15	*	5
employers—small establishments		3	8	1	3
managers—small establishments		5	26	*	8
professionals—self-employed		1	2	*	1
professionals—employees		7	5	1	4
ancillary workers & artists		6	14	19	13
supervisors—white-collar		*	*	2	1
junior white-collar		6	1	48	21
personal service		—	2	11	5
foremen—blue-collar		4	1	*	2
skilled blue-collar		30	4	1	13
semi-skilled blue-collar		14	15	5	11
unskilled blue collar		5	*	9	5
own-account workers (not professionals)		11	7	2	7
farmers—owners/managers		2	—	—	1
agricultural workers		2	—	—	1
Mean Cambridge scores					
All in work	all	26	44	37	34
	men	26	45	40	32
	women	29	42	36	37
Full-time workers	all	26	44	40	35
	men	26	45	40	32
	women	30	43	40	40
Part-time workers	all	25	39	31	32
	men	24	44	37	33
	women	25	38	31	32
Mean hourly earnings for employees (pence)					
All in work	all	660	852	545	648
	men	673	994	698	748
	women	548	650	508	536
Full-time employees (301 hours a week)	all	667	878	597	690
	men	675	997	702	750
	women	580	675	557	586
Part-time employees (, 30 hours a week)	all	487	576	449	463
	men	609	909	636	671
	women	429	535	442	449

Sources: 2% SAR, Great Britain, data for residents aged 16–64 years in employment, excluding student jobs and excluding the Armed Forces.

Integrated and Segregated Occupations

Social Class II compared to only one-fifth of sex-segregated occupations (Table 2.5). Sex-segregated occupations are dominated by Social Class III skilled occupations: white-collar jobs in the female sector and blue-collar jobs in the male sector. In contrast, the skilled occupations of Social Class III barely figure among integrated occupations. Semi-skilled occupations are adequately represented, but there is almost no unskilled work in the integrated sector, compared to one in ten jobs in the sex-segregated sector. Three-quarters of integrated occupations consist of Class I and II occupations, while three-quarters of the sex-segregated occupations are in Social Classes III to V.

Using Goldthorpe's class schema, two-thirds of integrated occupations are in the Service Class, while two-thirds of the sex-segregated occupations are in the other classes (Table 2.5). Again, integrated occupations have a small share of skilled and unskilled manual work. This class schema also shows

TABLE 2.5. *Class composition of sex-segregated and integrated occupations*

column/row/cell percent

	Type of occupation				% within each class				% female			
	Male	Mixed	Female	All	Male	Mixed	Female	All	Male	Mixed	Female	All
Goldthorpe Classes												
Higher service class	16	24	2	11	58	37	5	100	12	39	67	25
Lower service class	14	40	17	20	30	34	36	100	15	40	76	46
Routine non-manual	2	3	34	15	5	4	92	100	18	44	82	77
Personal service	—	—	18	8	—	—	100	100	—	—	90	90
Small proprietors, farmers	15	16	3	10	63	27	10	100	5	38	71	21
Lower technicians, foremen	8	2	2	4	77	7	16	100	7	27	67	18
Skilled manual workers	20	5	3	11	80	7	13	100	4	42	70	16
Semi- & unskilled workers	5	10	21	21	50	8	42	100	11	38	85	44
RG Social Classes												
I Professional	8	7	1	5	59	30	11	100	9	31	25	18
II Managerial & Technical	17	66	20	29	23	50	27	100	15	38	77	44
IIIN Skilled white-collar	7	5	50	23	11	5	84	100	19	43	83	74
IIIM Skilled blue-collar	44	8	6	21	80	8	12	100	4	47	64	15
IV Semi-skilled	19	15	13	15	46	21	32	100	15	51	88	46
V Unskilled	5	*	9	6	35	1	64	100	8	7	83	56
Total	100	100	100	100	39	22	39	100	10	40	80	44

Sources: 1% and 2% SARs, Great Britain, data for residents aged 16–64 years in employment, excluding student jobs. The 1% SAR provides data for Goldthorpe Classes and the 2% SAR is used for RG Social Classes.

female-dominated occupations in a new light, with one-fifth in the personal service class, a class that is exclusively female.

The high social and economic status of integrated occupations is reflected in their having the highest Cambridge scores for social status and the highest earnings. Cambridge status scores and earnings are discussed in more detail in Chapter 3, but it is worth noting here that they offer slightly inconsistent pictures. Cambridge scores show integrated occupations to have the highest status, and this is true for men as well as women, for part-timers as well as full-timers (Table 2.4). However, the peculiar scaling used means that female occupations are shown as systematically scoring higher in social status than male occupations—for men as well as women, for full-timers and part-timers. This *social* ranking is very different from the purely *economic* value of jobs reflected in earnings. Integrated occupations have markedly higher average hourly earnings; average earnings in sex-segregated occupations are markedly lower but also fairly similar. This pattern again persists across all groups, men and women, full-time and part-time employees. So while there may be some doubt about the relative social and economic status of male-dominated and female-dominated occupations, there is no doubt at all that integrated occupations have the highest rank on all dimensions, social and economic, and in terms of authority and independence.

WORKPLACE CHARACTERISTICS

Integrated occupations are concentrated disproportionately in London and the South-East region of England (Table 2.6), which is where the largest concentrations of professional and specialist workers are located. Highly sex-segregated workforces are more common in other regions of England and in Scotland and Wales. As Fielding has shown, the South-East, and London in particular, offer women more opportunities to climb occupational ladders than provincial areas (Fielding, 1992; Fielding and Halford, 1993).

Politicians often argue that growth and prosperity provide a faster route to equality of opportunity than is achieved by affirmative action policies. This is doubtful, at least as regards equal opportunities legislation, given that unequal pay for men and women was maintained over centuries of growth (Hakim, 1996a). However, there is some evidence for the USA that economic growth and prosperity provide a faster route to equalizing labour market outcomes than would be achieved by positive discrimination in favour of women or racial minorities (Feinberg, 1984, 1985). There is some indirect evidence to this effect also for Britain, in that a higher proportion of jobs in London and the relatively prosperous South-East region are in integrated occupations: 28% and 24% compared to 20% of jobs in the rest of Britain (Table 2.6).

TABLE 2.6. *Workplace characteristics of segregated and integrated occupations*   cell/column percent

	Type of occupation			
	Male	Mixed	Female	Total
Percentage of women whose workplace is:				
at home	5	7	3	4
no fixed place (home-based)	5	3	2	3
0–2 km from home	28	27	39	36
301 km from home	5	6	3	3
% who walk to work	11	11	19	17
Percentage of men whose workplace is:				
at home	2	6	2	3
no fixed place (home-based)	12	4	4	9
0–2 km from home	20	18	24	20
301 km from home	7	12	6	8
% who walk to work	7	7	12	8
Percentage of all workers whose workplace is:				
at home	2	6	3	3
no fixed place (home-based)	11	4	3	6
0–2 km from home	21	22	36	27
301 km from home	7	10	3	6
% who walk to work	8	9	18	12
Regional distribution of jobs				
London	10	15	13	12
Rest of South-East	20	23	20	21
Rest of Britain	70	62	68	67

Source: 2% SAR, Great Britain, data for residents aged 16–64 years in employment, excluding student jobs.

As regards travel to work patterns, female occupations are distinctively different from male and mixed occupations, but differences derive primarily from the sex differential in job choice which then becomes a characteristic of female-dominated occupations. Homework and travel to work patterns are analysed in Chapter 7, but the salient features of integrated and segregated occupations are noted here. (Chapter 7 also describes the recoding of the 'at home' category in Table 2.6.)

Integrated occupations have above average proportions of men and women working at home—6% compared to 2%–3% in the sex-segregated sector. Despite the popular view that women are trapped into working at home by child care duties (Allen and Wolkowitz, 1987; European Commission, 1995*d*), women and men are equally likely to work at home and female occupations do not have the highest rate of homeworking (Table 2.6). The higher level found among integrated occupations results from higher levels of self-employment in this sector, with 19% of the self-employed working at home and another 31% working from home as a base (see Table 7.8b). However, men are more than twice as likely as women to work from home as a base, or to have long journeys to work, while women as a group are more likely to work very locally, with short trips to work, often on foot.

Female occupations are distinctive in being located close to home, due to women's preference for local jobs offering short journeys to work. Women are almost twice as likely as men to work locally, within a 2-km radius of their home (36% compared to 20%), and twice as likely to walk to work (17% versus 8%), as shown in Table 2.6. The sex differential persists, to varying degrees, across all three types of occupation. So the travel to work patterns of integrated and segregated occupations are primarily a reflection of their sex composition. Even among part-timers, women are twice as likely as men to get to work on foot (see Table 5.7). Women's lower investment, in time and money, in transport to work echoes their lower investment, in time and effort, in obtaining educational qualifications.

In effect, employers have structured female occupations to accommodate women's distinctive preferences for part-time work, local jobs, and occupations requiring little or no investment in training and qualifications. Even on the basis of the limited information available from the 1991 Census, it is clear that it is female occupations, rather than integrated occupations, that provide the 'gender neutral' sector with low entry barriers easing transition into the labour market. The female sector is large enough to contain career occupations as well, comparable to the long-term career occupations in the integrated and male-dominated sectors. As a first approximation, about half of the female sector consists of 'career' occupations and about half consists of short-term jobs requiring no long-term commitment or investments, and with similarly reduced rewards and opportunities. The latter group would include the semi- and unskilled manual occupations identified by Goldthorpe's class schema (Table 2.5) and most part-time jobs.

It is well established that jobs in manufacturing industry are male-dominated while jobs in the service industries employ many women, and this pattern is repeated in the SARs data. However, integrated occupations are of particular interest. Some important manufacturing industries produce an above average number of integrated occupations: food and drink manufacture, the textile industry, and the manufacture of paper and paper products. However, service industries are the more important source of integrated occupations: insurance, business services, research and development, recreational services, air and sea transport, commission agents, personal services (that is, laundries, beauty parlours, hairdressing, and similar trades), real estate, public administration, retail distribution, and renting cars and equipment. There is no dominant type of industry, and they are drawn from the private as well as the public sector, from small and specialized as well as large industries. It is notable that the primary sector (agriculture, forestry, fishing), which is an important source of integrated occupations in less developed countries is a male-dominated sector in Britain, along with construction, ground transport, and the heavy manufacturing and engineering industries.

PERSONAL CHARACTERISTICS OF WORKERS

Analysis of the personal and household characteristics of workers in each of the three types of occupation again shows that the most important dividing line is between female-dominated occupations and integrated or male occupations. The one-quarter minority of women working in integrated and male occupations differs qualitatively from the three-quarters majority working in female occupations—the former being more career-oriented and the latter being more centred on family and home. Occupational choices reflect the polarization of working women, which is a long-term secular trend rather than a temporary and reversible phenomenon (Humphries and Rubery, 1992; Berger, Steinmüller, and Sopp, 1993; Burchell and Rubery, 1994: 109; Hakim, 1996a). More surprisingly, the small minority (14%) of men working in female occupations also differ substantively from the majority of male workers.

Women in female occupations are less likely to be single, divorced, cohabiting, or remarried; it is married women who gravitate to female occupations, which have an above average concentration of women in the 'conventional' family of two adults with dependent children. Their choice of job reflects greater priority being given to domestic activities than to paid work: they are less likely to work overtime, more likely to work part-time and to travel short distances to places of work close to home. In contrast, men working in female-dominated occupations are twice as likely to be single and young (aged under 25), still living in their parents' home, sometimes still in full-time education, and less likely than other men to have dependent children. Like women in these jobs, they also tend to work part-time, in local jobs. As shown in Chapter 6, some of them are students in full-time education, but student jobs are excluded from Table 2.7.

The combination of these two contrasting subgroups within the female job sector balances out to some extent, so that the summary profile of workers in female occupations looks no different from the overall profiles for integrated and male occupations. On the basis of personal and household characteristics, integrated and segregated occupations look identical in the aggregate. In all three groups three-quarters of workers live in owner-occupied housing, 4% are non-white, 29% have never been married, and 40% have dependent children living with them in the same household. In the aggregate, the three groups are distinguished by job characteristics, but not by personal charac-

TABLE 2.7. *Personal characteristics of workers in sex-segregated and integrated occupations*   row/cell percent

		Type of occupation			
		Male	Mixed	Female	Total
Women aged	16–24	10	17	73	100
	25–34	10	24	66	100
	35–44	8	21	71	100
	45–54	8	20	73	100
	55–64	8	17	75	100
	16–64	9	20	71	100
Men aged	16–24	63	16	21	100
	25–34	64	23	13	100
	35–44	62	26	12	100
	45–54	63	26	11	100
	55–64	63	24	13	100
	16–64	63	23	14	100
% non-white	men	3	6	8	4
	women	4	5	4	4
% with 11	men	42	42	37	41
dependent child	women	33	33	41	39
% in homes	men	70	68	71	70
with 21 earners	women	81	80	82	81
% in owner-	men	78	83	76	79
occupied homes	women	76	79	79	79
White workers		40	22	39	100
Non-white workers		29	28	43	100
Region: London		31	28	41	100
Rest of South-East		39	24	37	100
Rest of Britain		41	20	39	100

Source: 2% SAR, Great Britain, data for residents aged 16–64 years in employment, excluding student jobs.

teristics. Another conclusion is that sex-atypical workers are generally young, with older workers reverting to sex-typical occupations. But the trend is weak. The national distribution of male, female, and integrated occupations is repeated across all age cohorts of men and women, with little variation over the life cycle (Table 2.7).

SOCIAL RELATIONS AT WORK: DIVORCE AND REMARRIAGE RATES

Our primary interest in occupational segregation concerns the way it structures jobs and careers, opportunities and rewards within the workforce.

However, it also structures social interaction in the workplace to some degree. Workplaces are one of the many locations where people make friends, of both sexes, and meet potential marriage partners. Social interaction at work is not limited to people in the same occupation, but interaction is usually easier and more frequent between colleagues than across occupational boundaries. Humphries argues that in the nineteenth century, occupational segregation was prompted primarily by a concern to control sexuality, to avoid social contact between unrelated men and women in the workplace, to reduce or eliminate the potential for heterosexual liaisons (and hence illegitimate children) in social settings beyond family supervision (Humphries, 1987). This is no longer argued to be a principal function of occupational segregation in modern society at the end of the twentieth century, as contraception has replaced this prophylactic function of occupational segregation (Hakim, 1994). However, Murphy (1985) has argued that occupations which allow men and women to meet socially at work have the highest divorce rates, while occupations dominated by one sex (such as the police) have the lowest divorce rates. This thesis is tested in Table 2.8 and is broadly supported, although the impact of occupation type is tiny for men and only slightly larger among women.

Among ever-married men, the total divorce rate (with or without remarriage) is 20% and does not vary between segregated and integrated occupations. However, the remarriage rate for men is highest in integrated occupations, at 12% compared to 10%–11%. Among ever-married women,

TABLE 2.8. *Divorce and remarriage rates within integrated and segregated occupations*

	Divorced & remarried aged 16–64 as % of evermarried aged 16–64		Base numbers		
	Divorced not remarried	Divorced and remarried	Divorced not remarried	Divorced and remarried	Ever-married
Men in					
Male occupations	9	11	12,049	14,764	139,749
Integrated occupations	8	12	3,975	6,068	52,080
Female occupations	9	10	2,198	2,525	25,023
All occupations	8	11	18,222	23,359	216,852
Women in					
Male occupations	12	11	2,009	1,833	16,904
Integrated occupations	12	11	4,814	4,472	39,472
Female occupations	10	10	14,422	14,098	145,086
All occupations	11	10	21,245	20,403	201,462

Source: 2% SAR, Great Britain. Data for ever-married residents aged 16–64 years reporting a current or last job.

the total divorce rate (with or without remarriage) is higher in male-dominated and integrated occupations than in female-dominated occupations: 23% versus 20%, and the remarriage rate is also higher at 11% compared to 10%. Women in female-dominated occupations, who have the lowest probability of bumping into men at work and the lowest average earnings when they do work, have divorce and remarriage rates markedly lower than occur among women in occupations where men outnumber women and earnings are higher. Given the large numbers of cases in the 2% SAR, all differences between groups are statistically significant, but the size of the effect is small. Admittedly the test is not perfect. Social interaction at work is not limited to people in the same occupation and workplace size is probably important as well. Given the many social and cultural factors that might be expected to enhance or attenuate divorce and remarriage rates, it is perhaps remarkable that the sex composition of occupations, of itself, can make a significant contribution to a woman's chances of divorce and remarriage and to a man's chance of remarriage after divorce. It is also notable that, for women, the key dividing line is between female occupations and all others. A tentative conclusion is that, given their minority status in the workforce, working within a male-dominated or integrated occupation has a larger impact on women's lives, both private and professional, than it does for men who are anyway the dominant group.

The analysis of divorce and remarriage rates reminds us that occupations have a social side to them as well as the work task, that people bring their sexual identities to the workplace to some extent, that social relations in the workplace cannot be limited exclusively to work tasks. The positive side of this is that work colleagues sometimes choose each other as marriage partners. The negative side is that people may misjudge or mishandle relationships at work (or at social gatherings in the workplace) and fall into the trap of sexual harassment. It takes a minimum level of social skills to get this aspect of work relationships right, and these skills have to be learnt. The fallback option is to have sex-segregated workplaces and sex-segregated occupations in order to minimize the risks of sexual interaction in the workplace, as is the practice today in some Muslim societies, and as was often the practice in nineteenth-century Britain.

LABOUR TURNOVER

Our thesis that integrated occupations provide transitional jobs from which people are routed into other, more stable jobs, can be tested with labour turnover data and with information on occupation changes. This thesis predicts that integrated occupations will have the highest turnover rates, as they provide labour market entry and exit points. Alternatively, the preceding analyses in this chapter suggest that it is female occupations, rather than integrated occupations, that serve this role, and that female occupations will have the highest turnover rates.

A competing thesis is Jacobs's 'revolving doors' thesis which predicts that turnover rates are highest for women in male-dominated occupations. Jacobs's social exclusion or social control thesis stated that male colleagues refuse to provide the informal job induction process, the camaraderie and co-operative teamwork that new female entrants need to succeed, that male colleagues regularly ignore, harass, and undermine female colleagues in order to exclude them from male occupations (J. Jacobs, 1989*b*: 181–2). In effect he described the informal and invisible 'freezing out' mechanisms that complement and extend the formal exclusionary policies of patriarchal trade unions (Cockburn, 1983; Hakim, 1996*a*: 162–6). The thesis was plausible, resting as it did on patriarchy theory without ever using the term. However, the only evidence advanced was that Jacobs claimed to have shown that women entered, but were then forced out of male-dominated occupations to a greater extent than the ordinary quit rate for integrated and female-dominated occupations (J. Jacobs, 1989*b*: 142).

Analyses of labour turnover have to be presented separately for men and women because of the continuing sex differential in all measures of labour mobility: labour turnover, job tenure, and related measures of movement in and out of jobs and the labour market (Hakim, 1996*c*). The sex differential is found, to varying degrees, in all industrial societies, including the USA, Britain, and the rest of Europe (Hakim, 1996*c*). Labour turnover rates at the aggregate level can be constructed with the SARs information on jobs held in the last ten years. Turnover is defined as the proportion of men and women reporting a current or recent job who are not currently in work. Among people aged 16–64 years, 16% of men and 24% of women had left a job in the previous ten years (Table 2.9). These turnover rates, and the 50% mark-up in

TABLE 2.9. *Labour turnover rates among people of working age*

	Type of occupation	In work	Total not in work	Unemployed	Not working	Retired & Sick	Base 000s=100%
Men	Male	83	17	10	1	6	195
	Integrated	87	13	7	*	5	69
	Female	83	17	10	1	6	42
	All occupations	84	16	9	1	6	307
Women	Male	75	25	6	13	6	24
	Integrated	76	24	5	13	6	54
	Female	76	24	4	14	6	190
	All occupations	76	24	5	13	6	267

Source: 2% SAR, Great Britain. Data for residents aged 16–64 years reporting a current job or a job in the previous ten years, excluding student jobs.

the female rate, are completely typical of the rates and the sex differential reported in all other datasources for Britain since 1968, and they are not wholly dissimilar from turnover patterns in the USA and Western Europe (Hakim, 1996*c*). A European Commission report (1994*b*: 83–101) shows that Britain's 50% sex differential in labour turnover is typical of the European Union as a whole, even though labour mobility in Britain is above the EU average. So the picture obtained from the SARs is consistent with that from other sources, even if the measure employed is peculiar to the SAR files, and data for Britain is a reasonable approximation to the average European pattern of labour turnover. Turnover rates in the SARs can be calculated with student jobs excluded (Table 2.9) or included (Table 2.11). The sex differential is constant in both versions, with female turnover 50% higher than male turnover.

Women are most likely to leave jobs because they are quitting the labour force to become full-time homemakers, at least for a time, whereas unemployment accounts for most men who are not currently in work (Table 2.9). Contrary to all hypotheses, type of occupation has no impact at all; turnover rates are constant across all three occupation groups for men and women (Table 2.9). As shown in Chapter 5, the sex differential in turnover also persists, to varying degrees, across the full-time and part-time workforces with little or no impact of occupation type (see Table 5.10).

Another test of our thesis about transitional jobs is to look at the occupations of new entrants to the workforce: young people aged 16–25 years who are in transition from full-time education to full-time employment, or else the vacation and other jobs of students in full-time education. Student jobs are analysed in more detail in Chapter 6. Our interest here is whether they are typically in integrated or female occupations. We also look at the last jobs of people who classify themselves as retired[3] (Table 2.10).

Overall, female occupations are the most likely, and integrated occupations the least likely to provide jobs for labour market entrants, even among men: 70% of all jobs held by students (56% of men and 84% of women) were in female occupations (Table 2.10). To a lesser extent, female occupations also provide part-time jobs in the pre-retirement and post-retirement phase for men as well as for the majority of older women. However, most people make the transition from full-time work (in their main occupation) into full-time retirement without an intermediate phase of part-time work. So the

[3] In the population census, retirement is self-defined, but people whose primary status is 'retired' are those without any paid work. More detailed information on the retirement process, and the factors prompting people to classify themselves as 'retired' is provided by the 1988 Retirement Survey (Bone *et al.*, 1992). This survey explored the definitions of 'retirement' applied in the major government surveys (GHS, FES, and LFS) and showed that, among people around retirement age, self-classification produces a higher percentage of retired than official classifications of economic activity status, which invariably treat anyone with one hour's work per week as being in employment (Bone *et al.*, 1992: 22–9, 35–40).

TABLE 2.10. *Current and last jobs of students and the retired*

		% in each type of occupation		
		Male	Mixed	Female
Current & last jobs of students all		19	11	70
	full-time jobs	32	18	50
	part-time jobs	8	5	87
Male students	all	32	12	56
	full-time jobs	46	19	35
	part-time jobs	15	5	79
Female students	all	7	9	84
	full-time jobs	13	17	70
	part-time jobs	3	5	92
Last jobs of the retired	all	27	21	52
	full-time jobs	33	24	43
	part-time jobs	6	9	85
Retired men	all	57	26	17
	full-time jobs	57	26	17
	part-time jobs	38	17	45
Retired women	all	8	17	75
	full-time jobs	9	22	69
	part-time jobs	5	9	87
Current and last jobs of people aged				
16–24 years	all	35	16	48
	men	60	15	25
	women	10	17	73
	all FT	39	16	44
	all PT	10	8	82
55–64 years	all	40	20	40
	men	63	23	14
	women	8	17	75
	all FT	49	23	28
	all PT	9	11	80

Source: 2% SAR, Great Britain, data for residents aged 16–64 years.

transitional role of female occupations is much weaker at the end of working lives than at the start, as is also shown by data for age cohorts.[4] The occupations of the youngest and oldest people are shaped primarily by the existing national pattern of occupational segregation. None the less there is a small bias towards female occupations among young people. Among young men aged 16–24, one-quarter start out in female occupations, twice the national

[4] The 1988 Retirement Survey found that one-third of men and women aged 55–69 years said that their current or most recent job was not their main life job (Bone *et al.*, 1992: 7–8). Only small proportions of those who regarded themselves as retired were still doing paid work, almost always in a part-time job—11% of men and 6% of women (Bone *et al.*, 1992: 23). It seems likely that the recessions of the 1980s speeded up the transition into full retirement.

average for men (Table 2.10). What is certain is that integrated occupations do not serve as points of entry into and exit from the labour market.

Turnover rates are sex-specific, but they also vary by occupational grade. As a general rule, turnover is lowest in higher grade occupations and highest in lower grade occupations. For this reason, high turnover among women has often been dismissed by social scientists (though not by employers) as being due to their concentration in lower grade jobs. In fact, the available evidence has shown that women have systematically higher turnover than men in *all* grades of occupation (Hakim, 1996*c*: 6–7; see also Table 8.5). However very few datasets are sufficiently large to permit full analysis of turnover rates: only a small minority of people leave jobs in any given period, so datasets need to be really large to measure turnover reliably. For this reason the 2% SAR is used to present a full analysis of turnover rates by social class and SEG in male, mixed, and female occupations in Table 2.11. The results using the RG Social Classes are the clearest; Goldthorpe's classes and SEG tell the same story, with more detail.

The results in Table 2.11 refute a number of arguments. First, higher female turnover rates are not explained by their occupations or by the peculiar character of female-dominated occupations. With rare exceptions, women always have higher turnover than do men, typically 50% higher. The sex differential is smallest and sometimes even disappears in the lowest grade occupations, but in general it persists at all levels. Remarkably, the sex differential is highest in the highest grade occupations, those that require long years of education and training, that imply the highest levels of work commitment, and offer the greatest rewards: in the upper service class turnover rates are 8% for men and almost double at 14% for women; in the lower service class, turnover rates are 13% for men and 21% for women (Table 2.11).

Second, there are no fundamental differences between male, mixed, and female occupations in their turnover rates. Neither integrated nor female occupations have turnover rates that are well above average. In this table, where student jobs are included in the analysis, female occupations seem to have slightly higher turnover. Once student jobs are excluded, this excess disappears completely (Table 2.9). The exclusion of student jobs is perfectly legitimate since students in full-time education are not formally in the labour market. Female occupations provide labour market entry jobs, but this does not entail markedly higher turnover rates as a result, contrary to our thesis.

Third, women in male occupations do indeed have substantially higher turnover rates: 26% compared to 18% for men, but these rates are actually the gender-specific turnover rates observed throughout the entire workforce. In particular, there is no evidence that women are being pushed out of the highest grade and most rewarding male occupations by male exclusionary tactics, as J. Jacobs argues. If anything the contrary is true: female turnover is well *below* the female national average in male-dominated service class jobs, in

Integrated and Segregated Occupations

TABLE 2.11. *Turnover rates in sex-segregated and integrated occupations by class and SEG*

	Male		Mixed		Female		Total	
	M	F	M	F	M	F	M	F
All in work[1]	18	26	14	25	23	27	17	26
Goldthorpe Classes								
Upper service class	8	13	8	15	7	12	8	14
Lower service class	13	20	14	23	12	19	13	21
Routine non-manual	13	19	19	26	18	23	17	24
Personal service	—	—	—	—	40	32	40	32
Small proprietors, with employees	1	1	*	1	*	1	*	1
Small proprietors, no employees	11	13	13	20	10	11	11	15
Farmers	5	11	16	13	22	12	6	11
Lower technicians, foremen	16	27	12	27	19	25	16	26
Skilled manual workers	21	37	18	38	26	37	21	37
Semi- and unskilled workers	26	35	24	38	36	34	27	34
Agricultural workers	21	33	25	34	22	42	21	37
RG Social Classes								
I Professional	9	14	9	14	11	17	9	15
II Managerial, technical	11	18	11	18	13	20	11	19
IIIN Skilled	11	22	10	15	25	27	20	26
IIIM Skilled	18	31	18	30	20	31	18	31
IV Semi-skilled	23	32	23	39	40	32	24	34
V Unskilled	36	36	17	30	30	30	34	30
Socio-Economic Group								
employers and managers—								
large establishments	7	8	6	9	12	12	6	9
employers—small establishments	1	1	1	1	*	1	1	1
managers—small establishments	14	23	15	23	18	21	15	23
professionals—self-employed	2	6	3	4	3	6	2	5
professionals—employees	10	15	11	16	12	18	10	16
ancillary workers & artists	12	21	13	19	13	20	13	20
supervisors—white-collar	12	17	~	~	17	22	15	22
junior white-collar	12	25	26	29	27	27	22	27
personal service	—	—	29	24	34	34	34	33
foremen—blue-collar	16	23	15	26	17	22	16	23
skilled blue-collar	21	14	19	34	19	36	21	35
semi-skilled blue-collar	24	33	24	39	28	30	24	35
unskilled blue collar	38	37	17	30	35	30	37	30
own-account workers (not professionals)	10	12	12	19	8	9	10	15
farmers—owners/managers	5	10	—	—	—	—	5	10
agricultural workers	22	33	—	—	—	—	22	33
Armed Forces	10	23	—	—	—	—	10	23

Note: Student jobs are included in the calculation of turnover rates in this table.

[1] Includes inadequately described occupations.

Sources: 1% and 2% SARs, Great Britain, data for residents aged 16–64 years in employment, including student jobs. The 1% SAR provides data for Goldthorpe's Classes and the 2% SAR is used for the rest of the table.

male-dominated professional jobs, in male-dominated managerial and technical jobs (Table 2.11). Male-dominated occupations do not appear to offer a work environment that is any more exclusionary than are integrated and female occupations in line by line, occupation by occupation comparisons in Table 2.11.

Is this a case where the situation in Britain is completely at odds with trends in the USA, and where Britain is more successful at integrating women into the workforce? On closer examination, it emerges that the analysis carried out by J. Jacobs, based on data for 1967 to 1977, was too flawed to substantiate his 'revolving doors' thesis of social control mechanisms employed to freeze women out of sex-atypical occupations, even for the USA. Like so many other sociologists, Jacobs fell into the sample selection trap (Berk, 1983; Lieberson, 1985). By restricting his analysis to female occupation changers and thus to women employed over a period of ten years, it excluded a large proportion of female labour turnover in the USA, which would alter the balance of movements in and out of occupations (Hakim, 1996c: tables 13 and 14). Continuously employed women are a rare species, even in the USA. PSID data for the adult population in the USA show only 6 per cent of women compared to 64 per cent of men were in continuous full-time employment over the 13–year period 1968–1980 (Corcoran, Duncan, and Ponza, 1984: 177; Treiman, 1985: 218).

Furthermore, evidence from other USA studies, as well as evidence for Britain, contradicts Jacobs's thesis and is consistent with our results. Over the five years 1965–70, Sommers and Eck showed that labour force entries and exits in the USA were two to four times higher for women than men, across all occupations; after excluding differential labour force exit rates, there was no sex differential in occupational change rates, which were generally lowest, for women as well as men, in male-dominated professional and managerial occupations as well as in domestic service for women and farming for men (calculated from tables 3 and 4 in Sommers and Eck, 1977). Waite and Berryman (1986) found no evidence that being in a sex-atypical occupation increased turnover rates for young women or men in the USA. Recent USA research shows that, in the period covered by Jacobs's study, women in male-dominated occupations had significantly *greater* continuity of employment than women in female-dominated occupations (Rexroat 1992), a result which is wholly inconsistent with Jacobs's results and social exclusion thesis, but is consistent with our results for Britain.

A replication and extended analysis by S. Jacobs (1995) using work history data from a 1986 British survey also failed to corroborate J. Jacobs's thesis. She examined occupational changes over 15 and 25 years, for men and women, and found them to be largely stable within the three categories of male-dominated, female-dominated, and integrated occupations (S. Jacobs, 1995; see also Scott and Burchell, 1994: 141). Similarly a large degree of stability in type of occupation is found in the ONS 1% Longitudinal Study (OPCS, 1988) data on occupational change over the decade 1971–81 (Table 2.12). This analysis uses a definition of integrated occupations exactly the same as in Jacobs's analyses for the USA, namely occupations that are 30–70% female (50% 6 20%). On average, people have a major change of occupation once every four years among women and once every five years among men (or once every three years among men with broken employment records); over a decade virtually everyone will change occupation at least once (Elias and Main, 1982: 10). Yet most people remain in the same type of male, mixed, or female occupation that they were in a decade earlier (Table 2.12), so that the occupational structure is virtually identical at the start and end of the decade, apart from the growth of mixed occupations. The correlation coefficient between occupation type in 1971 and 1981 remains at about .40 for all subgroups shown in Table 2.12, varying only slightly or not at all between men and women, consistent with the results of USA studies (Rosenfeld and Spenner, 1992: 429). Occupational stability falls as an occupation increases in sex-atypicality. However, this pattern is the same among men and women. Among full-time workers, women are *more* likely to remain in male jobs than are men to remain in female jobs. This contradicts J. Jacobs's thesis that women are especially vulnerable to being 'frozen out' of male-dominated occupations by subtle (and crude) social control mechanisms; if anything, the social exclusion process is stronger for men in female jobs. Once again, a study restricted to women alone produced wrong conclusions.

REVERSION TO SEX-TYPICAL OCCUPATIONS

Unlike Jacobs's analysis, which was restricted to women, Table 2.12 compares men and women, full-time and part-time workers. This fuller analysis reveals a general tendency for people to leave sex-atypical occupations and move towards sex-typical occupations. This process is found among men and women to fairly equal degree, so any sociological explanation for this process has to apply equally to men and women. It is notable that people who leave integrated occupations generally move to sex-typical occupations by the end of the decade: most men leaving mixed occupations move to male occupations while most women leaving mixed occupations move to female occupations. This is the only finding which supports our thesis that integrated occupations provide transitional jobs which allow people to route themselves into stable sex-typical occupations.

In a sense, the surprising finding is that female turnover in managerial and professional occupations is well below the average for all women, and that most women, especially full-timers, do stick with their jobs in integrated and

TABLE 2.12. *Occupational change 1971–1981 among people in continuous employment*

	Type of occupation in 1971	Proportion (%) in each type of occupation in 1981				Totals for 1971 1 Base
		Male	Mixed	Female	Total	
All persons	Male	84	11	4	100	57
	Mixed	30	55	15	100	26
	Female	13	21	66	100	17
	Total	58	24	18	100	100
	Base for this group					131,600
All women	Male	37	29	34	100	11
	Mixed	10	61	29	100	39
	Female	7	21	72	100	50
	Total	12	38	51	100	100
	Base for this group					39,200
All men	Male	87	10	2	100	76
	Mixed	47	49	4	100	20
	Female	44	22	34	100	4
	Total	78	18	4	100	100
	Base for this group					92,400
Women working full-time only	Male	48	31	21	100	14
	Mixed	13	67	20	100	44
	Female	9	26	65	100	42
	Total	16	45	39	100	100
	Base for this group					17,700
Men working full-time only	Male	88	10	2	100	76
	Mixed	48	48	4	100	20
	Female	46	22	32	100	4
	Total	79	18	3	100	100
	Base for this group					88,500
All working full-time only	Male	86	11	3	100	66
	Mixed	37	54	9	100	24
	Female	20	25	55	100	10
	Total	68	22	9	100	100
	Base for this group					106,200
All with any part-time work	Male	49	22	29	100	17
	Mixed	10	56	34	100	34
	Female	6	18	76	100	49
	Total	15	32	53	100	100
	Base for this group					25,400

Note: Integrated occupations are those 30–70% female (50% 6 20%) using occupational classifications with 223 groups (1971) and 350 groups (1981). The classification of occupational groups is based on published 10% sample data from the 1971 and 1981 Population Censuses.

Source: ONS 1% Longitudinal Study, data for people aged 16 and over in England and Wales who were in employment in 1971 and 1981.

male-dominated occupations. Many professional and managerial jobs in consultancy, finance, management, research, or the mass media, for example, involve working hours hugely in excess of a normal working day or week, or else unsocial hours; many of these occupations involve regular business travel and other activities that eat into private lives. These all-consuming jobs are often attractive to young single people but become less attractive to older married people who may switch to less demanding occupations. Thus we might have expected female turnover in these jobs to be higher than it is, but for work-related reasons rather than due to male colleagues' attempts to discourage them from staying, actively or covertly.

The main finding from Table 2.12 is of a general drift away from sex-atypical occupations towards sex-typical occupations, a trend that is somewhat stronger among men than among women, especially among full-time workers. The most likely explanation is simply that working life is more psychologically and socially comfortable, or unproblematic, for many people when work colleagues are of the same sex, so that there is a natural tendency to drift back towards sex-typical occupations. The reversal to sex-typical occupations is 'natural' in the sense of being voluntary rather than forced on people by social institutions and work colleagues. Alternatively, men and women are equally hostile and unwelcoming to people of the opposite sex who 'invade' predominantly single-sex occupations. It appears that Jacobs's social exclusion thesis was accepted because it was consistent with fashionable feminist arguments rather than because the evidence was solid. J. Jacobs himself subsequently admitted that men and women in the USA *both* drift back to sex-typical jobs (Jacobs, 1993: 62). If the social control and social exclusion thesis is valid, then it applies *equally* to men and women, to male and female occupations, and ceases to be a distinctive factor.

Research is documenting the way that jobs are constructed by employers as female or male jobs, even in times of labour shortage during wars (Milkman, 1987; Bradley, 1989; Strom, 1989). But as noted by Bradley (1989: 229), one reason for this is the fact that women have preferred to work with women, men with men, partly as a demonstration of and confirmation of sexual identities (Matthaei, 1982: 194). Workers play an even more important role in gendering jobs than employers do. Workplace cultures are often heavily coloured by job incumbents: women regularly celebrate their private relationships and private lives at work and men celebrate their sexual exploits and leisure interests (Pringle, 1988: 95, 120, 225, 243; Reskin and Padavic, 1994: 134–41). Both feminine and masculine work cultures and associated institutions, such as clubs, can be experienced as exclusionary by men and women. For example, women can ostracize a female colleague who refuses to engage in discussions of private lives at work, while men can look down on a man who has no interest in cars, sport, or pin-ups. As yet we have little solid evidence on the informal 'freezing out' exclusionary processes, conscious or unconscious, applied by men and women to people in sex-atypical positions, and more generally to people who do not conform to gender stereotypes. This can include female colleagues at all grades, including professionals as well as secretaries, along with men refusing to co-operate with, or even work for, a female boss or manager (Hakim, 1996a: 114–18). Most of the time, masculine and feminine workplace cultures are unrelated to the nature of the work task; they are a gratuitous add-on. Quite often, it is the work culture that defines an occupation as male or female rather than the work task itself (Hakim, 1996a: 165).

In sum, two quite different tests of Jacobs's social exclusion thesis fail to produce any support for his arguments and reveal other social processes instead. Analyses of turnover rates in Table 2.11 and elsewhere (Hakim, 1996c) show a continuing sex differential and the marked impact of occupational grade, but few or no differences between male, female, and integrated occupations. Analyses of people who remain in employment over a decade (Table 2.12) show both men and women drifting back to sex-typical occupations, a trend that is stronger among men rather than women and is found even among people in continuous full-time employment. New explanations are needed for these patterns of occupational mobility and labour mobility.

CONCLUSIONS

This comparative analysis of the characteristics of integrated and sex-segregated occupations yields three important conclusions.

First, we have replaced the simple dichotomy of male and female occupations which has so far been the convention in research on occupational segregation with a threefold typology of male, mixed, and female occupations. The change works. What started out as an essentially statistical definition of integrated occupations as those grouped closely around the average sex ratio for the whole workforce (40% 6 15%) has developed into a typology that identifies important substantive differences between integrated occupations at the centre and sex-segregated occupations at the outer sides of the occupational structure. On every job characteristic examined, the small group of mixed occupations is raised above the sex-segregated sector, absorbing a disproportionate share of Service Class positions, managerial and professional occupations, the most highly qualified and highly paid jobs, with the authority of senior grades and/or the independence of the self-employed professional, craftsman, or business owner. In contrast, the sex-segregated sector presents two parallel occupational ladders centred on the middle and lower ground of routine white-collar work, skilled and unskilled blue-collar work.

The Service Class as a whole is split roughly one-third, one-third, one-quarter between male, mixed, and female occupations, a far more balanced picture than that hypothesized by virtually all the theories of occupational segregation, which present women as losing out massively to men. Maybe they did, when the theories were developed, in the 1960s. The two decades 1971–91 saw dramatic changes in the USA and Europe in women's preferences for professional and managerial careers instead of just jobs, and the pattern of occupational segregation has now been transformed in consequence (Reskin and Roos, 1990; Sokoloff, 1992; Hakim, 1992*a*; Rubery and Fagan, 1993). Most important, the best jobs in terms of earnings and (as we show in Chapter 3) status and prestige are now integrated occupations, shared proportionately by men and women, and not male-dominated occupations. Our results suggest the need for a dramatic reassessment of the current state of play on women's position in the labour market, on occupational segregation, and on the successes of equal opportunities policies—themes we return to in Chapter 10. In the meantime, the typology of male, mixed, and female occupations offers a major step forward in research on occupational segregation. As shown in Chapter 1, the typology offers a meaningful alternative approach for cross-national comparisons of occupational segregation in the USA and Europe. The discovery of qualitative differences between the integrated and segregated sectors means that the typology also provides a framework for linking macro-level analyses of national trends in occupational segregation to case studies of change processes in particular occupations and other micro-level research (Reskin and Roos, 1990; Hakim, 1993*b*: 304–6), as illustrated also by the case study of pharmacists in Chapter 9.

Second, the picture of stability, even inertia, presented by cross-sectional analyses of occupational segregation is misleading (Watts and Rich, 1992; Hakim, 1992*a*, 1993*b*; Rubery and Fagan, 1993). Even in decades when there is little or no *net* change in the overall pattern of occupational segregation, there is substantial *gross* change at the level of individuals. Workers are mobile even if the occupational structure is stable. Women are far more mobile than men, moving in and out of the labour market as well as switching between jobs and employers. Occupational change affects men and women equally, although it is less common than other changes (Hakim, 1996*c*). It is not appropriate to present occupational segregation as something that is imposed on people, locking them into inescapable occupational careers. On the contrary, there is a great deal of circulation between male, female, and mixed occupations and the dominant trend on this roundabout is the reversion to sex-typical occupations, even for people in the well-paid integrated sector. Women migrate towards female occupations and men migrate towards male occupations, when they are not there already. These results undermine the social exclusion thesis that men push women out of male-dominated occupations, especially the better paid and higher status occupations. On the contrary, female turnover in the Service Class is well below the average for all women, even if it remains well above male turnover.

Female turnover rates are broadly constant across male, female, and mixed occupations, even when social class and occupational grade are controlled. Turnover rates are gender-specific rather more than occupation-determined, and occupational grade has an even larger impact on male turnover than on female turnover. The occupational structure as a whole and occupational segregation in particular shape opportunities and the choices people make, but it is clear that a lot of real choices are being made within the existing system, producing change as well as renewal.

There is a tendency, both in academic and policy debates, towards the reification of occupational segregation as if it were a concrete social fact 'out there' that could impose itself on people against their will, as if it had causal powers. But occupational segregation is only a conceptual framework which is useful for making sense of the job choices people make and their consequent work experiences. Even in the cross-sectional data of the SARs, there is evidence that people are mobile between jobs and are constantly reviewing and renewing occupational preferences over the life cycle. Longitudinal data reveal change even more clearly.

Third, the profiles of integrated and sex-segregated occupations are shaped in part by the characteristics that workers bring to the labour market, and hence by continuing sex differentials in work orientations and labour market behaviour (Hakim, 1991, 1996a, 1996c; Hakim and Jacobs, 1997). Sex differentials are actually highlighted in integrated occupations, where one-fifth of women work part-time whereas one-quarter of men work extremely long hours, for example. But the main effect is to produce huge differences between male-dominated and female-dominated occupations. Female occupations are high turnover occupations because women as a group are more likely to move in and out of the labour market and because they constitute the majority of workers in the sector. Male occupations have low turnover because men are in the majority, and they shape the groups' profile. For this reason it is female-dominated occupations, rather than integrated occupations, that provide the bulk of labour market entry and exit jobs. Women themselves are often marginal participants in the labour market, a point developed further in Chapter 5, so it is female-dominated occupations that provide most of the jobs with low entry barriers, that tolerate high turnover, and do not impose major long-term demands on workers. The largest female occupations are in fact *gender-neutral* occupations, as is revealed by the listings in Annex B. Supermarket check-out operators and sales assistant jobs do not draw on any special domestic or feminine skills; they are jobs that can be learnt quickly and can be done by people with no special qualifications. The labels that are inevitably used in studies of occupational segregation, such as 'typically female', have given the false impression that there is something *intrinsically* or *necessarily* female about the jobs in question. In fact, many of them are low skill jobs anyone could do, young or old, male or female, black or white. Women themselves recognize this: women doing jobs they regard as 'women's work' are aware that the jobs rarely involve special skills and that men could also do them (Martin and Roberts, 1984: 30). As Dex (1987: 37) also found, the female-dominated sector consists of a combination of occupations that may exploit particular female talents—such as nursing and schoolteaching—and low-skill gender-neutral occupations that serve as labour market entry and exit jobs of the sort that we had expected to be integrated rather than taken up mainly by women. It is a myth that most female-dominated occupations exploit nurturant feminine skills and are thus undervalued (Kilbourne *et al.*, 1994; European Commission, 1994*c*: 59). Even social scientists doing research on occupational segregation, who might be expected to be better informed, repeat and endorse the stereotyped view that in modern Western societies women's work is characterized by an emphasis on providing services and taking care of people while men look after the material world (Kauppinen-Toropainen and Lammi, 1993: 92, 107), or that male occupations are 'technical' while female occupations involve 'caring', leading to the conclusion that a revaluation of women's caring work is needed to close the pay gap (Rubery and Fagan, 1993: 110, 117, 122). In fact, the most important female occupations are simply relatively low-grade jobs in office work or sales work, jobs with no customers or in which customers are normally treated impersonally and even ignored as individuals. Clerical work and sales assistant jobs are far more numerous than jobs in childcare or nursing, as noted in Chapter 1. There is nothing feminine about these jobs, and the interpersonal skills involved in the transactions are no greater than in all work relationships.

Fourthly, our results on female labour turnover shed new light on the thesis that one cause of occupational segregation is women's propensity to choose occupations that fit in with their anticipated family role and do not penalize them for spells out of the labour market (Polachek, 1979). The idea assumes an exceptional degree of forward planning, whereas research shows that many women are unable to predict their actual as opposed to their preferred marriage, fertility, and work patterns over the life cycle (Sandell and Shapiro, 1980), in part because so much depends on whom (and if) they marry (and whether they stay married). The continuing sex differential in labour mobility shows that women's employment histories are affected by their family roles, but that there is no clear association with choice of occupation. Women who choose male occupations quit them just as often as women who choose female occupations. On the other hand, gradual reversion to sex-typical occupations over the life cycle suggests that female occupations are in practice more compatible with family responsibilities (Dex, 1987), primarily because they offer a variety of reduced hours and part-time jobs, a topic considered further in Chapters 5 and 9. Studies in the USA have also found men and women drifting back to sex-typical occupations over time (Rosenfeld, 1984: 77; Rosenfeld and Spenner, 1992: 430; J. Jacobs, 1993: 62; C. Williams, 1993: 61, 79). Simpson *et al.* (1982: 1309) found that the sex composition of occupations did not explain the differences between their patterns of recruiting and retaining male and female labour forces in the USA, and concluded that females in male occupations are more like other females than like males in their labour market behaviour. So even if 'male' and 'female' occupations do not necessarily utilize specifically masculine or feminine skills and talents, they may still justify their sex-stereotyped labels by their compatibility with typically male and typically female employment histories over the life cycle (Hakim, 1996a: 132–8). This conclusion does not mean that breaks in employment have no impact on earnings, which is a separate issue (Hakim, 1996a: 180–1) and is addressed more fully in Chapters 3 and 4. The continued sex differential in labour turnover, especially in higher grade occupations, will necessarily have an impact on work experience and firm-specific experience, and hence on earnings in the long term (Suter and Miller, 1973).

Finally, the classification of occupations into male, female, and integrated provides a framework for situating case studies of particular occupations, and facilitates theoretical links between macro-level and micro-level studies of segregation in the labour market. For example, Breakwell and Weinberger (1987) studied female trainee technicians in the engineering industry, while McRae, Devine, and Lakey (1991) compared male and female engineers. Both these occupations are overwhelmingly male-dominated, and the two case studies point up the cultural stereotypes, personal and organizational characteristics which promote or impede successful integration into sex-atypical careers. The studies show the importance of full-time work, ability, and high levels of work commitment in breaking down sex-stereotypes and cultural barriers to women at all levels in the engineering industry. Laboratory experiments on mixed-sex task groups can then inform these policy-oriented studies, revealing the processes involved in creating and changing sex role socialization in task-oriented settings (Wagner, Ford, and Ford, 1986). Wharton and Baron's (1987) analysis of male employees' job satisfaction and self-esteem in integrated and segregated occupations suggests one explanation for the slow growth of integrated occupations: men seek to maintain patriarchal control over women and suffer from its loss, rather than from lower earnings in integrated occupations, so they avoid working in integrated occupations as far as possible.

Theories explaining occupational segregation are often tested with case studies of occupations that changed their sex label over a period of time, as illustrated by Strober's (1984) study of the feminization of public school teaching in the nineteenth century in the USA, Cohn's (1985) study of the feminization of clerical work in Britain and the USA, and Bradley's (1989: 178) case study of the feminization of shopwork. One of the most sophisticated sets of case studies is provided by Reskin and Roos (1990). Eleven case studies analyse the correlates and causes of rapid feminization in selected occupations over the period 1970–88 in the USA. Applying our classification of male, female, and integrated occupations, the case studies can be grouped into four categories:

- occupations that were male-dominated in 1970 but became integrated by 1988, such as bakers, bartenders, systems analysts, bank managers, pharmacists, and insurance sales;
- occupations that were integrated in 1970 but became female-dominated by 1988, including public relations specialists and insurance adjusters;
- occupations that remained integrated throughout the period, with an increasing female share, such as real estate sales and book publishing; and
- occupations that changed character completely, switching from male-dominated to female-dominated, the most notable example being typesetters and compositors, an occupation that swung from 17 per cent female in 1970 to 74 per cent female by 1988.

The case studies were combined with analysis of national statistics to identify the determinants and consequences of the feminization process, and to distinguish those that were occupation-specific or industry-specific from those occurring across the whole labour force. The authors adopted the assumption that it is ultimately employers who assign and withhold jobs (Reskin and Roos, 1990: 38). Following this logic, they concluded that the feminization of occupations conforms to job queuing and labour queuing processes. Although most employers continued to structure the labour queue around a gender queue, when the supply of men was inadequate—either because rapid job growth exhausted the supply or because men spurned the jobs as inferior to accessible alternatives—employers turned to women. They also did so when economic considerations made hiring women cheaper and when equal opportunities legislation and regulatory agencies made not hiring them potentially costly (Reskin and Roos, 1990: 63–4).

Unfortunately all the evidence presented by Reskin and Roos is equally consistent with the opposite of their preferred interpretation. Their evidence supports S. Goldberg's (1993: 108) thesis that men always choose occupations offering the highest pay and highest status while women balance a variety of criteria, including convenience factors such as part-time hours, when choosing jobs—in effect, that men chase money, power, and status harder than women so that any highly paid or high-status occupation inevitably *becomes* male-dominated. Goldberg points out that if the job queuing thesis was true, there would not be any male-dominated occupations with wages substantially below wages in female-dominated occupations. Although there has been a close association between earnings and occupational sex ratios in the USA, at least up to the 1980s, this is not equally true of Britain and other European countries. As shown above and in Chapter 3, integrated occupations have the highest average pay while male and female occupations have broadly similar and lower average earnings. The factual evidence compiled by Reskin and Roos supports the conclusion that the causal sequence is the opposite of the one they favour, and the opposite of the thesis that female-dominated occupations pay less well because feminine abilities are devalued (Reskin, 1988). Indeed at various points the authors recognize this, admitting that under normal conditions male workers are more important than employers in maintaining sex-segregated jobs; that female labour supply was equally important in the feminization of occupations in the USA; that changing social attitudes to the roles of men and women was a crucial factor in the 1970s and 1980s; and that in all the feminizing occupations roughly half of the women and up to 90% were able to work part-time and/or part-year even though very few of the men did this (Reskin and Roos, 1990: 64, 304, 305, 310).

Finally, cross-national comparisons demonstrate that changes taking place in one country do not necessarily happen elsewhere, that seemingly inexorable processes are in fact contingent on local conditions. For example the wholesale conversion of printing into a female occupation in the USA in the period 1970–88, apparently due to technological change, did not happen in Britain, despite equivalent technological change (Cockburn, 1983; Reskin and Roos, 1990: 275–98; Hakim, 1996a: 165–6). Similarly, Rubery and Fagan (1993: 61–111) were unable to explain contradictory trends and processes even within Western Europe in the 1980s—for example why women's share of computer professional occupations is rising steadily in some countries but is declining equally steadily in others (Rubery and Fagan, 1993: 110).

In sum, the available evidence from analyses of trends at the national level, from case studies of occupations, and from cross-national comparisons is consistent with at least two competing explanations for the existence and maintenance or decline of occupational segregation. For the time being we must conclude that workers and employers, women as well as men, contribute equally to the maintenance and renewal of occupational segregation in the workforce, with no single factor or theory pre-eminent in explaining change or why an occupation that is integrated in one country is sex-segregated in another.

3

Occupational Segregation, Social Stratification, and the Pay Gap

This chapter considers the relationship between occupational segregation, social stratification, and the sex differential in earnings. Social inequality and economic inequality are obviously linked (Marshall *et al.*, 1988). Their relationship to the sex-segregation of occupations is not self-evident. Hartmann was clear that occupational segregation is a patriarchal practice, being the primary mechanism in capitalist society for maintaining the superiority of men over women because it enforces lower wages for women in the labour market. But she was also clear that there are no social class exemptions from patriarchy, and that all men, workers as well as employers, contribute to the maintenance and constant renewal of occupational segregation and the maintenance of women's inferiority in the labour market (Hartmann, 1976: 139). Men enjoyed only the single oppression of capitalism, whereas women confronted the double burden of capitalism and patriarchy (Hartmann, 1976: 168). Subsequent writers have sought to develop the idea of interactions between class and sex inequalities, with no real success to date, as McRae (1990) points out. However, recent historical research has undermined Hartmann's thesis, showing that occupational segregation was introduced in the late nineteenth century to ensure the physical rather than the economic segregation of men and women (Humphries, 1987) and that trends in occupational segregation are not related to trends in the pay gap (Hakim, 1994, 1996*a*: 80–2, 170–7).

The information contained in the SARs is too limited to allow us to fully address these broad theoretical issues. However, the large size of the SAR files enables us to explore the relationship between occupational segregation, social stratification, and the pay gap in far more detail than is possible with ordinary sample survey datasets.

OCCUPATIONAL SEGREGATION AND SOCIAL STRATIFICATION

Occupational segregation and social stratification are theoretically separate areas of inquiry. Both deal with social and economic inequalities, and there is an extensive literature considering whether and how sexual and class inequalities are linked. One part of this literature discusses the advantages and disadvantages of merging explanations of gender inequality with class analysis (Walby, 1990; Fine, 1992). Fine (1992) insists that the oppression of women can be adequately incorporated into class analysis, but the general consensus now is that it is more appropriate to treat capitalism and patriarchy as separate but interacting. Another part of this literature considers whether the family or the individual is the appropriate unit for class analysis and, more specifically, whether wives should be allocated to social classes on the basis of their husband's occupation or on the basis of their own current (or last) occupation (Dex, 1990; McRae, 1990; Marshall *et al.*, 1995). Agreeing with Goldthorpe, McRae (1990) concludes that the task of explaining the existence and development of sex segregation in occupations should be kept separate from class analysis, in part because the two research topics will be affected differently by contemporary changes in the labour market.

Hakim (1996*a*) presents a further reason for keeping the two streams of research separate: increasing heterogeneity in female sex-role preferences and work orientations in rich modern societies leads to polarization of women's experiences in the labour market and the marriage market. Up to the early 1970s, women's upward social mobility through the marriage market produced mobility rates roughly equal to those of men through employment (Erikson and Goldthorpe, 1993: 231–77). However, the strategy of social mobility through the marriage market involves quite different choices—of educational qualifications, occupation, jobs, and area of residence, for example—from the strategy of seeking upward mobility through a personal employment career (Hakim, 1996*a*: 133). Women aiming for the homemaker career are more likely to take a degree in the arts, humanities, or a 'social' subject, followed by secretarial or clerical work in a large organization, than to take a degree in the natural sciences, engineering, law, medicine, or computer science followed by professional work. Rising numbers of women in higher education have changed women's employment patterns in the post-war period far less than is popularly believed (Blossfeld, 1987; Hakim, 1993*a*, 1996*c*) and the homemaker career has been reshaped rather than abandoned (Hakim, 1996*a*: 138). The polarization of women means that competing theories about women's position in class analysis may *both* be right—but for different groups of women. The key point is that women continue to have the option of determining their life chances and social status, and achieving social mobility, through the marriage market as well as through the labour market, whereas men are still restricted to employment careers. Unfortunately, there is no reliable way of differentiating the two types of women in most survey datasets, as they do not collect the necessary information on personal sex-role preferences and attitudes to the sexual division of labour (Hakim and Jacobs, 1997; Hakim, 1998*a*, 1998*b*). Also, some women switch between the two social mobility routes.

The 1% and 2% SARs only provide cross-sectional data, so a comparative analysis of women's and men's occupational mobility must be left to a study based on the census data in the ONS 1% Longitudinal Study (OPCS, 1988). Our objective here is to take advantage of the large SAR samples to map out the relationship between occupational segregation and social stratification—in practice, to demonstrate the absence of any association. Unlike most other chapters of this book, the analysis in this chapter relies exclusively on the 1% SAR as this is the only one providing all the required social stratification scales.

SOCIAL STRATIFICATION SCALES

There are three social stratification scales widely used in Britain: the Registrar-General's Social Class scale, the Goldthorpe class schema, and the Cambridge Scale. Two international scales are also available in the SAR files: the International Socio-Economic Index of occupational status (ISEI) and the Standard International Occupational Prestige Scale (SIOPS). All were used to test for any association between occupational segregation and social stratification in its many forms and shadings. There are many other scales used, in particular countries or datasets, but not available in the SAR files. Hierarchical ranking is the common feature of all the scales used to rank occupations, economic position, or status in the social hierarchy. The criteria used for or reflected in the ranking are variously described as occupational grade; occupational skill; occupational prestige; the general desirability of occupations; earnings and income; educational level and cultural capital; an underlying structure of social relations of deference, acceptance, and derogation; social stratification and social inequality. While the scales differ in conceptual framework and method of construction (see Annex A), they are highly correlated with each other in practice, and there is general agreement that the dimensions being measured all overlap heavily when continuous scales are collapsed into simplified 3–5 group classifications of broad social categories.

Whatever criteria are used to produce the classifications, or scales, they are usually linked, in Britain, to the Registrar-General's national classification of occupations or, for international classifications, to the ILO's International Standard Classification of Occupations (ISCO). Because these two classifications are used to code population census results, they are the most detailed classifications available to social scientists (Hakim, 1982: 178–80; ILO, 1990). The RG classifications are revised for each census and published the year before. The most recent editions are the OPCS *Classification of Occupations 1970*, the OPCS *Classification of Occupations 1980*, and the 1990 *Standard Occupational Classification* (SOC). Socio-Economic Group

(SEG) is a widely used summary classification of occupations, in addition to Social Class (see Annex A). This classification aims to group people whose social, cultural and recreational standards and behaviour are similar. However, clearly stated differences in the theoretical rationales for academic social stratification classifications do not, in practice, produce results that differ greatly between them or that differ greatly from the RG Social Class and SEG classifications.

SOCIAL CLASS AND OCCUPATIONAL SEGREGATION

Sharp differences between integrated and sex-segregated occupations are displayed more clearly by the RG Social Class classification than by Goldthorpe's class schema (Tables 3.1 and 3.2). Integrated occupations are the smallest group, but are distinctively high status, with no jobs in the lowest unskilled RG Class V and almost three-quarters of all workers in Classes I and II, as Scott and Burchell (1994: 133) also found with the much smaller 1986 SCELI dataset and using a different definition of mixed occupations (those with 30%–70% female workers). Male-dominated occupations include some professional occupations, which are virtually non-existent within the female-intensive sector (Table 3.1). Otherwise, male-dominated and female-dominated occupations are almost identical in their Social Class composition, apart from the well-known tendency for men to be concentrated in skilled blue-collar work while women are concentrated in skilled white-collar work—Social Classes III Manual and III Non-Manual respectively.

TABLE 3.1. *RG Social Classes by type of occupation*   column percentages

RG Social Classes	All in work					Full-time workers				
	Male occups.	Mixed occups.	Female occups.	All %	000s	Male occups.	Mixed occups.	Female occups.	All %	000s
I Professional	8	9	*	5	11	9	9	*	6	11
II Managerial & Technical	22	67	20	29	65	22	67	24	31	56
IIIN Skilled white-collar	6	7	48	24	52	6	6	52	20	37
IIIM Skilled blue-collar	42	6	7	21	47	42	7	8	24	44
IV Semi-skilled workers	17	11	16	15	35	16	11	14	14	26
V Unskilled workers	5	—	8	6	13	5	—	3	4	6
All classes	100	100	100	100		100	100	100	100	
Base 000s=100%	92	39	92	223		87	34	58	178	

Source: 1% SAR, Great Britain, data for residents aged 16–64 in employment.

Contrary to expectation, it is not male occupations which have the highest proportion of higher status occupations, but the small category of mixed occupations, a result that is repeated in the full-time workforce. As shown in Chapter 2, integrated occupations are the most highly qualified and have the highest proportion of self-employed people, which suggests that they fall in the primary internal and primary external segments of the labour market. Table 3.1 confirms again that the middle group of desegregated or mixed occupations on the boundary line between the male-dominated and female-dominated sectors is not a purely statistical category with no distinguishing features, but a qualitatively different sector of the labour market. In the integrated sector certificated skills and qualifications create a uniquely egalitarian and open labour market which overcomes the need to rely on sex stereotyping and statistical discrimination to allocate people to jobs, as in the past (Phelps, 1972; Cain, 1986: 724–9). Looking at it another way, there is less segregation in higher grade and highly qualified occupations than in lower grade occupations where there is greater reliance on informally acquired 'natural' skills.

The two groups of segregated occupations, male and female, are separated by horizontal segregation but have almost identical hierarchies within them. At the national level, vertical segregation is *not* a dominant feature of the workforce at the end of the twentieth century. This is a fundamentally important finding, as it overturns all theorizing to date, and the evidence to date for the USA (Rytina, 1981; Sokoloff, 1992) and Britain (Hakim, 1979). It is simply not the case that female occupations are concentrated disproportionately in lower grade work while the higher grade jobs are male-dominated, at least not in Britain in the 1990s. The pattern of occupational segregation is now very balanced, with male and female occupations having almost identical shares of professional, managerial, technical, white-collar, and blue-collar occupations. However, in terms of absolute numbers, there are more men than women in RG Social Class I and II occupations or, using Goldthorpe's class schema, in the Service Class (see Table 2.5) because male and mixed occupations dominate these classes. Sokoloff (1992: 26–8, 135–50) also found a very small number of female-dominated professions in the USA, a larger group of gender-neutral professions, with the majority of professions being male-dominated. However, most of the professions that were male-dominated in the USA in 1960–80 are found to be integrated professions in Britain in 1991—such as biologists and chemists, lawyers, pharmacists, opticians, dentists, physicians, vets, archivists, and designers. It is likely that the information for the USA is simply out of date. For example, pharmacy became an integrated occupation in the USA also by 1988, as noted in Chapter 9.

The picture obtained with Goldthorpe's class schema is broadly the same, with sharper detail (Table 3.2). Two-thirds of integrated occupations are in

TABLE 3.2. *Goldthorpe Classes by type of occupation*   column percentages

Goldthorpe Classes		All in work					Full-time workers				
		Male occups.	Mixed occups.	Female occups.	All		Male occups.	Mixed occups.	Female occups.	All	
					%	000s				%	000s
I	Upper service class	16	24	2	11	26	16	24	2	13	23
II	Lower service	14	40	18	20	45	15	41	21	22	39
IIIa	Routine non-manual	2	3	34	15	34	2	3	41	15	26
IIIb	Sales & service workers	—	—	18	8	17	—	—	12	4	7
IV	Petty bourgeoisie	15	16	3	10	23	14	15	3	11	19
V/VI	Skilled workers	28	6	5	15	34	28	7	6	17	30
VII	Unskilled workers	25	10	21	21	48	25	10	15	19	34
All classes		100	100	100	100		100	100	100	100	
Base 000s=100%		95	39	92	226		87	34	58	178	

Notes: the composition of Goldthorpe's Classes:

Upper service class: Higher grade professionals, administrators and officials; managers in large industrial estab-lishments; large proprietors.

Lower service class: Lower grade professionals, administrators and officials; higher grade technicians; managers in small industrial establishments; supervisors of non-manual employees.

Routine non-manual: Routine non-manual employees, higher grade (administration and commerce).

Sales and service workers: Routine non-manual employees, lower grade (sales and services).

Petty bourgeoisie: Small proprietors and artisans etc., with or without employees; farmers and smallholders; other self-employed workers in primary production.

Skilled workers: Lower grade technicians; supervisors of manual workers; skilled manual workers.

Unskilled workers: semi- and unskilled workers not in agriculture, etc.; agricultural and other workers in primary production.

Source: 1% SAR, Great Britain, data for residents aged 16–64 in employment.

the Service Class. Just over half of male-dominated occupations are manual occupations located in the working class; due to self-employment, another 15% are in the petit bourgeoisie. Just over half of female-dominated occupations are in the routine white-collar occupations of the Intermediate Class III with another quarter in the working class. The long-term trend of increasing vertical segregation of the workforce observed throughout the twentieth century (Hakim, 1979: 27–9) seems to have ended in 1971. It was no doubt halted, and reversed, by the sex discrimination and equal opportunities leg-islation introduced in the early 1970s, which facilitated a massive influx of women into professional, managerial, and technical top jobs (Hakim, 1992a). By the end of the twentieth century, the occupational structure was fundamentally altered. It can now be visualized as three triangles: male and female occupations are the two largest triangles sitting on their bases; driving a wedge between them is an inverted triangle of integrated occupations that combine desegregation with the superior employment conditions of the Service Class. Integrated occupations employ only one-fifth of the workforce but they account for one-third of the Service Class.

These results provide an explanation for contradictory findings from studies that dichotomize occupations into male and female, or that use a single continuous variable of % female (or % male) to characterize occupations (Rosenfeld, 1983; England, 1984; Kilbourne *et al.*, 1994). Half of male occupations are skilled and unskilled manual work and half of female occupations are skilled and unskilled white-collar work, so there is little scope for variation in occupational sex ratios, status, and earnings except in the top two classes, where integrated occupations are now dominant. The occupational structure is dominated by horizontal occupational segregation except in the top grades of highly paid professional, technical, and managerial occupations.

This conclusion is strengthened by measures of social status for full-time employees in the three types of occupation (Table 3.3). The ISEI occupational status scale and the SIOPS occupational prestige scale show that male and female occupations are virtually identical in average status and prestige. The two measures also yield very similar or identical average scores for men and for women in full-time employment, in part-time employment, in male-dominated and female-dominated occupations, whether full-time or part-time. The Cambridge social status scale gives a higher average score to women than to men, to female than to male occupations, 38 versus 29, because it takes account of wives often having husbands in higher status occupations, and a lifestyle that reflects the husband's status rather than the

TABLE 3.3. *Mean status scores for full-time employees in work*

	Type of occupation				All	All
	Male	Mixed	Female	all	men	women
All full-time employees in work						
ISEI	42	55	44	45	44	46
SIOPS	41	52	40	43	43	43
Cambridge scale	29	44	38	35	32	40
Goldthorpe's Service Class						
ISEI	62	62	56	61	62	59
SIOPS	55	58	55	56	56	56
Cambridge scale	51	53	57	53	52	53
Goldthorpe's other Classes						
ISEI	42	55	44	45	44	46
SIOPS	41	52	40	43	43	43
Cambridge scale	29	44	38	35	32	39

Source: 1% SAR, Great Britain, resident employees aged 16–64 in work, excluding student jobs.

wife's—a process that does not (yet) occur with men. The three scales are unanimous in reporting a significantly higher average social status, occupational status, and occupational prestige score for integrated occupations than for sex-segregated occupations (Table 3.3) and prestige scores within the Service Class indicate that integrated occupations contain the very highest grade jobs within this class (Table 3.3). The analysis in Table 3.3 focuses on full-time employees to offer consistency with subsequent analyses of the pay gap. It is notable that the ISEI and SIOPS scores show no status and prestige differences between full-time and part-time jobs in integrated occupations. It is only within sex-segregated occupations that there are clear differences in status and prestige between full-time and part-time jobs, for men and women.

These results confirm that male and female occupations form two parallel categories of work of equal average status and prestige, contradicting the feminist claim that greater rewards and higher status and rank accrue to male occupations and that female occupations are undervalued (C. Williams, 1993: 8, 29, 32–4, 49). It is integrated occupations that achieve these honours, which are therefore, by definition, equally accessible to women and men. However, the argument is supported by data on earnings.

Some comparative information for the USA is provided by Sokoloff's study of the professions 1960–80. She used the Nam–Powers occupational status scores, a socio-economic or social class indicator, not a status or prestige measure, and thus closer to the British Cambridge scale than to the ISEI or SIOPS measures in Table 3.3. Sokoloff reports that professional and technical occupations (roughly equivalent to Goldthorpe's Service Class but excluding all the managerial occupations) had Nam–Powers scores ranging from a low of 40 to a high of 99 (effectively the maximum score on the scale). Male-dominated professions had the highest occupational status (an average score of 95), integrated professions had slightly lower average status (91), female-dominated professions had the lowest average score (73), and technical occupations had similarly low average scores of 64 to 79 (Sokoloff, 1992: 26–8). These results for the USA may well be out of date in the 1990s, but they show male-dominated and integrated professions to have markedly higher socio-economic status than female professions in the USA. This picture contrasts sharply with the picture for Britain in the 1990s, suggesting that theories developed with reference to the USA labour market may simply not apply to European societies.

AVERAGE HOURLY EARNINGS AND THE PAY GAP

It has become received wisdom that occupational segregation is the key cause or facilitator of the pay gap between men and women. In Hartmann's most

extreme feminist formulation, developed further by Walby, occupational segregation is the key mechanism used by men to restrict and constrain women's
access to income and earnings, thus rendering them financially dependent on
men, forcing them to become domestic servants for their husbands
(Hartmann, 1976; Walby, 1990; Hakim, 1996a: 9–13). Recent analyses of historical trends in occupational segregation and pay inequalities between men
and women show, however, that there is not even a loose association between
the two, let alone a tight causal relationship (Hakim, 1994, 1996a: 80–2,
170–7). Furthermore, when studies examine jobs in sufficient detail, vertical
job segregation accounts for all the sex differential in earnings and the devaluation of feminine skills contributes almost nothing to explanations of the
pay gap (Sieling, 1984; Sloane, 1990; Kilbourne *et al.*, 1994: 706; Hakim,
1996a: 145–86). Our analyses of the large SAR datasets with the NES earnings estimates for employees were aimed at testing these conclusions once
again with a variety of occupational grade, social class, social status, and
related measures, as well as in relation to sex-segregated and integrated occupational groups.

The NES data in the SAR files provides an estimate of the average hourly
earnings of an employee of that age, sex, and occupation, working full-time
or part-time, living in London and the South-East or elsewhere in Britain
(see Annex A). The NES only covers employees, so no earnings estimates are
available for the self-employed in the SAR files. Earnings estimates for part-
timers exclude marginal workers with earnings below the income tax and
social insurance (called National Insurance in Britain) thresholds which
account for around 5% of all employee jobs (see Table 6.13). In practice, the
1991 Census also excluded these marginal jobs, as noted in Chapter 5, so
there is a good match between the two sets of data. Earnings estimates are for
the current jobs of employees in work, excluding student jobs which are
analysed separately in Chapter 6.

The earnings data in the SARs produce average hourly earnings that
closely match the NES published statistics for 1991 and NES-based analyses
of trends in the pay gap (Employment Department, 1991; Spence, 1992;
Payne, 1995). The sex differential in earnings, or pay gap, is the difference
between average male and female earnings. In practice most studies quote
average female earnings as a percentage of average male earnings.
Historically, men earned on average twice as much as women, even in the
same job, in part because physical strength used to be an important element
of most manual occupations, in part because it was accepted that men needed
to earn a family wage (Edgeworth, 1922). Despite small fluctuations,
women's pay remained at half of men's pay up to 1970 (Routh, 1980: 123;
Hakim, 1996a: 175). As part-time jobs are now common, the pay gap is normally measured by the *hourly* earnings (excluding overtime pay) of full-time
workers on adult rates of pay (Table 3.4). Overtime, incentive pay, and shift-

TABLE 3.4. *Trends in the pay gap 1886–1997: female earnings as percentage of male earnings*

| | Adult FT workers: hourly earnings, excluding overtime | | | Adult manual workers | |
	All	Non-manual	Manual	Hourly earnings	Weekly earnings
1886					52
1960				61	51
1970	64	53	62	60	50
1976	74	63	71	71	61
1984	74	62	69	70	61
1987	74	62	71	70	61
1989	77	63	70		
1991	78	67	71		
1993	79	68	71		
1995	80	68	73		
1997	80	69	72		

Source: Zabalza and Tzannatos (1988: 841), table 2 updated with annual New Earnings Survey data.

work premiums account for 11% of employees' gross weekly earnings—but these additions are far more important elements of men's pay, accounting for 23% of male manual employees' pay compared to 5% of female non-manual employees' pay, 13% of all men's pay and only 6% of all women's pay (Payne, 1995: 407). Gregory and Thomson (1990) and Sloane (1990) provide the fullest analysis of earnings in Britain and of explanations for the sex differential in earnings. Their conclusions echo those of Routh's (1980) earlier studies: that the pay structure is remarkably stable across time. Even in a period of dramatic inflation, rising unemployment, and upgrading of the occupational structure, pay relativities and skill differentials were maintained in the long run. However, their analysis only covers the period 1970–82, the period when equal pay legislation caused a sharp rise in female relative pay, from 64% in 1970 to 74% in 1976, after which it remained stable until 1987. In the late 1980s there was another increase in women's pay relative to men's which continued into the 1990s (Table 3.4) and is explained by changes in women's work orientations and employment patterns (Hakim, 1992a). Another feature of pay in the 1980s and 1990s is widening earnings differentials, especially in white-collar occupations (Spence, 1992: 582; Payne, 1995: 409). In general, white-collar occupations and jobs are more likely to have a variety of pay rates and grades and a larger wage spread than manual occupations, which often have only narrow pay bands in each workplace. Yet these grading differences in white-collar jobs are rarely recognized in occupational classifications. For example, retail shop managers are grouped together as a single category, combining everyone from managers of small local corner shops to managers of large department stores in urban centres, disregarding the huge variation in job grade and earnings within these jobs. This means we should expect to find a larger sex differential in earnings in white-collar jobs than in blue-collar jobs, and a larger pay gap in higher grade jobs than in lower grade jobs, as occupational classifications fail to keep pace with constant upgrading, differentiation, and specialization within the white-collar workforce (Hakim, 1996*a*: 151, 157).

OCCUPATIONAL SEGREGATION AND THE PAY GAP

Average hourly earnings in pence for full-time employees and all employees in sex-segregated and integrated occupations by social class are shown in Table 3.5. As 99% of the petite bourgeoisie class consists of the self-employed (see Table 8.3), this class is excluded from all the analyses using Goldthorpe Classes. The self-employed are dispersed across all six RG Social Classes (see Table 8.4), but our analyses show results only for employees in each Social Class. The RG Social Classes display a well-defined rising trend in average earnings as occupational grade and skill increase, and the pattern is repeated

TABLE 3.5. *Average hourly earnings by social class and type of occupation*

	All employees in work				Full-time employees in work			
	All	Male	Mixed	Female	All	Male	Mixed	Female
All classes	649	705	852	533	691	710	865	584
Goldthorpe classes								
Upper service	1119	1096	1183	923	1120	1094	1191	933
Lower service	891	915	853	906	899	919	865	915
Routine non-manual	545	784	668	528	567	795	708	547
Sales & services	388	—	—	388	416	—	—	416
Skilled workers	554	592	485	384	564	593	490	398
Unskilled workers	443	492	485	376	473	497	500	405
RG Social Classes								
I Professional	1114	1086	1203	811	1109	1081	1200	784
II Managerial & Technical	934	990	942	872	952	995	951	898
III Skilled white-collar	517	791	654	485	560	796	692	521
III Skilled blue-collar	527	557	481	394	536	559	486	409
IV Semi-skilled workers	462	521	489	400	489	527	504	420
V Unskilled workers	392	477	—	343	449	482	—	369

Note: The earnings estimates are average hourly earnings in pence (excluding any overtime pay) in spring 1991 for employees (excluding students with jobs) in each category in the table. £1 = 100 pence.

Source: 1% SAR, 1991 NES earnings estimates for resident employees in work, excluding students with jobs.

across male, mixed, and female occupations. This is not the case with Goldthorpe Classes, as the lowest average earnings are in the lowest grade of white-collar work, labelled Sales and Services, which are exclusively female-dominated occupations. The inclusion of the petite bourgeoisie would make for an even more bumpy distribution of earnings across classes.

Overall, mixed occupations have the highest earnings, male occupations have lower earnings, and female occupations have the lowest average earnings. But this general pattern is found only in the highest social class; in all other classes, and in both classifications, male occupations have the highest earnings and female occupations have the lowest earnings. It is this consistent pattern that leads to the conclusion that work done by women is less well rewarded, purely because it is done by women rather than because it is less skilled work, or because male-dominated trade unions and employers have ensured that men's work is disproportionately well rewarded so as to provide a family wage.

Even though they recruit few women, male occupations have the smallest pay gap (that is, the highest female earnings relative to men) followed by female occupations, with integrated occupations consistently displaying the largest pay gap, whichever social class classification is used (Table 3.6). There is no evidence that the pay gap is larger at the top of the occupational (or

TABLE 3.6. *Full-time employees: the pay gap by social class and type of occupation*

Goldthorpe Classes	Type of occupation			
	All	Male	Mixed	Female
All classes	78	90	74	80
Goldthorpe Classes				
Upper service	78	78	72	74
Lower service	81	81	72	78
Routine non-manual	79	78	75	84
Sales & service work	93	—	—	93
Skilled workers	67	79	74	75
Unskilled workers	76	81	75	79
RG Social Classes				
I Professional	87	86	81	88
II Managerial & Technical	75	77	71	74
III Skilled white-collar	76	83	75	86
III Skilled blue-collar	71	77	73	81
IV Semi-skilled workers	75	79	76	78
V Unskilled workers	76	85	—	86

Note: The pay gap is average female earnings in a category as a percentage of average male earnings in the same category.

Source: 1% SAR, 1991 NES earnings estimates for resident full-time employees in current jobs, excluding students with jobs.

social class) scale as we hypothesized; it is smallest in RG Professional Class I and in Goldthorpe's female-dominated Sales and Service work class. In fact, it is hard to see any pattern at all in the relationship between social class and the pay gap. So the overall conclusion is that the pay gap is largest in integrated occupations and smallest in sex-segregated occupations, contrary to patriarchy theory and feminist theorizing more generally.

The large size of the 1% SAR allows us to calculate female relative pay in part-time jobs as well, although there are quite a few empty cells and gaps in the table due to part-time jobs being concentrated among female occupations. In this case there is a tendency for the pay gap to be larger at the top of the occupational grade or social class scale, but the pattern is fairly weak. More interestingly, part-time jobs have low sex differentials in pay in sex-segregated occupations and the pay gap is largest within integrated occupations (Table 3.7). Overall, part-time earnings are highest for integrated occupations, but this is due in part to the absence of the lowest-paying jobs in the sales and services class and in part to small numbers in working-class jobs. In general, at each social class level, male occupations have the highest average earnings for part-time jobs and female occupations have the lowest earnings, the same pattern as for full-time jobs.

TABLE 3.7. *Part-time employees: the pay gap by social class and type of occupation*

	The pay gap by type of occupation				Average earnings by type of occupation			
	All	Male	Mixed	Female	All	Male	Mixed	Female
All classes	67	74	67	77	464	549	719	437
Goldthorpe Classes								
Upper service	68	60	72	~	1093	1155	1113	780
Lower service	71	60	63	67	821	723	691	865
Routine non-manual	89	~	87	91	467	537	466	467
Sales & services	106	—	—	106	365	—	—	365
Skilled workers	61	68	~	83	385	521	411	348
Unskilled workers	84	85	91	92	358	410	384	351
RG Social Classes								
I Professional	61	60	56	~	1251	1273	1246	~
II Managerial & Technical	65	60	66	63	798	750	846	785
III Skilled white-collar	92	65	81	100	412	607	488	409
III Skilled blue-collar	70	76	~	87	380	458	411	351
IV Semi-skilled workers	83	74	91	94	380	422	389	375
V Unskilled workers	92	112	—	92	337	388	—	335

Note: The pay gap is average female earnings in a category as a proportion of male average earnings in the same category.

Source: 1% SAR, 1991 NES earnings estimates for resident employees in work, excluding students with jobs.

Looking at the occupational structure as a whole, we conclude that the sex differential in pay is largest at the top of the hierarchy, among integrated occupations; it is lowest in the sex-segregated occupations which account for the bulk of working-class jobs. This pattern is found in both the full-time and part-time workforces. Once again, the small integrated group of occupations has distinctively different features separating it from the sex-segregated majority. Most important, there is no evidence that occupational segregation *per se* is a cause of the pay gap.

OCCUPATIONAL GRADE AND EARNINGS

A full analysis of the correlates and determinants of earnings lies beyond the scope of this study. Here we are concerned only with identifying and exploring systematic differences between sex-segregated and integrated occupations in the returns to occupational grade. More particularly, we are interested in any evidence of female-dominated occupations being devalued or less well rewarded, in part because women's concentration in a small number of occupations depresses wage rates in these 'overcrowded' jobs, in part because women's work is generally undervalued relative to work done by men, purely because women are second-class citizens. In any case, the SARs provide an inadequate basis for a full analysis of earnings because they do not contain information on some of the most important determinants of earnings, such as total work experience, tenure with the current employer (a measure of firm-specific expertise), tenure in the current job or occupation, risk-taking (Hakim, 1996a: 177–85), and the sex-role preferences, work orientations, and career commitment which are especially important for women (Hakim, 1991, 1996a, 1996b, 1996c; Hakim and Jacobs, 1997). The SARs only provide information on three key correlates of earnings: occupational grade, hours worked, and higher education qualifications. On occupational grade there is the advantage of a number of continuous measures of occupational status, prestige, and social status. On qualifications there is the advantage of clear distinctions between *grades* of tertiary level qualifications that are usually grouped together in most survey datasets; on the other hand, there is no information at all on secondary school and other qualifications at this level.

In practice, there proved to be little difference between the three measures of occupational grade: the correlation with earnings is roughly the same for all three (Table 3.8). Slightly higher correlations are obtained with the 2% SAR (Table 3.8), but this only contains the Cambridge social status scale, so our analyses rely on the 1% SAR. There is little or no difference between men and women, between male-dominated and female-dominated occupations. Occupational grade on its own accounts for at least half and as much as two-thirds of the variation in full-time employee earnings. Occupational grade by itself is the main determinant of earnings for men and women, in male and female occupations.

Integrated occupations stand out again, with occupational grade alone accounting for less than half of earnings variation among full-time employees (Table 3.8). Within the integrated sector, other factors collectively have a greater impact on earnings. These would include hours worked and qualifications, which were shown in Chapter 2 to display marked sex differentials. The SARs do not provide information on the other determinants of earnings, as noted above.

TABLE 3.8. *Correlations between occupational grade and earnings*

	Type of occupation				All men	All women
	Male	Mixed	Female	All		
Full-time employees in work						
ISEI	.77	.64	.69	.72	.77	.73
SIOPS	.73	.65	.76	.74	.77	.77
Cambridge scale	.76	.69	.74	.68	.77	.76
Cambridge scale (2)	.78	.70	.82	.70	.79	.79
Part-time employees in work						
ISEI	.60	.59	.59	.60	.64	.63
SIOPS	.59	.61	.77	.73	.69	.77
Cambridge scale	.56	.57	.74	.67	.65	.72

Note: (2) results based on the 2% SAR.

Source: 1% SAR, Great Britain, data for residents aged 16–64 years in employment.

The key point about these results is that occupational grade is *equally* important as a determinant of earnings in male and female occupations. There is no evidence here that female occupations offer lower financial returns to occupational grade. There is no evidence that sex-segregated occupations differ in the financial rewards for higher occupational grade, status, or prestige. These results may explain why equal pay for work of equal value adjustments generally have only a minor impact on earnings (Hakim, 1996*a*: 186) and they are consistent with earlier studies showing that vertical segregation *within* occupations is the principal explanation for women's lower relative earnings (Chiplin and Sloane, 1974; Sloane, 1990; Hakim, 1996*a*: 151) although women's discontinuous work patterns also reduce their earnings (Main, 1988*b*). These results also support Hakim's argument that there is greater scope for sex discrimination in the highest grade and best paid jobs, where the determinants of earnings are most complex and invisible (Hakim, 1996*a*: 182–5).

For completeness, results for part-time employees are also shown in Table 3.8. Occupational grade is a weaker determinant of earnings in part-time jobs, but correlations are generally stronger for women than for men, for female occupations than for male occupations. The returns to occupational grade are as good in female part-time jobs as in full-time jobs.

CROSS-NATIONAL COMPARISONS: BRITAIN AND THE USA

There is only one previous study of female relative earnings in sex-segregated and integrated occupations. Rytina's (1981) analysis for the USA used a slightly wider band to define integrated occupations as those with 40% 6 20% female workers rather than 40% 6 15% female workers, as applied in the British dataset. But this difference is too minor to account for the remarkable contrasts between the USA and Britain shown in Table 3.9. The two assessments of female relative pay are taken at equivalent stages after implementation of the respective equal pay laws in the USA and Britain. The 1976 USA survey was carried out thirteen years after equal pay was introduced in 1963 in the USA. The 1991 analysis for Britain presents the situation sixteen years after equal pay laws took effect in 1975 in Britain. So the comparison is meaningful, despite the wide gap in years between the two assessments.

The USA study found that the pay gap declined as the proportion of women in an occupational group increased. The effect was found at the level of individual occupations (with a correlation coefficient of 0.24 for 419 occupations) but is displayed most clearly when occupations are grouped into three bands, as shown in Table 3.9: female relative pay rises from 50% in male

TABLE 3.9. *Comparisons of female relative earnings in Britain and the USA*

| | USA | Britain | | | |
	All workers	Full-time year-round workers	All employees	Full-time employees	Part-time employees
Male occupations	50	62	86	90	74
Mixed occupations	55	66	73	74	67
Female occupations	62	70	74	80	77
All occupations	55	65	71	78	67

Notes: Male, mixed, and female occupations in Britain are defined as in Table 1.1 and throughout this book. For the USA, definitions differ slightly, as follows: male occupations are those with , 21% female workers; mixed occupations are those with 21%–59% female workers (40% 6 20%); female occupations are those with . 60% female workers.

Sources: Britain: 1% SAR and spring 1991 NES estimates of hourly earnings for resident employees in these occupations. USA: Rytina (1981: table 3) reporting 1976 Survey of Income and Education data on 1975 median annual earnings.

occupations to 55% in integrated occupations and to 62% in female occupations. Part-time workers clearly account for part of the trend, but it is still
present among full-time year-round workers: female relative pay rises from
62% in male occupations to 66% in integrated occupations to 70% in female-
dominated occupations.

Overall, female relative pay remained at a far lower level thirteen years
after the introduction of equal pay in the USA than it did in Britain: 55% in
the whole workforce and 65% among full-time year-round workers compared
to 71% in the whole workforce and 78% among full-time workers in Britain
sixteen years after equal pay was introduced. This disappointing result led
some USA policy-analysts to conclude that equal pay for work of equal value
was essential to raising female relative earnings, a conclusion that remained
controversial among economists, was never accepted by legislators, and has
since been shown to rest on an incomplete understanding of the determinants of trends in female pay (Goldin, 1990; Hakim, 1996a: 196–7). In
Europe, the European Commission proactively redefined Article 119 of the
Treaty of Rome to require equal pay for work of equal value, rather than
equal pay in the same job, and this wider interpretation was confirmed by the
European Court of Justice in 1982. So female relative pay in Britain (and the
rest of Europe) has probably been pushed up a little by the impact of equal
value laws in the 1980s. Given that equal value upratings rarely exceed 10%
and are typically in the range 5%–6% (Hakim, 1996a: 186), improvements in
human capital and increases in hours worked seem to be the more important
explanations for a sharp decline in the pay gap in the late 1980s in Britain
(Table 3.4) after the once-and-for-all sharp increase resulting from the impact
of equal pay laws in the mid-1970s.

However, the main difference between the USA and Britain in Table 3.9 is
not so much in the levels of female pay relative to men but in the absence of
any trend across the three types of occupation in Britain, and in the fact that
the pay gap is lowest in *male* occupations in Britain and in *female* occupations in the USA. Among full-time employees (the usual group for assessments of the pay gap between men and women) the pay gap is smallest in
male occupations and highest in integrated occupations in Britain: 10% and
26% respectively. Female occupations lie between these two extremes.
Differences between the three types of occupation are also much larger for
full-time employees in Britain than for full-time year-round workers in the
USA. Occupational segregation clearly has a quite different relationship to
pay levels among different industrialized Western societies, and results for
the USA are *not* necessarily indicative of patterns in Europe. (Similarly,
research results for Western European societies might not be indicative of
patterns in other countries.) This result weakens yet again the argument that
occupational segregation is crucial to maintenance of the pay gap between
men and women and that there is a direct causal link between the two.

CONCLUSIONS

Social mobility researchers have concluded that occupational segregation and social stratification are two separate structural features of the workforce, requiring separate analysis, with no important connections between sex inequality and class inequality (Erikson and Goldthorpe, 1993: 276–7). We draw the same conclusion. Social class divisions are repeated across male, female, and integrated occupations, with no stable links between social stratification and occupational segregation over time.

Up to 1971 there was increasing vertical occupational segregation in the workforce, with men taking larger shares of the highest grade occupations while women became concentrated in lower status occupations (Hakim, 1979). The trend was reversed after 1971. By 1991 a large and increasing proportion of the Service Class, the occupations offering the highest status, prestige, and earnings, were employing women as well as men. Chapter 2 discovered qualitative differences between male, female, and mixed occupations, suggesting that they constitute significantly different labour markets, but with female occupations the most distinctive of the three. In terms of their location within the social stratification system, it is integrated occupations that are distinctive. Male and female occupations form two parallel occupational hierarchies with equal average occupational prestige and social status. The sex-segregated sector is characterized by a large degree of horizontal occupational segregation, but not by vertical segregation. True, male occupations have higher average earnings than female occupations, and this disparity in rewards persists across social classes, possibly as a legacy of the family wage system. On the other hand, female occupations tend to have higher social status—substantially higher on the Cambridge social status scale and slightly higher on the ISEI index of occupational status. It may be that these two measures of rewards reflect the greater emphasis placed by men on earnings and by women on social characteristics when choosing jobs and occupations (Hofstede, 1980: 276–81, 1991: 79–108; Shamir and Salomon, 1985: 458; Marshall *et al.*, 1988: 208–10; Hakim, 1996*a*: 100–2).

Research on occupational segregation in the USA invariably finds male occupations scoring higher than female occupations on status, prestige, and earnings (Rytina, 1981; Sokoloff, 1992; J. Jacobs, 1993: 49). The pay gap is largest in male occupations and lowest in female occupations in the USA, leading to the conclusion that women suffer less discrimination in female occupations (Rytina, 1981). The situation in Britain is in marked contrast to that in the USA. By 1991 the top jobs in Britain were often integrated, and were distributed relatively evenly between male, mixed, and female occupations. Integrated occupations have the highest status and prestige and are among the highest paid. The pay gap is *lowest* in male occupations and *highest* in integrated occupations. Despite the similarities between the two 'liberal' welfare state regimes and relatively unregulated labour markets, it appears that there are fundamental differences so far unrecognized between the USA and Britain as regards the pattern of occupational segregation and its relationship with earnings. Similarly, Rubery and Fagan (1993: 109–11) found that countries within Europe have distinctive patterns of occupational segregation, with sharp contrasts alongside common trends, that seem to defy any single explanatory theory.

The link between occupational segregation and earnings differences between men and women is weak in Britain. The pay gap remains constant across classes, with only small variations, but is highest in integrated occupations. Although male occupations are systematically better paid than female occupations, the difference is small. On average, full-time workers in male occupations earn one-fifth more than people in female occupations, which is the same as the pay gap in the full-time workforce as a whole. Thus horizontal occupational segregation seems to be irrelevant, as Willborn (1989: 140–1) and Sloane (1994) also concluded, and vertical occupational segregation is no longer a major feature of the British occupational structure. Explanations for the large pay gap in integrated occupations, and in the workforce as a whole, require information that goes well beyond the SARs data. One explanation is that integrated occupations expose and highlight the sex differentials in sex-role preferences, work orientations, job choice, and work history and their impact on promotion up career ladders and earnings, as illustrated by the case study of pharmacists in Chapter 9. Another explanation is that the pay gap is due to invisible sex differences in job grade and authority, that is, vertical segregation within the integrated occupations. Only when these two explanations have been properly addressed and rejected can the remaining pay gap be attributed to sex discrimination.[1] Studies that employ adequately detailed information on job grade are able to explain all of the earnings difference between men and women. That is, vertical job segregation *within* occupations accounts for the entire pay gap (Hakim, 1996*a*: 149–52). For example, Spaeth (1979) found that indicators of authority and responsibility in occupations completely explained the earnings gap between men and women. He noted that this dimension is separate from occupational prestige or status; it is thus left unmeasured by the ISEI and SIOPS scales used in this analysis. This explanation is more consistent with the evidence

---

[1] Many studies use far too crude a classification of occupations or jobs to be able to measure the relative impact of sex discrimination, occupational segregation, and occupational grade, in addition to explaining earnings differences between part-time and full-time workers. Just one example is Rubery, Horrell, and Burchell's (1994: 217) analysis of 1986 SCELI data. The more sophisticated approach employed by Sloane (1994) produced very different results with the same data, leading to the conclusion that occupational segregation was not a key factor in explaining the pay gap and that the impact of sex discrimination was heavily determined by the method used and the underlying assumptions.

than the thesis that the devaluation of women's caring work produces the pay gap. As shown by the early equal value court cases in Britain and the early comparable worth cases in the USA, cooks are paid less than carpenters, and secretaries are often paid less than gardeners (Willborn, 1989). But trade union membership and collective bargaining for improved pay—or the lack of this activity among many women—seems to be a far more important factor than the failure to value a cook's caring skills when frying potatoes or a secretary's caring skills when bashing a keyboard. Another hidden factor that is never openly admitted in debates on equal pay is that until very recently most women accepted the idea of higher wages for men on the grounds that men were usually the main breadwinner in a family and needed a family wage, unlike most women. Even in the 1980s many women still accepted the idea that men should have priority over women in getting jobs during recession, because the idea of the breadwinner husband is still, for most women, an unquestioned fact of life, or aspiration (Hakim and Jacobs, 1997).

In sum, the relationship between occupational segregation and earnings only merits further research if datasets can provide information on the full range of social and economic factors that determine earnings, and also employ occupational classifications that are sufficiently detailed to identify the higher earnings of management grades within the increasingly specialized jobs of the Service Class. Such datasets are unfortunately all too rare. The more fruitful focus for future research would be the social processes that lead men to attain jobs of higher status and earnings more often than women. Even in the most enlightened organizations, sex discrimination, sometimes unconscious, is one factor in this process (Hakim, 1996a: 184). But that is not the same thing as research results that show sex to be one factor in the process.

4

Women with Discontinuous Employment Histories

An innovation in the 1991 Census was to obtain information on the last job held in the previous ten years (if any) for everyone not currently in work. The 1971 and 1981 Censuses had moved in this direction by collecting information on the last job of the unemployed and retired, but the 1991 Census went a lot further in collecting systematic information for a very much larger group of people who had recent work experience but no current job, either as employee or self-employed. In effect, the 1991 Census collected employment data for a ten years' reference period as well as the usual 'last week' reference period (Hakim, 1995a). The change had the greatest impact on data for women, who move in and out of jobs, and in and out of the labour market over the life cycle far more frequently than men, in the USA as well as in most European countries (Hakim, 1996c). The conventional 'last week' reference period for employment data has become less and less useful as women's labour force participation has become more discontinuous and dispersed across the whole life cycle instead of being concentrated in early adult life, before marriage and childbirth (Hakim, 1979: 10–12, 1996a: 132–9). The pure marriage career has almost disappeared in Britain although it remains very common in Greece and some other European countries (Hakim, 1997: 43). It has now been replaced by the modern marriage career, in which women work as secondary earners, often part-time, after marriage or child-bearing (Hakim, 1996a: 135–8, 1996b). This chapter analyses the SARs data on jobs held in the last ten years and provides an important complement to data on current jobs analysed in Chapters 2 and 3. The new data also provides an opportunity to test theories on the differences between women who work continuously and women with discontinuous work histories.

Hakim's thesis on the polarization of the female workforce and of women of working age (Hakim, 1996a) suggests that discontinuous women workers will be more similar to women currently working part-time than to women currently working full-time. The thesis also leads us to expect sharp differences between women in continuous employment and women with discontinuous work histories. Women with discontinuous work histories should display a lower investment in human capital and in employment careers than career-oriented women. More specifically, this chapter tests the hypothesis that women with discontinuous work histories have typically been working in female-dominated occupations, most often in part-time jobs.

Women with discontinuous work histories are defined, in practice, as those who had a job in the previous decade but are not currently working. The operational definition of women in continuous employment is simply women in current jobs, which is rather more of a simplification. In practice, the analysis compares women's *current* jobs with women's *last* jobs. The analysis covers men as well as women, to the extent that the data permit it, as is the practice throughout this book. However, women constitute the vast majority (96%) of non-working people with no other specific status (such as full-time student, unemployed, permanently sick or retired), and this is true both of non-working people with a job in the last ten years and of non-working people without a job in the last years, as shown in Table A1 of Annex A.

THE COMPOSITION OF THE NON-WORKING POPULATION

People of working age not currently in employment comprise five groups: students in full-time education, the unemployed, the permanently sick, the retired, and a residual group of non-working people with no other specific status. In all five groups, some people have had a job within the preceding ten years. Table 4.1 presents work experience within five ten-year age cohorts.

TABLE 4.1. *Work experience over the life cycle*

	Proportion of each age group who are:										Total
							All not currently in work				
	Retired		Non-working		Current jobs		With job in last 10 years		No job in last 10 years		
	N	%	N	%	N	%	N	%	N	%	N=100%
Women											
16–24	27	*	8,427	12	35,889	51	16,514	23	18,348	26	70,751
25–34	62	*	24,842	30	51,295	62	20,826	25	11,182	13	83,303
35–44	102	*	17,781	23	53,180	69	10,623	14	12,980	17	76,783
45–54	741	1	13,929	22	42,280	67	8,038	13	12,866	20	63,184
55–64	16,882	29	15,458	27	20,107	35	16,610	29	20,881	36	57,598
16–64	17,814	5	80,437	23	202,751	58	72,611	21	76,257	22	351,619
Men											
16–24	30	*	616	1	39,266	55	14,604	20	17,538	25	71,408
25–34	25	*	785	1	68,173	83	9,930	12	3,760	5	81,863
35–44	86	*	756	1	65,689	87	7,200	9	2,978	4	75,867
45–54	568	1	527	1	52,506	83	7,232	11	3,391	5	63,129
55–64	8,119	15	451	1	32,579	59	16,458	30	5,846	11	54,883
16–64	8,828	3	3,135	1	258,213	74	55,424	16	33,513	10	347,150

Source: 2% SAR, Great Britain, data for residents aged 16–64 years.

Students in full-time education aged 16–24 form the largest group of people without any (recent) work experience, with numbers balanced fairly evenly between males and females. The main reason for the larger numbers of women not currently in work compared to men (42% versus 26%) is that most women devote a portion of their adult life to full-time homemaking, often for a period of ten years or longer. This is clear from the penultimate column in Table 4.1: in all age groups from 25 to 54 there is a significant minority of women (13% to 20%) who have not done paid work for over ten years, in addition to the equivalent minority (13% to 25%) who have had a job in the last ten years. Between the ages of 25 to 64, at least one-quarter of all women are non-working with no other specific status. Over half of them have been out of the labour market for over ten years. In contrast, no more than 1% of men ever report themselves as non-working with no other status; half of them have recently held a job.

The majority of non-working people last worked in a female occupation (Table 4.2). This is due entirely to the predominance of women in the non-working population. The pattern of occupational segregation in the last jobs of the non-working population is almost identical to the pattern found among people in employment (Tables 4.2 and 2.1).

TABLE 4.2. *Non-working people: composition of group*

| | With job in last ten years: Type of occupation | | | | No job in last ten years | Base numbers |
	Male	Mixed	Female	Total		
Total	11	19	70	100		37,765
Men	61	20	19	100		1,627
Women	8	19	72	100		36,138
Total	5	9	32	45	55	83,572
Men	31	10	10	52	48	3,135
Women	4	9	33	45	55	80,437

Source: 2% SAR, Great Britain, data for residents aged 16–64 years.

JOB CHARACTERISTICS

For the rest of this chapter, the focus is on non-working people with no other specific status. It is not our purpose here to study the characteristics of the unemployed, the early retired, the permanently sick, and full-time students, groups that have been studied elsewhere in specialized surveys. Our focus is on the group that never attracts special attention: women (and men) who have dropped out of the labour market but do not classify themselves as 'retired' and thus leave open the possibility of a return to paid work at some future time. Roughly half of this group have had a job in the last decade and roughly half have not had any recent work experience. For the latter group, we have information on higher education qualifications but no other employment-related characteristics.

Non-working people with recent work experience are less well educated than people in employment: 11% and 18% respectively have tertiary level qualifications; 3% and 7% respectively have two or more such qualifications; 6% and 10% respectively have degree-level qualifications. This pattern of lesser qualifications is found among men and women, across all types of occupation (Tables 4.3 and 2.3). Non-working people with no recent work experience are even less well qualified than those who have had a job in the last ten years. For example, 3% of these women and men have higher education qualifications compared to 17% of women and 19% of men in employment (Table 4.3 compared with 2.3). No doubt there are similar differences in secondary school qualifications as well. The results support the thesis that women (and men) with discontinuous work histories have a much lower investment in human capital and in careers in the formal labour market than people in work; the lower the investment, the longer the period out of the labour market.

However, there is no evidence to support the thesis that non-working women are drawn primarily from the part-time workforce. As noted above,

TABLE 4.3. *Non-working people: higher qualifications*   column percent

Higher qualifications held		Non-working people with a job in the last ten years Type of occupation in last job				Non-working people with no job in last ten years
		Male	Mixed	Female	Total	
All	a higher degrees	1	1	*	1	*
	b first degrees	4	6	4	5	2
	c below degree level	3	4	7	5	2
	two or more	2	3	3	3	1
	none	92	89	90	89	96
Men	a higher degrees	1	2	2	1	*
	b first degrees	3	6	10	5	2
	c below degree level	2	6	4	4	1
	two or more	2	5	6	4	1
	none	95	87	85	90	97
Women	a higher degrees	1	1	*	*	*
	b first degrees	5	6	4	4	1
	c below degree level	4	4	7	6	2
	two or more	3	3	3	3	1
	none	91	89	90	89	97

Source: 2% SAR, Great Britain, data for residents aged 16–64 years in employment.

there is also no evidence that they were employed disproportionately in female occupations. Overall, there seem to be no differences between the current and last jobs of men and women considered separately. As regards regional and industry distributions, there are no important differences between current jobs and last jobs. No census information was collected on patterns of travel to work for previous jobs. One small difference is that the self-employed are greatly under-represented among last jobs (Table 4.4) because people who quit self-employment usually transfer to employee jobs (Bryson and White, 1996*b*).

The only notable difference is that jobs held in the previous ten years are of significantly lower status than current jobs, a difference that is reflected in social class, SEG, occupational grade, occupational prestige, Cambridge social status scores, and average earnings (Tables 4.4 and 4.5 compared to 2.4 and 2.5). Last jobs are concentrated disproportionately in lower grade white-collar work and in blue-collar work. This is particularly noticeable within the category of mixed occupations, where the usual dominance of higher grade occupations shrinks in favour of blue-collar jobs. This is one of the few findings consistent with our original thesis that mixed occupations provide high turnover labour market entry jobs as well as career jobs.

Earnings in previous jobs are lower than in current jobs for all subgroups, both within the non-working group and among all people with a recent job who are not currently in employment. This result is not due to inflation eroding the value of earnings in the last job. All earnings estimates refer to spring 1991 earnings for people in the occupation in question with the same characteristics (age, sex, hours worked, region of residence) as the person in the SAR sample. Lower average earnings in previous jobs are explained by their lower occupational grade compared to current jobs. People who stay in work continue to get promoted up occupational ladders and thus have higher earnings than people whose last job was held up to ten years previously. Since the NES earnings estimates do not control for job tenure or work experience, the lower earnings for jobs held in the last ten years are due exclusively to lower average occupational grade compared to current jobs. People whose last job was held over ten years ago will fall even further behind.

The lower grade of previous jobs compared with current jobs is reflected in lower mean scores on the Cambridge scale (Table 4.4), the ISEI occupational status scale, and the SIOPS occupational prestige scale, for full-time and part-time jobs, men and women. Correlations between occupational grade and earnings are just as strong for jobs held in the last ten years (Table 4.6) as for current jobs (Table 3.8), so there is no evidence of people leaving jobs because they were unfairly or poorly remunerated.

TABLE 4.4. *Non-working people: characteristics of last job*

	Non-working women by type of occupation				Non-working men
	Male	Mixed	Female	All	
Employment status					
Managers	12	30	1	6	8
Foremen	3	1	3	3	2
Small firm owner	*	*	*	*	*
Solo S/E	3	7	1	2	12
Other employees	82	62	95	90	79
Hours per week					
461	5	7	1	3	18
30–45	69	70	55	59	75
11–29	21	20	33	30	5
, 10	5	4	11	9	2
Socio-Economic Group					
employers and managers—large establishments	1	4	*	1	1
employers—small establishments	*	*	*	*	*
managers—small establishments	5	25	*	5	8
professionals—self-employed	*	*	*	*	1
professionals—employees	3	3	*	1	2
ancillary workers & artists	8	10	12	11	7
supervisors—white-collar	*	—	2	1	1
junior white-collar	13	1	53	40	9
personal service	—	3	14	11	3
foremen—blue-collar	2	1	*	1	2
skilled blue-collar	21	7	1	4	25
semi-skilled blue-collar	28	40	7	14	18
unskilled blue collar	6	*	11	9	12
own-account workers (not professionals)	2	6	1	2	9
farmers—owners/managers	1	—	—	*	*
agricultural workers	9	—	—	1	2
Mean Cambridge scores					
All recent jobs	23	32	33	32	26
Full-time jobs (301 hours)	23	33	36	34	26
Part-time jobs (, 30 hours)	21	29	29	29	26
Mean hourly earnings for employees (pence)					
All recent jobs	493	559	467	486	633
Full-time jobs (301 hours)	517	578	507	523	652
Part-time jobs (, 30 hours)	428	490	417	425	435

Source: 2% and 1% SARs, Great Britain, data for residents aged 16–64 years. Figures on employment status are from 1% SAR, and all other figures are from 2% SAR.

TABLE 4.5. *Social class of jobs held in last ten years by non-working people*   column percent

RG Social Classes		Women's previous jobs				Men's previous jobs			
		Male occups.	Mixed occups.	Female occups.	All	Male occups.	Mixed occups.	Female occups.	All
RG Social Classes									
I	Professional	4	3	*	1	2	4	4	3
II	Managerial & Technical	15	42	12	18	7	58	14	18
III	Skilled white-collar	13	4	53	41	4	6	36	10
III	Skilled blue-collar	24	11	6	9	48	10	11	34
IV	Semi-skilled workers	38	40	18	23	24	22	17	22
V	Unskilled workers	6	—	11	8	15	—	18	13
Total 00s=100%		29	63	260	350	10	3	3	15
Goldthorpe Classes									
I	Upper service class	9	13	*	3	6	12	2	7
II	Lower service	18	42	9	14	6	45	13	13
IIIa	Routine non-manual	3	5	30	24	1	2	22	5
IIIb	Sales & service workers	—	—	25	20	—	—	20	3
IV	Petty bourgeoisie	3	6	1	2	12	11	1	10
V/VI	Skilled workers	22	12	6	8	33	8	14	26
VII	Unskilled workers	45	22	29	30	42	22	28	36
Total 00s=100%		14	21	140	170	4	1	1	6

Source: 2% and 1% SARs, Great Britain, data for residents aged 16–64 years.
2% SAR used for data on RG Social Classes and 1% SAR used for data on Goldthorpe Classes.

TABLE 4.6. *Correlations between occupational grade and earnings for employee jobs held in last ten years*

	Type of occupation				All men	All women
	Male	Mixed	Female	Total		
ISEI	.70	.65	.61	.63	.70	.67
SIOPS	.67	.65	.76	.71	.73	.76
Cambridge scale	.68	.66	.75	.62	.69	.74

Source: 1% SAR, Great Britain, data for residents aged 16–64 years not currently in employment who held an employee job within the last ten years.

PERSONAL CHARACTERISTICS

In terms of personal characteristics, there is little evidence that women (or men) with discontinuous work histories are distinctive in any way, or that they differ in important ways from women (and men) currently in work (Table 4.7).

Ethnic minority women are more likely to follow the marriage career and have no recent work experience. There is the expected impact of dependent children keeping women at home. Only 40% of men and women in employment have any dependent children living with them, that is, children under the school-leaving age of 16 years (Table 4.7). The majority of men and, more especially, women with recent jobs have dependent children living with them: 57% and 77% respectively. The great majority of women with discontinuous work histories are married and financially dependent on their husband, living in one-earner households. The great majority of working women are also married, but they are part of households with two earners (or more). So far, the results seem to show that women with discontinuous work histories reflect a common but temporary phase in women's life cycle and work histories, a phase that affects all women equally.

HOUSING GROUPS

On closer inspection, this is not so. First, there is a clear polarization of choices in the 25–34-year age group. Almost half of women with discontinuous work histories are in the 25–34-year age group compared to only one-quarter of working women. Among working women, this is the age group where occupational attainment peaks, with 24% in integrated occupations (see Table 2.7) and the highest proportion in professional and managerial careers (37% compared to 31% among all working women). Secondly, housing type emerges as the second major influence on women's work patterns, and it reflects a permanent or at the least long-term lifestyle choice. Only 12% of men and women in work are in rented public housing, compared to 37% and 24% respectively of non-working men and women who had recently stopped working, and 45% and 30% respectively of non-working men and women who had not had a job for ten years or longer. The housing variable is probably highly correlated with the social class and earnings of the woman's husband. But as we had not foreseen that family circumstances other than the presence of young children would be important, information on spouses was not included in our SAR extract tape. So the housing variable is probably combining the effect of the family's social class (as determined by the husband's occupation) and the effect of the financial burden of

Discontinuous Employment Histories

TABLE 4.7. *Personal characteristics of working and non-working people*   column percent

| | Current jobs | | Non-working women | | All not currently in work | | | |
| | | | | | With job in last 10 years | | No job in last 10 years | |
	Men	Women	with recent job	no recent job	Men	Women	Men	Women
Age 16–24 years	15	18	15	7	26	23	52	24
25–34	26	25	44	20	18	29	11	15
35–44	26	26	20	24	13	15	9	17
45–54	20	21	11	22	13	11	10	17
55–64	13	10	10	27	30	23	18	27
% non-white	4	4	3	10	6	4	13	10
% with 11 dependent child(ren)	41	39	77	56	31	52	49	52
No earners in household	—	—	29	37	48	37	40	39
1 earner in household	30	19	62	46	29	46	26	38
21 earners in household	70	81	9	17	23	17	34	23
Heads of household	75	21	23	23	65	25	35	23
Spouses	6	62	73	73	5	58	3	53
Others in household	19	17	4	5	30	17	62	24
Family type								
Married, no children	22	24	13	24	28	23	12	22
Married, dependent child(ren)	42	35	55	39	29	41	45	40
Married, no dependent child	22	21	7	16	25	12	21	16
Cohabiting, no children	6	7	1	1	3	2	1	1
Cohabiting, dep. child(ren)	3	2	6	3	4	4	3	3
Cohabiting, no dep. child	1	1	*	*	1	*	1	*
One parent, dependent child(ren)	1	5	17	14	3	12	8	13
One parent, no dependent child	4	5	1	3	7	4	9	5
% in rented public housing1	11	12	24	30	27	23	33	30
% in owner-occupied housing	79	79	65	60	60	66	54	60

[1] Public housing is rented from local government agencies or from New Town authorities.
Source: 2% SAR, Great Britain, data for residents aged 16–64 years.

a large home purchase loan. Student loans are as yet a novelty in Britain, and tend to be small. House purchase loans are usually the first and by far the largest loans taken out by most adults, sometimes for 100% of the property value, and they are typically of long duration in Britain, with repayments usually spread over 20–30 years. In one sense, the impact of the husband's social class and that of owner-occupied housing are conterminous. Some couples choose to buy their own home, find that two salaries are needed to finance this purchase securely (especially in recession), and inevitably adopt somewhat more egalitarian sex roles in consequence, whether they started from this position or not. Other couples decide to rely on rented public housing, generally a far cheaper option, and the lower financial burden makes it easier for the wife to give up employment to become a full-time homemaker, so that highly differentiated sex roles are reintroduced or strengthened after children are born. Housing choices reflect and reinforce large social class differences in sex role preferences and norms about the sexual division of labour in the family (Vogler, 1994: 45, 55; Hakim and Jacobs, 1997).

The strong impact of housing choice on wives' employment patterns has not so far been addressed in the literature on women's employment. For example none of the SCELI reports considered the issue, although they did address household strategies and decision-making (Anderson *et al.*, 1994: 43, 59; Gallie and Vogler, 1994; McCrone, 1994: 96–7). The literature on housing and housing classes (Saunders, 1990; Forrest, Murie, and Williams, 1990) has focused on the social-psychological and political implications of home-ownership rather than on the implications for women's employment and work orientations. More recently, Holmans's (1993) careful study exposed the polarization of employment patterns in public and private sector housing, a long-term trend that accelerated in the 1980s due to government policies. Furthermore, new research on the 1980s shows that, *within* social classes, there was increasing polarization between dual-earner couples choosing to buy their homes and couples with a non-working wife living in public sector housing (Hogarth, Elias, and Ford, 1996). The link between wives' employment and housing type is of course well established in the ordinary knowledge that seems often to be missing from social science disciplinary knowledge (Lindblom and Cohen, 1979: 12–14; Scott and Shore, 1979).

The large impact of housing choice, and the particular sexual division of labour in the family associated with it, is reflected in turnover rates. Using the aggregate turnover rates that can be constructed in the SARs datasets (see Chapter 2), the labour turnover rate for women living in rented public housing was 28% compared to only 13% for women in owner-occupied accommodation, whether this was owned outright or owned with a house purchase loan still being paid off. In a sense, even these figures understate the stark differences between housing groups. Table 4.8 presents the same analysis as in Table 4.1, but comparing only women aged 20–59 in owner-occupied housing and in subsidized rented public housing. These two groups account for 89% of all women aged 20–59, so the analysis effectively covers almost all adult women. The contrasting employment patterns are remarkable. A clear majority (70%) of women living in homes they own (or co-own) are currently working compared to well under half (42%) of women in rented public

TABLE 4.8. *Employment patterns by housing type*

	Proportion of each age group who are:									Total
							All not currently in work			
	Retired		Non-working		Current jobs		With job in last 10 years		No job in last 10 years	
	N	%	N	%	N	%	N	%	N	%	N=100%
Women aged 20–59 years											
All	3,266	1	71,384	25	186,711	64	55,292	19	51,307	17	293,310
In owner-occupied housing	2,589	1	44,153	21	146,302	70	34,797	17	27,997	13	209,096
In rented public housing	489	1	19,605	40	20,533	42	12,439	25	16,206	33	49,176
Women aged 25–34 years											
All	62	*	24,623	30	50,645	62	20,522	25	10,908	13	82,075
In owner-occupied housing	33	*	13,657	24	39,043	70	12,831	23	4,207	7	56,081
In rented public housing	19	*	7,797	50	5,378	35	4,806	32	4,982	33	15,466

Source: 2% SAR Great Britain, data for residents aged 16–64 years.

housing. One-third of women aged 20–59 years living in rented public housing have not done any paid work for over ten years, compared to only 13% of
those who own their homes, and twice as many are non-working: 40% compared to 21% (Table 4.8). These results are not due to women in rented public housing being generally older than women who own or are buying their
own homes, either alone or with a partner. The same pattern is observed
among young women aged 25–34 years, with even sharper contrasts between
the two housing groups (Table 4.8). The financial burden of buying a home
undoubtedly prompts more wives to stay in employment, to postpone childbearing or return quickly to their jobs after having a baby, than is found
among wives in public housing. But another factor is the much greater acceptance of the sexual division of labour in the home among women and men in
working-class families, with women regarded primarily as homemakers and
men regarded as the principal breadwinners (Hakim and Jacobs, 1997).
Public sector housing facilitates, encourages, and maintains this 'traditional'
sexual division of labour in the working class.

Labour market analysts do not routinely seek to incorporate data on housing type and on husband's social class in studies of women's employment.
The human capital perspective has accustomed us to focusing on job-related
factors such as qualifications and work experience. The equal opportunities
and feminist perspectives also seem to make it almost illegitimate to refer to

women's private circumstances in analyses of women's employment decisions. Among sociologists, it is now fashionable to pretend that a husband's social class is not an important determinant of a woman's life chances, attitudes, and behaviour, and that reference should instead be made to a woman's own occupation and social class (Dex, 1990; McRae, 1990), as in the present analysis. When the data permit it, reference is usually made to numbers of dependent children, if any, as the most important 'private', non-labour market influence on women's employment decisions. Social class and housing, and their links to sex-role preferences and the sexual division of labour in families, are routinely excluded from 'economistic' labour market analyses and quite commonly excluded also from sociological studies too— as reflected in the design of the present analysis! Even when they have been included, the large social class difference in sex role preferences has been ignored in favour of a focus on the small sex differential in 'sexism' (Vogler, 1994).

CONCLUSIONS

The thesis that women with discontinuous work histories would be distinctive in their employment careers fails on the evidence. Women with discontinuous work histories have not necessarily been working in female occupations and in part-time jobs. On the contrary, women with recent work experience but not currently in employment have had jobs across the entire workforce, in full-time and part-time jobs, in male and integrated occupations as well as in female occupations. However, women with discontinuous work histories are less well qualified than working women, and those who have been out of the labour market for over ten years have even fewer qualifications. Differences between women who are currently working and women who have recently stopped working are generally weak as regards their employment characteristics, those that are public and visible to an employer. It is mainly in their private lives that clear differences emerge.

These results are due in part to the over-simplified, weak operational definitions of continuous and discontinuous employment that were imposed by the data. The majority of women currently in employment are not in fact continuous workers, but women who move in and out of the workforce. A 1988 national survey of 4,000 people aged 55 to 69 years living in private households found that only 10% of women compared to 56% of men had worked continuously throughout life, full-time and/or part-time, without any spells of unemployment or non-work (Bone *et al.*, 1992: 6). A recent study shows that the proportion of women of working age who are in continuous employment shrank in each successive age cohort after 1940, to only one in ten of women who entered the labour market in the 1960s (Hakim, 1996*a*: 139; see also Main, 1988*a*). Clearly continuous workers form a tiny proportion of the 58% of women who were in employment at the time of the 1991 Census. The great majority of working women already are or will become discontinuous workers. In effect, census data was not adequate to test the thesis properly.

The lack of differences between women's current and last jobs is consistent with the turnover rates reported in Chapters 2 and 5, which show that high female turnover is not concentrated in any single part of the labour market but is dispersed across all occupations and types of job, full-time and part-time. These results are also consistent with the finding that discontinuous employment is increasingly characteristic of both full-time and part-time women workers (Hakim, 1996*a*: 135–9). In effect, virtually all women have become discontinuous workers, so the lack of any marked labour market differences between working and non-working women is not surprising. The tiny minority of women in continuous employment (about 10% of women of working age) are almost certainly distinctive, but they are virtually impossible to identify except *post hoc*.

These results are of some policy significance. Social scientists have tried to argue that there is no significant sex differential in turnover rates (Hakim, 1996*c*) and that employers can predict who will quit jobs and who will stay (Light and Ureta, 1992), so that there is no case for differential human resource management policies to take account of women's different labour market behaviour. This seems doubtful. Childbirth is the main catalyst for women leaving the labour market, but recent studies repeatedly emphasize that women are taking shorter and shorter maternity breaks from their jobs (McRae, 1991, 1993; Macran, Joshi, and Dex, 1996). This is true, but it remains the case that only a one-third minority of women return to paid work while their children are young. Even in the 1990s the majority of mothers of very young children remain out of the labour force at least until the child reaches school age (5 years in Britain). The 1991–2 GHS shows that three-quarters (71%) of mothers do not work in the child's first year; two-thirds do not work in the child's second and third years; half (48%) stay out of work up to the child's 4th birthday and 57% up to the 5th birthday. Overall, two-thirds of mothers of children under age 5 remain out of the workforce. Only a tiny minority (11%) of mothers work full-time while their youngest child is under 5 years old, a constant proportion that is not affected by the child's age, indicating women who did not allow childbearing to interrupt their careers (Duncan, Giles, and Webb, 1995: 5–6). A high proportion of these women are in professional and managerial occupations, and can thus afford substitute childcare (OPCS, 1995: 54–5, 67). Even in the 1990s, the likelihood of a working woman returning to work after childbirth, to a job kept open for her by her employer as requested by the woman and as required by law, is only 50/50, which is no better than chance (Hakim, 1996*a*: 130).

This means it is still impossible for employers to predict how long a female employee will stay in a job—because it is impossible to predict whether a woman who explicitly commits herself to returning to work after childbirth will actually do so, and because there are no distinguishing employment characteristics that allow one to differentiate between continuous workers, discontinuous workers, and those who quit the labour market indefinitely after the birth of children. The information required concerns 'private' attitudes and circumstances that equal opportunities rules render it inappropriate to enquire about.[1]

Working and non-working women differ sharply in sex-role preferences and norms regarding the sexual division of labour in the family, and these differing preferences are associated with work histories (Hakim and Jacobs, 1997). The majority of women part-time workers and the majority of non-working women accept the sexual division of labour in the family that assigns the breadwinner role to the man and the homemaker role to the woman. The majority of women working full-time reject this sexual division of labour. These differences in sex-role preferences are associated with quite different work histories (Hakim and Jacobs, 1997), although a host of other factors also affect employment decisions. Most datasets do not include the relevant information on sex-role preferences and work orientations. Housing type and husband's social class are only loose proxies for information on norms and values, but at least this information is more likely to be available in survey datasets. We found that women's employment patterns differ significantly between housing groups. Working and non-working women are not differentiated by their labour market characteristics and studies which restrict their analyses to these variables alone will conclude, incorrectly, that sample selection bias is not a problem (Paci and Joshi, 1996: 20–1). Similarly, there are only limited behavioural differences between women who are financially dependent on their partner and those who contribute equally to household income (Joshi and Davies, 1996: 47). It is 'private' norms and values which differentiate between groups of women and remain the unobserved heterogeneity in most datasets on women's employment.

The family characteristics of women who had temporarily withdrawn from female occupations did not differ significantly from women who had recently held male occupations and integrated occupations. There is no evidence here that female occupations make it easier for women to remain in

---

[1] Maternity rights surveys reveal a sharp discrepancy between women's 'private' plans to return to work after the birth, or not, and women's formal statements to employers that they intend to return to work after the birth and wish their job to be held open for them (Hakim, 1996*a*: 127–9). In effect, maternity rights legislation forces women to lie about their 'private' intentions, which predict actual behaviour fairly accurately (Hakim, 1996*a*: 128).

employment during the childrearing phase, despite the higher proportion of part-time jobs on offer. Once again, the results deny that occupations impose certain employment patterns on people. They also imply that equal opportunities and sex discrimination legislation ensure that women do *not* choose their first main occupation with a view to its long-term compatibility with childrearing activities, that women are free to choose male occupations even if they do not necessarily stay in them throughout working life. Alternatively, women's sex-role preferences when young do not always last: they can change radically after they have children and discover that career success comes at a price, that the dedicated pursuit of promotion up career ladders is not compatible with a major involvement in family activities and children's development.

The 2001 Census will continue to collect information on jobs held previously, with refinements that enrich the research analysis potential of the data. One possible new question asks how long it is since the last job, with several response categories: less than 6 months, 6–12 months, 1–2 years, 2–5 years, 5–10 years, over ten years, and a separate tick box for people who have never done paid work. This would help to differentiate unemployed school-leavers who have never had a job from women who gave up work at marriage or childbirth, for example, and it provides useful extra detail on how long people have been out of the workforce. Occupational and other information will be collected for the last *main* job, which gives a better picture of a person's social status, earnings potential, and aspirations than the last job strictly defined. Finally, multiple coding of economic activity status last week will be significantly strengthened and facilitated by a separate question asking people to tick Yes or No for *each* of seven non-market activities and statuses: student in full-time education, retired, permanently sick/disabled, looking after the home or family, unemployed, waiting to start a job already accepted, and on a government training or employment scheme for the unemployed. All of these changes extend the analysis potential of the 2001 Census SARs microdata beyond the level reflected in this chapter. In particular, the 2001 Census will allow us to assess whether people in male, mixed, and female occupations differ in the length of their employment breaks, even if they do not differ in the incidence of such breaks.

In the meantime, the results presented here warn us against using information on 'current or last job' for women in research analyses, even though this greatly expands the sample of women for whom data on occupation (and social class) is available—by one-third or more compared to the group with current jobs. Previous jobs, even if restricted to the preceding decade, tend to be of systematically lower status and lower average earnings than current jobs. This is equally true for men and women. However, many more women fall into the 'previous job but not currently in work' category, so that the effect of including them is far greater in data for women than in data for men, invisibly depressing women's average occupational grade and earnings compared to men. This distortion is found in male, mixed, and female occupations, making it clear that it is simply the passage of time that is the key factor, as Erikson and Goldthorpe (1993: 242) argued. This is another topic on which the 2001 Census results should throw new light.

5

A Differentiated Part-Time Workforce: Marginal Jobs, Half-Time Jobs and Reduced Hours Jobs

The purpose of this chapter is to present a new classification of working hours which was developed through iterative analyses of the SAR files, and to show that it differentiates usefully between subgroups within the so-called part-time workforce, thus helping us to make sense of puzzles in cross-national comparisons of part-time work.

THE RISE IN PART-TIME EMPLOYMENT

Throughout Europe, and in most OECD countries, part-time work has been expanding, along with other types of non-standard employment. This new development has stimulated a substantial literature seeking to understand part-time work and to set it within an economic, social, and industrial relations context. Studies of part-time work in particular countries (Beechey and Perkins, 1987; Hakim, 1990b, 1991, 1993a; Hepple, 1990; Duffy and Pupo, 1992) are complemented by cross-national comparative reports (Goldthorpe, 1984; Neubourg, 1985; Dahrendorf, Kohler, and Piotet, 1986; Jenson, Hagen, and Reddy, 1988; Boyer, 1989; Lane, 1989; ILO, 1989; Rodgers and Rodgers, 1989; Dale and Glover, 1990; Hakim, 1990a; OECD, 1990, 1994: 73–100, 1995; Gladstone, 1992; Meulders, Plasman, and Vander Stricht, 1993; Pfau-Effinger, 1993; Pott-Buter, 1993; Bosch, Dawkins, and Michon, 1994; Meulders, Plasman, and Plasman, 1994; European Commission, 1994a, 1995a: 9, 17–18; McRae, 1995; Nätti, 1995; Rosenfeld and Birkelund, 1995; Wedderburn, 1995; Blanpain and Rojot, 1997; Blossfeld and Hakim, 1997; De Grip et al., 1997; O'Reilly and Fagan, 1998). The rise of part-time work has three characteristics that establish it as a new element in the labour market, qualitatively different and quite separate from the conventional full-time workforce: part-time jobs are growing faster than and sometimes replacing full-time jobs in the workforce; they are part of a broader trend towards diverse forms of non-standard or atypical employment contract and working hours; and they are mostly taken by women.

Part-time work also presents a challenge to social scientists: theories that work reasonably well in relation to a male-dominated full-time workforce fall apart in the context of the part-time workforce. Just one example is the fact that part-time employees (and working women generally) express high levels of satisfaction with their jobs, often greater satisfaction than is reported by full-time workers, or by men, with their objectively more rewarding, higher status, and better paid jobs (Hakim, 1991). This finding has been replicated in several separate national surveys, across Europe and in other industrial societies (Nerb, 1986: 19, 50–8; Curtice, 1993; Corti *et al.*, 1995: 54–7; Clark, 1996). Similarly, employees in temporary, casual, and fixed-term contracts report levels of job satisfaction equivalent to those of employees in permanent jobs (Clark, 1996: 196, 203). Employees with the lowest pay have the highest job satisfaction; after controlling for other variables, there is no correlation between earnings and satisfaction with the work itself in a national sample covering female as well as male employees (Clark, 1996: 195, 201). These results are due in part to sex differences in expectations and reference groups, and in part to selection effects—a problem that affects data for working women far more strongly than data for working men (Berk, 1983; Clark, 1996: 197–8; Hakim, 1996*a*: 120–44, 1996*c*: 14–24). But part-time work also exposes the narrow scope and sexist bias of conventional sociological and economic theory and research on the labour market, which has generally focused on men only, especially men in manufacturing industry, and adopted an antagonistic trade union perspective on part-time work (Hakim, 1997*a*: 47–52).

The rise of part-time work is explained by the entry into the labour market of people, mainly women, who remained out of market work when the only option available was full-time jobs. This is illustrated most clearly by the Netherlands, with an unchanging 20% full-time workrate among women; all the recent increase in employment rates was due to the creation of a new part-time workforce. Similarly in France, Britain, and Germany, full-time workrates have remained relatively stable at around 30%–40% of women of working age for as far back as the statistics go, so virtually all the recent change is due to the emergence of a new part-time workforce (Blossfeld and Hakim, 1997). The pace of change has of course depended on employers' willingness to create such jobs. But economic theory and supply and demand factors alone do not fully explain post-war developments. It is clear that socio-cultural factors are often crucial.

There are huge differences between countries in national levels of part-time work, and in the size and longevity of the post-war increase. In some countries, such as Britain, part-time work emerged soon after the Second World War when the marriage bar was abolished,[1] and has grown steadily

---

[1] The marriage bar was the formal rule, jointly enforced by employers and trade unions, that women had to leave paid employment on marriage. This rule effectively excluded all married women from the labour market, so that working women were necessarily single, widowed, or, rarely, divorced. The marriage bar became widespread in the second half of the 19th cent.

throughout the second half of the twentieth century. In contrast, Luxembourg and Italy have very small part-time workforces and very slow growth even by the end of the century. Figs. 1 and 2 illustrate the enormous variation in patterns of working hours among men and women and in the incidence of part-time work over the life cycle across Western industrial societies.

Table 5.1 ranks countries in the EU by the importance of part-time work among women, and shows that there is no simple association between part-time work and female employment rates. Within Europe, Finnish and Portuguese women (and to a lesser extent also French women) are distinctive in their commitment to continuous full-time employment in preference to unpaid childrearing activities or part-time work (Table 5.1 and Fig. 2). The source of this distinctive and long-standing commitment to employment has never been convincingly explained as yet, despite valiant attempts (Pfau-Effinger, 1993). In contrast, high female employment rates in the Netherlands, Britain, and Sweden depend heavily on very high levels of part-time work—about half of all women's jobs being part-time.

There are sharp contrasts between adjacent countries in northern and southern Europe with large similarities in social and economic conditions. Spain and Portugal have similar histories and economies and both have very little part-time work, but women's (full-time) employment rate in Portugal is roughly double that in Spain. There is a tendency to treat all Scandinavian countries as a fairly homogeneous group in labour market analyses, due to similarities in social and economic policies, yet Finland is distinctively different in having high female employment rates without substantial numbers of part-time jobs (Nätti, 1995) as illustrated by contrasts between Sweden and Finland in Table 5.1 and Fig. 2. In recent years both France and the Netherlands removed legal and other restrictions on part-time jobs and France also developed employment policies to promote part-time work. In the Netherlands the change of policy had an immediate effect, prompting massive growth in the female part-time workforce until it became double the size of the female full-time workforce by the mid-1990s. In France, the new

in Britain, and was abolished from the 1940s onwards, after a long campaign by women's organizations against employers and trade unions. For example, the marriage bar was abolished in the British Civil Service in 1946, but the Union of Post Office Workers maintained the marriage bar for its own employees until 1963. Abolition of the marriage bar constituted a fundamental change in women's workforce participation, and was a key factor in the rise of part-time work after the Second World War, yet it is only rarely mentioned by social historians, sociologists, and economists in Britain (Lewenhak, 1977: 41, 94, 215, 225–6, 265–6, 292; Walby, 1986: 57, 171–2, 204–7, 240). In the USA and other countries the marriage bar consisted of social and cultural norms dictating that wives should not engage in paid employment, which did not go as far as a legally enforceable rule, but had equally profound effects on patterns of female employment and earnings (Goldin, 1990). Pott-Buter (1993) reviews the very different pace of change in equal opportunities legislation and related attitudes across Western Europe, demonstrating their impact on female employment.

TABLE 5.1. *Cross-national comparisons of the salience of part-time work, 1995*

	Working age population 15–64 millions	Total employment millions	Employment rates % of working age population			Part-time workers % of all employed		FTE employment rate
			All	Men	Women	Women	Men	Women
USA	165.8	119.4	72	79	65	25	11	57
European Union								
Netherlands	10.5	6.7	64	75	53	67	17	35
UK	37.4	26.2	70	77	63	44	8	49
Sweden	5.5	4.0	72	73	72	43	10	57
Denmark	3.5	2.6	76	83	68	36	10	56
Germany	54.8	34.9	64	73	54	34	4	45
Belgium	6.7	3.8	57	67	46	30	3	39
France	36.9	22.3	61	69	53	29	5	45
Austria	5.3	3.8	71	80	61	27	4	53
Ireland	2.3	1.3	56	69	42	23	6	37
Luxembourg	0.3	0.2	77	98	56	21	1	50
Spain	25.9	12.0	46	62	32	17	3	29
Finland	3.3	2.0	62	64	60	16	8	55
Italy	38.9	19.9	51	67	36	13	3	34
Portugal	6.7	4.4	65	75	56	12	4	53
Greece	6.8	3.8	56	75	39	8	3	37
EU15	244.8	148.0	60	71	50	31	5	42
Other European countries								
Poland	23.9	13.8	58	64	52	13	9	49
Slovenia	1.4	0.9	62	66	58	2	1	57
Hungary	6.8	5.5	81	85	77	2	1	76

Notes: The FTE (full-time equivalent) employment rate assumes that most part-timers work half-time hours, so that two part-time workers are equivalent to one full-time worker.

Figures for the USA relate to the population aged 16–64 instead of the population aged 15–64 and part-time jobs are slightly underestimated compared to European countries. USA CPS statistics define part-time workers as people whose weekly hours, in all jobs, total less than 35 hours, rather than people working part-time in their main job.

Part-time work is self-defined in the EU Labour Force Survey, with some variation between countries in the upper limit for what are regarded as a part-time hours.

Sources: EU Labour Force Survey data for 1995 and other sources reported in European Commission, *Employment in Europe 1996*, and estimates from other sources for 1995 for Eastern Europe and for the USA reported in Blossfeld and Hakim (1997: table 1.1).

policies met with dismay and resistance rather than enthusiasm among women trade unionists and social scientists and part-time work grew very slowly (Blossfeld and Hakim, 1997).

Some of the sharp contrasts within Europe are diminished or even resolved by replacing the conventional headcount measure of employment by a Full-Time Equivalent (FTE) measure as shown in Table 5.1. (FTE rates take account of differences in hours worked by counting two part-time jobs as equivalent to one full-time job.) On the face of it, the Netherlands and Greece are at opposite poles in Europe with 67% and 8% of working women in part-time jobs and with 53% and 39% of working women in employment. After

A Differentiated Part-Time Workforce

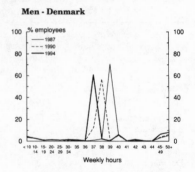

Fig. 1. Distribution of usual hours worked per week in European Union member states, 1987–1994

Source: European Commission (1995*a*), *Employment in Europe 1995*, pp. 183–6, reporting EU Labour Force Survey data.

Men - Ireland

Men - Italy

Men - Luxembourg

Men - Netherlands

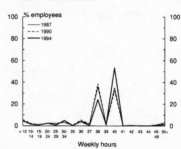

Men - Portugal

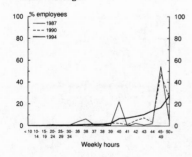

Men - UK

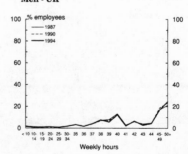

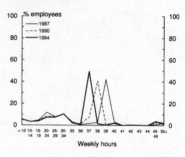

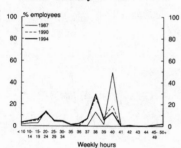

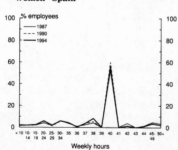

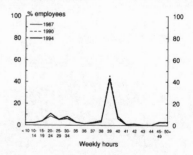

FIG. 1. *cont.*

Women - Ireland

Women - Italy

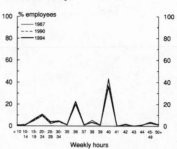

Women - Luxembourg

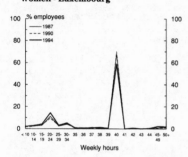

Women - Netherlands

Women - Portugal

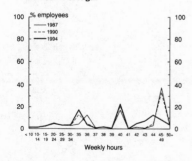

Women - UK

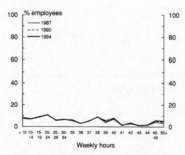

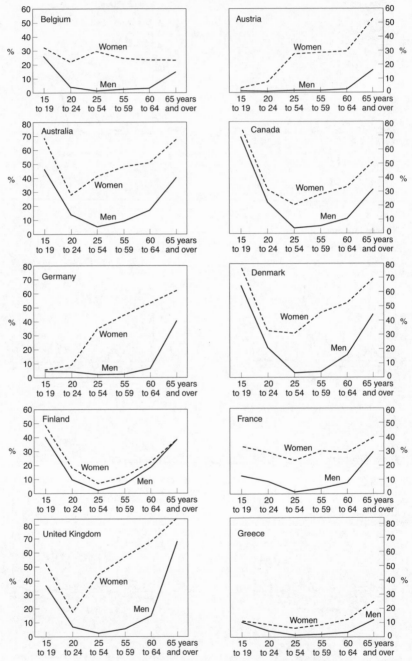

FIG. 2. The share of part-time jobs in total employment by age and sex in the EU, the
Source: Unpublished 1993 data supplied by OECD, Paris, for all countries except Japan. Data for

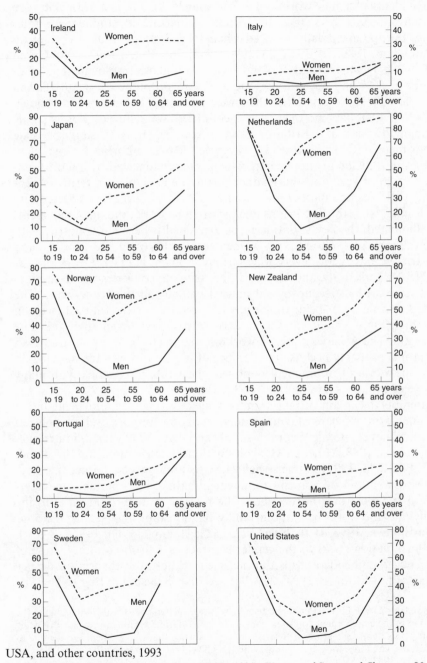

USA, and other countries, 1993

Japan refer to 1985–87 and are taken from OECD (1994), *Women and Structural Change*, p. 86.

conversion to FTE rates, Greece and the Netherlands are shown to have almost identical female workrates at 37% and 35% of women of working age respectively. As others have also found, disparities in employment rates across Europe are greatly reduced when FTE figures are used (European Commission, 1989: 19, 1993: 33, 1996: 33–5; Pott-Buter, 1993: 205). On an FTE basis, Denmark and Finland have the highest employment rates in Europe at 56% and 55% of working age women, followed by Austria and Portugal with 53%.[2] Spain has the lowest FTE employment rate for women at 29%. Differences between other countries are reduced. For example Germany, France, and Britain are revealed as having very similar female employment rates near the EU average. Most importantly, the clear north–south divide in simple employment rates is replaced by a more complex picture of variation that cannot readily be explained in terms of economic variables, the industrial structure, and the importance of agriculture and fishing. Once the distortions due to part-time work (and unemployment) are eliminated, the key variation to be explained is between countries with high full-time workrates among women such as Portugal and Finland, and countries with very low levels of female involvement in market work such as the Netherlands, Italy, and Greece. In between are countries where employment rates are pushed up by substantial volumes of part-time work. The USA is also shown as being unlike any EU country in that American women have high employment rates that derive principally from high full-time workrates. The American female workforce seems to be less polarized than in Europe, probably because the absence of a generous welfare state makes part-time work an impractical option in the USA, in contrast with many European countries (Hakim, 1996a, 1997a).

Attempts to explain variations in the scale of women's employment and in part-time work in terms of country socio-economic profiles, welfare policies, or in terms of economic theory of supply and demand have had limited success (Rubery, 1988; Mincer, 1985; Pott-Buter, 1993; Rosenfeld and Birkelund, 1995; Blossfeld, 1997). Some social scientists are now concluding that adequate explanations of women's employment have to incorporate some reference to socio-cultural norms about the roles of women (and men) in the family and the workforce, about family relationships and gender relations (Pfau-Effinger, 1993; Pott-Buter, 1993: 322; Hakim, 1996a, 1996b, 1997a). One formulation refers to the gender contract as a socio-cultural feature of each society embedded in institutions such as the tax and social insurance system (Pfau-Effinger, 1993: 389–90; see also Sainsbury, 1996). The key

---

[2] Sweden's 57% FTE workrate, and female workrates generally, are misleading due to the inclusion in the employment count of women at home full-time on long parental leave while retaining job rights, a feature of Swedish labour statistics that makes them seriously non-comparable with those for other countries. See OECD (1991), Jonung and Persson (1993) and Pott-Buter (1993: 208).

problem with this approach is that it fails to account for the diversity of sex-role preferences and family models *within* countries (Hakim, 1996*b*). Preference theory notes that family roles and relationships are in practice negotiated at the micro-level, within couples and families, and that individuals may accept, modify, or reject the prevailing societal norms on the role of women at home and at work. The clearest indication of this is the rise of voluntary childlessness in industrial societies after the contraceptive revolution of the 1960s gave women independent control over their own fertility, even though there was no change in societal models of the family as including offspring and no change in societal approval of motherhood (Hakim, 1996*a*: 125–6, 183, 208). Thus even within societies with well-defined ideal-type models of the family and sex-roles, there is diversity of preferences at the individual level which inform employment choices across the life cycle (Hakim, 1996*a*: 208, 1998; Hakim and Jacobs, 1997).

Clearly, values and sex-role preferences are only one factor among the many that determine employment behaviour. However, new research in the 1990s suggests that sex-role preferences and values are becoming more influential in women's employment choices than they were in the past when employment was driven primarily by economic necessity. For example, Thomson's analysis of the 1994 British Social Attitudes Survey indicated that women's employment decisions are now informed *primarily* by their conceptions of women's role at home and at work and only secondarily by practical factors such as childcare problems or financial need. Careful checks indicated that attitudes to the mother's 'proper' role in the family were not just a form of self-justification or *post-hoc* rationalization (Thomson, 1995: 80–3). The increasing impact of sex-role norms is underlined by research on women who have invested in higher education qualifications and thus have access to better paid jobs. Analyses of the 1991 British Household Panel Study data show that sex-role preferences have an even greater impact on employment decisions among highly qualified women than among women with no qualifications or secondary school qualifications at best, as highly qualified women can afford to choose between competing lifestyles, given homogamy (Hakim, 1996*b*: 186, 1997*a*: 42). Finally, Pott-Buter's detailed historical and comparative analysis of women's employment in seven northern European countries led her to conclude that preference theory offers the only explanation for the continuing exceptionally low female employment rate (measured on a full-time equivalent basis) in the Netherlands as compared with Belgium, France, Denmark, Germany, Sweden, and Britain (Pott-Buter, 1993: 203–8, 322). Sex-role preferences play a key part in women's choice between full-time work, part-time work, or no market work at all (Hakim, 1997*a*, 1998).

Another puzzle of part-time jobs is the large variation in their characteristics and location within the workforce. In Sweden and Denmark, part-time workers have the same status and employment rights as full-time workers, whereas they were partially excluded from statutory employment rights until 1994 in Britain, remain excluded from the tax and social insurance system in some countries, and were not even recognized by statute law until very recently in Italy and Greece (Hakim, 1995*b*: 441; Rubenstein, 1996: 8; Blanpain and Rojot, 1997; Blossfeld and Hakim, 1997). We would argue that explanations for the growth of part-time work have to be more precise about the nature of the activity itself. The key argument of this chapter is that there are three types of part-time job, which do not exist in all countries and may exhibit different trends. By grouping together everything that is not full-time work into a single category of part-time work, previous studies have effectively not been comparing like with like.

THREE TYPES OF PART-TIME JOB

The classification of three types of part-time work presented in this chapter was proposed as a potential solution to the problems of comparative research in Europe (Hakim, 1993*b*: 291). Operational definitions of the three types of job were developed through an iterative process of testing various cut-off points in analyses of the British 1% and 2% SARs and assessing their appropriateness in the wider European context. The resulting classification has four key features. It is first of all empirically based, and differentiates meaningfully between types of part-time job and types of part-time worker at the micro-level in British data. Second, the classification is informed by the European Commission's macro-level analyses of data for the whole of the EU and incorporates distinctions that have been found meaningful at the macro-level in European research. The links to European research are set out more fully later on in the section on comparative perspectives. Here we note that the classification proved useful in a comparative analysis of part-time work across Europe and the USA (Blossfeld and Hakim, 1997). Third, the classification is informed by several reviews of the research literature on part-time work, on employers' labour use strategies and policies, and on the characteristics of part-time workers (Hakim, 1987*c*, 1990*a*, 1990*b*, 1993*b*, 1996*a*, 1997*a*). Fourth, the classification is informed by decisions of the European Court of Justice (ECJ) on cases concerned with part-time jobs or part-time workers, usually in the context of the continuing debate on indirect sex discrimination (Hakim, 1996*a*: 193–200).

Britain provides an especially apposite case study as well as offering the enormous advantage of a very large dataset for research on workforce minorities. Fig. 1 shows clearly that Britain is unique within Europe in that weekly working hours are spread across the whole spectrum, especially for women and to a lesser extent for men. All other European countries display high concentrations around average full-time hours, typically 37–41 hours a week. The slow decline in working hours moved the peaks to the left, down the scale, between 1987 and 1994. But in most cases the high concentrations around average full-time hours (for men and women) and around average part-time hours (for women) still remain in 1994. Britain is the only country where working hours are sufficiently dispersed, for men and women, across the complete range of weekly hours, to allow us to test a variety of cut-off points to differentiate the three groups. This wide dispersion of working hours is due to the relatively unregulated character of the British labour market, as compared with other European economies (Bosch *et al.*, 1994; Hepple and Hakim, 1997; Blanpain and Rojot, 1997). Britain is otherwise a fairly representative case study, with rates of part-time work and employment rates that are around the middle of the distribution for European countries, as shown in Table 5.1.

Part-time work is rare among men (Table 5.1), and is taken up at different points in the life cycle (Fig. 2). Male part-time work seems to be relatively homogeneous: across Europe, the USA, and other industrialized countries, male part-timers tend to be the very young and students or else older people approaching retirement (Fig. 2). For men, part-time work functions as a transition into or out of the workforce (Meulders *et al.*, 1994: 17; OECD, 1994: 84–6; Nätti, 1995). The British SARs are uniquely valuable in providing sufficiently large datasets to allow us to analyse part-time work among men as well as women.

The substantial literature on part-time work has been reviewed by Hakim (1997*a*), who developed a sociological perspective on part-time work to replace the earlier, policy-centred perspectives. Her argument is that permanent or long-term part-time work is a qualitatively different type of labour force involvement to the conventional full-time continuous employment which characterizes male work histories. Part-time work is more than a wholly marginal and amateur contribution to the workforce, but it does not require the same commitment to the employment career as full-time jobs— in time, effort, and personal identity. What makes it a distinctive choice is its subordination to other life interests, mainly but not necessarily non-market activities, so that it becomes a qualitatively different kind of instrumental work. For many (but not all) women and some men, part-time work is subordinate to the family-centred non-market activities which are easily subsumed under the label of 'childcare responsibilities'. But the primary interest may lie elsewhere. For some people paid employment may take second place to their political activities, voluntary community work, religious activities, sporting activities, artistic or creative activities. This alternative work orientation is covered by economists' concept of the *secondary earner*, someone who relies on another person as the primary earner and contributes a partial or secondary income to the collective pot (Pott-Buter, 1993: 301–2; Hakim,

1996*a*: 65–74). Almost all primary earners hold 'standard' full-time jobs; part-time jobs are taken almost exclusively by secondary earners. However, not all secondary earners take part-time jobs—in some countries the only choice is between full-time jobs and no job at all. And not all wives become secondary earners. In the USA, for example, secondary earners typically have full-time jobs and pay for private childcare, and black women in the USA and Britain often remain primary earners throughout life (Hochschild, 1990; Hakim, 1996*a*: 65–74). Students in full-time education and young people in transition between full-time education and full-time employment are another group of secondary earners who constitute substantial numbers of part-time workers. But very few students have part-time jobs, as shown in Chapter 6.

The three distinct types of part-time work, which exhibit differential rates of growth and do not exist in all countries, as is evident from the distributions of working hours across Europe shown in Fig. 1, are reduced hours jobs, half-time jobs, and marginal jobs, all involving hours shorter than conventional full-time jobs of 37 hours or more per week.

Reduced hours jobs are those with weekly hours a little shorter than usual full-time hours: 30–36 hours a week. In Britain certain full-time jobs involve hours in the 30–36 range, in particular white-collar jobs in the public sector which require 8–hour days with a one-hour lunch break, making a 35-hour working week. In Norway, the definition of part-time work was changed in 1989: part-time employees are now those working less than 37 hours a week with the exception of people working 30–36 hours a week, who classify themselves as full-timers (Nätti, 1995: 355). In other European countries, anyone working less than full-time hours is automatically classified as a part-time worker, including people with a small reduction in their daily hours. Reduced hours work is the dominant form of part-time work in East Germany (Marshall *et al.*, 1995: 6) and Sweden, and it is treated as a separate category in France[3] (Blossfeld and Hakim, 1997). Many 'part-timers' in Sweden and Denmark are working 30 hours a week (6 instead of 8 hours a day, for example) and would be classified as full-time workers in Finland, Britain, and Holland. Tilly (1991: 11) calls these jobs 'retention jobs', noting that they are still rare in the USA. Reduced hours work is often organized in response to an employee's request. It is thus more of a personal choice, involves no change of occupation or employer, and is normally a temporary arrangement, with the worker returning to normal full-time hours when children have reached a certain age, for example. The analysis which follows shows that reduced hours workers and jobs are most appropriately classified with long full-time workers and jobs, as they already are in some countries, rather than with part-timers.

[3] In France, reduced hours jobs typically consist of normal full-time hours on four days a week, allowing women to stay at home on Wednesdays when schools are closed.

Half-time jobs are those with 11–29 hours a week, with the highest concentrations around 20 hours a week. This type of part-time work is the dominant type in Britain, Germany, France, Belgium, the Netherlands, and Luxembourg (Fig. 1). Half-time jobs are typically organized by the employer on a permanent basis, often as separate jobs from the full-time jobs in their establishment, with people recruited directly and specifically for these long-term jobs. This means that different terms and conditions, or different employee benefits may be offered to the full-time and part-time workforces, and there may be no arrangements for transfers between the two groups.

Half-time jobs can include job-shares: with an employer's agreement, two people agree to share one full-time job, each doing half the hours, with special arrangements for co-ordination between the two job-sharers. Despite a government policy of promoting job-sharing as a solution to unemployment in Britain in the 1980s, job-sharing schemes never took root among employers, and most schemes were abandoned early on. However, the idea of job-sharing took root among working women. Although women do not have any legal right to obtain part-time work or job-sharing arrangements with their employer, a series of well-publicized industrial tribunal cases in Britain produced judgements that the employer had engaged in indirect sex discrimination against female employees in not permitting job-shares or part-time work and in failing to produce any objective justification for the refusal (Rubenstein, 1996: 35, 39–40). Job-share schemes have been promoted as a solution to unemployment in other European countries, but again with little success (Kravaritou-Manitakis, 1988: 55–9). Job-shares are equivalent to reduced hours jobs in that they involve no change of occupation or employer, can be temporary, with the women returning to full-time work at some point, and they necessarily enjoy the same terms and conditions as full-time employees.

Marginal jobs are defined here as those with up to 10 hours a week. Marginal jobs always involve very few hours a week, such as one-day-a-week jobs, are often exempted from income tax and social security contributions, and are frequently excluded from statutory employment rights or employer benefits (Schoer, 1987; Hakim, 1989*a*, 1989*b*; ILO, 1989; Meulders *et al.*, 1993: 82–5; Meulders *et al.*, 1994: 30–1; OECD, 1994: 95; Sainsbury, 1996; Wickham, 1997: 146). In some countries, the threshold is higher. For example in Germany, people working less than 15 hours a week and with low earnings are excluded from social insurance: 2 million women and 1 million men fell into this category in 1992. One-third of women working part-time in Germany are in marginal or casual jobs (Büchtemann and Quack, 1989: 115). In Britain, people with weekly earnings below a certain threshold do not have to pay social insurance contributions (and are thus excluded from social welfare benefits) and do not pay income tax. Estimates of the size of this group range from 2 to 4 million marginal workers, most of them (about

75%) being employees (Hakim, 1989*b*: 488; European Commission, 1995*b*: 140). Marginal jobs are very popular in the Netherlands: one-third of part-timers work less than 10 hours a week (Pott-Buter, 1993: 206; see also Plantenga, 1995: 284). In the USA, unpaid family workers working less than 15 hours a week are not considered employed and are excluded from employment statistics. In line with existing practice, jobs with less than 12 or less than 8 hours a week have been excluded from EC proposed directives on atypical workers which aim to improve the rights of part-timers (Wedderburn, 1995: 68). In the Netherlands, for example, an employee must work more than 14 hours a week to earn the right to a guaranteed minimum wage, to be protected against unfair dismissal, or to vote for the workers' representatives (OECD, 1994: 96). In Ireland, new protective labour legislation for part-time workers only covers employees working at least 8 hours a week on a regular basis (Wickham, 1997: 146).

Marginal jobs do not exist in all countries, or at least they are not visible in national statistics. In heavily regulated Western European countries and in some developing countries, marginal jobs exist mainly in the 'irregular' or 'underground' economy (Thomas, 1992: 119–255; Hakim, 1989*b*, 1992*b*, 1996*a*: 38–40). Marginal jobs seem to exist only when the tax and social insurance system, employment law, employer policies, and labour supply all combine to create a favourable climate. As the German government argued in *Nolte v Landesversicherungsanstalt Hannover* before the ECJ, these small jobs readily disappear into the underground economy if they are burdened with the full range of legal, tax, and other regulations. In December 1995 the ECJ accepted this argument and ruled in the *Nolte* case that the exclusion of low-paid marginal workers (working less than 15 hours a week) from the German statutory social security scheme was permissible, even though considerably more women than men are affected. Marginal workers in Germany are not subject to contributions and are also excluded from sickness benefits and the national pension scheme. This landmark judgement established the legality of treating marginal workers with small earnings differently from part-time workers working over 15 hours a week and with more substantial earnings. This case is of particular interest as it reached the opposite conclusion to a 1989 ECJ ruling on marginal workers and to an equivalent case decided by the House of Lords in Britain in 1994. In *R. v Secretary of State for Employment, ex parte Equal Opportunities Commission*, which involved adjudicating between the Equal Opportunities Commission and the government, the House of Lords refused to accept that there might be objective justification for the exclusion of marginal workers (working less than 16 hours a week) from statutory employment rights given that more women were affected (Hakim, 1995*b*: 441; Rubenstein, 1996: 8). The government argued that the exclusion of marginal workers from burdensome legislation encouraged employers to create more small part-time jobs. But it relied exclusively on arguments from economic theory without any supporting evidence, and lost the case to the EOC. The 1994 House of Lords decision on marginal workers was in line with a 1989 ECJ ruling on another German case, *Rinner-Kühn v FWW Spezial-Gebäudereinigung GmbH & Co. KG.* In this case, the ECJ ruled that the German government failed to offer objective justification for the exclusion from sick pay schemes of part-timers working less than 10 hours a week or less than 45 hours a month, the majority of whom are women. The combination of these judgements means that there continue to be fundamental differences between European countries in the legal status of marginal part-time workers, despite the harmonization of European law.

In other cases, the ECJ has ruled that part-time workers must be treated the same as full-time workers, enforcing the principles of non-discrimination and equal treatment rigorously, without the bias in favour of women that some feminists expect from equal opportunities legislation. The ECJ has consistently refused to allow part-timers better than pro rata benefits or any arrangement that would leave part-timers advantaged compared with full-timers (Hakim, 1996a: 190–200). For example, in *Stadt Lengerich v Helmig* the ECJ ruled that there is no discrimination contrary to European law where a collective agreement providing overtime supplements will be paid only when the normal working hours for full-time workers are exceeded. This decision involved six joined cases from Germany on whether Article 119 requires employers to pay part-timers overtime supplements when they work in excess of their own contractual hours. Helmig was a teacher working 19.5 hours a week instead of full-time teachers' 38.5 hours a week who demanded the same 25% overtime supplement when she worked longer hours than usual. The ECJ decided that as part-time and full-time employees were paid the same overtime rates there was no unequal treatment and no discrimination. The Advocate General's Opinion which preceded the ECJ ruling noted that full-time hours were uniform and fixed, by statute or by collective bargaining, whereas part-time hours can vary from 5 to 35 hours a week. Paying overtime supplements to part-timers on an individual basis would create inequality of treatment. The ECJ's argument implicitly recognized the diversity of part-time jobs which is made explicit in our new classification, with three distinct groups working less than 'standard' full-time hours. If separate overtime payments were to apply to part-time workers, there would not just be one extra rate but at least three, and potentially a multitude.

Half-time jobs are the jobs most commonly thought of as part-time jobs, and they alone have most or all of the characteristics that differentiate part-time from full-time jobs. However, the label 'part-time' is applied to all jobs requiring less than normal full-time hours, including reduced hours jobs that differ exclusively in a slight reduction in weekly hours, often negotiated individually, thus overlapping with jobs where the same reduction has been achieved collectively for particular groups of full-time workers.

Marginal jobs are invariably included with other part-time jobs but clearly constitute a qualitatively different group, whose involvement in the labour market, in terms of hours and earnings, cannot seriously alter their social status and personal identity which derives from their other, full-time activity— as housewife, artist, or student, for example. Marginal jobs include one-day-a-week jobs, sometimes labelled 'vertical' part-time work, Saturday jobs, or 'casual' jobs because they are often temporary or short-term.[4] In some European countries, such as Denmark, the great majority of marginal jobs are taken by students in full-time education, and student jobs clearly account for much of the recent expansion in male as well as female marginal part-time work in the Netherlands, Denmark, and Britain (OECD, 1994: 78–82; see also Plantenga, 1995: 282). In these three countries jobs with less than 16 hours a week accounted for 15%, 10%, and 10% respectively of all employee jobs in 1990 compared to less than 5% in other EU12 member states (Watson, 1992: table 16). Marginal jobs are insignificant in terms of total hours worked but are increasingly significant in headcount employment.

BASIC FEATURES OF PART-TIME JOBS

Our analysis relies principally on the SARs, but the LFS also provides relevant data, in Tables 5.2 and 5.3. The minimum hours definition of a 'proper' full-time job was set at 37 hours a week excluding overtime and meal breaks. This definition is used in several EU countries, including Germany, and it is consistent with the hours of full-time workers in Britain (Bosch *et al.*, 1994; Blanpain and Rojot, 1997; Blossfeld and Hakim, 1997). In Britain in 1991, the national average for full-time workers (defined here as employees working over 30 hours a week, hence grouping together people in reduced hours jobs and long full-time jobs) was 44 hours, made up of 39 basic hours plus 2.3 hours average paid overtime plus 1.9 hours average unpaid overtime (Table 5.2). Women in full-time jobs generally work shorter hours than men, largely because they are less likely to do overtime, and average 40 hours per week compared with men's 45 hours. Average hours for part-timers (in effect, half-time workers and marginal workers grouped together in Table 5.2) are about one-third those for full-timers at 17 hours a week. Part-time jobs have less variation in total hours, with almost no differences between men and women and negligible amounts of overtime.

---

[4] The 1981 GHS shows that roughly half of all part-timers were in 'horizontal' part-time jobs, which involve short working hours on all five days of the working week, and roughly half were doing 'vertical' part-time jobs and working only one, two, three, or four days a week. About one in ten part-timers were working only one day a week and another one in ten were working only two days a week (OPCS, 1983: 114). However, new working time arrangements, such as annualized hours contracts, are eroding these distinctions (Wareing, 1992).

TABLE 5.2. *Employees' average usual total, basic, paid, and unpaid overtime hours, Great Britain, 1991*

	Weekly hours worked			
	Total hours	Basic hours	Paid overtime	Unpaid overtime
All employees	37.4	34.0	1.9	1.5
Full-time	43.6	39.4	2.3	1.9
Part-time	16.9	16.2	0.4	0.2
All male employees	43.6	39.0	2.8	1.9
Full-time	45.3	40.5	3.0	2.0
Part-time	15.7	15.3	0.3	0.2
All female employees	30.2	28.4	0.9	0.9
Full-time	40.3	37.5	1.2	1.7
Part-time	17.0	16.4	0.4	0.2

Note: Part-time jobs have up to 30 total usual hours a week excluding meal breaks (usual basic hours plus usual overtime); full-time jobs have total usual working hours over 30 hours per week excluding meal breaks.

Source: Spring 1991 Labour Force Survey results reported in Watson (1992: 550).

An important feature of part-time work is that hours are not only shorter but typically *fixed*, so that work is far less likely to spill over into private life. Labelling part-timers as part of the 'atypical' or 'flexible' workforce has obscured the fact that it is full-time workers who are most likely to have variable hours, due to shift work, overtime, and other arrangements (Watson, 1992: 542, 1994: 242; Naylor, 1994: 476). As a result, part-timers are rarely eligible for a variety of additional payments for shift work, overtime, and unsocial hours that significantly boost full-time earnings relative to part-time earnings and male pay relative to female pay (Payne, 1995: 407). As noted earlier, the ECJ decided these arrangements are not sex discriminatory.

Full-time jobs can be subdivided into those where overtime is common and those where little overtime is worked. Alternatively long full-time jobs can be subdivided into those attracting paid overtime (most ordinary employee jobs) and those where unpaid overtime is the norm, typically professional and managerial jobs (Hepple and Hakim, 1997: 676). However, the SARs do not provide any information on overtime hours and there does not seem to be any other widely used or non-arbitrary cut-off point for identifying jobs with exceptionally long hours. Analyses of the SARs revealed some differences between full-timers working 37–45 hours a week and those working 46 hours or more; these were largely attributable to the fact that people working over 45 hours are usually men (83% of the total). Jobs that regularly require people to work 46 hours or more a week, excluding meal breaks and overtime, will typically extend to 48 hours or more a week after overtime hours are added in. These jobs are labelled as having 'overtime' hours of the sort that are banned by the European Commission's Social Charter recommended average maximum of 48 hours a week. Thus the large category of full-time jobs is sometimes subdivided into reduced hours jobs (30–36 hours a week), long full-time (37–45 hours a week), and overtime jobs (46 or more a week).

The dividing line drawn here is very slightly different from the conventional statistical definition of part-time work in Britain and Holland. The conventional British definition used in Table 5.2 classifies jobs with exactly 30 hours a week as part-time jobs, whereas the new classification used in Tables 5.4 to 5.10 (and throughout this book) classifies them as reduced hours jobs. This small but theoretically and empirically important adjustment of the key dividing line explains why analyses for Britain using the new classification do not agree exactly with official analyses based on the conventional definition of part-time work. Just over two per cent of the workforce aged 16–64 years works 30 hours a week, and moving this group above the dividing line into reduced hours jobs reduces part-time jobs to 18% of all employee jobs (2% for men and 37% for women) and to 10% of all self-employment jobs (4% for men and 29% for women). In the following tables, results are shown separately for men and women only if there are substantive differences between them. Otherwise, results are given for all workers aged 16–64 years.

The great majority of part-time workers choose this option in preference to a full-time job, a key factor in their greater job satisfaction. Throughout Europe, involuntary part-time work has remained a minority element in the part-time workforce, despite small fluctuations in response to recession and economic downturns (Hakim, 1990a; OECD, 1990, 1995). Involuntary part-time work is identified in the LFS (Table 5.3) as part-timers who say they could not find a full-time job, and the percentage fluctuates between 6% and 17% over the decade 1984–94 (17% to 33% for married men and 4% to 9% for married women). One important category among part-time workers is students aged 16 and over in full-time education. In Britain this category grew from 344,000 in 1984 to 673,000 in 1994 and from 7% to 11% of the part-time workforce (Table 5.3). As shown in Chapter 6, students with part-time jobs during the academic year generally have marginal jobs, typically one-day-a-week jobs, as they normally take full-time jobs only during the summer vacation. This chapter does not separately identify students among part-time workers, as the subject is dealt with more fully in Chapter 6. However, certain features of the part-time workforce, such as its high labour turnover, are strongly affected by the inclusion of student jobs, so some analyses are repeated with and without students.

TABLE 5.3. *Reasons for choosing part-time work, United Kingdom, 1984–1994*

column percent

	Percentages of employees and self-employed working part-time[1] who gave each reason for taking a part-time job			
	1984	1987	1991	1994
All persons (thousands)	4,913	5,316	5,730	6,121
Student	7	8	10	11
Ill/disabled	1	1	2	1
Could not find a full-time job	10	9	8	13
Did not want a full-time job	68	65	63	74
Other reasons[2]	14	17	18	1
Married[3] men (thousands)	290	313	392	449
Student	1	1	2	3
Ill/disabled	5	4	5	4
Could not find a full-time job	19	23	19	33
Did not want a full-time job	52	45	48	59
Other reasons[2]	23	28	26	*
Non-married[3] men (thousands)	280	346	406	547
Student	53	53	61	57
Ill/disabled	3	3	2	2
Could not find a full-time job	18	20	13	25
Did not want a full-time job	17	14	14	16
Other reasons[2]	10	11	10	*
Married[3] women (thousands)	3,591	3,850	3,965	4,144
Student	*	*	*	1
Ill/disabled	1	1	1	1
Could not find a full-time job	6	6	5	9
Did not want a full-time job	79	77	75	89
Other reasons[2]	13	16	18	1
Non-married[3] women (thousands)	752	807	966	1,179
Student	26	30	32	30
Ill/disabled	2	2	2	2
Could not find a full-time job	17	14	12	20
Did not want a full-time job	42	37	37	48
Other reasons[2]	14	18	16	*

[1] Part-time status is self-defined in this table.

[2] 'Other reasons' includes cases where no reason for working part-time was given. For 1984–91, 'other reasons' was one of the valid responses to the question. From 1992 onwards this category was dropped, and only includes people who gave no reason. Hence exact comparisons before and after 1992 cannot be made.

[3] From 1989 onwards 'married' includes cohabiting couples.

Source: Extracted from Beatson (1995: Table 2.4), reporting UK Labour Force Survey data.

The 1991 Census included a direct question asking about usual weekly working hours, excluding meal breaks and overtime, in a person's main job (ignoring any second jobs). Before this, the general question on economic activity invited employees to classify themselves as working full-time or part-time. Since the 1950s the statistical definition of part-time work has been jobs involving 30 or fewer hours each week. From 1984 onwards, part-time status has been self-defined in the LFS, to facilitate an immediate question on reasons for working part-time (Table 5.3). In addition, information is collected on usual and actual hours worked (basic and overtime), to permit analyses of the sort presented in Table 5.2. There is almost complete agreement between self-classified part-time status and the statistical definition of hours worked: 98% of people working over 30 hours a week see themselves as full-time workers and 95% of people working up to 30 hours per week see themselves as part-timers (Watson, 1992: 542; Naylor, 1994: 477). The same pattern is found in the Census SARs data (Table 5.4). However, the SARs analysis in Table 5.4 reveals an important difference between men and women in their conceptions of a full-time job. Men who classified themselves as working 'full-time' were almost all working 37 or more hours a week compared to two-thirds of women, with another one-third working reduced hours. One-fifth of men who classified themselves as 'part-time' workers were working 30 hours a week or more, presumably because they were working shorter hours than the usual full-time hours in their jobs. In contrast, almost all women who classified themselves as 'part-timers' were working less than 30 hours a week (Table 5.4). So when men and women talk about 'full-time' jobs they are often talking about very different hours schedules, even within a single country. This raises some doubts about the European Commission's heavy reliance on self-classified status as full-time or part-time workers in the European LFS, as inconsistencies will be magnified further in cross-national comparisons, as in Table 5.1. The analysis here and throughout this book classifies people by usual hours worked and thus avoids the problem. Full-time jobs typically consisted of 42 hours a week whereas reduced hours jobs typically consisted of 35 working hours a week. The most common half-time job involved 20 hours a week, and marginal jobs most frequently consisted of 7–8 hours a week or one-day-a-week jobs.

The main defect of the 1991 Census data is an undercount of marginal jobs, especially student jobs. A comparison of the results of the spring 1991 LFS and the 1991 Census shows that the more detailed questioning of the LFS identifies larger numbers of small jobs of the sort that are easily overlooked in a self-completion exercise like the population census. The 1991 LFS identified 5% more men and women in employment than the census, around 780,000 men and 530,000 women aged 16 and over. The largest single addition was an extra 542,000 student jobs plus another 210,000 marginal jobs held by housewives. Of the 1.2 million extra jobs counted by the LFS,

TABLE 5.4. *Self-classification as part-time employee and usual work hours*   row percent

Self-classification of hours worked	Hours worked in current job by employees				Base 000s =100%
	Full-time 371	Reduced hours 30–36	Half-time 11–29	Marginal hours 1–10	
All employees					
Full-time	82	17	1	*	320
Part-time	2	5	74	19	76
Male employees					
Full-time	89	11	*	*	204
Part-time	12	10	63	15	5
Female employees					
Full-time	69	29	1	*	115
Part-time	1	5	75	19	71

Source: 2% SAR, Great Britain, data for resident employees aged 16–64 years.

840,000 were marginal jobs of less than 16 hours a week (Sly, 1994*a*). This demonstrates that marginal jobs are often not regarded as 'proper jobs' worth reporting in a survey. It also means that the SARs count of marginal jobs should be increased by about one-half, and that the number of student jobs in spring 1991 was about three times as many as were counted by the 1991 Census.

WORKRATES IN THE FOUR CATEGORIES OF WORKING HOURS

Differences between men and women in patterns of work across the life cycle are shown in Table 5.5. Among prime-age men (25–54 years), at least 80% are in continuous employment across the life cycle, almost invariably in long full-time jobs. Among prime-age women, two-thirds are in employment, but only one-quarter are in full-time jobs with long hours. From the age of 25 to 54, jobs with less than 37 hours a week are dominant, employing one-third to one-half of women. Women are also the slowest to enter the workforce when young and the first to quit employment permanently after the age of 55. This pattern is repeated across all member states of the EU, to the European Commission's consternation (1997: 34–5).[5] The equal importance of

[5] The Commission is forced to admit that there is a significant level of economic inactivity among young people aged 15–24 and among older people aged 50–64 years, and that women are far more likely than men to be non-working with no specific status. The Commission is unable to explain these sex differentials. In contrast, dramatic inter-country variations in

full-time and part-time jobs throughout women's work histories is demonstrated clearly by the comparative workrates in Table 5.5. Throughout life, part-time jobs are the exception for men, held briefly and dropped quickly in favour of full-time work or, among men aged 55–64 years, full-time retirement.

These differences in workrates derive from the sexual division of labour in the household, with men typically being the main breadwinner, hence most likely to be identified as the head of household on census forms, and wives typically being secondary earners. The roles of primary and secondary earner clearly determine full-time and part-time workrates to a great extent (Table 5.5). Among heads of household (both men and women) who are usually main breadwinners, 59% work long full-time hours. Among spouses, only 25% work long full-time hours. The incidence of full-time work among spouses is even lower than for other members of the household (Table 5.5).

CHARACTERISTICS OF FULL-TIME AND PART-TIME WORKERS AND JOBS

In terms of workers' personal characteristics, workplace, and job characteristics, there are important substantive differences between long full-time jobs, reduced hours jobs, half-time, and marginal jobs (Tables 5.5–5.9). However, the main dividing line is between people working 30 hours a week or more and people working less than 30 hours a week. It is more appropriate to group reduced hours jobs with long full-time jobs than to label them as part-time work, as is the practice in Germany and Scandinavia.

Reduced hours jobs with 30–36 hours a week are a small category compared to long full-time jobs, as shown by the base numbers in Table 5.6. But separating the two reveals a profound difference between the male and female workforces which is concealed by the conventional distinction between full-time and part-time work. Women constitute almost half the workforce aged 16–64 years, but they remain a minority of workers in the 'proper' full-time workforce dominated by men (Table 5.6). Only 13% of men are in jobs with less than 37 hours a week, compared to 56% of women. Long full-time workers are typically men (69% of the total) whereas reduced hours workers are typically women (63% of the total). A very high proportion of women nominally working 'full-time' are working fixed reduced hours of 30–36 a week, whereas few men are in this category. The contrast between

employment rates among prime-age women are assumed, without evidence, to be explained completely by 'unrecorded' participation in homeworking, family enterprises, and unpaid community work. In fact, the available evidence does not support this assumption: there are no sex differentials in unpaid voluntary work and community support activities, and the volume of understated homeworking and other 'hidden' paid work is far too small (Hakim, 1996*a*: 26–51) to explain the massive sex differentials in complete economic inactivity (nonworking in this chapter) throughout the life cycle.

TABLE 5.5. *Full-time and part-time workrates by age and position within household*

cell percent

		Hours worked in current or last job				
		Full-time 371	Reduced hours 30–36	Half-time 11–29	Marginal hours 1–10	All working as % of age group[1]
Women aged	16–24	33	11	4	1	51
	25–34	29	12	15	5	62
	35–44	25	13	25	6	69
	45–54	24	13	24	5	67
	55–64	10	6	14	4	35
	16–64	25	11	16	4	58
Men aged	16–24	45	6	1	*	55
	25–34	71	8	1	*	83
	35–44	74	8	1	*	87
	45–54	72	7	1	*	83
	55–64	48	6	3	1	59
	16–64	63	7	1	*	74
Relationship within household:						
head		59	9	4	1	72
spouse		25	10	21	5	61
other		42	8	3	1	53

Note: Workrates show the percentage of an age group who are currently in work.

[1] Includes people not stating hours worked.

Source: 2% SAR, Great Britain, data for people aged 16–64 years.

men's very long hours and women's generally shorter hours is much greater than has so far been recognized, even *within* the nominally full-time workforce. This factor is obviously of greater importance in explaining the sex differential in pay among full-time workers than has so far been recognized.

Reduced hours jobs make it easier for women to remain in nominally 'full-time' work throughout the life cycle, whereas women in long full-time jobs are disproportionately younger women, aged under 35 years, and disproportionately single (Table 5.6). For men, both long full-time and reduced hours jobs provide employment across the life cycle.

One difference between reduced hours jobs and long full-time jobs is that the former have relatively fixed hours whereas the latter often include overtime, paid or unpaid. Some people work well beyond 45 hours a week: 10% of British workers aged 16–64 years work 46 hours a week or more (up to 82 hours a week), and the great majority of them are men. The sex differential in working hours runs all the way through the hours distribution. Women form 17% of people working 46–82 hours a week, 34% of people working

A Differentiated Part-Time Workforce

TABLE 5.6. *Personal characteristics of full-time and part-time workers*

row/column percent

		Full-time 371	Reduced hours 30–36	Half-time 11–29	Marginal hours 1–10	Total
All		67	14	15	4	100
Men		87	10	2	1	100
Women		44	19	29	8	100
% female		31	63	91	86	47
Women aged	16–24	26	20	8	18	19
	25–34	30	27	22	23	26
	35–44	19	23	29	26	23
	45–54	15	18	24	18	18
	55–64	10	13	18	16	13
	16–64	100	100	100	100	100
Men aged	16–24	16	19	34	60	17
	25–34	25	26	16	10	25
	35–44	24	22	13	8	23
	45–54	20	17	13	7	19
	55–64	15	16	25	15	16
	16–64	100	100	100	100	100
% single (never	M	29	36	48	68	30
married)	F	38	31	9	19	27
% with 11	M	40	35	32	48	39
dependent child	F	34	36	53	63	42
% non-white	M	4	6	7	7	4
	F	5	5	2	3	4
% in owner-occupied accommodation		75	80	77	77	76
Relationship within household:						
head of household		60	43	20	20	50
spouse of head		20	38	71	59	32
other		20	19	9	21	18
Region:	London	11	19	9	9	12
	Rest of South East	20	21	20	23	20
	Rest of Britain	69	60	71	68	68
Bases N=000s	All	378	79	83	25	565
	Men	260	29	7	3	300
	Women	118	50	76	22	265

Source: 2% SAR, Great Britain, data for residents aged 16–64 years reporting a current or last job, including student jobs.

TABLE 5.7. *Workplace characteristics of full-time and part-time workers*   column/row percent

	Hours worked in current or last job				
	Full- time 371	Reduced hours 30–36	Half- time 11–29	Marginal hours 1–10	Total
Percentage of women whose workplace is:					
At home	3	2	3	10	4
0–2 km from home	29	30	46	50	36
301 km from home	4	4	2	2	3
% who walk to work	12	12	24	32	17
Percentage of men whose workplace is:					
At home	3	3	9	11	3
0–2 km from home	20	16	25	25	20
301 km from home	8	11	4	5	8
% who walk to work	8	7	13	14	8
Percentage of all workers whose workplace is:					
At home	3	3	4	10	3
0–2 km from home	23	25	44	48	27
301 km from home	7	7	2	2	6
% who walk to work	9	10	23	31	12
Industries with varied working hours:					
64/65 (part) Shops (excluding cars)	52	9	30	10	100
661 Restaurants, cafes, etc.	52	12	24	12	100
662 Bars, pubs	41	7	35	17	100
664 Canteens, messes	29	16	36	19	100
81 Banking & finance	34	53	11	2	100
82 Insurance	41	51	7	1	100
92 Sanitary services	50	10	27	13	100
93 Education	37	28	24	11	100
95 Medical services	52	15	29	4	100
96 Other services	37	20	36	7	100
97 Recreational services	58	16	19	7	100

Note: The impact of including student jobs is to increase the percentage of male marginal workers who walk to work from 14% to 19% and to increase the percentage of male marginal workers whose workplace in within 2 km of their home from 25% to 37%.

Source: 2% SAR, Great Britain, data for residents aged 16–64 years in employment, excluding student jobs.

37–45 hours a week, 63% of those in reduced hours jobs, 91% of workers in half-time jobs, and 86% of people in marginal jobs.

Marginal workers are the smallest group in the workforce, a bare 4%. Half-time workers are a larger group with 15% of all workers, equal in size to the reduced time workforce. Marginal workers are distinctively different from half-time workers in all respects. Male marginal workers are typically young single men aged under 25, on the margins of the workforce: many are students, as shown in Chapter 6, or are in transition between full-time education and full-time employment. Women outnumber men four to one because, in addition to the young single female students there are substantial numbers of prime-age married women with children who hold marginal jobs. In general, men take part-time jobs early in the life cycle and transfer quickly to full-time jobs, working longer hours when they marry and have children to support, whereas women generally drop out of full-time jobs in favour of jobs with shorter hours as they marry and have children. The polarization of male and female work histories is clearly displayed with the new classification.

In contrast, full-time and part-time workers do not differ at all on other characteristics. A constant three-quarters of all workers, male and female, are in owner-occupied accommodation rather than in rented accommodation. Only 4% of men and of women belong to non-white ethnic minorities and they are found in all four categories of working hours. All four categories of working hours are found across Britain, although London has an above aver-age share of the public sector jobs that offer reduced hours.

Long full-time and reduced hours workers constitute the mainstream of the workforce. Marginal workers and, to a lesser extent, half-time workers, are located outside the workforce, with some other dominant social identity such as parent, homemaker, or student. This is illustrated most concretely by the distance between home and workplace and patterns of travel to work. A three-quarters majority of people in long full-time and reduced hours jobs travel over 2 km to get to work, by car or public transport, and 7% travel over 30 km to work. In contrast, half of all part-timers work in the close vicinity of their home, or even at home; one-third of marginal workers and one-quarter of half-timers walk to work (Table 5.7). Not surprisingly, part-timers invest little extra time in travel to work for short hours jobs. But this also means that their choice of jobs is restricted to those available in the neigh-bourhood, which is typically a residential area. This understandably low investment in travel to work time among part-timers is correlated with high concentrations working in retail shops and other service occupations and industries located in or near residential areas. As shown in Chapter 7, *local* part-time jobs have the lowest status and earnings (see Tables 7.5 and 7.6).

It is frequently observed that part-time work and all forms of labour flexi-bility are concentrated in the service industries. In some cross-national com-parative studies the relative importance of the service sector is virtually the only correlate of part-time working (Rosenfeld and Birkelund, 1995) and countries with a small service sector never have much part-time work (Blossfeld and Hakim, 1997). Clearly, manufacturing companies engaged in industrial mass production dominated by Fordist work processes have not found it easy to accommodate or utilize flexible or non-standard jobs, includ-ing part-time work. But the primary sector (agriculture, forestry, fishing, and mining) and the majority of service industries have an equally inflexible work organization, based on long full-time jobs almost exclusively. It is only particular industries in the service sector that have been able to reorganize to utilize part-time workers, or else to create reduced hours jobs for large parts of their workforce. Interestingly, these seem to be alternatives, as they are only rarely found together—in educational institutions, for example. Table 5.7 lists eight industry groups where jobs with less than 37 hours a week are substantially above the 33% national average. Together, these industries account for only 23% of all jobs whereas the service sector as a whole accounts for 68% of all jobs in Britain.

The retail distribution industry provides large numbers of part-time jobs (and very few reduced hours jobs) but only in specific areas: shops selling domestic goods but not shops selling cars and other vehicles, for example. The hotel and catering industry also provides a lot of part-time jobs, but again in specific areas rather than throughout. Half of all jobs in banking, finance, and insurance are reduced hours jobs, but part-time jobs are not important (Table 5.7). In medical and other services, half-time jobs have grown to become a major part of the workforce. Educational institutions differ from all other industries in having a very low level of long full-time jobs (37%) and substantial numbers of reduced hours, half-time, and marginal jobs (28%, 24%, and 11%). Alongside these industries, there are others where long full-time jobs remain the norm, such as wholesale distribution, repairs and servicing motor vehicles, research and development, and the whole transport and communications industry. In other service industries, the distribution of working hours is similar to the national average, as illustrated by business services, public administration, and personnel services. There is nothing natural or inevitable about service industries providing many part-time jobs and accommodating flexible working hours; most do not, even in Britain. Those that do have chosen to accommodate women's preferences for shorter working hours and employ a lot of women. But this too is not inevitable but a 'man-made' development, literally. In Germany, retail shops had rigidly inflexible working hours until the late 1990s, and provided very few part-time jobs compared with British shops, despite tax and social insurance regulations favouring marginal jobs of less than 15 hours a week.

The new classification shows that reduced hours jobs have the highest proportion of highly qualified occupations: one-quarter of all workers have at least one higher education qualification and 10% have two or more (Table 5.8). Long full-time jobs, half-time jobs, and marginal jobs do not differ to any important degree, with 84%–88% of workers having no qualifications or only secondary school qualifications.

The 1991 Census identifies the proportion of men and women aged 18 and over with any type of higher education qualification, that is, any post-secondary school qualification, ranging from the vocational qualifications of nurses and teachers (level c) to university degrees (level b) and postgraduate degrees (level a). At first sight, men and women seem to be equally well

TABLE 5.8. *Job characteristics of full-time and part-time workers* column percent

	Hours worked in current or last job				
	Full-time 371	Reduced hours 30–36	Half-time 11–29	Marginal hours 1–10	All jobs
Goldthorpe Classes					
Higher service class	11	14	3	5	10
Lower service class	20	25	12	10	19
Routine non-manual	12	29	19	13	16
Personal service	4	7	24	31	9
Proprietors, farmers	11	5	3	4	8
Lower technicians, foremen	5	2	2	1	4
Skilled manual workers	14	5	4	2	11
Semi- and unskilled workers	23	14	34	35	24
RG's Social Class					
I Professional	5	5	1	1	4
II Managerial, technical	28	35	17	14	27
IIIN Skilled	18	36	40	34	25
IIIM Skilled	27	10	7	5	21
IV Semi-skilled	17	11	20	27	17
V Unskilled	5	3	15	19	6
Estimated hourly earnings (pence)					
Current jobs Men	731	907	660	708	748
Women	573	614	448	453	536
All	683	722	461	470	648
Previous jobs Men	639	771	475	392	633
Women	511	571	420	400	484
All	582	626	426	398	546
Higher qualifications held by grade					
All a higher degrees	1	2	*	1	1
b first degrees	8	13	4	5	8
c below degree level	7	11	7	6	8
two or more	6	10	4	4	6
none	84	75	88	88	83
Men higher qualifications by grade					
a higher degrees	2	3	2	2	2
b first degrees	8	19	11	8	9
c below degree level	6	12	6	3	7
two or more	6	15	9	6	7
none	84	66	81	87	82
Women higher qualifications by grade					
a higher degrees	1	1	*	1	1
b first degrees	7	9	4	4	6
c below degree level	9	10	7	7	9
two or more	7	7	4	4	6
none	83	79	89	88	84
Current jobs: % self-employed					
with employees	5	2	1	1	4
without employees	9	5	5	6	8

Source: 1% and 2% SARs, Great Britain, data for residents aged 16–64 years reporting a current job or a job in the last ten years, including student jobs. The 1% SAR is only used to provide data on Goldthorpe classes.

qualified. As noted in Chapter 2, there is in fact a marked difference in the *level* of the higher qualifications held by men and women: women typically obtain qualifications below degree level (for example in nursing and school-teaching) and men typically obtain first and higher university degrees. As shown in Chapter 2, men are on average more qualified than women in all occupations. By aggregating all post-secondary school qualifications into a single undifferentiated category, many studies have failed to identify the sex differential in qualifications which plays a part in explaining promotion patterns and vertical occupational segregation. Put simply, women are more likely to qualify as nurses than as medical doctors, and there is a very substantial earnings differential as well as quite different career ladders for these two professions, even if both require post-secondary school studies. The qualifications gap is now found to be concentrated in jobs with less than 37 hours a week, that is, in jobs where women outnumber men four to one. Within reduced hours jobs which recruit the most highly qualified personnel 22% of men compared to 10% of women have degrees or higher degrees, 15% of men versus 7% of women have two or more higher education qualifications (Table 5.8). The qualifications gap is equally significant in the part-time workforce, with twice as many men as women holding university degrees or higher qualifications. The pattern is repeated across male, female, and integrated occupations. These findings comprehensively overturn the feminist thesis that the overqualification of women part-timers is the result of sex discrimination. Instead, it appears that the limited range of part-time jobs often leads to workers' qualifications being underutilized or wasted, at least in the short term. But it is men who stand to lose most from this process, a fact that is of course not revealed by studies that look exclusively at female part-timers.

It is a commonplace that part-time jobs tend to be of lower skill and status than full-time jobs: jobs in management are less likely to be offered on a part-time basis than clerical jobs, semi-skilled, and unskilled service jobs. Table 5.8 shows that it is reduced hours jobs rather than long full-time jobs that have the largest proportion of Service Class occupations: 39% versus 31%, compared to only 15% of part-time jobs. It is thus reduced hours jobs rather than long full-time jobs that have the highest average hourly earnings: £7.22 an hour compared to £6.83 for long full-time jobs and £4.60 an hour for part-time jobs. The pattern is the same for men and women, current jobs and previous jobs (held within the last ten years). Interestingly, the Cambridge scores for social status suggest that long full-time jobs have the same social status as part-time jobs, with an average score of 33. Only reduced hours jobs achieve a higher average score of 42. The pattern is similar among men and women, but men in part-time jobs and women in long full-time jobs both tend to be in higher status jobs, implying that sex-atypical employment situations are most acceptable, or most enduring, when the particular job held is of above-average status.

Chapter 3 shows that the pay gap is larger in the part-time workforce than in the full-time workforce (see Tables 3.6 and 3.7). The analysis here has revealed just two of the many explanatory factors that remain undocumented and unmeasured in most survey datasets: substantial sex differentials in part-timers' educational qualifications and in their willingness to travel long distances to work. Hidden factors such as these must contribute much of the explanation for the higher sex differential in earnings in the part-time workforce. Chapter 7 considers other factors contributing to lower average earnings in part-time jobs.

PART-TIME WORK AND OCCUPATIONAL SEGREGATION

Because of men and women's contrasting patterns of employment and work hours across the life cycle, the sex composition of occupations differs substantively between full-time and part-time jobs (Table 5.9). As noted in Chapter 1 (see Table 1.1), the full-time and part-time workforces are highly segregated, and they also display conflicting trends in occupational segregation. After 1971, as a result of equal opportunities legislation and changes in the occupational structure, occupational segregation has been falling in the full-time workforce, while the part-time workforce is becoming more segregated (Hakim, 1993*b*, 1996*a*: 166–9; see also S. Jacobs, 1995). Using the new classification of part-time work in Table 5.9, the SARs confirm this picture.

TABLE 5.9. *Occupational segregation and working hours*   column percent

	Hours worked in current or last job				
	Full-time 371	Reduced hours 30–36	Half-time 11–29	Marginal hours 1–10	All jobs
All working in:					
male occupations	50	19	8	8	38
mixed occupations	23	22	12	8	21
female occupations	27	59	80	84	41
Men working in:					
male occupations	67	41	34	28	63
mixed occupations	22	28	18	13	22
female occupations	11	31	48	59	15
Women working in:					
male occupations	13	7	5	4	9
mixed occupations	27	18	11	8	19
female occupations	60	75	84	88	72

Source: 2% SAR, Great Britain, data for residents aged 16–64 years reporting a current job or a job in the last ten years, including student jobs.

By 1991, one-quarter of full-time jobs were integrated (or mixed), employing men and women in proportion to their numbers in the whole workforce. In contrast, part-time jobs consisted almost exclusively of female-dominated occupations with very few integrated occupations (Table 5.9). In reduced hours jobs women predominate at 63% of the workforce (see Table 5.5) and the majority of jobs are in female-dominated occupations: 59% compared to 27% for conventional full-time jobs. In terms of its occupational composition, the reduced hours category is distinctive.

As shown in Chapters 2 and 3, integrated occupations are by far the most highly qualified and include many of the highest grade jobs. In addition, they include the full range of working hours, whereas male occupations are heavily weighted towards long full-time jobs and female occupations are heavily weighted towards jobs requiring less than 37 hours a week. As noted in Chapter 2, our original hypothesis, which proved incorrect, was that mixed occupations would be the most 'open' occupations, offering men and women the easiest access to the labour market, and hence with the most mobile workforce and highest turnover rates. The SAR analyses show instead that female-dominated occupations perform this function because they are in fact gender-neutral low-skill jobs rather than requiring specialist feminine skills. Another reason for female occupations providing workforce entry and exit jobs is that they include by far the highest proportion of part-time jobs, double the average for all occupations, thus facilitating job sampling among students and young people and gradual withdrawal from employment among older workers. We might therefore expect female part-time jobs to have the highest labour turnover. However, an earlier study concluded that turnover rates remained gender-specific rather than occupation-specific throughout the post-war decades (Hakim, 1996*c*: 11–14, 24) and this is confirmed by the SAR results for 1991.

LABOUR TURNOVER

There has been a long-standing debate in Britain over whether the higher turnover rates observed in the part-time workforce are a feature of the jobs in question or a characteristic of the workers in these jobs (Hakim, 1995*b*: 439). Some social scientists even went so far as to deny that there is now any sex differential in labour turnover, insisting that the differential had disappeared with rising female employment (Hakim, 1995*b*: 443). Several independent studies using different datasets have now confirmed that there has been little or no change in the sex differential in labour turnover and job tenure in the post-war decades: women still have turnover rates 50% higher than among men (Gregg and Wadsworth, 1995; Burgess and Rees, 1996; Hakim, 1996*c*). The 1991 BHPS showed that labour turnover differs little between highly qualified women and women with only secondary school or no qualifications: about 8% drop out of the workforce in the course of a year, and about 30% have less than one year's tenure in the job (Corti *et al.*, 1995: 50–1). Hakim also showed that the continuing sex differential in labour turnover is found in all Western industrial societies, in the USA as well as in Europe, and is attributable to the personal characteristics of women and part-time workers, notably their different work orientations and sex-role preferences, rather than to job characteristics (Hakim, 1996*a*, 1996*c*, 1997*a*). The SAR analyses further confirm these conclusions from a very different dataset.

As noted in Chapter 2, the labour turnover measure constructed within the SAR data is not the conventional one, and relies on the fact that job details are reported for anyone who held a job in the previous ten years. Labour turnover rates are defined as the percentage of people with a job in the last ten years who are not currently in work (Table 5.10, see also Table 2.11). The rates thus cover a longer period than the conventional measure reporting movement in and out of jobs, or the labour market, over a 12–month period (Hakim, 1996*c*). None the less, the sex differential is exactly the same: labour turnover among women is 50% higher than among men, at 26% compared to 18% (Table 5.10). It is worth noting that any under-reporting of last jobs held in the previous decade is more likely to affect part-time jobs than full-time

TABLE 5.10. *Labour turnover rates[1] by type of occupation and hours worked in current or last job*

Type of occupation	Full-time 371		Reduced hours 30–36		Half-time 11–29		Marginal hours 1–10		All jobs	
	a	b	a	b	a	b	a	b	a	b
Women working in:										
male occupations	26	25	22	20	26	25	29	23	26	24
mixed occupations	24	23	18	17	25	24	25	21	25	24
female occupations	28	26	23	22	25	23	33	22	27	24
Men working in:										
male occupations	17	16	17	16	28	22	50	29	18	17
mixed occupations	13	12	12	10	21	15	32	17	14	13
female occupations	19	16	18	14	43	19	75	21	24	17
All women	26	25	22	21	25	23	32	22	26	24
All men	16	15	16	14	34	19	62	23	18	16
All persons	19	18	20	18	25	23	36	22	21	19

[1] Labour turnover rates are defined as the percentage of people with a job of a given type in the last ten years who are not currently in work. Turnover rates are calculated in two versions:

    a for all people with a current or last job, including student jobs;

    b for all people with a current or last job, *excluding* student jobs.

Source: 2% SAR, Great Britain, data for residents aged 16–64 years reporting a current job or a job in the last ten years.

jobs, so that any understatement of labour turnover will affect part-time jobs more than full-time jobs. People are far more likely to overlook a marginal or half-time job held some years ago than to forget a full-time job held some years ago. So the sex differential in labour turnover, and the differential between part-time and full-time jobs, is more likely to be understated than overstated by the SAR measure.

Turnover rates in Table 5.10 are calculated in two versions:

a including student jobs, and
b excluding student jobs.

Although students are classified as out of the labour market, the jobs they hold are sometimes included in employment statistics. In the SARs, student jobs are included among all jobs with hours and occupation information. Thus the first version of the turnover rate corresponds to conventional labour turnover analyses and is comparable with national statistics (Hakim, 1996c: 6–12).

Using the conventional measure (version a), female labour turnover rates are almost constant across the four categories of working hours, with a small increase to 32% in marginal jobs. Among the tiny group of men in marginal jobs (albeit numbering 3,468 in the 2% SAR), turnover reaches 62%, and turnover doubles from the 18% average for men to 34% in half-time jobs. This suggests that part-time jobs do have an effect, increasing labour turnover among women and even more strongly among men. This interpretation appears unlikely, given information in Tables 5.5 and 5.6 showing that half-time jobs are far too rare to be a stable or accepted type of work for men, especially among prime-age men, who readily drop them in favour of a proper full-time job. Most male half-time workers are either young (16–24 years) or else older workers (55–64 years) who are moving into or out of the workforce—hence creating above average turnover rates compared to men in full-time jobs. However, the most important factor was found to be student jobs specifically.

After excluding student jobs (version b), turnover rates are revealed to be gender-specific rather than specific to particular working hours and/or types of occupation (Table 5.10), as found also in Chapter 2 (see Table 2.9). The overall turnover rate for all occupations is reduced from 21% to 19%, and turnover rates now become uniform, varying little around 16% for men and 24% for women. Turnover rates remain constant within sex-segregated and integrated occupations (Table 5.10). As shown in Chapter 6, the great majority of student jobs are part-time jobs in female-dominated occupations, with exceptionally high turnover rates. The higher turnover in part-time jobs and female occupations is eliminated almost completely after student jobs are excluded from the analysis in Table 5.10. However, men in marginal jobs still have turnover rates higher than for men in other jobs and close to female turnover rates. In sum, the sex differential in turnover rates is repeated in the SAR datasets and the higher turnover rates for half-time and marginal jobs are due primarily to the personal characteristics of women in these jobs and, for men only, to the effects of being in jobs that are clearly atypical for men in every respect.

These results suggest that most of the sharp fall in job tenure in part-time jobs since 1986 (Hakim, 1996a: 142, 1996c: 8) could be due to the dramatic rise in student jobs in the same period (see Chapter 6). Although there has been a small general decline in average job tenure in recent decades (Burgess and Rees, 1996), part-time jobs have been affected far more than full-time jobs, leading some to conclude that employers were expanding the number of marginal jobs in order to evade social insurance costs and employment protection rights, even when there was no evidence of such policies (Beechey and Perkins, 1987: 155). An alternative explanation seems to be the doubling of part-time jobs held by students (see Chapter 6), who are formally outside the labour market anyway. Although student jobs are a tiny proportion of all part-time jobs, their exceptionally high turnover rates (well over 100%) mean that they have a disproportionate impact on turnover rates, especially on male turnover (which is otherwise very low) and on rates for part-time jobs. The inclusion of student jobs in labour market analyses would also contribute to an apparent reduction in the sex differential in turnover rates. The reason this factor is so difficult to detect and measure, and has so far remained hidden, is the inconsistent treatment of student jobs in official employment statistics, as noted in Chapter 6. Statistical conventions have not been modified to keep abreast of social change and innovation in the labour market.

A COMPARATIVE PERSPECTIVE ON PART-TIME WORK

Even within European labour markets part-time work means very different things, and cross-national comparisons are often not comparing like with like (Jonung and Persson, 1993). The differing size and importance of the four categories of working hours in any country contributes to the puzzling diversity of patterns of part-time work across industrial societies and to the weak correlations with other social and economic factors even in studies limited to Europe (Bruegel and Hegewisch, 1994; McRae, 1995). For example, Rosenfeld and Birkelund (1995) were obliged to limit their analysis to a narrow group of Northern European and Anglo-Saxon countries: the USA, Canada, Australia, Britain, West Germany, Denmark, Sweden, and Norway, excluding Japan, Southern Europe, and socialist states, in order to obtain reasonable correlations between the proportion of female employees in part-time jobs and other socio-economic indicators; even then, the most important correlate was simply the industrial structure, as measured by the proportion of women working in the public sector. This is hardly a new or major finding. The weak results obtained to date in cross-national comparisons of part-time work are due to the failure to differentiate between the different forms of part-time work. There are qualitative differences between reduced hours jobs, half-time, and marginal jobs and many countries do not have all three types.

OECD and EC reports have recently started to distinguish between the three types of part-time work to show, for example, that marginal work of under 10 hours a week is of growing importance among women both in countries with little part-time work, such as Ireland, and in countries with substantial part-time workforces, such as the Netherlands, Britain, Denmark, and even Germany (European Commission, 1994*a*: 108–12; Meulders *et al.*, 1994: 16; OECD, 1994: 78–82). In the Netherlands, Britain, and Denmark, marginal work grew over the decade 1983–92, so it is becoming more rather than less important, in part due to the growth of part-time jobs held by students in full-time education. In the European Community as a whole, most women working 30–34 hours a week regard themselves as full-time workers, and the European Commission now regards a full-time classification as most appropriate for these reduced hours workers, thus reserving the label 'part-time' for people working 10–29 hours a week, and classifying marginal workers as a qualitatively different group (European Commission, 1994*a*: 116). On this basis, they found much less variation in levels of part-time working among women across Europe than is indicated by the Labour Force Survey statistics routinely reported each year (see Table 5.1). This new classification may eventually be adopted for European Commission reports but most research analyses continue, as yet, to apply a variety of definitions of part-time work, thus magnifying the cross-national differences to be explained. One study that did adopt the new definition of part-time work (jobs with less than 30 hours a week) showed that the popularity of part-time work has been greatly underestimated by the Commission. The 1990 Eurobarometer found that the majority of women aged 20 to 60 years with children preferred not to work at all (60%) rather than to work part-time (29%) or full-time (11%), and most women aged 20 to 60 years without children preferred to work only part-time (43%) rather than full-time (24%) or not at all (33%). In Denmark and East Germany, part-time work was the preference of half to two-thirds of all women with and without children (European Commission, 1991: 127).

A study of part-time work in West Germany found that *regular* half-time jobs were the most popular type of part-time work. It also found that differences between half-time and marginal workers were just as great as differences between full-time and half-time workers, with marginal jobs growing fastest of all in Germany (Büchtemann and Quack, 1989: 115–30). Marginal workers were usually young people, often students, and the majority were employed in small firms with fewer than 20 employees. Marginal workers had a substantially lower investment in educational qualifications and training than full-time or half-time workers; almost half had no qualifications at all, and over half reported their job as unskilled. Marginal workers also had higher turnover rates and many spells out of the labour market. Because marginal workers are exempted from social security contributions in Germany and because of a special 10% flat-rate tax relief for low-income earners, female marginal workers had net hourly wages slightly higher than among regular half-time workers. However, almost all part-time workers were living in households with at least one other earner, usually a full-time worker (Büchtemann and Quack, 1989: 115–30). In sum, the characteristics that differentiate marginal workers and half-time workers seem to be similar in West Germany and Britain.

The new classification proved useful in a cross-national comparative analysis of part-time work in Europe and the USA (Blossfeld and Hakim, 1997; Hakim, 1997*a*). For example, Sweden is regularly held up as an exemplary model, with its family-friendly and egalitarian policies, and its equal treatment of full-time and part-time workers. However, most part-time jobs in Sweden are simply reduced hours jobs which are labelled as full-time work in countries such as Britain, so that equal treatment is true by definition. Employment conditions for half-time and marginal workers is the real issue—that is, the group conventionally labelled as part-time workers in Britain. Marginal jobs and workers do not exist in all countries. They provide the source of the most extreme images of exploited part-time workers, yet the ECJ has ruled that they may legitimately be excluded from social insurance systems, as noted above, and many of them are students who are not formally in the labour market.

By differentiating between types of part-time job, the new classification helped to identify part-time workers as secondary earners whereas full-time workers are typically primary earners. The *secondary earner* is someone who relies on another person as the main breadwinner and contributes a partial or secondary income to the collective pot (Hakim, 1996*a*: 69–74). The qualitatively different work orientations and job preferences of secondary earners explains why part-timers express more satisfaction with their lower status and less well paid jobs than do full-timers with their objectively 'better' jobs. Half-time and marginal jobs are clearly not 'proper' jobs from the perspective of a main breadwinner. But they can be constructed by employers to be attractive to secondary earners, who are less concerned with earnings and promotion prospects than with convenience factors (such as short and/or flexible work hours, a location sufficiently close to home to minimize travel time and costs, and unpaid time off work for domestic reasons) and with social aspects of the jobs (such as pleasant co-workers and management). These characteristics are not 'natural' features of service sector jobs—they must be designed into part-time jobs by innovative employers, or else employers must design jobs that tolerate high turnover rates (Hakim, 1997*a*). Tax incentives and legal changes favouring the creation of part-time jobs are not enough in isolation: employers must exert some imagination, as well as a knowledge of *local* labour supply, to create a permanent part-time work-force—as happened in Britain. Changes of regulations favouring part-time jobs in Italy and Greece did not have any significant impact on the labour market, whereas a change of policy in the Netherlands produced an immediate and dramatic increase in part-time jobs (Blossfeld and Hakim, 1997). Employee attitudes are also important. The idea of the dependent or semi-dependent wife is sometimes accepted, sometimes rejected in the sex-role preferences of men and women, and there is great variation in sex-role preferences *within* as well as *between* European countries. Thus the diversity of working hours and the emergence of a permanent part-time workforce illustrated by the Netherlands and Britain depend heavily on employers recognizing and building on the heterogeneity of women's sex-role preferences and work orientations (Hakim, 1996*a*, 1997*b*).

Scholars are now rejecting conventional economic activity rates and employment rates as inappropriate socio-economic indicators for cross-national comparative studies in favour of more robust and meaningful measures—such as full-time equivalent employment rates (Büchtemann and Quack, 1989: 115; Hakim, 1993*a*: 109–14; Pott-Buter, 1993: 204–8; Sainsbury, 1996: 110; Zighera, 1996). Our solution to the problem of cross-national comparisons is very different from Jonung and Persson's (1993) proposal, reiterated by Zighera (1996), for a new measure of average weekly market hours per person of working age. This measure was calculated for Britain and added to the comparisons presented by Jonung and Persson (Table 5.11). Market hours workrates per head of population show that

TABLE 5.11. *Cross-national comparisons of average market hours per person of working age*

	Men	Women	F/M ratio
Britain 1991 16–64	29.8	17.2	57.7
USA 1989 16–64	32.2	21.0	65.2
Finland 1989 16–64	27.7	21.4	77.3
Norway 1989 16–64	28.2	16.5	58.5
Sweden 1989 16–64	29.3	20.7	70.6
Sweden 1989 20–64	33.4	22.5	67.4
Sweden 1988 20–64	31.9	22.2	69.6
Britain 1991 20–64	31.4	17.7	56.4

Sources: 2% SAR, Great Britain, data for residents aged 16–64 years, and data for other countries quoted in table 4 in Jonung and Persson (1993: 270).

women in Britain do rather less market work than women in Sweden, Finland, and the USA, and just over half of the hours worked by men in Britain. However, the new measure is almost as uninformative as the head-count economic activity rate it replaces. It still focuses on group averages for all men and all women. The new classification of part-time jobs is more informative, and can be adapted to a greater variety of applications, as demonstrated in this chapter and the next.

CONCLUSIONS

In Germany, and many other European countries, a part-time job is any job requiring less than the 'standard' week of 40 hours (Hörning *et al.*, 1995: 35; Blanpain and Rojot, 1997). This approach is far too broad, failing to differentiate between three qualitatively different categories of shorter working hours: reduced hours jobs, half-time jobs, and marginal jobs. In Britain, a far lower threshold has been applied in national statistics, with part-time jobs defined as jobs with up to 30 hours a week. This definition is more appropriate, but it is still necessary to reclassify jobs with 30 hours a week (6 hours a day instead of 8) as reduced hours jobs, and thus a type of full-time job, rather than as part-time work. The SARs analysis has shown that the main dividing line is between half-time jobs and reduced hours jobs, and that marginal jobs constitute a separate category of part-time work—in terms of the personal characteristics of workers and job characteristics. The new classification is consistent with European Commission analyses, takes account of ECJ decisions on part-time workers, and has proved meaningful in comparative research on Europe and the USA.

Part-time work is diverse rather than homogeneous, as the single label implies, and one type of so-called 'part-time' work is really full-time work. New labels and a new classification are necessary to help us understand the *variety* of innovations created by part-time jobs. Another social change that has emerged slowly and has also been hidden by statistical conventions is the part-time student job. Employment patterns among students in full-time education are analysed in Chapter 6. In this chapter we discovered that student jobs are sufficiently important within the part-time workforce to distort conventional labour market analysis: high turnover rates in part-time jobs disappear after student jobs are excluded from the analysis. This suggests that new statistical conventions for student jobs are needed urgently. At the very minimum, research analyses and statistics should in future state explicitly whether student jobs, and other marginal jobs, are included or excluded. It is student jobs that explain the marked difference in labour turnover between full-time and part-time jobs in Denmark, for example (Hakim, 1996c: 9).

It has already been shown that the full-time and part-time workforces are polarizing as regards occupational segregation (Hakim, 1993*b*), skill and employment benefits (Rubery, Horrell, and Burchell, 1994: 229). Declining occupational segregation in the full-time workforce is counterbalanced and concealed by rising occupational segregation in the part-time workforce; the two conflicting trends cancel out, giving an illusion of stability instead of revealing change and development in the labour market. This polarization is extended by differentiation of the full-time and part-time workforces in terms of all the characteristics examined here, plus other characteristics reviewed in the research literature, such as work orientations and job satisfaction. Part-time jobs are not just diminutive versions of full-time jobs. As some social scientists are now recognizing (Hörning *et al.*, 1995), part-time workers are a new and qualitatively different element in the labour force, people for whom paid work is not the dominant or exclusive centre of their life.

It follows that different policies or benefits may be appropriate for part-time workers or, more generally, for secondary earners. So far, the European Commission has refused to recognize the existence of secondary earners. All policy analysis is written on the assumption that *all* workers are primary earners who have a full-time lifelong career which is only interrupted temporarily and involuntarily by the need to care for young children or the elderly, and that part-time work is taken by women mainly or exclusively when caring for others (European Commission, 1995*b*: 21, 138–41). Yet the Commission's own analyses in the same report demonstrate clearly that this is not the case. There are huge differences across the EC in the percentage of wives who state they are not working because of 'family reasons' *even when they have no child*, ranging from 20% in Portugal and Denmark to 80% in Holland and Italy (European Commission, 1995*b*: 142). Similarly, there are large differences between countries in the percentage of married women *without children* who work full-time, ranging from 60% in Portugal to 20% in the Netherlands (European Commission, 1995*b*: 142). Part-time work is almost non-existent in all southern European countries whereas it is a common (rather than atypical) form of employment for women in most northern European countries (European Commission, 1995*b*: 142). Similarly, European Commission discussion of the minimum wage does not take account of the expanding numbers of secondary earners: it insists that all wages should be adequate to provide a reasonable standard of living for an adult, or complete family, ignoring the fact that wage-earners differ qualitatively in work orientations, job priorities, and financial needs.

Secondary earners may work shorter hours on a permanent basis. Or they may take full-time jobs on a seasonal or periodic basis. Discontinuous employment is another equally acceptable alternative for some. Dedicated policy-makers working full-time in long-term careers must accept that employment may be the centre of life for them, but will not necessarily be the centre of life for all adults. The alternatives multiply in wealthy post-modern societies. The post-modern perspective on part-time work (Hörning *et al.*, 1995) seems to be more appropriate than the social problem perspective that the European Commission seeks to impose on all analyses of women's employment and part-time work.

These arguments carry most weight in relation to people in marginal jobs. Marginal workers are not aiming for or achieving economic independence. Most of them are not acquiring employment rights or benefits and remain outside the social insurance system. Even if they are given access to employment benefits, such as employers' pension schemes, the low hours worked and high turnover of marginal workers means that the benefits accrued would be of trivial value, and possibly outweighed by administrative costs. Marginal workers obtain benefits as dependants rather than as workers (Sainsbury, 1996). It is time to recognize that the inclusion of marginal work in headcount employment has become a serious distorting factor in labour market and social policy analysis.

6

Working Students:
Students in Full-Time Education with Full-Time and Part-Time Jobs

As Britain moved from an élite to a mass higher education system in the 1980s and 1990s, the number of students with jobs increased. In some cases this was prompted by financial necessity, in part because the value of government subsidies for students' living expenses (called 'grants' in Britain) fell in the late 1980s and early 1990s. The relative decline in funding for higher education and the consequential increasing employment of students became hotly debated public policy issues in the 1990s. A survey carried out in 1995 for the National Union of Students (NUS, 1996) concluded that students in higher education were being forced into part-time work, providing a million-strong pool of cheap labour for employers, but damaging their studies in the process.

However, it is clear that financial need has not been the sole, nor even the main driving force behind the rising trend in student jobs. First, student workrates have been increasing steadily for as far back as data are available, and the increases are found in all age groups, among men and women, among teenagers in secondary school as well as students in higher education. Second, all research to date in Britain and the USA shows that student workrates are, if anything, higher in the most affluent households and among the more able young people; there is no evidence that most students are pushed into taking jobs by low household income or parental unemployment. On the contrary, rising student employment reflects the changing social and economic status of young people and the changing relationship between education and employment. It is a complex and sociologically interesting phenomenon rather than a simple story of financial hardship.

STUDENT JOBS IN BRITAIN

Many secondary school teenagers have regular jobs delivering newspapers or helping in a shop on Saturdays.[1] Others earn money through what is

---

[1] A 1982 survey of employment patterns in retail shops found that Saturday staff, usually schoolchildren, formed a significant component of the workforce in small independent shops, but were more numerous in national chain stores (Craig and Wilkinson, 1985).

technically self-employment: babysitting, lawnmowing, or car-washing for neighbours and family friends. Paid work is more common among 16–18-year-olds in full-time education than among children under the school-leaving age of 16 years, due to legal restrictions on the employment of children. Until recently, student jobs were seen as a rarity, or confined to summer holidays in most cases. In the 1990s a series of studies based on widely differing sources revealed a continuous long-term increase in the proportion of students in full-time education who held part-time jobs during the academic year rather than just in the summer holidays, so that student jobs reached substantial numbers, on a year-round basis.

An analysis of FES data for 1968–91 showed that over one-quarter of a century annual part-time workrates[2] among young people aged 16–18 years in full-time education rose from 40% to 59%. The largest increases were in female annual workrates, rising from 43% to 63% by 1991 compared to 37% rising to 53% for young men. The biggest increases were not in employee jobs but in self-employment, such as babysitting, especially among girls, and girls were more likely to have multiple sources of income from work (Micklewright, Rajah, and Smith, 1994). All studies agree that student term-time jobs are almost invariably marginal jobs, typically 6–10 hours a week, and very often one-day-a-week Saturday jobs (Hutson and Cheung, 1992; Micklewright *et al.*, 1994: 79; Dustmann *et al.*, 1996: 86; Lucas and Ralston, 1997). The biggest increases in student jobs were in the 1980s, in a period of rising youth unemployment, demonstrating that the demand for marginal or 'casual' workers is relatively unaffected by the economic cycle, or is even counter-cyclical (Micklewright *et al.*, 1994). The LFS shows that between spring 1984 and spring 1988 the percentage of young people aged 16–19 in full-time education who had a part-time job rose from one-quarter to one-third (Hutson and Cheung, 1992). The 1992 and 1993 LFS showed that one-third of 16- and 17-year-olds in full-time education had a part-time term-time job (Sly, 1993, 1994*b*). The FES also shows annual workrates of 35% or just over for employee jobs among 16–18-year-olds, or annual workrates of 50% and over when all forms of paid work are included, in particular occasional, casual, and self-employment jobs. Summertime workrates are always higher at 50%–60% of the age group. By 1991, 53% of male students and 63% of female students aged 16–18 years had some paid work at some point in time in the preceding 12 months (Micklewright *et al.*, 1994). The 1994 LFS counted three-quarters of a million students with paid work in the summer, compared to 663,000 in the spring (Dex and McCulloch, 1995: 35–7).

---

[2] Annual workrates report the percentage with paid work of any sort within the previous 12 months, and are thus much higher than conventional workrates, which report the percentage with paid work of any sort in the 'last week' before interview. For technical reasons, the FES analyses reported annual student workrates rather than the narrower 'last week' workrates.

Workrates peak among teenagers at school and are significantly lower among older students. In summer 1994, only 32% of higher education students aged 20–24 had a summer vacation job compared to about 40% of schoolchildren aged 16–19 (NUS, 1996: 5). The expansion of student employment meant that by the 1990s student jobs had become a significant minority element in the part-time workforce, and the LFS started to monitor their numbers more carefully. Over the decade spring 1984 to spring 1994 the number of students with part-time jobs rose from 7% to 11% of the part-time workforce at a time when the part-time workforce itself expanded from 4.9 million to 6.1 million (Beatson, 1995: 16, see also Table 5.3). In effect, the number of student part-time workers doubled over the decade 1984–94, from 343,000 to 671,000. By spring 1995 the number of student part-time jobs reached 752,000, then rose by another 28% in just two years to reach 960,000 in spring 1997 or 15% of the 6.4 million part-time workforce. If anything, the pace of change is gaining momentum rather than slowing down. The size, the longevity, and the universality of the changes in student jobs indicate that the new trend has causes going wider than a simple reduction in student grants, although that may also be a significant catalyst in particular cases.

Poverty, or low household income, is an insignificant factor in the rise of student jobs. This conclusion is drawn from separate analyses of two national datasets with excellent information on household income and student earnings: FES data for 1968–91 and the 1958 cohort study known as NCDS (Micklewright *et al.*, 1994: 81–4; Dustmann *et al.*, 1996: 88). This is also the conclusion of several independent small-scale studies of students in particular localities using depth interviews (Roberts *et al.*, 1987; Hutson and Cheung, 1992). Both types of study, quantitative and qualitative, find that student workrates are equally high, or even higher, in the most affluent homes. Roberts *et al.* (1987) looked specifically at Saturday jobs among 16–19-year-olds and concluded that these earners are educational high achievers from affluent homes. They note that employers like their ability to learn things quickly and the up-market atmosphere they help to create, as found also by Lucas and Ralston (1997). Hutson and Cheung (1992) also found that Saturday jobs are held at some time by about two-thirds of teenagers in full-time education across the whole social class spectrum, and that there is no significant association between Saturday working and the student's spending allowance (or 'pocket money') given by their parents, largely because such allowances are very standard, with little variation across social classes, a conclusion drawn also by Dustmann *et al.* (1996: 93) using the NCDS. Some affluent parents would give their children additional funds to pay for holidays and other luxuries, but the general tendency was to restrict funds to teenagers, in order to teach them money management and to restrict over-consumption, given the commercialization of young people's leisure. Finally, student workrates are substantially higher in households where the father is working, and higher still if the mother is also working, as compared with households where the head is unemployed or otherwise inactive: a difference of about 20 percentage points (Micklewright *et al.*, 1994: 81; Dustmann *et al.*, 1996: 88).

Hutson and Cheung note that teenagers spend all their earnings on themselves, generally on luxuries rather than necessities: fashion clothing, music, nightclubs, drink, and hobbies. All their earnings constitute discretionary income, and for most of the 16–19-year-olds an important reason for doing paid work was to obtain *independent* money. Part-time term-time jobs might be extended into full-time work during the summer holidays in order to earn spending money that gave them psychological and financial 'independence' from their parents, establishing their identity as individuals and a degree of autonomy within the family. Most also enjoyed the new responsibilities of paid work, which increased their feelings of competence and self-esteem. The relatively low-skilled and low-paid jobs taken by full-time students in shops, supermarkets, and fast-food outlets are very similar to the full-time jobs taken by school-leavers, at least in terms of hourly pay, so they did not feel 'exploited' by employers (Hutson and Cheung, 1992; Micklewright *et al.*, 1994: 80). The conclusion to be drawn from Hutson and Cheung's interesting study is that for many young people jobs are a *necessary* adjunct to remaining in full-time education beyond the minimum school-leaving age of 16 in order to obtain better qualifications. In effect, the increase in student jobs is driven by the rising proportion of young people in full-time education, a conclusion drawn also by the OECD (1996: 128–33). Parents continue to treat their offspring in full-time education as dependent children rather than as adults. Part-time jobs give young people some degree of 'independence' and a taste of adult social status, as well as work skills, which makes the long years of social and economic dependence while in full-time education more tolerable. It is clear that this 'need' for a job does not apply to all young people, with a good deal of self-selection operating (Griliches, 1980). For example, among 16–17-year-olds in full-time education in autumn 1993, one-third had a part-time job; one-fifth would have liked a job and a few were actively seeking one; but almost half had no desire for paid work (calculated from figures supplied in Sly, 1994*b*: 333). It seems likely that academically oriented students will have less interest in paid work while those with 'real world' interests are more likely to seek a part-time job. However part-time working is significantly *positively* associated with intellectual ability (Dustmann *et al.*, 1996: 88), so ability *per se* is not a selection factor, any more than financial need. In sum, the rise in student jobs has been supply driven rather than demand driven, and there is evidence that employers see it this way (Lucas and Ralston, 1997).

Most of the studies reviewed so far focus on students aged 16–19 years, but the results can be expected to apply also to students aged 20 and over in higher education, who are fewer in number and far more difficult to study. Older students often live separately from their parents, and they often have multiple sources of income, so any relationship between parental income and student employment could not be assessed as easily as with teenagers living at home. Given the evidence that two-thirds or more of all secondary school students have some experience of gainful work and of regular part-time jobs, with consumption patterns to match, it seems likely that those who continue into higher education will maintain these tastes and behaviour patterns, with self-selection into student jobs becoming even more sharply defined.

STUDENT JOBS IN THE USA

Student employment has a longer history in the USA, with its emphasis on entrepreneurial values and the 'self-made man' and where it is possible for students to finance their way through college by part-time (and sometimes full-time) employment, often in on-campus jobs designed for students. We might expect to find a stronger association between family poverty or low income and student employment in the USA, but here too there is none. Patterns of student employment are broadly similar to those reported for Britain (Griliches, 1980; Meyer and Wise, 1984; Michael and Tuma, 1984; Ehrenberg and Sherman, 1987). The only important difference is the huge race differential in student employment: white girls and boys are far more likely to have jobs than are black girls and boys (Michael and Tuma, 1984), a finding that argues against the thesis of financial necessity as the catalyst for student employment.

Employment rates for white teenagers in school rise steadily from over one-quarter of 14-year-olds to over half of 17-year-olds, with no difference between boys and girls. Workrates are much lower among black and Hispanic teenagers: around 10% of 14-year-olds rising to one-third of 17-year-olds had a (part-time) job while in school, again with no difference between girls and boys (Michael and Tuma, 1984: 467). Student jobs are typically marginal jobs, averaging 8–10 hours a week among teenagers, but reaching half-time jobs of 20 hours a week among college students (Michael and Tuma, 1984: 467; Ehrenberg and Sherman, 1987: 6).

It is estimated that two-thirds of all college students work at some time while they are in college (Griliches, 1980: 297). One study found 20%–45% of students had part-time jobs and 10%–36% had concomitant full-time jobs depending on the type of college attended (Meyer and Wise, 1984: 134). Another estimate states that half of all college students have part-time jobs (Ehrenberg and Sherman, 1987: 6).

Research in the USA has focused on whether student jobs adversely affect educational attainment, aspirations, or subsequent labour market experience. Overwhelmingly, studies found that having paid work while a student is associated with success in education and in the labour market. Selection effects are assumed to be an important intervening factor: it is the most able, motivated, and successful students who are likely to have a job while studying, thus gaining valuable work experience and social skills as well as educational qualifications. However, some studies also find that the least able students also have jobs, smoothing their way into full-time employment as an alternative to extended education (Griliches, 1980; Michael and Tuma, 1984; Meyer and Wise, 1984; Ehrenberg and Sherman, 1987). One study showed that a real-world part-time job held during high school had a large impact on subsequent success in gaining full-time employment, whereas vocational training during high school had little or no impact on subsequent employment (Meyer and Wise, 1984: 127). Absence of the expected negative impacts on attainments in school or college, or later on, is consistent with the failure to find any significant associations between student part-time employment and family characteristics or financial need. Apart from the well-established ethnicity differential in workrates noted above, people with student jobs are not a special group.

In sum, research in the USA also supports our conclusion that student employment is a necessary consequence of young people having extended periods of full-time education. Student jobs blur the boundary line between full-time education and full-time work, dependence and independence, and allow a gradual transition into the labour market. However, this new phenomenon has only recently been addressed in labour market research.

STATISTICAL INNOVATIONS:
DOUBLE CODING OF ECONOMIC ACTIVITY

Students in full-time education who also hold jobs, during the academic term or during vacations, provide a classic example of the new developments that were concealed by traditional census coding and classifications—in this case rules for the single coding of economic activity status. Developments in IT provided a *technical* solution to the constraints of single coding of census questions. This chapter demonstrates that our theoretical and conceptual frameworks must also be developed and amended, in order to fully address the fact that people may have multiple activities, and to produce new rules for identifying their main activity (which may be part-time) and for analysing relationships between primary and any secondary activities or second jobs.

In the 1980s, technical improvements and falling data processing costs meant that double coding of the economic activity question became feasible in the 1991 Census. Double coding allows people to be classified as having two concomitant statuses instead of identifying a single overriding status among multiple codes. For example, students in full-time education who also have a part-time job (such as a Saturday job) are counted under both these statuses, instead of solely as students (and hence economically inactive) under conventional single-coding rules. Technically, multiple coding of survey questions has long been possible—as illustrated by the widespread practice of allowing people to tick two or more replies to attitude questions in small-scale surveys covering a few thousand people. But multiple coding does create extra work as well as extra possibilities—and these are multiplied millions of times over in the context of the population census, which covers 55 million people, of whom 27 million were economically active in 1991.

Double coding of economic activity status exposes the artificiality of the rules invented to select one overriding status in single-coding systems and reveals how technology has constrained our conceptual frameworks. The one-hour-a-week minimalist definition of employment endorsed by the ILO ensures that *any* paid employment is identified by censuses and statistical surveys. In effect, national statistics give priority to economic status over social status, so that a full-time housewife who does one hour's paid childminding a week for a neighbour is classified as economically active and 'in employment' rather than by her main social status and activity of housewife, and hence economically inactive (Hakim, 1996*a*: 23–5). The only exception to this rule, applied in censuses up to and including the 1991 Census, is that students in full-time education are invariably coded *first* to this status, and hence classified as economically inactive, even if they also do one hour's paid work in the reference week. In the 1980s, government statisticians began to break this rule and the LFS now classifies working students as part of the workforce, leading to some confusion over the labour market status of young people (Sly, 1993, 1994*b*) and inflating headcount employment by 3.5 per cent.[3] In other sources the official count of *jobs* may include jobs held by full-time students (people technically outside the labour force) whereas a count of *workers* normally excludes students.

It is not the case that the complexity of multiple statuses was a new development in the 1980s, resulting from workforce restructuring, as argued by some commentators, as in Handy's discovery of the 'portfolio worker'

---

[3] It is not clear when the rule was first overridden by government labour statisticians in order to boost headcount employment during recession. From 1985 onwards, the GHS has included student jobs in headcount employment, a fact which is highlighted in all GHS reports as a source of discontinuity. However, the 1991 Census coding of economic activity maintained the convention of all students in full-time education being outside the labour market: any jobs held are coded as a secondary status in the SAR files. Two articles by Sly (1993, 1994*b*) based on the LFS advertise the change in procedure. Both articles point out that the ILO one hour's work a week minimalist definition means that student jobs 'can be' counted in the LFS employment statistics, but the articles do not explicitly state or justify this major change of the classification rules which substantially inflates headcount employment. The 874,000 student part-time jobs counted in the spring 1996 LFS added 3.5% to headcount employment.

(Handy, 1984, 1994: 175–9). This complexity has always existed in reality, but was simply ignored by government statisticians who were obliged to make do with the simplistic picture obtained from single-coded employment status, dictated by technical feasibility. Over time, they even made a virtue out of necessity. This simplistic conceptual framework was in line with, and further reinforced by national social insurance rules which also insist on a person having only one status—of full-time employment, full-time unemployment, full-time education, or full-time economic inactivity. Each status dictates whether social insurance contributions should be collected from the worker or whether social insurance benefits should be paid to them, underlining a sharp dividing line between payers and recipients. In reality, people have often had multiple activities and multiple statuses—but this complexity has routinely been ignored by national statistics and public policies that classify everyone to a single main status.

The reality of people holding multiple jobs or having multiple statuses was acknowledged from the earliest population censuses, with rules invented to identify a main job or status. For example, the 1851 Census *Report* states that 'the double occupations are as great a source of difficulty as the varying degrees of the subdivision of labour in the manufacturing and other districts. The same person is a member of parliament, a magistrate, a landed propri-etor, and an occupier of land; in a lower circle, an innkeeper and a farmer; a maltster and a brewer; a fisherman in the season, a farmer or a labourer in the rest of the year. The enumerators were instructed to this effect, that a per-son following more than one distinct trade may insert his occupations in the order of their importance; and in the classification the first occupation was generally taken' (Hakim, 1980: 578). The multiple activities of housewives also presented problems. Between 1831 and 1911, the British population cen-sus tried out a series of different approaches to classifying the economic and social status of wives, ending with the current practice of treating wives engaged exclusively in unpaid domestic work as economically inactive (Hakim, 1980: 554–62). Full-time housewives sometimes had marginal jobs or did seasonal work to supplement the household's income on a regular or periodic basis—for example, taking in lodgers, taking in laundry (Davidoff, 1979; Lewis, 1984), or doing seasonal harvest work, such as hop-picking, which served also as a summer holiday for the family (O'Neill, 1990). The fact that the population censuses did not count all these part-time and sea-sonal jobs, led feminists to argue that the census 'undercounted' women's work. In fact there is no evidence that the census undercount of women's work is any greater than the census undercount of men's work (Hakim, 1996a: 19–59). If anything, the undercount has probably affected men more than women as men are generally more likely to have second jobs and are equally likely to do unpaid voluntary work (Hakim, 1996a: 38, 45). The USA, with a higher degree of job mobility and double-jobbing, adopted a broader and more flexible framework for national labour force statistics, yet they too show far lower levels of economic activity among women than among men. For over 30 years in the USA, statistics on the percentage of the population in employment at any time in the past 12 months have been published as well as statistics on the numbers employed in the last week (Hakim, 1996*a*: 65). This broader measurement does not radically alter the picture of a substantial sex differential in labour force participation (Clogg *et al.*, 1990; Hakim, 1996*c*: 20), a conclusion drawn also by Jonung and Persson (1993: table 4; see also Table 5.11). Even when women's multiple activities are fully counted, their workrates remain lower than for men (Hakim, 1996*a*: 51).

The fragmentation of employment brought about by the recessions of the 1970s and 1980s, and the workforce restructuring of the 1990s is not as new as some suggest. It is rather that multiple job-holding and complex economic statuses were concealed by national labour force statistics that classified everyone to just one status. Improvements in IT now permit us to routinely collect data on second jobs, to double code questions, and to analyse data in more detail than before. At the same time, there clearly are innovations in the workforce of the 1980s and 1990s that have not yet been explored. Just one of these is the expansion of paid employment among schoolchildren and students, a group that for many decades was effectively excluded from the labour market not only by statistical definition but also in reality. This innovation is clearly linked to the growth and diversification of part-time jobs explored in Chapter 5.

NEW COMBINATIONS OF WORK AND STUDY

Countries that have élite higher education systems, with fewer than 10% of any age cohort entering university and other tertiary educational institutions, generally have few students doing paid work, because students come from the wealthier sections of their society and/or because governments subsidize higher education costs for this élite minority group. Countries that have mass higher education systems, with around 30% or more of any age cohort entering tertiary educational institutions, generally have many students who help to fund their education by paid employment as well as by taking student loans. Working students are also more common in countries where tertiary level qualifications can require 5–9 years of study in contrast with the 3–4 years required for a B.Sc. degree in Britain in a system that only exceptionally permits a student to repeat an examination or a year of study.[4]

---

[4] Students also proceed more slowly through the educational system in countries that allow students to repeat years. In Canada, Belgium, Finland, Norway, Sweden, Ireland, Belgium, France, Greece, and Spain, for example, a substantial proportion of 20-year-old students are in upper secondary schools rather than in university. In contrast, three-quarters of 20-year-old students in the USA and the UK are in university (OECD, 1996: 149).

Working students are widely accepted, not only in the USA, but also in Nordic European countries, where the highest rates of part-time working are found among young people under 20 and people aged over 60 rather than among prime age women (Nätti, 1995; see also Fig. 2). Denmark, Finland, Sweden, and Norway have long had working students, who typically have part-time, and temporary, jobs, during term as well as in vacation, in part because students may remain in higher education institutions, repeating years where necessary, up to the age of 30. In Finland, for example, half the students in higher education have jobs during the term. University studies usually take 5–8 years and the grant system does not cover all living costs. In addition, every fifth high-school student and every third vocational school student works during the school term. Among all students who work while studying, 39% have part-time jobs. Most (70%) young people aged 15–24 working part-time say they work part-time because of their studies (Nätti, 1993, 1995: 356). In contrast, the unforgiving British higher education system expects students to work intensively year-round and to complete their course in a fixed number of years. This system allows (or forces) a student to complete a BA or B.Sc. degree within 3–4 years and a Ph.D. within 3–4 years, so that it is possible to graduate with a Ph.D. by the age of 24 or 25, after 6 years intensive study. In the British context, holding even a part-time job during term-time could pose a threat to a student's educational progress. On the other hand, many students take jobs, full-time or part-time, during the long summer vacation. So even in the context of the British educational system, students often gain work experience of some sort during their years in higher education.

Three developments have increased the chances of students having some work experience. First, more people aged 25 and over are returning to full-time education to gain additional qualifications, sometimes after many years of full-time employment. In the 1980s and 1990s, universities and other institutions created many new postgraduate and post-experience courses aimed at this group. Mature students sought extra qualifications to enhance promotion prospects within their existing occupation, or else to enable them to change their occupation. For example, mature students often invested in a Master of Business Administration (MBA) to enhance their earnings and career prospects, or else to achieve a major change of direction in their career. In these cases, students resigned from their job (or took unpaid leave) and studied full-time, funded by their own savings, bank loans, and any government grants available to them. They would typically seek a new job after graduation.

In the second case, mature students are funded by their employers, who sponsor or 'second' them to study full-time for an extra qualification, or even for a first degree. These students continue to be paid as a full-time employee by their employer throughout their studies, often with a contractual requirement to continue working for their employer for a minimum number of years after graduation, so that the employer's investment is recouped. The key feature of this group is that they remain full-time employees throughout their spell as full-time students. Both statuses are combined equally, and both would be reported with double coding of economic activity.

The third development is the creation of educational courses which include a spell of full-time employment aimed at providing students with 'hands on' experience of applying their new skills in a real-life work setting. The spell of employment may consist of three months with an employer, at the minimum, but often consists of a full year's employment which is 'sandwiched' between the second and fourth years of a four-year B.Sc. degree instead of the usual three-year course without any work experience. During their third 'sandwich' year, students become full-time employees while remaining enrolled as full-time students, a combination of statuses that can be reported in double-coded census questions.

In addition to these situations combining two apparently incompatible statuses, there are many other arrangements, formal and informal, enabling people to combine full-time or part-time study with full-time or part-time employment. These arrangements expanded in the 1980s and 1990s as jobs became increasingly skilled, with increased emphasis on training by employers, and as IT developments forced people to retool and retrain by taking courses of varying durations. And finally, in addition to the new arrangements, there are of course the traditional forms of apprenticeship, which combine education with on-the-job training while working full-time with an employer. Apprenticeships are especially common in manual occupations, but are also found in professional and other white-collar occupations, where a variety of specialist labels are used to describe them, such as 'articled clerk' with a firm of lawyers (solicitors), the 'pupillage' with a barrister's practice, the 'internship' or 'houseman' in the medical professions. Population censuses used to identify apprentices as a separate category in the past; however, the status was excluded from the 1991 Census economic activity question and classification (see Fig. 3 in Annex A). The decision seems odd, in the context of the increasing overlap between education and employment described above, and the move towards identifying working students. Thus we cannot identify what proportion of working students were in some form of apprenticeship, or were sandwich students—the two situations where employment activity is designed to contribute positively to the educational experience. Information on employer training more broadly defined is now collected in the LFS. The autumn 1995 LFS showed that 14% or around 3 million employees of working age (seasonally adjusted) received training related to a current or future job in the four weeks prior to interview. LFS results for 1995 indicated a levelling off in training rates for employees in the 1990s, after a slow but steady increase from 8% in spring 1984.

In sum, current developments are eroding the boundary line between education and employment among adults as well as teenagers in secondary school. In the past, it was possible for people to 'complete' their education (or apprenticeship) once and for all and then enter employment with, at the most, additional on-the-job training specific to the employer's business. The new pattern is for spells of full-time and part-time education and full-time and part-time employment to be interspersed throughout adult life, sometimes with two full-time statuses held simultaneously. Double coding of economic activity helps us to identify and analyse this innovation. Theoretical and conceptual frameworks also need to be developed to fully exploit this richer data and to understand the new phenomenon of lifelong learning. The analysis which follows is one step in this direction.

DOUBLE CODING IN THE 1991 CENSUS SARs

Annex A shows the economic activity question used in the 1991 Census (see Fig. 3). Respondents are invited to tick all boxes that apply, but hardly anyone ticked more than one. There is no explicit statement that up to three responses would be coded on the computer file for each person aged 16 and over and, in practice, only two statuses, at most, are present in the SAR files released for research analysis, so the term 'double coding' is more accurate than multiple coding. There is no information on how well double coding worked in the 1991 Census, nor even on how it was expected to work. The census quality check only assessed the validity of answers and undercoverage, not whether the double coding of economic activity worked well. The economic activity question had a higher than usual gross error rate: 11% in 1991 compared to 8% in 1981, followed by the daily journey to work question, with gross error rates of 8% in 1991 compared to 8.6% in 1981. Census processing was delayed by six months by the discovery that half a million people in employment had been incorrectly classified as students, due to incorrect assumptions about how people would record students with jobs during the Easter vacation (Thompson, 1995: 216, 224–6). This error was detected and corrected; it is possible that smaller errors were not detected. Our SAR analyses suggest that census form-fillers made far less use of the multiple tick option than they might have, and there is evidence that the Census Office only expected single ticks on the question (Thompson, 1995: 224). Everyone aged 16 and over was assigned a primary economic activity status, as usual. Only 5% of people aged 16–64 years and only 5% of people in employment were also identified as having a second status, which is low, given what is already known about the number of people who have second jobs (5%–6% of the workforce, on average), quite apart from other combinations, such as working students and people who have retired on an employer's pension but who also have a part-time job, an increasingly common development in the 1980s (Bone *et al.*, 1992). The 1991 Census count of working students is clearly understated, in part because the census form would often be filled in by students' parents rather than by students themselves. Apart from identifying working students in a few tables of the *Economic Activity* report (see Annex A), the Census Offices published no statistics from the exercise.

In addition, it is well known that the 1991 Census missed an estimated 2.2% of the resident population, a higher undercount than in previous censuses, and one that was not explained by the census quality check (Thompson, 1995: 214). The undercount was highest among people aged 20–29: 6% nationally, 9% for men and 3% for women (OPCS and GROS, 1994*a*: 9; Thompson, 1995: 215). It was also higher in inner city areas, especially in London. The controversial new poll tax (community charge) seems to have been one factor, plus a more widespread alienation from government and authority, in addition to the usual problems of high geographical mobility among young people. It was also thought that a loosening of ties to particular households meant that fewer people regarded themselves as having a usual, permanent address (Thompson, 1995: 214–15), a new and potentially permanent problem for the census.

The census undercount reduces the total counts for students aged 16–24 and for working students aged 16–24. However, it is not the cause of the lower jobcount among male students, especially in London, in Table 6.1 and in the SARs, and the consistently lower workrates among male students. All studies of student jobs in Britain, both quantitative and qualitative, find workrates are consistently higher among women than among men, an interesting reversal of the sex differential in workrates in the adult workforce (Hutson and Cheung, 1992; Sly, 1993, 1994*b*; Micklewright *et al.*, 1994; Dustmann *et al.*, 1996; Lucas and Ralston, 1997). The LFS also shows that student workrates are generally lower in metropolitan areas, such as London and Manchester, and higher outside metropolitan areas: 27% compared to 40% among 16–17-year-olds in full-time education (Sly, 1994*b*: 332).

The spring 1991 LFS estimates the number of student jobs at 645,000, almost three times as many as the 226,000 counted by the 1991 Census (Sly, 1994*a*: 89). This is not strictly an estimate of the census undercount, as the LFS and census differ in so many ways as not to produce directly comparable statistics. In particular, the census statistics refer to a single week in April 1991, whereas the spring LFS presents averages for a three-month period (March, April, and May) which generally gives a higher employment count. None the less, the comparison shows clearly that the census count hugely understates the level of student employment in spring 1991. Workrates for all groups should probably be doubled to approximate to reality. On the other hand, the *pattern* of results on student jobs in the census is otherwise a close

Working Students

TABLE 6.1. *National statistics: working students and workrates by age and ethnic group*

Age and ethnic group	Total			Men			Women		
	All students	Working students	Work rates	All students	Working students	Work rates	All students	Working students	Work rates
Total	1,911,832	235,050	12	947,073	103,419	11	964,759	131,631	14
16	515,815	50,543	10	256,385	21,128	8	259,430	29,415	11
17	339,519	58,462	17	158,561	24,432	15	180,958	34,030	19
18	253,805	43,119	17	120,860	18,871	16	132,945	24,248	18
19	175,673	21,168	12	88,140	9,855	11	87,533	11,313	13
20	151,734	14,497	10	78,118	6,881	9	73,616	7,616	10
21–24	281,911	24,443	9	150,938	12,062	8	130,973	12,381	9
25–29	82,625	8,765	11	45,533	4,339	10	37,092	4,426	12
30–34	44,409	4,870	11	22,242	2,203	10	22,167	2,667	12
35–39	29,510	3,634	12	11,994	1,351	11	17,516	2,283	13
40–44	19,467	2,772	14	6,969	999	14	12,498	1,773	14
45–49	8,767	1,456	17	3,270	591	18	5,497	865	16
50–54	3,845	784	20	1,698	392	23	2,147	392	18
55–59	1,140	258	23	582	160	27	558	98	18
60–64	842	117	14	446	71	16	396	46	12
65+	2,608	162	6	1,253	84	7	1,355	78	6
Whites	1,681,082	222,312	13	821,639	97,125	12	859,443	125,187	15
Black Caribbean	20,991	1,807	9	8,690	661	8	12,301	1,146	9
Black African	28,789	1,775	6	16,981	989	6	11,808	786	7
Black—other	10,589	902	9	4,749	362	8	5,849	540	9
Indian	59,027	2,943	5	31,805	1,482	5	27,222	1,461	5
Pakistani	31,656	1,048	3	18,850	664	4	12,806	384	3
Bangladeshi	10,536	315	3	5,802	204	4	4,734	111	2
Chinese	24,094	1,076	4	13,582	534	4	10,512	542	5
Asian	20,387	1,015	5	11,782	521	4	9,620	494	5
Other	23,657	1,857	8	13,193	877	7	10,464	980	9
People born in Ireland	11,874	1,409	12	5,741	648	11	6,133	761	12

Source: *1991 Census-Economic Activity*, tables 1 and 2, reporting 100% statistics for residents aged 16 and over.

duplicate of the pattern of results in the LFS, where direct comparisons can be made. There does not appear to be any differential under-reporting in the census.[5]

The published data and our SAR analyses refer to people who are resident in Britain, thus excluding the minority of foreign students and other students not normally resident in Britain. The 5% with a second status constitute 37,517 people aged 16–64 years in the 2% SAR, of whom 9,574 identified paid employment as their second status. (Two-thirds simply identified their second status as 'other inactive'.) Working students account for almost half

[5] For example, Sly (1993: 308) reports 30% of 16-year-olds and 42% of 17-year-olds having paid work in autumn 1992, with workrates systematically lower for boys than for girls (30% versus 40%). The census workrates for 16- and 17-year-olds are much lower, but the pattern of results in Table 6.1 is the same as in the LFS.

of these, 4,440 in the 2% SAR, 1,960 men and 2,480 women. Given the rule that students in full-time education are invariably coded *first* to this status, and the instruction on the census form that employees on training courses paid for by the employer should not be treated as students, there are no cases of employees (full-time or part-time) who are classified as students (full-time or part-time) in their second status.

No use was made of the double-coded data in the official report on *Economic Activity*, apart from the addition of a separate code identifying working students in the basic classification of economic activity which is used in tables 1–4 of the report (OPCS and GROS, 1994*a*). The published 100% counts of economically active students (including a few reporting themselves as unemployed rather than in work) are analysed in Table 6.1, and occasional reference is made to these published statistics later on. The inclusion of 'unemployed' students makes little sense, and raises student workrates (strictly, economic activity rates) in the published statistics and in Table 6.1 by one percentage point on average (just under one point for women and just over one point for men).

Some key limitations of all the census data on working students (both published and in the SARs) should be noted. The data cover all students in full-time education aged 16–64 who are resident in Great Britain, thus combining data for secondary school children aged 16–18 and higher education students aged 19 and over. There is no information on what educational courses people are registered for, nor on the type of institution they attend. There is information on any higher education qualifications already held, but the vast majority of students have none. Some students are still living in the parental home, while others have already left home, so the group is socially diverse, as reflected in the age structure. Finally, it has to be said that analysis of the SAR data on students with jobs is more difficult, and requires more care than analysis of data for the normal workforce.

NATIONAL ESTIMATES

The 1991 Census identified some 2.3 million students in full-time education, over 2 million of them students aged 16–24 years. About 400,000 were non-residents who are excluded from Table 6.1, reducing the resident student total to 1.9 million. One in three students had some recent work experience, but only eleven per cent were reported as having a job in the census reference week, which was 14–20 April 1991 (Tables 6.1–6.4). For most educational institutions this week was part of the Easter vacation period, when students could have taken a temporary job, full-time or part-time. The national total for economically active students in spring 1991 is 235,000 in the 100% statistics (Table 6.1), a student workrate of 12% (11% in employment and 1% who are unemployed). However, the national total falls to 214,520 economically active or 207,200 in work in the 10% statistics—both giving a student workrate of 11%, the same as in the SARs. Grossing up to national estimates from the SARs shows about 210,000 students with a current job in April 1991 plus another 500,000 who had held a job within the previous ten years (Tables 6.2–6.3). Overall, some 710,000 students had some recent work experience. The published census statistics cover a few 'unemployed' students looking for a job as well as those with a current job, with information on the ethnic composition of working students (Table 6.1). Our analysis classifies students reporting themselves as 'unemployed' with those reporting a previous job.

TABLE 6.2. *National estimates of male and female students with and without work experience, 2% SAR*

	Total		Men		Women	
	N	%	N	%	N	%
Students with concurrent jobs	4,296	11	1,889	9	2,407	12
Students with a previous job (within last 10 years)	9,381	23	4,702	23	4,679	23
All with work experience	13,677	33	6,591	32	7,086	35
Students with no recent work experience	27,173	67	13,751	68	13,422	65
All students in full-time education aged 16–64 years	40,850	100	20,342	100	20,508	100

Source: 2% SAR, Great Britain, data for residents aged 16–64. Numbers should be multiplied by 50 to obtain national estimates.

TABLE 6.3. *National estimates of male and female students with and without work experience, 1% SAR*

	Total		Men		Women	
	N	%	N	%	N	%
Students with concurrent jobs	1,945	11	843	9	1,102	12
Students with a previous job (within last 10 years)	3,734	20	1,844	21	1,890	20
All with work experience	5,679	31	2,687	30	2,992	32
Students with no recent work experience	12,555	69	6,244	70	6,311	68
All students in full-time education aged 16–64 years	18,234	100	8,931	100	9,303	100

Source: 1% SAR, Great Britain, data for residents aged 16–64. Numbers should be multiplied by 100 to obtain national estimates.

The almost complete absence of sex differences in student jobs, in workrates, and in all the other analyses in this chapter is notable and contrasts with sharp sex differentials in adult life. Young men and women are equally likely to seek paid work, and sex discrimination is clearly not a problem. Similarly, if there are any advantages for subsequent employment careers, young men and women benefit equally.

The great majority (88%) of students' *current* jobs are part-time jobs with less than 30 hours a week, whereas most (60%) *previous* jobs were full-time jobs involving over 30 hours a week. Because data on hours worked are so central to the analysis, we classify students as having work experience (now or previously) only if they also supplied information on their occupation and hours worked. This requirement reduced the base number of current jobs very slightly, from 4,440 to 4,296 in the 2% SAR, which left the subgroup unchanged at 11% of the 41,000 full-time students. This requirement also reduced the number of students identified as having a previous job to 9,381 and 23% of full-time students. People who did not provide information on hours worked would probably be those whose last job was of short duration or finished some years ago. They were grouped together with students with no recent work experience, raising numbers slightly to 27,173 and 67% of all full-time students (Table 6.2). The occupations of those not providing hours data were examined and found to be a close parallel to the occupations of those with hours data, so their exclusion does not affect our results.

Tables 6.2–6.4 present the base numbers for students with and without work experience which underlie the subsequent analyses, and show the composition of the SAR samples. The great majority (91%) of students are aged 16–24 years, and so are students with current jobs. However, there are important age differences between groups (Table 6.4). Students with no recent work experience are the youngest group, with 95% aged under 25 years. Students with a previous job are a distinctly different group, combining students aged 16–24 years (82%) whose previous job may have been a short-term summer vacation job, and mature students aged 25–64 years (18%) who have experienced long-term full-time employment.

WORKRATES AMONG STUDENTS

Previous jobs could have been held at any time in the decade 1981–91, although it seems clear from the results described below that full-time students reporting previous jobs were referring to jobs held within the last year or before they started their course. Precise workrates can only be calculated for current jobs, held in the 'last week' (Tables 6.1 and 6.5). Inevitably this understates student employment levels. Many more students hold a job at some point in the year, particularly during the summer months, as noted

TABLE 6.4. *National estimates of working and non-working students by age*

	Students with work experience			No recent work experience	All FT students aged 16–64	
	Current job	Previous job	All		N	%
All students						
16–24 years	3,918	7,298	11,216	25,799	37,015	91
25–34	217	1,425	1,642	970	2,612	6
35–44	117	518	635	321	956	2
45–54	33	126	159	73	232	1
55–64	11	14	25	10	35	*
Total	4,296	9,381	13,677	27,173	40,850	100
Male students						
16–24	1,729	3,695	5,424	13,041	18,465	91
25–34	97	777	874	554	1,428	7
35–44	37	187	224	128	352	2
45–54	16	36	52	24	76	*
55–64	10	7	17	4	21	*
Total	1,889	4,702	6,591	13,751	20,342	100
Female students						
16–24	2,189	3,603	5,792	12,758	18,550	90
25–34	120	648	768	416	1,184	6
35–44	80	331	411	193	604	3
45–54	17	90	107	49	156	1
55–64	1	7	8	6	14	*
Total	2,407	4,679	7,086	13,422	20,508	100

Source: 2% SAR, Great Britain, data for residents aged 16–64. Numbers should be multiplied by 50 to obtain national estimates.

earlier. A measure of any work experience (in the last ten years) is shown in Tables 6.5 and 6.6 and approximates to the annual student workrates reported earlier from the FES. At age 16, only 14% of students have ever had a job, according to the census. The proportion rises rapidly to 38% by age 19 when they leave school, then rises more slowly during the higher education years to reach 55% by age 24 (Table 6.5).

Student workrates show the percentage with a job of any sort in each age group. Student workrates peak at ages 17–18, then decline to about 10% at ages 19–24 years. Young people in secondary school aged 16–18 have higher workrates than do students in higher education. The vast majority of current jobs are marginal jobs involving no more than 10 hours a week, typically an 8-hour one-day-a-week job. However, 4%–5% of students aged 17–24 years had a job with longer hours, typically half-time, but sometimes full-time hours. In some cases this means that financial necessity forces a student to hold a full-time job at the same time as studying. In other cases it means that a full-time employee is seconded by an employer to study full-time for another qualification. Unfortunately, there is no way of differentiating these two categories, to see which is more important.

Workrates among mature students aged 25–54 are markedly higher, reflecting the higher proportion of employees sponsored by employers to study full-time, as well as other combinations. Marginal jobs are rare among male mature students. Marginal jobs account for almost half the jobs done by female mature students, and here again they probably reflect financial necessity rather than a desire to fill in time or the search for relevant work experience.

There are very few full-time students aged 55–64 years, about 2000 nationally, with slightly more men than women (Tables 6.1 and 6.4). Base numbers in the SARs were too small to calculate workrates for women in Table 6.5, but men in this age group had the very highest workrates, typically involving full-time jobs, as confirmed by the 100% statistics in Table 6.1.

One notable finding is that students in ethnic minority groups are significantly more likely to devote themselves exclusively to their studies: 79% of non-white students have never held a job compared to 65% of white students. Only 4% of ethnic minority students had a current job compared to 11% of white students; only 17% of ethnic minority students had previously held a job compared to 24% of white students (Table 6.6). As in the USA, white students in Britain are almost twice as likely as ethnic minority students to gain some experience of paid work while in full-time education. One factor

TABLE 6.5. *Student workrates based on current jobs by age*   row percent

Age	Males		Females		All students		Students with recent work experience
	All jobs	Marginal jobs	All jobs	Marginal jobs	All jobs	Marginal jobs	
16	7	5	10	8	9	7	14
17	15	10	17	13	16	12	27
18	13	8	16	10	14	9	32
19	9	4	9	4	9	4	38
20	7	2	9	4	8	3	43
21	6	2	9	4	7	3	46
22	6	2	7	3	6	2	45
23	6	2	6	2	6	2	49
24	5	1	9	3	6	2	55
16–24	9	5	12	8	11	7	30
25–34	7	2	10	4	8	3	63
35–44	10	1	13	6	12	4	66
45–54	21	3	11	5	14	4	69
55–64	48	10	~	~	31	6	71
Total 16–64	9	5	12	8	11	6	33

Source: 2% SAR, Great Britain, data for resident students in full-time education aged 16–64.

TABLE 6.6. *Workrates among white and ethnic minority students*

Percentage of all students with work experience	White students			Other students		
	M	F	T	M	F	T
Current job	10	13	11	3	5	4
Previous job	24	24	24	18	17	17
Any job	34	36	35	21	22	21

Source: 2% SAR, Great Britain, data for resident students in full-time education aged 16–64.

may be awareness of racial discrimination in Britain, which discourages black, Asian, and Chinese schoolchildren and students from seeking part-time or summer holiday jobs (Brown, 1984). Alternatively, ethnic minorities are more likely to live in poor neighbourhoods where part-time jobs and odd jobs such as babysitting and car-cleaning are less readily available. Another factor could be the higher value placed on learning and scholarship in other cultures, particularly Buddhism. Cultural differences would also help to insulate ethnic minority students from the commercialized consumer culture that requires high spending on clothes, alcohol, and entertainment. A third factor may simply be that ethnic minority students have to work harder at their studies because English will often be a second or third language for them rather than their first language. Probably all factors combine to produce significantly lower workrates among non-white groups.

The 100% statistics in Table 6.1 are especially useful for checking this result for small minority groups in the SARs, and the results are unequivocal: whites are twice as likely to be in employment (strictly, economically active in this table) as are resident students in the ethnic minority groups, with the lowest workrates among Chinese and Asian students. The absence of any differences in workrates between men and women in each ethnic group identified in Table 6.1 confirms that social and cultural factors are dominant, not financial need. Ethnic minority groups are generally less affluent than the dominant white community, yet they are more likely to ensure that their children devote themselves exclusively to their studies while they remain in full-time education. Separate cultures which protect them to some degree from the dominant white consumer culture probably helps in this process. The Buddhist culture, in particular, places exceptionally high value on education and scholarship as valuable in themselves, not merely as vocational training.

PERSONAL CHARACTERISTICS OF WORKING
AND NON-WORKING STUDENTS

There are no differences between working and non-working students in personal and family characteristics. As a group, students differ completely from the general population of working age: they are young and often still live with their parents, who constitute the joint heads and main earners in the household. They are almost all single and have no children of their own, though this fact is obscured by their living in the parental home with other dependent children under 15 years, who are younger siblings of the student rather than their own children (Table 6.7). Largely due to the presence of mature students, the group with previous work experience but no current job is more likely to contain students who have married, who maintain their own household (typically in privately rented accommodation), earn their own living, and have children. But the differences are relatively small. Most notable is the finding that there are no marked differences between students currently in work and students who have never held a job, or between working students and all students in general, at least not in terms of visible personal and family characteristics. If we use owner-occupied housing as an indicator of greater affluence, then students with a current job are in more affluent homes than students in general. But there is no difference in housing tenure between students with and without work experience (Table 6.7).

In sum, there is no evidence that working students are distinctive in any obvious way, or are more likely to come from poorer families. Any differences between working and non-working students must lie in their attitudes to work, money, and education which are not reflected in census data. Here, as elsewhere in the analysis, there are no sex differences at all within each subgroup of students with and without work experience. These results are consistent with previous studies of student employment in Britain and the USA.

THE CHARACTERISTICS OF STUDENT JOBS

A remarkable finding is that students' current and previous jobs include every occupation listed in the 1990 SOC at the level of 73 Major Occupational Groups, and this was true for women as well as for men. At the more detailed level of 371 occupational units (in practice 358 groups in the SARs), there was at least one man and at least one woman in almost every occupational group for previous jobs, which outnumber current jobs three to one. So student jobs are dispersed across the entire occupational structure, even if the numbers in each occupational group are usually tiny. Many of these jobs seem to be related to students' course of study. In these cases

TABLE 6.7. *Personal characteristics of working and non-working students* column percent

	Students with work experience			No recent work experience	All FT students aged 16–64	All persons aged 16–64
	Current job	Previous job	All			
Marital status						
Single	94	88	90	97	95	31
Ever-married	6	12	10	3	5	69
Ethnic group						
White	96	91	92	86	88	95
Other	4	9	8	14	12	5
Number of earners in household						
None	*	22	14	15	15	14
Only one	5	31	22	28	27	29
Two or more	95	47	64	57	58	56
Higher education qualifications						
None	94	84	87	96	93	85
1	4	12	10	3	5	9
2 or more	2	4	3	1	2	6
Housing tenure						
Owner-occupier	84	72	77	78	71	73
Other	16	28	23	22	29	27
Region						
London	10	14	13	15	14	12
Rest of South-East	24	21	21	19	20	19
Rest of Britain	66	65	66	66	66	69
Position in household						
Head of household	7	18	14	4	8	46
Spouse of HOH	3	8	7	1	3	33
Other member	90	74	79	95	89	21
Lifestage						
Age 16–24:						
single, with children <15 in household	38	16	24	36	32	5
single, no children in household	47	45	46	47	47	10
in couple, no children in household	5	11	9	8	8	3
in couple, children <15 in household	3	4	3	4	4	2
Age 25–54, single or couple:						
no children in household	4	15	11	3	5	31
with children <15 in household	3	9	7	2	4	33
Age 54–64	*	*	*	*	*	16

Sources: 2% SAR for the top part of the table; 1% SAR for the bottom part of the table.

TABLE 6.8. *Occupations of students in full-time education*   column percent

	Current jobs			Previous jobs			All with work experience
	M	F	T	M	F	T	
Students aged 16–64 years							
72 Sales assistant and check-out operators (a)	39	48	44	16	27	21	28
62 Catering occupations (b)	10	16	13	7	11	9	10
95 Other jobs in sales and services (c)	15	11	13	8	8	8	9
All other occupations	36	25	30	70	55	62	53
Total	100	100	100	100	100	100	100
Students aged 16–24 years							
72 Sales assistant and check-out operators (a)	42	52	47	20	32	26	33
62 Catering occupations (b)	10	16	13	8	14	11	12
95 Other jobs in sales and services (c)	16	11	13	9	9	9	10
All other occupations	32	21	27	63	45	54	45
Total	100	100	100	100	100	100	100

Notes: (a) the occupation includes: sales assistants, retail cash desk and check-out operators, petrol pump forecourt operators; (b) the occupation includes: chefs, cooks, bar staff, waiters, waitresses; (c) the occupation includes: hospital and hotel porters, kitchen porters and hands, counterhands, catering assistants, shelf-fillers, lift and car park attendants, window cleaners, road sweepers, cleaners, domestics, and similar jobs.

Source: 2% SAR.

students are clearly gaining relevant work experience, for example in computing or as lawyers' clerks, with rates of pay above the average for student jobs (Lucas and Ralston, 1997). However, current jobs are dominated by just three occupations, which account for more than two-thirds of all jobs held by students aged 16–64, and for three-quarters of all jobs held by students aged 16–24 (Table 6.8). Jobs held previously by full-time students show far less concentration in these three occupations and include many more higher grade jobs, due to the presence of mature students with long-term work experience

Among women, the three main student jobs accounted for three-quarters of current jobs and half of previous jobs, compared to two-thirds and one-third respectively for men. Among students aged 16–24 years, the degree of concentration is even more marked (Table 6.8). The three main types of student jobs are in catering (including waiters and waitresses, bar staff, and cooks), sales work (mainly as sales assistants, retail cashiers, check-out operators, and some petrol forecourt attendants), and miscellaneous other service jobs (most commonly kitchen assistants, counterhands, cleaners, and shelf-fillers in supermarkets). These are gender-neutral jobs with no particular connection with feminine skills, even though they are female-dominated in terms of their sex composition nationally, as noted in Chapter 2. It is notable that integrated occupations, which employ both men and women, are not the main source of student jobs, as had been expected. The high turnover and part-time occupations that provide the source of four-fifths of all current student jobs are female-dominated occupations (Table 6.9, see also Tables 2.10 and 2.11). This is especially true of marginal jobs (with ten hours a week or less), but it is also true of half-time jobs and reduced hours jobs (see Table 5.10). Female-dominated occupations are the source of jobs taken by young men and women almost equally, because male and female students are generally found in equal numbers in all four categories of work hours, with only a slight balance towards men (61%) in long full-time jobs and a slight balance towards women (62%) in marginal jobs held by students. Since jobs previously held by students were often long-term full-time jobs, the usual pattern of occupational segregation is more in evidence, particularly within full-time jobs.

TABLE 6.9. *Student jobs: occupational segregation* column percent

Type of occupation	Men			Women			All students with work experience		
	Current jobs	Previous jobs	All jobs	Current jobs	Previous jobs	All jobs	Current jobs	Previous jobs	Total
Male	20	36	32	4	8	7	11	22	19
Mixed	7	15	12	5	12	9	6	13	11
Female	73	49	56	91	80	84	83	65	70
Total	100	100	100	100	100	100	100	100	100

Note: Male occupations are those with <25% female workers; mixed occupations are those with 25%–55% female workers; female occupations are those with >55% female workers.

Source: 2% SAR.

The high degree of concentration in just three occupations, found especially among *current* jobs, produces a similar concentration in just two RG Social Classes and two Goldthorpe Classes (Table 6.10). It is only when we move away from analysis of occupational grade and class, which display no important sex differences, to the analysis of occupational segregation that we find any sex differences between students, working or non-working. Two-thirds of student jobs, and often the vast majority, are in female-dominated occupations, whether they are done by men or women. Marginal jobs in particular are almost exclusively (88%) in female-dominated occupations. The only exception are the jobs held previously by men: in this group a substantial minority of male-dominated occupations appears, especially in the case of full-time jobs (Table 6.9). It appears that working students, almost all of them part-time workers, are only in competition with married women part-time workers and older, semi-retired workers, for jobs. These results further confirm the pronounced and growing segregation of the part-time workforce (Rubery, Horrell, and Burchell, 1994: 229; Hakim, 1993*a*, 1993*b*, 1996*a*, 1997), which recruits large numbers of 'marginal' or transient workers who are on the edge of the labour market.

Within the British workforce as a whole, marginal and half-time jobs are rare, accounting for 4% and 14% of jobs respectively (Table 6.10, see also

TABLE 6.10. *Characteristics of jobs held by full-time students*   column percent

	Current jobs			Previous jobs			All with work experience	Total workforce
	M	F	T	M	F	T		
Hours worked per week								
Full-time 37+	12	6	9	54	35	45	33	68
Reduced 30–36	3	2	3	14	16	15	11	14
Half-time 10–29	32	27	29	15	22	18	22	14
Marginal <10	53	64	59	17	27	22	34	4
Total full-time	16	8	12	69	51	60	45	82
Total part-time	84	92	88	31	49	40	55	18
Distance to work								
Works at home/no fixed place	5	4	4	..	..	..	..	11
0–2 km	46	47	46	..	..	..	..	27
3–4 km	19	18	19	..	..	..	..	15
Over 5 km	30	31	31	..	..	..	..	47
Transport to work								
Works at home	2	2	2	..	..	..	..	5
Walks to work	24	24	24	..	..	..	..	12
Uses transport	74	74	74	..	..	..	..	83
Social Class								
I Professional	2	1	2	7	2	5	4	4
II Managerial, technical	7	8	7	16	14	15	13	26
IIIN Skilled	45	57	52	31	49	40	44	24
IIIM Skilled	7	2	4	11	4	7	7	21
IV Semi-skilled	25	26	26	25	26	25	26	17
V Unskilled	12	6	8	9	4	7	7	6
Other (a)	2	*	1	1	1	1	1	2
Goldthorpe Classes								
Service class	7	6	6	23	16	19	15	29
Routine non-manual	6	8	7	13	21	17	14	15
Personal service	38	54	47	17	32	25	32	8
Proprietors, farmers	1	*	*	1	*	1	1	9
Lower technicians, foremen and skilled manual workers	6	2	4	9	4	6	6	15
Semi- and unskilled workers	42	30	35	37	27	32	33	24

Notes: (a) Inadequately described, not stated, and Armed Forces.

Sources: 2% SAR for the top part of the table; 1% SAR for the bottom part of the table.

Chapter 5). However, the overwhelming majority of students' current jobs are marginal jobs and half-time jobs, accounting for 59% and 29% respectively of all current student jobs (Table 6.10). Full-time jobs are a rarity, and may indicate cases where an employee is sponsored by an employer to study full-time at a higher education institution.

Student jobs are distinctive in other ways, and once again the consistent absence of sex differences is itself remarkable. Students typically choose very local jobs—half take jobs within a 2 km distance from their home, compared to one-quarter of workers nationally (Table 6.10). One-quarter of students walk to work, double the national average for all workers. These features reflect the lower investment in travel time that is typical of people with marginal jobs, as shown in Chapter 7.

The aggregate 1991 NES earnings information assigned to employees in the SARs provides estimated 1991 earnings for students' current and last jobs. Table 6.11 shows average hourly earnings excluding overtime payments for all young people aged 16–24 and for students aged 16–24. On average, students earned £3.46 an hour in current jobs and £4.23 an hour in previous jobs. In the workforce generally, previous jobs have lower average earnings than current jobs, reflecting the fact that people who stay in the workforce continue to be promoted up occupational ladders to reach higher job grades and earnings (see Chapters 3 and 4). This effect is found even among young people aged 16–24 (Table 6.11). Among students, however, previous jobs tend to be higher grade and better paid than currently held jobs, which are typically part-time only (Table 6.11). For students with jobs in catering, average hourly earnings were £3 for current jobs and £4 for previous jobs. For students with jobs as sales assistants, average hourly earnings were £3.15 for

TABLE 6.11. *Estimated average hourly earnings (pence) for young people and students aged 16–24*

All young people aged 16–24	Current jobs		Previous jobs		
	Men	Women	Men	Women	
Male occupations	503	516	477	449	
Mixed occupations	655	567	579	455	
Female occupations	461	436	380	376	

Students aged 16–24 years	All jobs	Current jobs	Previous jobs	Men	Women
Male occupations	498	430	514	492	531
Mixed occupations	531	513	535	573	492
Female occupations	360	329	380	367	357
All jobs	396	346	423	421	373

Source: 2% SAR, Great Britain, data for resident employees aged 16–64.

current jobs and £3.24 for previous jobs. Despite the relative uniformity of student jobs, there is a small sex differential in hourly earnings: female students earn £3.73 an hour compared to £4.21 among male students. Even in the group of female-dominated occupations which provides most student jobs there is a tiny sex differential, £3.57 for women versus £3.67 for men. The sex differential is largest in the group of integrated or 'mixed' occupations (Table 6.11) as was also found in Chapter 3. The sex differential in earnings emerges even before young people fully enter the labour market.

Among students with work experience, previous jobs outnumber current jobs by 3 to 1, whereas in the workforce as a whole current jobs outnumber previous jobs by 4 to 1. This demonstrates very clearly the fundamental difference between student jobs, which are taken on a temporary or short-term basis, even if the job itself is permanent, and normal jobs, which are typically taken on a long-term and permanent basis. Labour turnover in the student workforce is so high that the term ceases to have its normal meaning. Although part-time workers have always had higher turnover rates than full-time workers (Hakim, 1996*c*), student turnover rates are vastly higher for all jobs. As we have shown in Chapter 5, student jobs are a crucial factor distorting national turnover rates, especially in marginal jobs (see Table 5.10). In the relatively unregulated British labour market employers are not restricted in their use of temporary workers (Hepple and Hakim, 1996), so temporary jobs recruit many social groups, not only students. In the highly regulated Nordic countries, where there are many restrictions on temporary jobs, between one-third and two-thirds of all temporary jobs are taken by young students, and 30% of young people aged 15–24 have temporary jobs (Nätti, 1993: 455).

In sum, student work experience covers the whole range of occupations in the labour market but student jobs are typically semi-skilled or unskilled jobs requiring little specific training (apart from the student's existing education), are available in the immediate neighbourhood, are frequently available on a part-time basis, and tolerate the high turnover rates typical of students. As regards the characteristics of student jobs, the results of this analysis are consistent with those of the 1995 NUS survey and other studies.

THE IMPORTANCE OF STUDENT JOBS IN THE MARGINAL WORKFORCE

These results suggest that the recent growth of marginal jobs could be explained almost entirely by the growth of student jobs. In fact, student marginal jobs account for a minority of all marginal jobs in Britain, no matter what evidence is used. The census SARs show student marginal jobs to constitute 16% and 22% of current and previous marginal jobs respectively

TABLE 6.12. *The overlap between marginal jobs and student jobs*

	Hours worked in current/previous job				
	Full-Time 37+	Reduced 30–36	Half-time 11–29	Marginal <11	Total
Workforce aged 16–64					
current jobs	304,655	63,701	61,829	15,954	446,139
previous jobs	73,108	15,831	21,096	9,169	119,204
Students aged 16–64					
current jobs	383	113	1,256	2,544	4,296
previous jobs	4,173	1,439	1,708	2,061	9,381
Students aged 16–24					
current jobs	281	77	1,138	2,422	3,918
previous jobs	2,870	1,111	1,365	1,952	7,298

Source: 2% SAR, Great Britain, data for residents in employment.

(Table 6.12). These are underestimates, given the census undercount of young people and student jobs. But the census also undercounted marginal jobs generally, as noted in Chapter 5, so the proportions may be fair. The spring 1991 LFS counted 2,687,000 jobs with less than 16 hours a week (Sly, 1994*a*); even if all 645,000 student jobs in the LFS involved fewer than 16 hours a week, student jobs would still contribute only 24% of these short part-time jobs.

Consistent evidence is also found in LFS data on the earnings of part-timers. Employees and self-employed with weekly earnings low enough to remain below the threshold where social insurance contributions become payable are almost invariably working part-time (Hakim, 1989*b*: 476–80, 1992*b*). The most recent analysis of these workers, based on spring 1995 LFS data for employees, shows that 14% are men aged 16–24 and 19% are women aged 16–24 (Table 6.13). This is the main age group for student jobs, but also for the first jobs of school-leavers, many of whom leave school without any qualifications. (In winter 1995/96, among people of working age, 25% of women and 17% of men had no qualifications.) Altogether one-third of jobs with earnings low enough to be exempt from paying social insurance contributions are held by young people aged 16–24 years. The analysis in Table 6.13 uses a totally different approach from the census analysis of marginal jobs in Table 6.12; they are strictly not comparable. However, both analyses show that jobs held by young people, including student jobs, account for a minority of jobs with very low hours and/or very low earnings. Prime age married women secondary earners form the dominant group among employees in marginal jobs with low earnings (Table 6.13) and they are also the dominant group among the self-employed with very low earnings (Hakim, 1989*b*:

TABLE 6.13. *Employees with low, marginal earnings, spring 1995*

	Employees earning less than social insurance threshold (£58 per week)		As percentage of all employees in each age group
	000s	%	
Men aged			
16–24 years	312.5	14	17.8
25–49	73.9	3	1
50–64	47.6	2	2.3
total	434	19	..
Women aged			
16–24 years	423	19	25.1
25–49	1017.4	45	15.4
50–64	390.3	17	20.3
total	1831	81	..
All with low earnings	2265	100	..

Source: Spring 1995 Labour Force Survey, data for employees in work aged 16 and over.

477, 1992*b*, 1996*a*: 26–32). Similar results are reported for West Germany (Büchtemann and Quack, 1989).

What people in marginal jobs have in common is that they are not earning a living but obtaining supplementary income while remaining substantially dependent on some other source of funds—parents, spouse, an employer's occupational pension, or state grants and subsidies. The expansion of student employment has clearly contributed to the growth of the marginal workforce towards the end of the twentieth century, but working students remain a minority element in the marginal workforce in Britain and are outnumbered by wives for whom a job is almost a hobby.

CONCLUSIONS

Work experience can be both beneficial and detrimental to students. On the one hand, early work experience facilitates the transition from full-time education to full-time employment, as young people have a better idea of what to expect in the world of work, are more informed in their choice of jobs (hence make fewer mistakes), acquire work skills, and are more attractive to employers. The new 'sandwich' courses are designed to capitalize on this advantage. There is evidence from the USA that vocational training has no beneficial impact after graduation, but that students with real experience of paid work are more likely to find jobs quickly on leaving full-time education and obtain higher wages than students who did not have part-time jobs while studying (Meyer and Wise, 1984; see also Michael and Tuma, 1984). However, there is also a danger that students' educational attainment is reduced by competing activities that bear no relationship to their studies— such as a Saturday job as a shop assistant, or evening jobs as barman or wait- ress, which are the typical student jobs. Successful completion of a course, or maximum educational benefit, requires exclusive full-time study, it is argued. In the USA, Ehrenberg and Sherman (1987) found no impact of term-time part-time jobs on college exam results. However in Britain, there is evidence from the NCDS that educational attainment is lower among secondary school students who have a part-time job (Dustmann *et al.*, 1996: 94–9), pos- sibly because of the unforgiving educational system. Self-selection into employment will magnify both these effects of paid work while studying.

The SARs confirm that self-selection is important. Cultural factors tend to keep ethnic minorities out of paid work while they are in full-time education, whereas most white young people gain some work experience while studying. There is no evidence that financial need or poverty are key factors pushing students into jobs; if anything they come from the most affluent homes. Any differences between working and non-working students must lie in their atti- tudes to work, education, money, and consumption which are not reflected in the limited behavioural data collected by the census and labour force sur- veys.

The SARs provide national samples of working students large enough to calculate workrates (albeit understated), to assess patterns of student jobs across age and social groups, and to permit detailed examination of student jobs. Our findings are consistent with previous studies. In particular, sec- ondary school students have higher workrates than students in higher edu- cation; ethnic minority groups have consistently lower workrates than the white majority, a factor that may contribute to their higher educational attainment at secondary school level; there are no significant sex differences in levels and patterns of student employment; student jobs are concentrated in the same three occupations for both men and women. Despite the absence of sex differences throughout the findings on current student jobs, occupa- tional segregation is in evidence in the jobs held previously by students, par- ticularly full-time jobs, which are more likely to have been held long-term. The sex differential in earnings also emerges early, even before full entry into the workforce. The results also indicate that students and prime-age married women are potential substitutes in the part-time workforce and are poten- tially in competition with each other for marginal and half-time jobs, which are typically in female-dominated occupations. Student jobs contribute between one-fifth and one-quarter of all marginal jobs; the expansion of stu- dent jobs clearly contributed to the expansion of part-time jobs, in particu- lar marginal jobs, in the 1980s and 1990s. The separation of the part-time and full-time workforces is underlined by the presence of students in the part-time workforce, a group that has conventionally been regarded as outside the labour market.

The once well-defined boundary between full-time education and full-time employment has broken down. Education and employment are now combined by a minority of students across the life cycle. With the trend towards lifelong learning, this pattern will become more common, in all age groups and in all rich modern societies. A recent study by the OECD (1996: 128–33) showed that the percentage of 18-year-old and 22-year-old employed men and women who are simultaneously attending school rose in almost all member states in the decade 1984–94, sometimes by substantial amounts (Table 6.14). By 1994, around half or more of employed 18-year-olds in the USA, Canada, Denmark, the Netherlands, and Australia were also attending school; among 22-year-olds, the percentages fell to 15–25 per cent. Some countries, such as France and Spain, have no tradition of student employment and young people are often jobless for a long time after they leave full-time education. It is notable that the trend towards combining employment and education is found even in France and Spain, with sharp increases in the percentage of employed 18-year-olds who were also attending school, and smaller increases among 22-year-olds. The OECD analysis does not examine hours worked, but it seems likely that most or all of these young people are combining full-time education with a (marginal) part-time job. The above analysis excludes apprenticeships, which continue to be important in Germany, Denmark, Luxembourg, Britain, and Australia, especially for young men (OECD, 1996: 118–19).

These results give us another reason for rejecting the one-hour-a-week minimalist definition of employment that has become the ILO standard. This minimalist definition of a job allowed the British government to give the misleading impression of massive job creation in the 1980s and early 1990s, and is now being used in the LFS to reclassify working students as 'workers' with 'jobs' rather than as inactive students. If marginal jobs with ten hours a week or less were excluded from headcount employment, virtually all working students would automatically be excluded, along with other marginal workers. The inclusion of student jobs in the employment count is at the very least confusing, given that students themselves are normally excluded from the definition of the workforce, and potentially seriously misleading. There is a case for counting marginal jobs, but not for treating them as equivalent to a 'proper job' which might potentially be of interest to an unemployed school-leaver or a prime-age man who is a primary breadwinner and cannot understand why he remains unemployed while married women and students readily find jobs. There is no overlap between the labour market of 'proper' jobs for primary earners and the labour market of marginal jobs taken exclusively by secondary earners with another main status, including students.

Working Students

TABLE 6.14. *Cross-national comparisons of working students, 1984 and 1994*

	Percentage of the employed who are also attending school at:			
	age 18		age 22	
	1984	1994	1984	1994
Men				
Australia	41.7	43.9	14.9	18.0
Belgium	7.1	11.5	4.9	3.8
Canada	46.1	68.1	14.0	22.8
Denmark	23.9	50.8	6.4	15.9
France	1.9	15.6	1.9	9.4
Germany	5.8	12.0	2.0	5.8
Greece	5.8	5.1	2.0	2.7
Ireland	5.9	10.8	3.5	3.7
Italy	2.1	2.6	2.4	3.0
Luxembourg	0.9	5.6	1.6	1.4
Netherlands	23.7	55.1	13.7	25.6
Portugal	10.2	16.6	7.9	10.2
Spain	2.0	11.3	0.6	6.6
United Kingdom	14.6	21.9	6.6	7.9
United States	43.8	46.3	9.2	12.0
OECD unweighted average	15.7	25.1	6.1	9.9
Women				
Australia	21.8	51.8	12.8	22.1
Belgium	3.2	6.7	2.5	2.7
Canada	47.1	72.1	14.6	27.9
Denmark	32.5	63.5	9.6	15.6
France	5.7	27.6	3.8	16.2
Germany	7.3	15.4	2.3	5.9
Greece	2.1	8.5	4.4	3.6
Ireland	6.9	23.3	2.3	3.7
Italy	2.5	2.3	2.1	3.5
Luxembourg	3.1	4.2	0.0	3.2
Netherlands	18.8	65.7	10.3	16.5
Portugal	4.0	15.8	8.0	16.4
Spain	0.5	17.8	0.9	12.3
United Kingdom	18.1	33.0	3.2	7.8
United States	42.9	45.6	7.3	13.2
OECD unweighted average	14.4	30.2	5.6	11.4

Notes: In this analysis attending school excludes apprenticeships which combine education with on-the-job training while in full-time employment.

Source: Extracted from table 4.10 in OECD (1996: 132) reporting analyses of LFS, CPS, and other sources. Data for Ireland refer to 1984 and 1993. Data for the Netherlands refer to 1983 and 1994. Data for Portugal and Spain refer to 1986 and 1994.

Grouping the two together in headcount employment statistics is becoming increasingly misleading as the marginal workforce grows in size.[6] Different statistical treatment of the mainly seasonal and part-time work of students also distorts cross-national comparisons, especially for young people aged 15–25 years (Bosch *et al.*, 1994: 23).

Another inescapable conclusion is that we need to devise better conceptual frameworks for the analysis of multiple activities and statuses, especially when these activities may all be of equal weight, or part-time, so that none dominates the others. The 1991 Census report on *Economic Activity* effectively sidestepped the issue by only reporting people's primary economic activity. The present analysis demonstrates the wealth of information which remains to be exploited in the SARs. With the economic activity question redesigned to encourage greater use of multiple response in the 2001 Census (see Chapter 4), the value of the information will increase. However, analyses of the data will require innovation and imagination, breaking away from the rigidities and standardized reporting formats that have so far constrained employment statistics.

[6] The focus here is on marginal jobs taken by students, but the same issues arise at the other end of employment histories. The trend towards early retirement from age 50 onwards, funded by employers' occupational pensions, has increased the number of marginal jobs taken by older people who regard themselves as essentially retired. This means that hugely different statistics on retirement can be produced for people aged 55–69, depending on whether retirement is self-defined or whether the ILO rule is applied to classify anyone doing one hour's work a week as part of the workforce (Bone *et al.*, 1992: 20–40). For example, among men aged 55–59 years, 21% regarded themselves as retired, but only 3% would be classified as retired in the LFS.

7

Homework and Travel to Work Patterns

When the results of the 1981 National Survey of Homeworking were published (Hakim, 1984, 1985, 1987*b*, 1988*a*), they aroused controversy because they revealed a picture of homeworking very different from the one being offered at the time by local and national pressure groups (Rubery, 1989: 52; Phizacklea and Wolkowitz, 1995: 31–2). There was feminist and left-wing political resistance to the conclusions that many homeworkers were men; that most women homeworkers did not have young children at home; that white-collar jobs greatly outnumbered low-paid manufacturing homework jobs; that rates of pay and earnings varied a great deal rather than homework being universally poorly paid work; that the majority of homeworkers seemed to be self-employed and often worked for a variety of employers rather than being clear-cut cases of dependent labour working for a single employer on a continuous basis; that most homeworkers were satisfied with their jobs; and that homeworkers had negative views of trade unions, seeing them as organizations that served the interests of well-paid male workers, with little or no interest in the problems of low-paid female workers, especially if they worked part-time and on an intermittent basis at home. All these results were questioned, doubted, and rejected, by trade unions, pressure groups, and academics sympathetic to them, on the basis of local studies which necessarily had small and unrepresentative samples and concluded that homeworkers were women, forced to work at home by childcare responsibilities and hence exploited by unscrupulous employers (Allen and Wolkowitz, 1987; Huws, 1994; Phizacklea and Wolkowitz, 1995). However, all studies of homeworking undertaken since the 1981 National Homeworking Survey have in fact confirmed the results of that first nationally representative survey of homeworkers (Huws, 1994; Granger, Stanworth, and Stanworth, 1995; Phizacklea and Wolkowitz, 1995; Felstead, 1996; Felstead, Jewson, and Goodwin, 1996; Felstead and Jewson, 1997; Stanworth and Stanworth, 1995, 1997), even those explicitly designed to overturn those findings (Phizacklea and Wolkowitz, 1995; Felstead, 1996). Furthermore, cross-national comparative studies and research in other countries have generally produced broadly similar pictures of manufacturing and white-collar homework towards the end of the twentieth century (Hartmann, Kraut, and Tilly, 1986: 144–7; Morokvasic *et al.*, 1986; Varesi and Villa, 1986; Applebaum, 1987; Boris and Daniels, 1989; Rodgers and Rodgers,

1989; Schneider de Villegas, 1990; Lui, 1994; Meulders, Plasman, and Plasman, 1994; European Commission, 1995c, 1995d, 1995e).

At the beginning of this century, most jobs in the labour market, and hence also most homeworking jobs, were in the manufacturing industries and in blue-collar occupations. The composition of the workforce then changed radically over the century (Routh, 1965, 1987) so that by the late 1990s half of all jobs were in white-collar occupations and most jobs were in the service sector. These changes occurred also in the homeworking labour force, but the change remained hidden until pressure group activities in the 1970s created a resurgence of political and media interest in a type of work that was widely believed to have become virtually extinct. Subsequently, the impact of information technology on work organization, the growth of telecommunications, and political concern at the environmental impact of the growth in commuting and car usage led to positive interest in homework, telework, and flexiplace work as technically feasible and socially advantageous complements to, or even substitutes for, office-based work (Shamir and Salomon, 1985; Di Martino and Wirth, 1990; European Commission, 1995c, 1995d, 1995e). There are now a host of new reasons for monitoring the size of the homework labour force and its characteristics in the 21st century. Homework today is agreed to be an innovation, recreated in fundamentally new forms, rather than a throwback to nineteenth-century small-scale manufacturing production units. It is also agreed that homework has wider implications for the future shape of work and employment relationships, for the meshing of employment and family lives, and even for the globalization of work and enterprises (Schneider de Villegas, 1990). Improvements in telecommunications permit many white-collar jobs to be relocated almost anywhere in the world and to a lesser extent homework facilitates the spatial relocation of work away from urban centres. Despite these new developments, homeworkers remain a tiny minority in the labour market in all industrial economies, and they are sufficiently geographically dispersed to pose difficulties for research.

This chapter presents the first update of the 1981 National Survey of Homeworking, presenting equivalent nationally representative statistics on homeworking—this time using the 1991 Census SARs in place of the special interview survey linked to the 1981 Labour Force Survey. From 1992 the LFS has periodically included questions designed to identify homeworkers and home-based workers. Although no special additional information is collected in these LFS surveys, the standard LFS data on the workforce is thus available also for the minority group of homeworkers. Our analyses of the census SARs are thus complemented by LFS statistics on homeworkers in the mid-1990s (Tables 7.1 and 7.2).

One advantage of the SARs data is that it allows us to set homeworking in the wider context of travel to work patterns, because homework was identified within questions on the daily journey to the place of work and the means of transport used for the longest part, by distance, of the daily journey to work. Distance between the home and the workplace was office-coded, on the basis of responses to questions in the census which included tick-boxes for people who worked mainly at home and for people working from a home base with no fixed place of work (such as salesmen). Similarly, there was a tick-box identifying homeworkers in the question on transport to work. The census questions thus differ substantially from the question used in the LFS to identify homeworkers, which has separate tick-boxes for people working *at* home and people working *from* home as a base (Table 7.1). One advantage of the LFS data is that family workers are also identified, so the overlap between these groups can be shown (Tables 7.1 and 7.2). And of course the LFS is carried out on a continuous basis, so that trends can be monitored.

However, the ultimate advantage of the SARs data over the LFS is in providing a far larger sample, permitting more detailed analysis and far more reliable national estimates than the LFS. This fact is invariably hidden by the practice of presenting LFS statistics grossed up to national estimates, as shown in Tables 7.1 and 7.2. Even academics who analyse LFS microdata have concealed the small size of the LFS sample by refusing to quote base numbers for any of their analyses (Felstead, 1996). In practice, the LFS sample provides well under 1000 cases of homeworkers in any one quarter, compared to 21,000 cases in the 2% SAR raw data and 15,000 homeworker cases in the edited data.

EDITING THE CENSUS DATA ON HOMEWORKERS

The 'raw' census data on homework is invalid and has to be edited before analysis can proceed. Some 5% of all persons in employment, 5% of men and 5% of women, ticked the 'mainly at home' box when answering the census questions on travel to work. Published 10% sample statistics (Table 7.3) and unpublished small area statistics both present unedited census statistics on people working 'at home' and analyses based on them are unfortunately incorrect, despite being commissioned and published by the Department of Employment (Felstead and Jewson, 1995; Felstead, Jewson, and Goodwin, 1996: 13–19).

Analysis of the 2% SAR showed that two groups of people ticked the 'mainly at home' boxes: people who work at home and people who live at their workplace. The latter group includes farmers whose home is on the farm, people running pubs and shops who live in flats attached to the enterprise, and live-in occupations in communal establishments. People who live in accommodation that is supplied with, or attached to, their job are in a fun-

TABLE 7.1. *Homeworkers and home-based workers, 1995*

thousands

	All	Men	Women
Homeworkers			
Employees and self-employed			
working in own home (main job)	631	213	418
Full-time	312	160	152
Part-time	317	53	265
Whom they work for:			
an outside organization	112	35	76
on their own account	353	149	205
a family business	165	29	136
Managers and administrators	158	72	87
Professionals	82	51	32
Associate professional/technical	101	49	54
Clerical & secretarial	114	*	108
All other occupations	177	40	138
Unpaid family workers working in			
their own home	56	~	47
Home-based workers			
People doing paid work in different			
places using home as a base			
(main job)	1731	1368	364
Full-time	1295	1157	137
Part-time	303	126	177
Second jobs total	342	171	172
Working at home	180	67	114
Working from home as a base	162	104	58
Homeworkers as % of all main jobs	3%	2%	4%
Home-based workers as % of all main			
jobs	6%	9%	3%
Base—all employees and self-			
employed:			
main jobs	24944	13812	11132
second jobs	1261	530	731

Note: ~ National estimates below 10,000, which are typically based on less than 30 unweighted cases.

Source: Labour Force Survey, Great Britain, spring 1995 not seasonally adjusted, as reported in *Employment Gazette*.

damentally different situation from people who provide their own housing and then engage in gainful work in or from their own home. The two groups have to be separated in order to get a clear picture of the social and economic circumstances of homeworkers as distinct from tied housing. (See Annex A for further details.) The problem arises with interview surveys as well as the

Homework and Travel to Work

TABLE 7.2. *Homeworkers and family workers, 1995 and 1996*

	Homeworkers			Family workers		
	as % of employment	1996	1995	as % of employment	1996	1995
		thousands			thousands	
Men aged 161	..	..	..	..	..	..
Men aged 16–64	1.3	177	190	0.2	28	30
Women aged 161	4.2	486	465	0.7	82	93
Women aged 16–59	3.8	424	404	0.6	66	76
of whom:						
with dependent child(ren)	6.1	241	238	0.9	36	44
aged 0–4 years	7.5	107	98	1.1	16	19
aged 5–10	5.9	82	90	0.8	11	15
aged 11–15	4.6	52	50	~	*	10
no dependent child , 16 (may include dependent child(ren) aged 16–18 in full-time education)	2.6	183	166	0.4	30	32
All persons 16–59/64	2.4	601	594	0.4	94	106
All persons 161 (estimate)	2.6	670	670	0.5	120	130

Source: Labour Force Survey, Great Britain, spring 1995 and 1996, not seasonally adjusted, as reported in *LFS Quarterly Bulletin*.

census (Hakim, 1987*b*: 8, 18, 22–3, 253–4) and thus affects the LFS statistics as well.

After people living at their workplace were reclassified as having live-in jobs rather than being homeworkers, the edited census data shows only 3% of the workforce (3% of men and 4% of women) to be homeworkers in 1991 (Table 7.4). As found also in the 1981 National Homeworking Survey, people working in different places using their home as a base outnumber homeworkers by two to one, and most people working from a home base are men. The census labels these workers as having 'no fixed place' of work—as illustrated by plumbers who carry out repairs in customers' homes. This group was identified by a separate tick-box in the census travel to work questions, as they did travel to work but not to any fixed place. The edited SAR data produces a fourfold classification, with the largest group being ordinary workers who do their jobs on-site at a separate workplace (Table 7.4).

It is notable that in 1991 women constituted just half of homeworkers (Table 7.4), compared with 71% in the 1981 survey. It appears that men have been taking up homework at a faster rate than women, prompted in part by repeated recessions, large-scale redundancies, and early retirement schemes in the 1980s and 1990s.

TABLE 7.3. *Homework in the context of travel to work patterns*

	Total in employment	Works mainly at home		Walks to work		Workplace is ≤ 2 km from home					Home-based, but no fixed workplace[1]	
						walks to work	other transport	total				
		N	%	N	%			N	%		N	%
All persons	23,452,230	1,146,890	5	2,769,990	12	2,284,730	3,057,600	5,342,330	23		1,453,980	6
Men	13,125,010	631,550	5	1,032,020	8	788,800	1,430,160	2,218,960	17		1,173,620	9
Women	10,327,220	515,340	5	1,737,970	17	1,495,930	1,627,440	3,123,370	30		280,360	3
of whom, working:												
31+ hours	5,886,200	243,670	4	693,010	12	610,910	816,910	1,427,820	24		89,200	2
16–30 hours	2,561,980	105,460	4	538,220	21	457,100	480,010	937,110	37		92,610	4
1–15 hours	1,586,340	122,330	8	473,740	30	402,570	297,820	700,390	44		75,880	5
not stated	292,700	43,880	15	33,000	11	25,350	32,700	58,050	20		22,670	8

[1] A few of this group may also walk to work.

Source: Tables 1 and 7 in *1991 Census-Workplace and Transport to Work* (1994) reporting 10% sample data for Great Britain, employees and the self-employed aged 16 and over in employment.

TABLE 7.4. *Revised national estimates for homework*

	All		Men		Women		Women as % of all
	N	%	N	%	N	%	
Homework (working at home)	15,407	3	7,675	3	7,732	4	50
Working from home (no fixed place)	28,404	6	22,980	9	5,424	3	19
Live-in jobs (live at workplace)	6,377	2	4,226	2	2,151	1	34
On-site jobs in separate workplace	410,776	89	223,332	86	187,444	92	46
All in employment	460,964	100	258,213	100	202,751	100	44

Source: 2% SAR, Great Britain, data for people aged 16–64 years in employment, excluding student jobs.
Numbers should be multiplied by 50 to obtain national estimates.

TRENDS IN HOMEWORK AND HOME-BASED WORK

The separation of home and work imposed by the Industrial Revolution and the creation of large manufacturing establishments is slowly being reversed as a result of the information technology revolution, and as the service sector replaces manufacturing as the main source of employment in many Western industrial economies. Information technology allows white-collar jobs to be done at home, or almost anywhere, and the telephone network begins to replace public transport systems and the car as a means of getting the work and the worker together.

Manufacturing homework has survived, and may even have increased temporarily in the 1990s, due to the general trend towards subcontracting (Boris and Daniels, 1989; Hakim, 1990*b*) but it is clear that white-collar homework is now the dominant form. From the 1970s onwards, but particularly after the 1980s when personal computers, laptops, and portable telephones revolutionized homework, traditional manufacturing homework became overshadowed by white-collar homework: professional, technical, artistic, administrative, and clerical work carried out as a personal or family business or undertaken for employers on diverse contractual terms. A major research programme on homework in Britain carried out by what was then the Department of Employment (now part of the Department for Education and Employment) documented these developments and their social, economic, employment law, and policy implications (Cragg and Dawson, 1981; Hakim and Dennis, 1982; Leighton, 1983; Huws, 1984; Kay, 1984; Hakim, 1984, 1985, 1987*b*, 1988*a*). In the 1990s there has been much speculation about future trends, with some commentators predicting that half the workforce in Britain could be working at or from home at least some of the time by the beginning of the 21st century. However, it is difficult to measure the extent of homeworking and to monitor trends at the national level, even if we restrict our attention to people who work exclusively or mainly at home and ignore the very much larger number who do so occasionally or at certain times of the year (such as IT specialists, schoolteachers, and academics). The censuses, LFS, and special surveys all show clear evidence of an increase in homework, but a slower increase than some commentators claim. There is a great deal of change and innovation in this area, with innovation often assumed to imply growth.

Surveys of homework invariably reveal large overlaps between work done in or from home, self-employment, work in a family business, second jobs, part-time work, 'live at work' arrangements, temporary jobs, and intermittent work, leading to some confusion in the literature over numbers in each category and over which groups should be included or excluded from counts. Only a specially designed personal interview survey can attempt to separate out all these overlapping aspects, and homework has so far remained far too small a labour force minority to justify more than occasional national studies. As a result most studies are small and local, so that results are distorted by the enormous diversity and local variation within the sector (Allen and Wolkowitz, 1987; Felstead, Jewson, and Goodwin, 1996). Cross-national comparisons remain a hit-and-miss affair (Meulders *et al.*, 1994: 147–59). Population censuses and the LFS can only include very simple questions, so the chances of people being misclassified, incorrectly included, or incorrectly excluded are much greater than in special surveys. None the less, the best measure of change over time in Britain comes from the census, due to the consistency of question-wording and data processing procedures in 1981 and 1991.

The 1981 Census included questions on workplace address and transport to work very similar to the 1991 Census questions. The 1981 Census identified a total of 2.2 million people in England and Wales whose home and workplace were linked, consisting of 777,000 people who ticked the 'mainly at home' box and another 1,431,000 people who ticked the 'no fixed place' box in response to questions about the journey to work (Hakim, 1987*b*: 22–3). Further analysis showed that many people who 'live at work' had classified themselves as working 'mainly at home'. They should have said they walked to work (to adjacent premises), even if the distance was measured in metres rather than kilometres. For example 70,000 people living and working in hotels and other residential establishments and 150,000 people who held their residential accommodation by virtue of their employment or with a job, shop, farm, or other business ticked the 'mainly at home' box. Thus at least 220,000 or 29% of the people who ticked the 'mainly at home' box had 'live-in' jobs and it is possible that there were also others less easily identified (Hakim, 1987*b*: 22–3). If 'live-in' jobs are excluded, the 1981 Census identified some 560,000 people working 'mainly at home' and 1.4 million people with 'no fixed workplace', a total of just under 2 million workers in England and Wales whose work was linked to their home. Uprating the figures by 10% to include Scotland, there were 2.2 million such workers in 1981, 616,000 homeworkers and 1.54 million working from home as a base.

The 1991 Census 10% sample statistics for Great Britain identified 2.6 million workers whose work was linked to their home: 1.147 million who ticked the 'mainly at home' box and 1.454 million people working from home with no fixed workplace (Table 7.3). Analysis of the SARs shows that at least 29% of the 1991 Census figure for homeworkers again consists of 'live-in' jobs. Thus of the 1.147 million reporting they worked 'at home', 71% or 814,000 would be homeworkers, a clear increase of 200,000 on our equivalent 1981 Census estimate of 616,000 homeworkers in Great Britain. Thus over the decade 1981–91, there was a 32% increase in the number of people working 'mainly at home', but little or no change in the numbers working from home as a base.

The LFS yields virtually identical figures on homework and home-based work in spring 1994, 1995, and 1996. The stability of the figures seems to invalidate the popular idea of substantial under-reporting in particular groups (such as ethnic minorities), which should cause more variation in annual figures. More important, the LFS national estimates for the mid-1990s are very close indeed to the edited 1991 Census figures, suggesting that there were no further increases in homework in the 1990s. This means that the 2% SAR results are not in fact dated and provide an adequate picture of homeworking at the end of the twentieth century.

The 1995 LFS gives a national estimate of 2.3 million workers working at or from home: 630,000 working mainly at home, 56,000 family workers working mainly at home, and 1.6 million working from home as a base. In both the edited 1991 Census statistics and the 1995 LFS estimates, homeworkers constitute 3% of the workforce and people working from home constitute 6% of the workforce. LFS data for the mid-1990s suggests that manufacturing homework did increase, from 60,000 homeworkers in 1981 (Hakim, 1987*b*: table 3.1) to 85,000 homeworkers in 1994 (Hakim, 1996*a*: table 2.5). But virtually all the increase in numbers was in non-manufacturing homework, in white-collar work, and in self-employment. Four-fifths of homeworkers now work on their own account or for a family business (Table 7.1), which explains the high proportion of 'managers' among homeworkers. These results are entirely consistent with the SAR analyses presented below.

If 1991 Census statistics are compared with national estimates from the 1981 National Homeworking Survey, the growth in homework is very much larger than when 1981–91 Census statistics are compared. The 1981 special survey identified 1.7 million people whose home and workplace were linked in some way or 7% of the 1981 workforce in England and Wales (Hakim, 1987*b*: 19, 1988*a*: 613). Of these, 260,000 (1% nationally) worked mainly or solely *at* home; 710,000 (3% nationally) worked *from* home as a base; and 738,000 (3% nationally) lived at their workplace. On this account, the number of homeworkers, and of people using their home as a base, more than doubled between 1981 and 1991. However, there are real problems of comparability between these two data sources, especially as regards the classification of live-in jobs.

NATIONAL TRAVEL TO WORK PATTERNS

Until recently, homework was presented as a forced choice, poorly paid work taken mainly by women obliged to stay at home with their young children. The 1991 Census allows us to place homeworking in the context of travel to work patterns, which show clearly that women generally work closer to home than do men, and that this is closely associated with women's preference for part-time jobs (Table 7.3).

As working hours decline, the proportion of women walking to work increases steadily, from 12% among full-timers to 21% among half-timers and then to 30% among people in marginal jobs. The proportion working less than 2 km from home similarly rises from 24% for full-timers to 37% among half-timers and then to 44% for women in marginal jobs (Table 7.3). The association is indisputable. There is a large overlap between the group that walks to work and those with a workplace within 2 km of their home: 76% of men and 86% of women who walk to work are going to a workplace that is very local. Nationally, one-quarter of the workforce works locally in the sense that they walk to work and/or have a workplace no more than 2 km from home. However, women are almost twice as likely as men to work locally: 33% compared to 19% of men walk to work and/or have a workplace that is very local. Even women with full-time jobs are more likely than men to work locally: 26% compared to 19%. However, working locally is closely associated with part-time jobs: 40% of women working 16–30 hours a week and 49% of women working less than 16 hours a week have local jobs. This is not surprising, in a way. However, it has never been noticed before that a key feature of about half of all part-time jobs is that they are also *local neighbourhood jobs*, sufficiently close to residential areas to enable people to walk to work and/or travel less than 2km from home. Similarly, a study based on the USA 1960 Census PUS showed that occupations with a high proportion of part-time workers also had a high proportion of women walking to work—the classic examples being salesworkers, hairdressers, and waitresses (Darian, 1975: 256).

Given that most wives are secondary earners, contributing less than 30%

of household income, increasing journey times significantly reduce a wife's decision to continue working (Andrews, 1978). If they work short hours, women are even less likely to invest in the time, energy, and cost of a long journey to work. The effect is to restrict them to the type of job available in local neighbourhoods. It seems likely that it is the preference for *local* jobs as well as for *part-time* jobs that leads women to be heavily concentrated in relatively low-paying sales assistant jobs, in the shops and supermarkets close to residential neighbourhoods and suburban areas. Women will be concentrated in small workplaces for the same reason. In other words, the tendency for women in part-time jobs to have lower hourly earnings than women in full-time jobs (see Chapters 3 and 5), which is usually presented by the EOC and others as indicating sex discrimination by employers, may actually be the result of job preferences which restrict choices to such a narrow local labour market that sales assistant jobs and clerical jobs are the only ones available in large numbers, even if they underutilize a woman's qualifications and work experience. The greatest variety of jobs, and the highest paid jobs, are in urban centres and thus require a longer journey to work.

The SARs provide two indicators of the nature of jobs available in local labour markets as compared with jobs available in larger and more distant labour markets: the average Cambridge status score (which is available for all jobs, both employee and self-employed) and average hourly earnings in employee jobs (Table 7.5). The Cambridge scores show that local jobs tend to be lower grade and lower status than jobs requiring longer journeys to work. Local jobs are also concentrated lower down the earnings distribution. Employee jobs available in wider labour markets pay on average 27% more than the employee jobs available in local labour markets. In part this is due to a different mix of full-time and part-time jobs being available locally and in wider labour markets. Using the definition of part-time work developed in Chapter 5 as jobs with less than 30 hours a week, 29% of jobs in local labour markets are part-time jobs compared to only 12% of jobs in wider labour markets. But only 2% of men work part-time, whether in local or wider labour markets. So the difference is, in practice, a feature of the female workforce only: half (47%) of jobs held by women in local labour markets are part-time jobs compared to one-quarter (28%) of jobs held by women in wider labour markets. It seems appropriate to compare earnings in full-time and part-time jobs separately for local and wider labour markets in Tables 7.5 and 7.6.

Tables 7.5 and 7.6 show that transferring from a wider labour market to a local labour market entails an average fall in earnings of 21% for employees, with little or no difference between men and women, between full-time and part-time workers. If anything, it is men rather than women who lose most from such a transfer. Changing from a full-time to a part-time job has a similar impact, a fall of 11% for the tiny minority of men who make this change and a 23% fall in earnings for women. But the falls are always larger in local

TABLE 7.5. *The limitations of local labour markets*

	Part-time jobs held by			Full-time jobs held by			All current jobs held by		
	Women	Men	All	Women	Men	All	Women	Men	All
Local jobs , 2 km from home (excluding homework jobs)									
mean Cambridge status score	28	28	28	35	28	32	32	28	31
mean hourly earnings (pence)	412	549	417	537	661	605	477	657	548
Jobs involving travel over 2 km from home									
mean Cambridge status score	34	36	35	41	34	37	39	34	37
mean hourly earnings (pence)	485	731	502	610	783	723	576	781	695
All jobs									
mean Cambridge status score	32	33	32	39	32	35	36	32	34
mean hourly earnings (pence)	449	671	463	586	750	690	536	748	648

Source: 2% SAR, Great Britain, data for residents aged 16–64 years in employment, excluding student jobs.

TABLE 7.6. *Average fall in employee earnings produced by specified job changes*

	A. Change from wider labour market to a local labour market (excluding homework jobs)			B. Change from a full-time job to a part-time job		
	PT jobs	FT jobs	All jobs	Local jobs	Other jobs	All jobs
Women	–15%	–12%	–17%	–23%	–20%	–23%
Men	–25%	–16%	–19%	–17%	–7%	–11%
All	–17%	–16%	–21%	–31%	–31%	–33%

Source: Table 7.5.

labour markets than in wider labour markets. The analysis in Table 7.5 is not concerned with a worker's individual earnings potential. It describes the array of jobs available in practice in different labour markets, to show that, independently of the earnings forgone by choosing a part-time job instead of a full-time job, workers who also restrict themselves to a local neighbourhood job will experience a substantial additional drop in earnings, as noted also by Sloane (1994: 178, 197).

Travel to work patterns are rarely included in analyses of the determinants of earnings and the wage gap. Even when the information is included, regression analyses tend to assign relatively low importance to this factor (even if statistically significant) because they show results after controls for other factors or 'all other things being equal'. But other things are *not* equal in the real world and regression analyses can produce misleading results. As Lieberson (1985: 83) points out, the *ceteris paribus* situation may never occur in reality. In practice, the choice of a local job as well as part-time hours entails some restriction in the choice of occupation. In the real world, all possible combinations of occupation, work hours, and location are not available to every individual, no matter where they live, and certain choices lead inexorably to others in a causal sequence that is never incorporated in regression analyses of earnings.

One example is an analysis of wage differentials at age 33 in the British 1958 cohort study, the NCDS, which showed that full-time women and men had roughly the same average daily journey to work, in minutes, while women working part-time had significantly shorter journeys, of 15 minutes instead of half an hour for full-timers. Journey time was identified as a statistically significant correlate of earnings, but 'all other things equal' it had a relatively small impact on earnings (Paci and Joshi, 1996: 56). Our analysis in Tables 7.5 and 7.6 shows that, in reality, choosing to work locally has a significant impact on the range of jobs available and therefore on earnings.

Homeworking can now be seen as an extreme version of the general tendency for women to work closer to home. This perspective explains why it is attractive to many women who do not have young children at home, and is generally more attractive to women than men. This perspective also explains the huge sex differential in working from home as a base with no fixed workplace: men are three times more likely to do this than are women, and on this point there is complete agreement between the census (Tables 7.3 and 7.4) and the LFS (Table 7.1).

Research in the USA has also found that women's work trips are shorter than men's, whether measured in time or physical distance, and that work trips vary with work hours, occupational grade, and earnings. Married women in particular select jobs closer to home because their shorter work hours reduce the earnings return to commuting and because their domestic activities increase the cost of longer commutes. Average job tenure among wives has been found to be half that for spouses, implying turnover rates double that for spouses. However, women are more likely to stay in jobs closer to home; shorter work trips are associated with longer job tenures, with the effect strongest for women (Madden, 1981).

The sex differential in daily commuting to work patterns is great enough to produce gender-specific local labour markets in Britain. Travel To Work Areas (TTWAs) defined on the basis of total commuting flows for women are generally much smaller and more numerous than equivalent TTWAs defined from data for men. Disparities between male and female TTWAs are greatest in the most urbanized regions, where 40 female TTWAs can be identified in areas with only 8 male TTWAs (Green *et al.*, 1986). What this means is that a single labour market identified by men's commuting patterns divides into five separate smaller female labour markets when we look at women's travel to work patterns instead—a drastic narrowing of job options.

National Travel Survey (NTS) data for 1965 to 1993 (Department of Transport, 1988, 1993, 1995) show that the sex differential in commuting trips remained constant in the second half of the twentieth century despite the increase in women's employment, probably because rising economic activity rates were due primarily to the substitution of part-time jobs for full-time jobs among women (Hakim, 1993*a*, 1996*a*: 60–5). Commuting trips between home and work have been getting longer over time, increasing by about 50% between 1972 and 1991, but the sex differential has remained constant in the population of working age. Average journey distances for men working full-time are 40% higher than for women working full-time, and average journey distances travelled by women with full-time jobs are 60% higher than among women working part-time. These differentials persisted at least until 1986, after which the NTS stopped reporting full analyses of commuting patterns. However, recent NTS results confirm that substantial sex differentials in commuting and other travel persisted across all age groups well into the mid-1990s. It might be thought that the sex differential in journey length, and the larger differential between women working full-time and women working part-time could be due to their occupations or the occupational composition of the three groups. In fact both differentials persist across all grades of occupation. So the occupational composition of the three groups is not the explanation. Finally, there are even larger sex differentials in work-related travel undertaken in addition to daily commuting to work journeys.

It is interesting that the marked and persistent differences between men and women working full-time, and between full-time women and part-time women, in travel to work patterns have been lost from sight in recent research on the sex differential in earnings and occupational attainment, along with other factors that have an important impact on earnings in the long run, such as risk-taking behaviour (Chauvin and Ash, 1994). Human capital theory focuses our attention on the personal characteristics and work experience of employees. Social structural and institutional explanations for the pay gap focus our attention on sex discrimination and the characteristics of industries and employers (Gregory and Thomson, 1990; Sloane, 1990; Blau and Ferber, 1992). In between this dual focus on workers and employers, we have lost sight of all the other intermediary factors that play an important part in matching people to jobs in specific labour markets. Social science theory can prove just as blinding as common-sense thinking.

KEY FEATURES OF HOMEWORK

The growth in homework has not substantively changed the profiles of home-workers and of people working from home as a base, other than to further

Homework and Travel to Work

reduce the relative importance of manufacturing homework (Tables 7.7 to 7.10). The long-term increase in numbers of white-collar homeworkers means that the relatively constant numbers of manufacturing homeworkers are steadily dwarfed and reduced in importance. In 1981 one-quarter of homework jobs were in blue-collar occupations (Hakim, 1987*b*). By 1991

TABLE 7.7. *Job grade and earnings of homeworkers*

	At home	Home-based	Live in	Separate workplace
Socio-Economic Group (column percent)				
employers and managers—large establishments	*	*	1	6
employers—small establishments	15	7	10	2
managers—small establishments	8	5	12	8
professionals—self-employed	4	2	1	1
professionals—employees	1	1	4	4
ancillary workers & artists	14	9	5	13
supervisors—white-collar	*	*	*	1
junior white-collar	12	6	2	23
personal service	3	1	6	5
foremen—blue-collar	*	1	*	2
skilled blue-collar	2	9	*	14
semi-skilled blue-collar	2	5	3	12
unskilled blue collar	1	5	1	5
own-account workers (not professionals)	37	48	5	3
farmers—owners/managers	—	*	39	*
agricultural workers	—	1	11	1
Mean Cambridge scores (employees and self-employed)				
All in work	all	40	28	39	34
	men	38	26	40	33
	women	41	38	37	37
Full-time workers	all	39	27	39	35
	men	38	26	40	33
	women	40	40	37	39
Part-time workers	all	41	34	32	32
	men	41	32	36	33
	women	41	35	32	31
Mean hourly earnings for employees (pence)				
All in work	all	646	663	572	648
	men	880	705	627	749
	women	537	577	500	535
Full-time employees	all	760	693	589	690
(301 hours a week)	men	888	703	627	752
	women	599	635	522	586
Part-time employees	all	528	566	441	457
(, 30 hours a week)	men	835	758	541	658
	women	506	538	424	444

Sources: 2% SAR, Great Britain, data for residents aged 16–64 years in employment, excluding student jobs and the Armed Forces.

only 5% of homeworkers were in blue-collar jobs compared to one-third of the on-site workforce (Table 7.7). The 1994 LFS showed only 13% of all homeworkers to be working for manufacturing industries (Hakim, 1996*a*: table 2.5).

The minority status of blue-collar homework was a key finding of the 1981 National Homeworking Survey and the result most frequently challenged. It was argued that if a suitably narrow policy-oriented definition of homework were adopted, manufacturing homework would emerge as the dominant form, thus placing centre stage the problems of low-paid manual jobs and the attached health and safety risks. In reality, such a definition identified only 100,000 homeworkers in 1981, of whom less than half were engaged in manufacturing homework (Hakim, 1987*b*: 41). A more recent attempt to demonstrate the large size of the homework workforce vulnerable to exploitation by employers claims to have obtained a national estimate of 250,000 homeworkers from the 1994 LFS on the same definition, but only one-quarter were employed by manufacturing businesses (Felstead, 1996: 233–5). Furthermore, the estimate of 250,000 homeworkers is clearly not based on the same definition and is extremely dubious since it is double the size of the 1994 LFS estimate of 120,000 homeworkers 'employed by an outside organization', hence employees, rather than 'working on their own account', hence self-employed (Hakim, 1996*a*: table 2.5). Even the most determined advocacy research activists are finally admitting that homework is dominated by white-collar occupations: professional and technical jobs, clerical and secretarial jobs, and a huge variety of service sector jobs (Phizacklea and Wolkowitz, 1995: 95, 125–7; Felstead, 1996: 233). People doing childcare work, including childminders, constitute 5% of all homeworkers in 1991, between 40,000 and 45,000 in Britain, a substantial increase on the national estimate of 28,000 in England and Wales in 1981. People in a variety of clerical and secretarial occupations outnumber people in textiles and garment-making by a factor of five to one. There are no typical or representative homeworking occupations.

It is thus not surprising that people doing homework are equally or more highly qualified than the average on-site worker, and are doing higher status jobs which normally attract equal or higher earnings than the average on-site employee job (Table 7.7 and 7.8a). Another myth disposed of by the SARs is the idea that female-dominated occupations provide the majority of homework jobs, rendering female homeworkers vulnerable to exploitation due to overcrowding in these occupations or to the low value placed on women's work. In fact it is integrated occupations that provide the largest single category of homework jobs: 42% compared to 22% of on-site jobs (Table 7.8a), in part because so many homeworkers describe themselves as proprietors and managers of their own business. Overall, the homework workforce is the most integrated of the four groups identified in Table 7.8a.

TABLE 7.8a. *Job characteristics of homeworkers*   column percent

		At home	Home-based	Live in	Separate workplace
Higher qualifications held					
All	a higher degrees	2	1	1	1
	b first degrees	11	5	5	9
	c below degree level	8	6	7	9
	two or more	8	4	7	4
	none	79	88	87	81
Men	a higher degrees	3	*	1	2
	b first degrees	14	4	6	11
	c below degree level	8	4	5	8
	two or more	10	3	5	8
	none	76	92	88	80
Women	a higher degrees	1	1	1	1
	b first degrees	9	10	4	7
	c below degree level	8	13	9	10
	two or more	6	9	3	6
	none	82	76	87	83
Occupational segregation					
All	male occupations	28	70	53	37
	mixed occupations	42	14	28	22
	female occupations	30	16	19	41
Men	male occupations	46	83	63	61
	mixed occupations	45	11	23	24
	female occupations	9	5	14	15
Women	male occupations	11	15	33	9
	mixed occupations	39	24	38	19
	female occupations	50	61	29	72

Source: 2% and 1% SARs, Great Britain, data for residents aged 16–64 years in employment, excluding student jobs. The table is based on the 2% SAR, except for data on employment status in the main job taken from the 1% SAR. See Annex A for details of the two types of data on self-employment in the SARs.

Beyond this, the usual differences between working men and women emerge among homeworkers. Part-time jobs (especially marginal jobs) are far more common among homeworkers than among on-site workers: 29% compared to 17% (Table 7.8b). However, it is women who do the part-time homework jobs; male homeworkers, and those working from home as a base, almost invariably work full-time hours. Men are much more likely to be self-employed than are women working at home: 79% compared to 55% (Table 7.8b). Indeed, one important finding from this analysis is the large overlap between homework and self-employment. Two-thirds of all homeworkers and almost as many people working from home as a base are self-employed. Over half of the solo self-employed are working at home or from home as a base rather than in separate premises (Table 7.8b, see also Table 8.7).

Table 7.8b. *Job characteristics of homeworkers* (continued)   cell/row/column percent

			At home	Home-based	Live in	Separate workplace
% self-employed (by type) among homeworkers and others						
All	all self-employed		67	61	53	6
	with employees		50	54	29	3
	without employees		17	7	24	3
Men	all self-employed		79	68	59	8
	with employees		21	9	26	4
	without employees		58	59	33	4
Women	all self-employed		55	33	40	3
	with employees		12	2	19	2
	without employees		43	31	21	1
Employees			1	3	1	95
men working	full-time (301 hours)		3	8	2	87
	part-time (, 30 hours)		10	17	1	72
women working	full-time (301 hours)		3	2	1	94
	part-time (, 30 hours)		5	4	*	91
Self-employed			19	31	6	44
men	solo S/E		15	46	5	34
	small firms		12	15	8	65
women	solo S/E		41	21	6	32
	small firms		21	2	10	67
Employment status (main job)						
Managers			9	5	14	13
Foremen			*	1	1	5
Other employees			22	31	24	76
Self-employed with employees			18	7	25	3
Self-employed without employees			51	56	36	3
Usual weekly hours (excluding overtime and meal breaks)						
All	461		28	22	61	9
	37–45		32	54	27	59
	30–36		11	9	4	15
	11–29		17	11	6	14
	up to 10		12	4	2	3
Men	461		39	26	70	15
	37–45		43	62	18	81
	30–36		10	7	10	2
	11–29		6	4	2	2
	up to 10		2	1	*	*
Women	461		18	5	43	3
	37–45		21	22	29	41
	30–36		13	15	9	20
	11–29		28	40	14	29
	up to 10		21	18	5	7

Source: 2% and 1% SARs, Great Britain, data for residents aged 16–64 years in employment, excluding student jobs. The table is based on the 2% SAR, except for data on employment status in the main job taken from the 1% SAR. See Annex A for details of the two types of data on self-employment in the SARs.

Homework and Travel to Work

TABLE 7.9. *Personal characteristics of homeworkers*   row/cell percent

		At home	Home-based	Live in	Separate workplace
Women aged	16–24	1	1	1	97
	25–34	4	2	1	93
	35–44	5	3	1	91
	45–54	5	3	1	91
	55–64	5	3	2	90
	16–64	4	3	1	92
Men aged	16–24	1	7	1	91
	25–34	2	9	1	88
	35–44	3	10	2	85
	45–54	4	10	2	84
	55–64	5	9	3	84
	16–64	3	9	2	86
% non-white	men	6	2	2	4
	women	4	3	3	4
% with 11	men	41	43	38	41
dependent child	women	56	41	38	38
% in homes	men	69	67	72	70
with 21 earners	women	88	79	87	81
% in owner-	men	87	81	41	79
occupied homes	women	89	82	28	79

Source: 2% SAR, Great Britain, data for residents aged 16–64 years in employment, excluding student jobs.

TABLE 7.10. *Ethnic minority homeworkers: national estimates*

	Men		Women	
	Works at home	Home-based	Works at home	Home-based
White	7195	22437	7387	5275
Black Caribbean	27	142	18	54
Black African	16	32	16	11
Black—other	11	33	6	10
Indian	199	164	146	29
Pakistani	56	78	24	6
Bangladeshi	26	7	5	—
Chinese	78	8	66	13
Other—Asian	25	30	35	14
Other—Other	42	49	29	12
Total	7675	22980	7732	5424

Source: 2% SAR, Great Britain, data for residents aged 16–64 years in employment, excluding student jobs. Numbers should be multiplied by 50 to obtain national estimates.

Homework must be understood within the context of self-employment (see Chapter 8) as well as in comparison with ordinary on-site employee jobs.

PERSONAL CHARACTERISTICS OF HOMEWORKERS

The 2% SAR's huge sample of 15,000 homeworkers confirms conclusively two key findings from the 1981 special survey: dependent children are not the primary catalyst for women to take up homeworking and the vast majority of homeworkers (88% compared to 79% of on-site workers) own their own homes (usually with a house purchase loan still being paid off). The financial burden of house purchase is more likely to be the catalyst pushing mothers to take up homework than are young children *per se* (Table 7.9). Admittedly, homeworkers are far more likely to have children under the age of 16 at home than are women working at a separate workplace: 56% compared to 38%. Even so, only half of all female homeworkers do have a child at home and half do not, so this cannot be the decisive factor. It is questionable whether homework is advantageous for mothers of young children, since it is not possible to do paid work efficiently and care for children at the same time. The main advantage of homework is in eliminating the journey to work and in achieving flexibility of working hours. Work can be done in short bursts during the day, in the evenings, or at weekends, and thus be interspersed with domestic activities across the whole week. Unsocial hours are worked because the homeworker chooses to do so rather than because they are a necessary feature of the task being done.

Another important finding is that many homeworkers are now men. Men have always dominated the group working from home as a base, and there has always been a minority of men living in tied accommodation or working at home, occasionally or regularly (Finch, 1983: 53–67). In the 1980s the number of male homeworkers increased sharply, a trend which will change the public stereotype of homeworkers in the long run. Regional variations are not shown in Table 7.9. Region has no effect on the distribution of homework and other jobs except for a reduced percentage of live-in jobs in London, an area where farms are far less common than elsewhere in Britain.

There has been some debate over the importance of homeworking among ethnic minorities and migrant communities, who may seek to conceal their activities if they are working in the informal economy (Morokvasic *et al.*, 1986; Varesi and Villa, 1986; European Commission, 1995*d*, 1995*e*; Phizacklea and Wolkowitz, 1995). The census SARs allow us to provide the first reliable nationally representative statistics on ethnic minority homeworkers (Tables 7.9 and 7.10). The advantage of the census data here is twofold. First, the census is a compulsory data collection with 100% coverage of the population, so there is no possibility of ethnic minority groups being excluded or failing to participate. (As noted in Chapter 6, the census undercount was concentrated among young people and students, who are highly mobile.) Second, the large SAR samples provide a reliable basis for counts of ethnic minority workers, certainly a far more reliable basis than the much smaller LFS samples.

The proportion of non-whites among homeworkers is only very slightly above the national average for the on-site workforce, 5% versus 4% (Table 7.9). This national average will obviously vary across areas, with some cities having high concentrations of ethnic minority homeworkers while others have none at all. But at the overall national level, ethnic minority home-workers remain a tiny minority, just as they are in the population. Among non-white homeworkers, Indians form the largest single group, followed by the Chinese (Table 7.10). People from the Indian subcontinent taken together (India, Pakistan, and Bangladesh) constitute 4% of male homeworkers, 2% of female homeworkers, 1% of men working from home, and 1% of women working from home as a base. Grossing up the 2% SAR figures produces national estimates of 23,000 homeworkers for this group as a whole (14,000 men and 9,000 women). The next largest group is the Chinese, with 7,500 homeworkers (4,000 men and 3,500 women). Even if figures for the Indian group are doubled, to allow for a large degree of under-reporting of home-work by women, ethnic minority groups constitute less than 10% of all home-workers, a small minority by any standards. Even though ethnic minorities are overrepresented among homeworkers, they remain a tiny proportion of the whole workforce.

CONCLUSIONS

Homework and work done from home as a base are growing, though more slowly than some forecasters have predicted. By 1991 homeworkers and people working from home as a base constituted 3% and 6% of the workforce respectively, and these figures remained stable to the end of the 1990s. When compared with the results of the 1981 Census, these figures suggest a one-third increase in homeworking, but no change in the numbers working from home as a base. When compared with the results of the 1981 National Homeworking Survey, the figures suggest much larger increases in home-working, but the two sources are not fully comparable.

A workforce that was shown to be heterogeneous even in 1981 (Hakim, 1987*b*) is becoming increasingly diverse and heterogeneous as it grows in size. Almost without exception, every occupation identified by the 1990 SOC at the level of 73 Major Occupational Groups had at least one homeworker in it. There is no occupation in the labour force that is not carried out at or from home as well. Similarly, homeworkers themselves are a heterogeneous group, displaying just as much diversity in personal and family characteristics as the workplace-based workforce. In particular, men are just as likely to work at home as women, and they are far more likely to work from home as a base as well. There is no evidence that homework, and other forms of work linked to the home, are in any sense peculiarly feminine in character. By 1995 one-quarter of households in Britain owned a home computer. Although these are often used for games as well as serious tasks, it helps to explain why 30% of men and 25% of women worked at home at least part of the year in 1995 and provides a basis for the expansion of telework in the future.

The huge overlap between homework and self-employment is explored further in Chapter 8. However, the dominance of self-employment is one of the two distinguishing characteristics of homework. The other is that the homework labour force has the lowest level of occupational segregation and the largest proportion of integrated occupations in the entire labour force. In this respect, it differs completely from the part-time workforce, which, as noted in Chapter 5, is strongly segregated from the full-time workforce and consisted almost entirely of female-dominated occupations.

Feminist orthodoxy has produced a disinclination to notice or address continuing sex differentials in work orientations and in labour force partici-pation (Hakim, 1991, 1995*b*, 1996*a*, 1996*b*, 1996*c*; Hakim and Jacobs, 1997). In line with the National Travel Survey and other sources, the census SARs confirm the continuing sex differential in patterns of travel to work. Women in Britain and the USA generally work closer to home than do men; they are twice as likely to work locally. Women produce much smaller Travel To Work Areas (TTWAs) than do men. This has a significant impact on the nature and variety of the jobs available to them, reducing their potential earnings simply due to the restricted range of work available in very local labour markets. Homeworking can be seen as an extreme version of the general tendency for women to work closer to home. The characteristics of local labour markets are an important intermediary factor in the process of matching people to jobs and they shape expectations for everyone working in the locality.

8

Small Firms and the Solo Self-Employed

The historical decline of self-employment came to a halt in 1965 in Britain and in the 1970s in most other industrial societies. Most countries have experienced a revival of self-employment since then, albeit uneven in some cases, but the growth in Britain up to 1990 was spectacular and attracted special attention (OECD, 1992: 155, 172–3). This new rising trend prompted vigorous public policy debate and a great deal of new research on the causes of the upturn in self-employment, whether the revival had similar characteristics across all industrialized countries, the role of public policy (on unemployment, on taxes, on state benefits, and on promoting an enterprise culture), and on the characteristics of the new entrepreneurs (OECD, 1986, 1992; Curran, 1986; Hakim, 1988b; Steinmetz and Wright, 1989; Storey, 1994). The new research programme on self-employment and the enterprise culture drew contributions from labour economists, labour sociologists, labour lawyers and psychologists, from specialists in management, industrial relations, banking and finance, as reflected in the contributions to edited collections (Stanworth, Westrip, and Watkins, 1982; Watkins, Stanworth, and Westrip, 1982; Lewis, Stanworth, and Gibb, 1984; Curran, Stanworth, and Watkins, 1986) and in numerous reviews (Curran, 1986; Hakim, 1988b; Storey, 1994). This made for a rich research literature (Stanworth and Curran, 1976; Scase and Goffee, 1980, 1981, 1982; Curran and Burrows, 1986, 1987, 1988; Meager, 1991, 1992; Meager, Court, and Moralee, 1994; Stanworth and Stanworth, 1995, 1997; Bryson and White, 1996a, 1996b). It also meant that contributors were often addressing quite different questions, only loosely linked to each other.

NEW PERSPECTIVES ON THE SELF-EMPLOYED

In Britain the total number of self-employed fell steadily until 1965, rose a little then fell again to a low of 1.9 million in 1977–8, then grew rapidly from 1979 to 1990, after which numbers stabilized, with some fluctuation, in the 1990s. Growth rates were largest in non-agricultural self-employment (Hakim, 1987c, 1988b: 426). As a percentage of the workforce in employment, self-employment effectively doubled in the 1980s, from 7% in 1965 to 13% of the workforce by 1991. Growth was fastest among the solo self-employed (who have no employees at all) and among women, whose share grew from 20% in 1971 to 25% by 1994 (Beatson, 1995: 9). The growth of self-employment in Britain was larger and faster than in any other OECD country, so it attracted special attention in all the recent literature, but there were similar developments in other industrial societies including the USA and Japan (Blau, 1987; OECD, 1986, 1992; Steinmetz and Wright, 1989; Sengenberger, Loveman, and Piore, 1990; Daly, 1991; Meager, 1991, 1992; Meager *et al.*, 1994). The phase of rapid growth has now ended, but the new higher levels of self-employment have become a permanent feature of the workforce. Some concluded that a change of a fundamental nature has occurred in rich modern societies, making self-employment more attractive (Blau, 1987: 447). Alternatively, self-employment, like homework, is being reconstructed and recreated in new forms for the 21st century.

However, most academic researchers took a pessimistic view, arguing that high unemployment was the driving force behind the increase, which was presented as little more than a countercyclical trend in Western Europe and North America (Staber and Bögenhold, 1991). This narrow explanation was challenged on the evidence as simply unproven (Meager, 1991, 1992). Other social scientists also showed that the countercyclical response to unemployment from the 1970s onwards provided only a small part of the explanation for the reversal of the long-term decline (Steinmetz and Wright, 1989; Storey, 1994: 25–48). Involuntary self-employment and forced choices resulting from unemployment or redundancy accounted for only a small part of the increased flow into self-employment in Britain (Hakim, 1988*b*: 433–8, 1989*d*; Meager *et al.*, 1994). Special studies of new recruits to self-employment in the 1980s found that even when unemployment or redundancy was the catalyst prompting a reassessment of goals, a change of direction, and a change of work style, there were almost always other, positive aspirations as well, for the independence and autonomy of freelance work or running their own business (Bevan *et al.*, 1988; Carter and Cannon, 1988*b*; Hakim, 1989*d*). Even among female copy-editors forcibly reclassified as home-based freelances by publishers, one-quarter were converted to the ideology of autonomy and independence (Granger *et al.* 1995).

The sustained higher rate of self-employment seems to be due to a combination of other factors with a long-term impact rather more than to recession and high unemployment (Storey, 1994: 25–48). Technological change, which allows many white-collar jobs to be done almost anywhere, is relevant, as it facilitates setting up small businesses and home-based freelance work, as noted in Chapter 7, an impact far more important than the more attention-grabbing special case of teleworking (European Commission, 1995*e*). The continued decline of manufacturing in favour of the expanding service industries is also important, even if it is often dismissed as merely 'compositional change' in the industrial structure (Steinmetz and Wright, 1990). The fragmentation of enterprises, employers' increased interest in subcontracting, and the expansion of all forms of 'flexible' employment contracts as a response to recession and economic uncertainty are also significant (Streeck, 1987; Hakim, 1988b: 438–44, 1990a, 1990b; Beatson, 1995; Dex and McCulloch, 1995). Employers' muddled and uncertain planning (Hakim, 1990b) led some academics to doubt that such non-strategic thinking could have any lasting impact on labour usage (Pollert, 1991). None the less, the slow but steady decline in 'standard' full-time permanent employee jobs continued throughout the 1980s and into the 1990s, from 70% of the workforce in 1981 to 62% by 1993 (Hakim, 1996a: 43). In the long term, these trends support the theory of Piore and Sabel (1984) that modern economies are moving towards flexible specialization in both product demand and in labour use strategies, even though early tests of the theory claimed it was as yet unproven anywhere except in the original research site in Northern Italy (Storey, 1994: 42–3).

Research in industrial sociology and the sociology of work has generally focused on large organizations. The argument has been that large employers account for most jobs and most workers, and this justifies research on the labour process in complex organizations rather than on smaller and simpler workplaces. However, the most recent estimates for 1991 (Storey, 1994: 20–5) and 1993 (Dale and Kerr, 1995: 464) show that businesses employing over 100 people accounted for only 50% of all jobs in the UK; small firms with 1–10 workers provided 28% of UK employment, an increase on 20% of employment in 1979; enterprises with 11–99 workers accounted for another one-quarter. In the European Union as a whole, just over half of all employment is in enterprises with less than 100 employees, with some variation between countries. The USA is distinctive in having two-thirds of all employment in enterprises with over 100 employees and half in enterprises with 500 employees or more (Storey, 1994: 20–5). The importance of very small firms (and workplaces) is hidden by the fact that they are excluded from many national surveys (to spare them the trouble of form-filling, *inter alia*) and by some conventions in statistical surveys. For example, the British Census of Employment always excluded sole proprietors with no employees, and the British Workplace Industrial Relations Surveys have so far excluded workplaces with fewer than 25 employees. The population census and labour force surveys classify 'large' employers as those with 25 or more employees and 'small' employers as those with 1–24 employees. However, these 'small' employers typically have just 1–4 employees, well below the cut-off point (Hakim, 1988b: 430, 1989c: 33, 1989d: 288). The Census of Employment shows that almost half of all businesses that employ staff have less than five employees, about four-fifths have fewer than 25 employees, and only 5%–6% have more than 100 employees. The typical enterprise is a small business even if the typical employee works for a large organization. Due to the growth of the service sector, small firms and small workplaces are likely to contribute a larger share of the total in the 21st century. The fragmentation of enterprises and subcontracting reinforce the trend.

The glamorous image of the self-employed is of the risk-taking entrepreneur as presented by Schumpeter (1934), the initiator of 'gales of creative destruction' through the introduction of totally new products—and services, we would now add. It was an essentially Schumpeterian concept of the enterprise culture that the British government promoted in the 1980s, emphasizing the role of the self-employed and small firms in economic development through innovation, job generation, and wealth creation. However, even in the advanced economies of Western Europe, the enormous number of small businesses means that most small firms and most self-employed seek only to make a living from existing technology and well-established forms of enterprise rather than to change the world with innovative and radical new ideas. The ideology of self-employment today contains two separate strands. The first emphasizes independence, autonomy, flexibility, choice, and the freedom of being 'your own boss'. The second stresses financial rewards, the idea of earning more money than as an employee, and of reaping the rewards of one's own labour. People who have recently set up their own business mention both these attractions, but it is notable that the 'independence' motive is mentioned twice as often and seems to be twice as important as the 'financial rewards' motive (Hakim, 1989*d*: 289). Most owner-managers of existing small firms are also not entrepreneurial. They are simply repeating an existing, well-proven type of business, such as the corner shop, and many of the self-employed simply prefer to 'own their own job', for example as an independent plumber, hairdresser, or small accountancy service (Stanworth and Curran, 1976; Curran, 1986: 17; Curran and Burrows, 1987: 165–8). Only ten per cent of existing small firms in Britain seek rapid expansion and another one-third seek only slow steady growth. Over half of all small firms and the self-employed do not seek any growth or expansion at all; the majority of this group are sole traders who employ at most two people, including themselves, and many of them work from a home base (Hakim, 1989*c*: 33; see also Stanworth and Curran, 1976; Scase and Goffee, 1980: 91). Only half of new entrants to self-employment in the 1980s sought to create a growing business; the other half had no plans to expand their business in the future and sought only to 'own their own job'. People who regarded themselves as involuntary entrants, forced into self-employment by unemployment or the lack of alternatives, were most likely to seek only to provide themselves with a job and a living income, but half of the voluntary entrants into self-employment had equally limited aims. Entrepreneurs with aspirations for building a business form a minority of the self-employed and small firms, even among optimistic new entrants (Scase and Goffee, 1980: 161–5; Hakim, 1989*d*: 291). An even smaller minority will be building a business with innovative products and services.

Sociologists of social stratification have not been interested in the contribution of the self-employed to the economy but in their relationship to other social classes (Marshall *et al.*, 1988). Due to their particular market situation, the self-employed are classified as the petite bourgeoisie, an anachronistic class located between the bourgeoisie and the proletariat, or between the Service Class and the working class, who escape domination and exploitation by the bourgeoisie. Strictly speaking, the petite bourgeoisie consists of the solo self-employed, those who neither buy the labour of others nor sell their own, but in practice Goldthorpe assigns small proprietors and artisans working with employees as well as those working alone to the class (Erikson and Goldthorpe, 1993: 37–9). In Wright's (1985) class schema, the precise number of employees becomes crucial: 'capitalists' are those with 10 or more employees, 'small employers' have 2–9 employees, and the 'petite bourgeoisie' have only one or no employees (Rose and Marshall, 1986). These distinctions may seem arbitrary, but they have been found to identify significantly different natural groupings within the small firm sector (Hakim, 1989*c*: 37) as well as differences in work orientations, self-assigned class, and voting patterns (Marshall *et al.*, 1988).

The two social class classifications implicitly refer to (male) full-time workers seeking a breadwinner or family wage rather than to the part-time self-employment in the service industries that became increasingly common in industrial societies in the 1980s, especially among women. They also do not deal with the increasingly common situation of the small firm which has several or many workers in addition to the owner, all of whom are self-employed rather than employees, as illustrated by the taxi-cab service. However, the most important distinction has always been between what are called 'small firms' in this chapter, that is, the self-employed with employees, and the solo self-employed without any employees but who may be assisted by other members of the family. This distinction is drawn fairly clearly and consistently in the Socio-Economic Group (SEG) classification used in the British population census and in most other statistical surveys of households (see Annex A). Although technically self-employed, unpaid family workers are treated as a separate group in Britain and in the European LFS, if they are counted at all (Sly, Price, and Risdon, 1997: 102). Studies that include family workers among the self-employed reveal much higher levels of self-employment among women (Kovalainen, 1993).

The employment law perspective has so far been structured around a sharp distinction between 'wage slave' and 'entrepreneur', to use Drake's (1968) labels. In English and American law, the employment law distinction between the employee hired to do the employer's bidding (and potentially eligible for various employment rights and benefits) and the autonomous self-employed worker who delivers a finished product or service rests heavily on legal tests of control, mutuality of obligation, the provision of premises, tools, and equipment, and whether someone is 'in business on their own account'. In the majority of cases, the distinction is clear-cut, but there has always been a grey area on the boundary line where decisions on the 'correct' employment status are finely balanced, based on precise details of the work relationship and national legal precedents, giving rise to a substantial labour law literature on where the line has been and should be drawn (Linder, 1989*a*, 1989*b*, 1992). In all countries, agriculture and the construction industry have always employed substantial numbers of self-employed as well as employees, who may well work side by side, on site, both supplying their own hand tools. In these industries, the distinction between employee and self-employed can be a matter of custom and practice, and also varies with unemployment levels and the economic cycle, but those involved are clear about the differences and their consequences. Self-employment rates have always been relatively low in manufacturing, certainly lower than rates in service industries. Difficulties in operationalizing the traditional legal distinction between the employee's contract of service and the self-employed's contract for services are most common in service sector industries and occupations. Difficulties, or the arbitrariness of decisions at the margin, seem to be increasing with the expansion of 'flexible' employment contracts—such as 'consultants' hired for their expertise who advise rather than follow orders; businesses which consist entirely of the talents and experience of the staff; employees on fixed-term contracts that may be for 3–6 years and run longer than the average job; and the erosion of workplace-centred control systems as a result of developments in information technology. In certain types of work, such as homeworking, there is no clear and simple rule for deciding the correct employment status in law (Leighton, 1983; Hakim, 1987*b*). Some commentators have argued that social welfare and employment rights should be offered to all workers, on the grounds that the old distinctions no longer work, and maybe never did work (Hepple, 1986; Linder, 1989*a*, 1989*b*, 1992).[1] As yet, few social scientists and labour lawyers have recognized that the old criteria of risk, control, responsibility, and innovation are gradually ceasing to be pivotal in the context of an unprecedented degree of economic uncertainty deriving from the need for continuous rapid adjustment to a market that has become

---

[1] The usual argument is that social security and employment rights should be extended to all workers *because* the distinction between the solo self-employed and the employee is no longer clear-cut. But the second argument is not in fact a necessary basis for the first. One can argue that certain important rights and benefits should be universally accessible, even if there are differences between subgroups. For example, in Britain, access to health care is universal and does not depend on employment status. Similarly sex and race discrimination laws apply universally, both in and beyond the labour market. In the same vein, some would argue for a universal guaranteed basic income (or negative income tax). The case for universal access to social security benefits and employment rights does not depend on the argument that there are no important differences (objective or subjective) between employees and the solo self-employed.

permanently more turbulent and volatile (Streeck, 1987); extensive public sector employment (where private sector criteria rarely apply); and increasing levels of expertise in most occupations. Today, task complexity and authority level have become the key features differentiating occupations (Spaeth, 1979; Parcel and Mueller, 1983). Some degree of uncertainty attaches to all jobs, and risk-taking can be an important determinant of earnings in employee jobs as well as freelance jobs (Chauvin and Ash, 1994). Similarly, employee jobs at virtually all grades benefit from some degree of autonomy (Marshall *et al.*, 1988: 50–8, 116–22).

The rising trend in self-employment is not readily explained by existing social and economic theory, which generally regards the petite bourgeoisie as doomed to extinction. One response has been to doubt, deny, or dismiss the trend as illusory, insisting that the new freelance workers are really casual employees in disguise because they have low and irregular earnings, or work mainly for one organization at any one time, or do not have the complete autonomy of the craftsman (Dale, 1986; Linder, 1989*a*, 1989*b*; Linder and Houghton, 1990; Rainbird, 1991; Linder, 1992). However, neither class position nor employment status are determined by the level of earnings or tax position, and many of these arguments ignore the very real differences in the *degree* of autonomy and independence that the self-employed perceive between their position and someone doing the same job as an employee. University academics in Western Europe (even the most dissatisfied) enjoy a degree of autonomy and independence in their work, and a degree of flexibility in working time, especially over the year, that go far beyond the wildest dreams of the vast majority of ordinary employees, especially as these benefits are enjoyed in combination with security of employment. Academic social scientists are thus uniquely poorly placed to judge the weight that a homeworker, freelance, or small firm owner may attach to achieving some small *increase* in autonomy and independence in their work, as compared with doing the same job as an on-site employee under the immediate control of the employer (Scase and Goffee, 1981). Occupational self-direction—the use of initiative, thought, and independent judgement at work—has a powerful impact on psychological well-being and general health (Kohn and Schooler, 1983; see also Kohn *et al.*, 1990). Even housewives, who work without pay, value their autonomy and the independence of 'being your own boss' when compared with the subordination of a more remunerative employee job (Oakley, 1974). Qualitative research testing population census questions has shown that in Britain the solo self-employed are aware of major differences between 'freelances' who mainly work for one or two companies or an agency, and can thus rely on a fairly regular supply of work, and other self-employed who work for many companies and are regularly seeking new clients. However, all the solo self-employed, including the 'freelances', regard themselves as significantly different from employees, even if they are subject to market forces instead of an employer's control (Scase and Goffee, 1981). For most, the extra work autonomy is a major goal, which can out-weigh profit-maximization and even the almost universally low, irregular, and variable earnings of self-employment (OECD, 1986: 62, 1992: 162; Evans and Leighton, 1987; Linder, 1992: 69; Meager *et al.*, 1994; Eardley and Corden, 1996). It is the desire for some degree of autonomy that prevents many of the self-employed from expanding their business, as this almost invariably leads to taking on other workers and thus the responsibilities of a manager and an employer (Stanworth and Curran, 1976: 107; Scase and Goffee, 1982: 189–90; Rainbird, 1991: 212).

The census SARs do not provide any special information on the self-employed. It is simply their enormous size that provides us with the largest sample of the self-employed that is available from any source, and thus allows us to explore some of their characteristics in more detail and with greater pre-cision than is possible with interview survey datasets. The SARs allow us to look further at some of the issues reviewed above, in particular the location of the self-employed in the class structure. However, our primary interest is exploring the features of female self-employment, partly because it was female self-employment that grew fastest in the rapid growth period of the 1980s, partly because self-employment was found in Chapter 2 to be an important feature of integrated occupations. We might thus expect to find some connection between these two aspects of self-employment. Finally, we look at the link between self-employment and homework, which also experi-enced rapid growth in the 1980s, as shown in Chapter 7.

NATIONAL ESTIMATES

The 1991 Census offers two counts of the self-employed in Britain, which dif-fer by 7% in raw numbers (Table 8.1) or by 5% after reweighting the 10% sam-ple to adjust for sampling error (OPCS and GROS, 1994a: 8). That is, about 5% of the self-employed are technically the employee of their own incorpo-rated business and are removed from the count. The 1981 Census also offered two counts, which differed by 11% (Hakim, 1988b: 423). The problem is even larger in the USA population census and CPS (the equivalent of the LFS), with the two counts differing by 11% in 1967, 24% in 1982, and 26% in 1983 (Steinmetz and Wright, 1989: 989, 1990: 737).

In strictly legal terms, the self-employed are restricted to owners (sole pro-prietors and partners) of unincorporated businesses. Working proprietors or managers of incorporated businesses are classified as employees in statistical surveys because that is their status in law and for tax and social insurance purposes. These distinctions are often ignored by self-employed respondents to the census and LFS, who report the reality of generating their own income and being their own boss rather than working as hired labour. Self-classification as self-employed is thus correct as regards sociological analysis. However, statistical offices routinely reclassify the self-employed as employees if the name of the firm they work for suggests it is their own business (OECD, 1992: 155–6). In Britain, office corrections are made only to the 10% sample data that is used for the fullest analyses (and provides the SARs) but not to the basic 100% counts (Table 8.1). The recoded 10% sample data is technically correct but substantively wrong. Overall, the census and statistical surveys such as the LFS *under*estimate the true level of business ownership (OECD, 1986: 43–4). For example, it has been shown for the USA that business ownership is in fact 60%–75% larger than the percentage of people reporting themselves as self-employed (Haber, Lamas, and Lichtenstein, 1987: 18).

TABLE 8.1. *National estimates: small firms and the solo self-employed*

	Men		Women		Total		S/E as % of all aged 16 and over		
	N	%	N	%	N	%	M	F	T
100% counts									
Total	2,373,764	100	704,672	100	3,078,436	100	11	3	7
Small firms	787,981	33	255,984	36	1,043,965	34	4	1	2
Solo self-employed	1,585,783	67	448,688	64	2,034,471	66	8	2	5
10% counts									
Total	2,230,610	100	642,580	100	2,873,190	100	11	3	7
Small firms	705,600	32	228,340	36	933,940	33	4	1	2
Solo self-employed	1,525,010	68	414,240	64	1,939,250	67	7	2	5
							as % of workforce aged 16+ in each hours band		
Usual weekly hours worked									
31+ hours	1,912,440	93	367,540	63	2,279,980	87	16	6	13
16–30 hours	108,400	5	135,900	23	244,300	9	27	5	8
Up to 15 hours	35,110	2	78,470	14	113,580	4	16	5	6
Total, hours stated	2,055,950	100	581,910	100	2,637,860	100			
Hours not stated	174,660	8	60,670	9	235,330	8	37	21	31
Total	2,230,610	100	642,580	100	2,873,190	100	17	6	12

Source: 1991 Census, Great Britain, 100% and 10% sample statistics as reported in tables 1 and 3, *Economic Activity*, data for residents aged 16 and over in employment.

Businesses are more likely to be incorporated as they increase in size and turnover. The main effect of reclassifying owners of incorporated businesses as ordinary employees is to reduce to almost nil the number of employer-managers of 'large' organizations with 25 or more employees. These few large firms are grouped together with small firms in all tables of this chapter, to report a single figure for 'small firms' with employees (typically less than five) as compared with the solo self-employed with no employees. The reclassification of employment status has a much smaller impact on the numbers of solo self-employed: a difference of 5% in raw numbers (Table 8.1) or 3% after reweighting the 10% sample, compared to 11% and 9% respectively for small firms (OPCS and GROS, 1994*a*: 8).

In 1991 women contributed 44% of the workforce or 39% on an FTE basis, but only one-third of all full-time employment and one-third of full-time permanent employee jobs (Hakim, 1996*a*: 43, 155, 173). Their share of self-employment remained substantially lower, at 22%, reflecting women's lower propensity to engage in risk-taking compared with men (Chauvin and Ash, 1994; Hakim, 1996*a*: 183). Men are almost four times more likely to be self-employed than are women: 11% of men aged 16 and over compared to a bare 3% of women. The solo self-employed outnumber small firms with employees by two to one, with no difference between men and women (Table 8.1). However, self-employed women work far shorter hours than men, even when working full-time, and one-third are working part-time, almost as many as among employees. There is no evidence that self-employment is used as a route into shorter and more convenient work hours: the percentage of the female workforce who are self-employed is constant at 5%–6% across all hours bands. In fact, self-employment serves this purpose for men rather than for women (Table 8.1).

In the 2% SAR, there are self-employed people, both men and women, with and without employees, in 65 out of the 73 occupation units listed. The eight occupations without any self-employed include army and police officers, sales assistants and check-out operators, receptionists, telephonists, civil service clerical officers, and managers in transport and storage. The occupations with substantial numbers of self-employed include construction workers, electricians, plumbers, carpenters, taxi-drivers, sales representatives, lawyers, accountants, management consultants, writers, artists, sports professionals, childminders, sewing machinists, bookkeepers, teachers, health professionals, and managers/proprietors in a range of service industries such as hairdressers and restaurateurs.

THE SOCIAL CLASS LOCATION OF THE SELF-EMPLOYED

The self-employed are concentrated disproportionately in the petite bourgeoisie, but they are in no way restricted to it. On the contrary, they are found in all of the RG Social Classes, and in the Service Class as well as the working class, for reasons displayed most clearly by the SEG classification (Tables 8.2 to 8.4).

In Table 8.2 some of the self-employed recoded as employees are added back into the self-employment statistics. Four-fifths of the small firm owners are classified as employer-managers and about four-fifths of the solo

TABLE 8.2. *SEG composition of the self-employed workforce*

SEG		Small firms		Solo S/E		All S/E	
		Men	Women	Men	Women	N	%
1/2	Employers and managers (with employees)	9,856	3,590	—	—	13,446	24
3	Professionals—S/E	2,175	274	1,555	325	4,329	8
5.1	Intermediate non-manual	339	189	2,384	1,560	4,472	8
12	Own-account workers (with family workers)	—	—	23,856	5,745	29,601	52
13/14	Farmers	955	157	1,616	245	2,973	5
15	Agricultural workers	29	26	200	91	346	1
	Inadequately described	453	168	782	339	1,742	3
	Totals	13,807	4,404	30,393	8,305	56,909	100

Source: 2% SAR, Great Britain, data for residents in employment aged 16–64.

TABLE 8.3. *Goldthorpe class composition of small firms, the solo self-employed and employee workforce*

		Small firms	Solo self-employed	Managers	Foremen & supervisors	Other employees	Total
Goldthorpe classes							
Upper service class	M	1,685	1,404	7,782	—	10,069	20,940
	F	391	534	2,934	—	3,514	7,373
Lower service class	M	63	1,028	14,724	1,263	11,002	28,080
	F	93	756	8,040	2,501	14,358	25,748
Routine non-manual	M	—	—	—	184	9,204	9,388
	F	—	—	—	640	33,916	34,556
Personal service	M	—	—	—	—	2,847	2,847
	F	—	—	—	—	21,727	21,727
Proprietors	M	4,491	13,220	—	—	—	17,711
	F	1,610	3,240	—	—	—	4,850
Farmers	M	499	1,015	299	—	—	1,813
	F	104	202	60	—	—	366
Lower technicians, foremen	M	—	—	—	5,164	4,470	9,634
	F	—	—	—	1,699	646	2,345
Skilled manual workers	M	—	—	—	—	25,226	25,226
	F	—	—	—	—	5,782	5,782
Semi-unskilled workers and agricultural workers	M	134	—	38	96	36,194	36,462
	F	69	—	18	13	31,167	31,267
All self-classified as self-employed	M	6,872	16,667	22,843	6,707	99,012	152,101
	F	2,267	4,732	11,052	4,853	111,110	134,014

Source: 1% SAR, Great Britain, data for employed residents aged 16–64 years.

self-employed are classified as 'own account' workers. Own account workers are self-employed persons engaged in any trade, personal service, or manual occupation not normally requiring training of university standard and having no employees other than family workers. Jobs that do require university level education are classified as self-employed professionals, and own-account farmers are treated as a separate category. However, ordinary agricultural workers also appear as self-employed with and without employees. The SEG classification shows clearly why the self-employed are found in all classes, with only half in SEG 12 which is usually classified as the petite bourgeoisie. There is far less homogeneity in the group than is assumed by the single label of petite bourgeoisie. The self-employed include a great variety of social statuses, occupational grades, and earnings levels, as is shown by their location in Goldthorpe's class schema in Tables 8.3 and in the RG's Social classes in Table 8.4.

TABLE 8.4. *Job characteristics within the self-employed workforce* column percent

	Small firms			Solo S/E			All S/E		All employees	
	M	F	All	M	F	All	M	F	M	F
Type of occupation										
Male	47	14	39	73	18	62	65	17	63	8
Integrated	49	70	54	22	50	28	31	57	22	18
Female	4	16	7	5	32	10	4	26	15	74
Hours worked										
Overtime 46+	58	38	54	34	20	31	42	27	12	3
Full-time 37–45	36	31	35	53	27	47	47	28	75	41
Reduced 30–36	4	13	6	8	17	10	7	16	10	20
Half-time 11–29	1	14	4	4	26	9	3	21	2	29
Marginal 1–10	1	4	1	1	10	3	1	8	1	7
Higher qualifications held										
a higher degrees	1	1	1	1	1	1	1	1	2	1
b first degrees	18	9	16	6	11	7	10	10	10	7
c below degree level	5	8	6	4	7	5	5	7	8	10
two or more	10	7	9	4	7	4	6	7	8	6
none	76	82	78	89	81	87	85	81	80	83
RG Social Class										
I Professional	16	7	14	5	4	5	9	5	7	2
II Managerial, technical	42	58	46	23	45	28	29	50	29	27
IIIN Skilled white collar	10	25	14	8	27	12	9	26	12	40
IIIM Skilled blue collar	25	6	20	49	6	40	41	6	31	7
IV Semi-skilled	5	3	5	10	16	11	8	12	16	16
V Unskilled	2	1	1	5	2	4	4	1	5	8

Source: 2% SAR, Great Britain, data for residents in employment aged 16–64 years.

In Goldthorpe's class schema, roughly equal numbers of small firm owners and solo self-employed appear in the Upper Service class and small numbers appear also in the Lower Service class. Small proprietors and farmers form the two largest classes, but small business owners are also found among semi-skilled and unskilled workers (Table 8.3). The self-employed appear in all the RG's Social Classes, with the highest concentrations in the managerial/technical Class II and in skilled manual work Class IIIM (Table 8.4). The stereotype of the self-employed as a tiny homogeneous category falling into a single social class is unfounded and needs to be replaced. The self-employed may be a small category but it is an internally heterogeneous one.

OCCUPATIONAL SEGREGATION AMONG THE SELF-EMPLOYED

Occupational segregation is far less pronounced among the self-employed than in the employee workforce (Table 8.4). Women in particular achieve a very different occupational profile when working as solo self-employed or as small business owners. Only 32% of the solo self-employed and 16% of small firm owners were in female-dominated occupations compared to 74% of female employees. There is clear evidence here that the jobs most readily offered to women by employers are not necessarily the jobs preferred by women. This problem does not arise for men, who are even more likely to be working in male-dominated occupations when they are solo self-employed than is true of male employees generally. Self-employed women are significantly different from women employees while self-employed men differ relatively little from employees. This suggests that one of the special attractions of self-employment for women is the opportunity to escape from the sex-role stereotyping of abilities and interests that pervades the employee workforce. Over half (57%) of all self-employed women are in integrated occupations compared to just 18% of female employees (Table 8.4). The proportion of women who are self-employed is also far higher within integrated occupations: 17% compared to 2% for female occupations (see Table 2.3)

These results must be read in terms of personal choice as well as social structural constraints on job choice. By 1991, after a decade of exceptional growth, self-employed women had become significantly different from other working women on a number of measures. It is also clear that female-dominated occupations provide just as much potential for self-employment as do male-dominated occupations. For example, the personal service and clerical occupations dominated by women provide ample scope for creating small firms or working as solo self-employed: female typists and secretaries, hairdressers, beauticians, caterers, and childcare staff could potentially be self-employed just as often as male plumbers, electricians, and carpenters. The low female self-employment rate in female-dominated occupations must therefore be read as reflecting women's own preferences for working as subordinate employees in enterprises managed by others. In fact there are often equal or larger numbers of male self-employed in female-dominated occupations such as catering and dressmaking. The recent rise in women's self-employment in Western Europe is notable precisely because the sex differential in self-employment rates has been universal (Loutfi, 1992). These results support theories presented by Goldberg and others stating that men are far more likely than women to have a drive to achieve the higher positions in any society (S. Goldberg, 1993; Hakim, 1996*a*: 5–9). This would explain why men more often seek the autonomy of being 'their own boss' in all grades of job, no matter how high up or down the occupational ladder. If they cannot be masters of the universe, they can at least be master of their own small firm, or of their own lives.

Consistent evidence comes from the integrated occupation of pharmacy described in Chapter 9, which provides a wide range of opportunities, in most Western European countries, for full-time and part-time work, employee jobs, self-employment, and small businesses. In this context of relatively unconstrained choice, women typically choose employee jobs while men are far more likely to choose self-employment in their own pharmacy business (Crompton and Sanderson, 1990: 65–88; Crompton and Le Feuvre, 1996). Indeed, ethnic minority men are more likely to establish their own pharmacy business than are white women. It seems fair to assume that the degree of discrimination differs little between highly qualified ethnic minority men and white women, so the differential rates of self-employment must be due to the sex differential in work orientations and ambitions.

Women's avoidance of self-employment is partly due to their preference for defined, low-risk activities and partly due to their preference for fixed as well as shorter working hours. One fundamental difference between the employee workforce and the self-employed is that the self-employed work systematically longer hours, *far* longer hours. This is true of women almost as much as men (Table 8.4). Almost half of self-employed men *usually* work over 46 hours a week (excluding overtime) compared to only 12% of employees; one-quarter of self-employed women usually work over 46 hours a week compared to 3% of employees. These long hours are most common among small firm owners: in this group half regularly work 'overtime' hours and part-time workers are virtually non-existent. But one-third of the solo self-employed also report regular work hours far longer than the normal 'long' full-time hours of 37–45 hours a week (Table 8.4).

Self-employed women, especially the solo self-employed, are generally better qualified than female employees, as shown by the percentage with degree-level qualifications and the percentage with two or more higher education qualifications (Table 8.4). This is a recent development (Daly, 1991: 115–16). Self-employed men working alone are systematically less well qualified than employees, as most are working in skilled blue-collar trades, while small business owners are markedly better qualified than male employees generally, and better qualified than female small firm owners too, a finding which helps to explain the greater numbers of men in the Upper Service class in Table 8.3. Working women are a self-selected group who are not representative of all adult women (Hakim and Jacobs, 1997). The SARs reveal that self-employed women are an even more self-selected group, who differ from female employees as well as from non-working women.

LABOUR TURNOVER

Labour turnover is most commonly studied in relation to the employee workforce (Hakim, 1996c). The literature on small firms and the self-employed indicates that turnover in this sector may not be very different, overall, from employee turnover, although it seems to be far more polarized: exits from self-employment or running a small firm are exceptionally high in the first year or two, then fall rapidly to insignificant levels for people who have established themselves (Hakim, 1987b, 1988a, 1988b; Storey, 1994). Since the solo self-employed are not eligible for unemployment benefits in periods when they have no work, variations in workloads are reflected in varying levels of annual turnover and profitability as well as in labour turnover rates. This may explain the almost non-existent turnover rates among owners of small firms and the relatively low turnover rates for the solo self-employed in Table 8.5. In addition, turnover among the self-employed tends to mean switching back into an employee job rather than becoming unemployed or leaving the labour market (OECD, 1992: 166; Bryson and White, 1996b: 56–7). So many of those who had left self-employment jobs would reappear within the

TABLE 8.5. *Labour turnover rates[1] by employment status and hours worked*

	Full-time 37+	Reduced hours 30–36	Half-time 11–29	Marginal hours 1–10	All men	All women	All persons
Managers	14	14	17	17	12	20	14
Foremen/supervisors	17	18	15	26	15	22	18
Other employees	23	22	26	37	22	29	25
Small firm owners	*	1	*	0	*	1	*
Solo self-employed	10	9	6	12	10	14	11
All	19	19	25	35	18	27	22

[1] The percentage of people with a job of a given type in the last ten years (including student jobs) who are not currently in work, including student jobs.

Source: 1% SAR, Great Britain, data for residents aged 16–64 years reporting a current job or a job in the last ten years.

employee workforce, thus reducing the aggregate turnover rates for the self-employed in the SARs. These factors may contribute to lower turnover rates among the self-employed in Table 8.5. None the less, it is notable that the 11% turnover rate for the solo self-employed is half the 20% turnover rate in the employee workforce.

The 1991 Census turnover rates for the solo self-employed are remarkably consistent with all other sources: annual turnover rates of 10% for partnerships and 12% for sole proprietors as measured by annual VAT deregistration rates (Storey, 1994: 86) and an annual turnover rate of 9% or 10% for the self-employed throughout the 1980s as measured by the LFS (Daly, 1991: 124; Meager *et al.*, 1994: 14). Self-employment turnover rates are consistently low across all hours worked and similar to turnover rates among managers (Table 8.5). This makes sense, as people working on their own account are in effect managing their own work as well as doing it. It is notable that the sex differential in turnover rates discussed more fully in Chapter 2 is observed to apply equally to employees and the solo self-employed, and to be highest for managerial employee jobs and lowest for non-supervisory employee jobs. Although self-employed women are distinctive in many ways, they still exhibit a significant 40% mark-up in turnover rates which is only a little lower than the 50% average mark-up for the female workforce noted in Chapter 2. Studies based on the LFS (Daly, 1991: 124; Meager *et al.*, 1994: 17) report a very similar sex differential in annual turnover rates for the self-employed throughout the 1980s.

PERSONAL CHARACTERISTICS

The self-employed do not differ from employees in their personal characteristics, apart from the fact that they are generally older, on average, so they have the profiles of an older age group, in terms of being married, having children, and having bought their homes (Table 8.6).

Not surprisingly, it is rare for young workers aged 16–24 to be self-employed, but it is three times more frequent among young men than among young women. Among women, age has no effect on the propensity to be self-employed after the age of 25, which remains at a steady level of 2%–3% small firm owners and 4%–5% solo self-employed (Table 8.6). Among men, the propensity to choose self-employment increases quickly so that 20% of men are self-employed from the age of 35 onwards. The transfer to being solo self-employed occurs at younger ages than the decision to create (or take over) a small firm. So it is clearly not only the advantages of greater work experience and better access to capital or other resources as one grows older that create opportunities for self-employment, for the rising trend is restricted to men, at the end of a decade with a massive increase in female self-employment

TABLE 8.6. *Personal characteristics of self-employed workers*

row/column/cell percent

		Small firms	Solo S/E	All S/E	All employees
Men aged	16–24	1	6	7	93
	25–34	4	11	15	85
	35–44	7	13	20	80
	45–54	8	13	21	79
	55–64	6	14	20	80
Women aged	16–24	*	2	2	98
	25–34	2	4	6	94
	35–44	3	5	8	92
	45–54	3	4	7	93
	55–64	3	4	7	93
Region:	London	10	14	12	12
	Rest of South-East	21	23	22	20
	Rest of Britain	70	63	66	68
% non-white	men	7	4	5	4
	women	6	5	5	4
% single	men	10	23	19	31
	women	8	18	14	28
% with 1+	men	53	42	45	40
dependent child	women	48	46	46	38
% in homes with	men	70	66	67	70
2+ earners	women	88	82	84	81
% in owner-	men	90	82	84	78
occupied homes	women	87	85	86	78

Source: 2% SAR, Great Britain, data for residents in employment aged 16–64 years.

(Carter and Cannon, 1988*a*, 1988*b*). Clearly, there is also a sex effect here. For some reason women are less attracted to being 'my own boss', or they are more comfortable with the role of the subordinate employee.

It seems reasonable to conclude that the lack of interest in self-employment among women as compared with men is a lack of interest in greater responsibility and has the same source as the well-documented fact that, on average, female employees are less interested in promotion than male employees (Hakim, 1991, 1996*a*: 108–9). It is true that those women who do seek promotion routinely experience sex discrimination, due to the sex role stereotyping that produces a masculine model of the manager (Hakim, 1996*a*: 184). However, it is also true that a substantial proportion of women do *not* seek promotion, greater responsibility, or authority roles at work, either through promotion within internal labour markets or through self-employment in the external labour market, due to a weaker motivation to achieve the top jobs and perhaps also to prejudiced sex-stereotyping among women themselves (P. Goldberg, 1968). Both factors contribute to vertical occupational segregation and women's lower share of the top jobs, as noted in Chapters 2 and 9.

Self-employed women are a small and selective group, but the SARs do not tell us in what way they are different, apart from being sufficiently committed to their work to put in far longer hours than the average employee. Qualitative research on female entrepreneurs helps to fill the gap. All this research is very recent, prompted by developments in the 1980s (Watkins and Watkins, 1982, 1984; Carter and Cannon, 1988*a*, 1988*b*; Granger *et al.*, 1995; Stanworth and Stanworth, 1995, 1997). It indicates that women who become solo self-employed, or start their own business, are strongly motivated towards a career of some sort and have spent a large proportion of their lives in employment. The great majority have some family connection with self-employment. (However, Bannock and Stanworth, 1990, show that this is generally true of the self-employed.) The search for independence and autonomy is just as important as among men. Some studies find it to be the primary motivation (Carter and Cannon, 1988*b*). Some studies find it to be a secondary motivation (Granger *et al.*, 1995). Female entrepreneurs are generally less likely than men to regard profitability and growth as primary goals, but accept them as an objective measure of success. Many report frustration with career blocks in their previous employee jobs, with lack of recognition and reward for their work, and no offers of career progression on the same basis as male colleagues (Carter and Cannon, 1988*a*). One architect describes the classic 'glass ceiling' problem as follows:

When I first qualified, I expected problems in managing construction sites, but it was really very easy. The problems I didn't expect to find were my employers not seeing me as management potential. I found it very difficult to ask for pay rises and more seniority, though I found it easy to take on responsibility in the office   (Carter and Cannon, 1988*a*: 568)

At the same time, one-third of solo self-employed women (and virtually no men) are working part-time hours, suggesting that their objectives may differ little from those of other part-time workers.

THE OVERLAP WITH HOMEWORK AND HOME-BASED WORK

Home and workplace are closely connected for most of the self-employed: half are working at home or from home as a base (Table 8.7). Small firm owners, who employ others, are less likely to work at or from home, and one-fifth have separate but local premises. The solo self-employed, who are by far the largest group, typically work at home (21%) or from home as a base (41%). In both groups, women are most likely to work at home, as illustrated by the

Small Firms and the Solo Self-Employed

copy-editors studied by Stanworth and Stanworth (1995, 1997), and men are most likely to work from home as a base, as illustrated by the construction workers studied by Scase and Goffee (1981)—one-third of the total in each case. The sex differential in travel to work patterns noted in Chapter 7 is maintained and even enhanced among the self-employed, although it remains sharp among employees (Table 8.7).

TABLE 8.7. *Workplace and travel to work patterns among the self-employed*

	S/E with employees			S/E without employees			All S/E		All employees	
	M	F	All	M	F	All	M	F	M	F
Percentage of people who work:										
at home	12	21	14	15	41	21	14	34	1	2
no fixed place (home-based)	14	3	12	46	21	41	36	14	4	2
0–2 km from home	20	26	21	8	10	8	12	15	22	37
30+ km from home	4	3	3	3	2	2	3	2	9	3
walk to work	5	9	6	3	5	3	3	6	9	17

Source: 2% SAR, Great Britain, data for residents in employment aged 16–64 years.

CONCLUSIONS

For both men and women, self-employment provides a greater degree of independence and autonomy than can be achieved in ordinary employee jobs. Academic social scientists have often been unable to appreciate this point because they enjoy a degree of autonomy, independence, and flexibility, as employees, that is normally achieved only by the self-employed. Because so many university academics have never held a job in the real world, they have no experience of the constraints of ordinary employee jobs requiring regular daily attendance at work with fixed daily hours for 48 weeks of the year across the whole of adult life. Nor can they appreciate the effects of all their work being constantly subject to supervision, quality assessment, monitoring, and assessment on a weekly, monthly, or annual basis, often by a superior who is regarded as mediocre, non-competent, or biased. Although university academics hold employee contracts providing job security, regular pay increments, and all the other benefits offered by large employers, they enjoy at the same time all the advantages of the self-employed in terms of freedom to plan their working day and week, freedom to go into their workplace or not (so long as lectures and classes are covered), freedom to teach what they want within very broad limits and, until the late 1990s, there was virtually no monitoring of their work and performance, certainly none that carried consequences. Academic social scientists are thus uniquely poorly placed to judge the validity of statements by the self-employed that they enjoy the independence, autonomy, and flexibility it offers as compared with doing the same job as an on-site employee. Among both men and women, this is the most important benefit of self-employment, as the financial advantages are uncertain, variable, or even non-existent.

Otherwise, self-employment serves quite different purposes for men and women. Men typically remain in the same male-dominated occupations, doing the same work but with the psychological advantage of being 'a boss', a status that is available at all occupational grades, from the service class to the working class. The highly qualified women who have been entering self-employment recently are often using it to escape the sex-stereotyping and sex discrimination that colour experiences even in the most enlightened organizations. For other women, it is a route into greater hours flexibility and part-time work without being obliged to switch to the low-status and low-paid occupations available in local labour markets (see Tables 7.5 and 7.6). Occupational segregation is significantly lower among the self-employed than in the employee workforce.

When they move into self-employment, men and women take with them the special features of their employment behaviour in the employee workforce: women often work part-time hours; men generally work longer hours than women; women have higher turnover rates than men; women are far more likely to do white-collar work while men are concentrated in blue-collar work; women are more likely to work at home or close to home while men work from home as a base and are generally more mobile.

The analysis demonstrates important differences between small business owners who employ staff and the solo self-employed (who are assisted by family workers at most), as well as important differences between the solo self-employed and employees. The number of freelances and other self-employed working without assistants increased by over one million in the 1980s, effectively doubling in just a decade, leading some commentators to argue that they formed a new variety of exploited wage labour rather than 'genuine' members of the petite bourgeoisie. We have shown that the self-employed are dispersed across the entire class structure and cannot be understood exclusively within the stereotype of the petite bourgeoisie. It appears that stereotypes of the self-employed are out of touch with recent developments.

Finally, it appears that the link between home-ownership and self-employment has been exaggerated (Curran and Burrows, 1988). Nationally, 13% of all owner-occupiers are self-employed (18% of men and 7% of women) as compared with 9% of people renting public sector accommodation (12% of men and 4% of women). The difference is significant but relatively small. It is sometimes argued that it is easier for home-owners to obtain a loan to start a business, using their home as security for the loan. In practice, such loans are rare: only 1% of owner-occupiers had such a loan in 1981; loans for housing investment and other uses were three times more common (OPCS, 1983: 49–50). Another thesis is that people who have achieved the autonomy and independence of home-ownership are also more likely to seek the autonomy and independence of self-employment. Our analysis suggests that any such effect is weak, raising self-employment rates by 50% on average, compared to people renting public housing. Home-ownership may well provide ontological security, as Saunders (1990) argues, but this seems to have little or no impact on work orientations and risk-taking behaviour.

9

The Drug Dealers: A Case Study of Pharmacy, an Integrated Occupation

In this chapter the 1% census SAR is used for a case study of pharmacists. Looking at a particular occupational group allows us to draw together the themes of previous chapters, to provide a more rounded view of one example of an integrated occupation, and to consider the links between themes. Chapters 9 and 10 synthesize the analysis and draw conclusions. The approach here is an empirical synthesis, via a strategic case study, while Chapter 10 focuses on theoretical conclusions and policy implications.

Pharmacists were chosen for our case study for two reasons. First, this is now an integrated occupation, with roughly equal numbers of men and women holding a pharmacy qualification and/or working as pharmacists. Second, and equally important, there has been a shortage of pharmacists throughout the second half of the twentieth century, in particular throughout the 1970s, 1980s, and 1990s when equal opportunities legislation created a new climate of opinion on women's employment. At a time when repeated recessions limited job opportunities in some professions and industries, there have always been plenty of jobs for pharmacists, who have been able to choose work arrangements to suit themselves. Pharmacy is not only an integrated occupation, but also one that has been expanding and has escaped the constraints of recession. These characteristics pertain to the USA as well as Britain, with similarities and differences between the two countries.[1]

Normally, the 2% SAR would be the logical choice for case studies of special groups, due to its larger size. In practice, this chapter has to rely exclusively on the smaller 1% SAR as it is the only one containing the detailed classifications of occupation and of educational qualification subjects that enable us to identify pharmacists. This means that the case study samples are relatively small, with 350 qualified pharmacists identified by their highest qualification, 302 pharmacists identified by the occupation of their current or last job, and 247 people who are pharmacists on both criteria.

[1] The choice of pharmacy as a case study was prompted in part by Crompton's research on this profession in Britain and other European countries, and this chapter draws on her reports (Crompton and Sanderson, 1990: 65–88; Crompton and Le Feuvre, 1996; see also Crompton and Harris, 1998), and in part by the existence of an equivalent case study of pharmacy in the USA (Reskin and Roos, 1990: 111–27; see also Sokoloff, 1992: 82–9). In both Britain and the USA pharmacy became an integrated occupation over the two decades 1970–90.

PROFILE OF A PROFESSIONAL LABOUR MARKET

Pharmacy became a degree-entry profession in 1967 in Britain. Prior to that, the Pharmaceutical Society of Great Britain, founded in 1841, examined and registered pharmacists. The profession is heavily regulated. Registration remains compulsory, and there is a mandatory one year's on-the-job training after completion of educational courses. Under the terms of the British National Health Service, only a qualified pharmacist can dispense Health Service prescriptions. Regulations relating to the sale of drugs and dispensing of prescriptions require a qualified pharmacist to be in attendance at all times. These rules create a permanent demand for locum pharmacists to cover the lunch breaks, holidays, and other absences of pharmacists working in hospitals and community pharmacies, in addition to the wide range of conventional jobs. Throughout the post-war decades there has been a relative shortage of pharmacists and the profession has expanded continuously. In 1963 the Pharmaceutical Society had 26,000 pharmacists registered. The 1991 Census counted 37,000 qualified pharmacists (Table 9.1).

In the first half of the twentieth century, pharmacy was a heavily male-dominated profession. It is estimated that numbers of women in pharmacy rose slowly from about 10% in 1941 to 15% in the 1950s, to about 20% in the 1960s, to 25% in the 1970s and 33% in 1981 (Crompton and Sanderson, 1990: 75–6). By 1991 women constituted 45% of people aged 18 and over with any qualification in pharmacy and 48% of all people working as pharmacists (Table 9.1).

An even older professional body is the Society of Apothecaries, founded in 1617 in Britain. This has also acted as a qualifying body, based on a seven-year apprenticeship. Today, the Society of Apothecaries persists as a licensing body for dispensers, who are qualified but low-level assistants to pharmacists. This is now a virtually all-female occupation. Entry qualifications are O-levels or equivalent secondary school diplomas and training consists of two years' work under the supervision of a pharmacist, followed by exams (Crompton and Sanderson, 1990: 72, 87). The occupation of dispenser is not separately counted in census statistics and it seems possible that some dispensers reported themselves, or were coded as, pharmacists in the 1991 Census. Some 5% of the female pharmacists in the SAR samples report no higher education qualifications at all (see Table 9.5) and it seems possible that these women are in fact qualified dispensers rather than qualified pharmacists.

The shortage of pharmacists is not expected to last beyond 1999 in Britain. But pharmacists will always need to use locums to cover for holidays and other absences, so part-time and temporary jobs should continue to be widely available, along with permanent and full-time jobs. The other advan-

TABLE 9.1. *Qualified pharmacists: activities and occupations*

	All		Men		Women	
	N	%	N	%	N	%
Highest qualification in pharmacy						
Total	35,960	100	19,560	100	16,400	100
Higher degree	2,140	6	1,360	7	780	5
First degree	33,020	92	17,890	91	15,130	92
Sub-degree level	800	2	310	2	490	3
Any qualification in pharmacy						
Total	37,320	100	20,410	100	16,910	100
Occupations of those in employment						
Managers and administrators	2,770	7	1,970	10	800	5
Professionals:						
pharmacists	22,520	60	11,700	57	10,820	64
other professions	1,280	3	850	4	430	3
Associate professionals						
health-related	300	1	90	*	210	1
other occupations	560	2	330	2	230	1
Clerical and secretarial	140	*	40	*	100	*
Craft and related	30	*	10	*	20	*
Personal & protective service						
health-related services (nurses, etc.)	10	*	—	—	10	*
other occupations	90	*	40	*	50	*
Sales	340	1	230	1	110	1
Plant and machine operatives	70	*	30	*	40	*
Other occupations/Not stated	220	1	80	*	140	1
Total in employment	28,330	76	15,370	75	12,960	77
Unemployed/government schemes	280	1	160	1	120	1
Economically inactive (students, permanently sick, retired, and other non-working)	8,710	23	4,880	24	3,830	23

Source: Tables 6 and 14B in *1991 Census—Qualified Manpower, Great Britain*, reporting 10% sample statistics for residents aged 18 and over with one or more higher education qualification in pharmacy.

tage of pharmacy as an occupation is that local jobs are available in community pharmacies as well as jobs in hospitals, pharmaceutical companies, and related businesses. Career ladders exist in both types of work. For example the Boots company, a retailer-cum-pharmacy chain of shops, traditionally required all shop managers to be pharmacists, thus providing opportunities for community pharmacists to move up into management.

A few of the people who obtain one qualification in pharmacy go on to obtain a higher qualification in another subject, and many people with a qualification in pharmacy do not work as pharmacists (Tables 9.1 and 9.2). Movement up into management is the most common pattern, but tiny numbers of qualified pharmacists, both men and women, work in a variety of lower grade occupations, some of them health-related, but many of them not (Table 9.1). The census information is too general for us to know whether, or how, the pharmacy qualification is being used. For example, sales representatives may be agents for pharmaceutical companies; people in advertising may be working on pharmaceutical company advertising campaigns. Equally, jobs in advertising and sales may have no connection with a pharmacist's training. A minority of people have important changes of direction in their employment career after they start work. However, there is no difference between men and women in this regard: both are equally likely to work in professional and managerial occupations, although men are twice as likely to reach management grades. On average, three-quarters of all qualified pharmacists aged 18 and over are in work, and only 5% are in associate professional or lower grade occupations (Table 9.1).

TABLE 9.2. *National estimates of the pharmacist workforce*

	Total		Men		Women	
	N	%	N	%	N	%
Totals	25,750	100	13,620	100	12,040	100
Full-time employees	14,800	57	8,170	60	6,630	55
Part-time employees	3,070	12	480	4	2,590	22
Solo self-employed	3,190	12	1,320	10	1,870	16
Small firms	4,380	17	3,520	26	860	7
Unemployed	220	1	130	1	90	1
Students with jobs	100	*	20	*	80	1
All employees	17,870	69	8,650	63	9,220	77
All self-employed	7,570	29	4,840	36	2,730	23
All other	320	1	150	1	170	1

Source: Table 4 in *1991 Census-Economic Activity* report presenting 10% sample data for Great Britain, residents aged 16 and over in employment who report their occupation as pharmacist.

LABOUR TURNOVER AND NON-WORKING WOMEN

The permanent demand for pharmacists is reflected in virtually no unemployment, relatively low turnover rates, and a very low incidence of women dropping out of the labour market (Tables 9.2 and 9.3). In effect, anyone who wants a job can get one and anyone who is not working is doing so from choice.

Pharmacists can be identified by their qualifications or by their occupation, but the characteristics of the profession are almost identical in each case

TABLE 9.3. *Key characteristics of the pharmacist workforce*

	All	Men	Women
Pharmacists defined by qualifications			
Percentage of people in work who are:			
solo self-employed	11	4	18
small firms	17	28	4
Percentage of employees working part-time	16	2	30
Turnover rates (%)	13	8	18
% non-working	5	—	11
Percentage in each type of occupation:			
male	9	11	7
mixed (pharmacist)	84	84	83
female	7	5	10
Pharmacists defined by occupation			
Percentage of people in work who are:			
solo self-employed	13	6	21
small firms	18	32	4
Percentage of employees working part-time	17	3	30
Turnover rates (%)	14	9	19
% non-working	6	1	12

Source: 1% SAR, Great Britain, residents aged 16–64 years.

(Table 9.3). Either way, only one per cent are unemployed, with no difference between men and women (Tables 9.1 and 9.2). Labour turnover rates for people working in integrated occupations average 14% for men and 25% for women (see Table 2.11). Among pharmacists, whether identified by qualifications or by occupation, turnover rates are significantly lower: 8% for men and 18% for women (Table 9.3). As shown in Chapter 4, one-quarter of all women aged 16–64 are non-working women who have temporarily dropped out of the labour market (see Table 4.1), and about half of them have not had a job for over ten years. Among pharmacists, whether identified by qualifications or by occupation, there are no male drop-outs and the non-working rate among women is relatively low at 11%–12% (Table 9.3). All of the non-working women had a job within the previous ten years, suggesting that spells out of the labour market are of relatively short duration among pharmacists. Most of them were young (aged 25–34 years), married, with children under the age of 16 years at home.

Another indicator of the strong demand for pharmacists is the relatively high level of part-time working in a professional occupation. As noted in Chapters 2 and 5, integrated occupations generally offer few opportunities for part-time work: 19% of women in integrated occupations are working part-time compared to 43% of women in female occupations (see Tables 2.3

and 5.9). In contrast, 30% of female employee pharmacists have part-time jobs (Table 9.3) and when the self-employed are included, the proportion working less than 30 hours a week is even higher at 39% of women (Table 9.5).

OCCUPATIONAL GRADE, EARNINGS, AND THE PAY GAP

The great majority of people qualified as pharmacists work in the integrated occupation of pharmacist (Tables 9.1 and 9.3) and are thus located in the Higher Service Class or in RG Social Class I (Table 9.4). Once again, there are virtually no differences between men and women. Pharmacists are a homogeneous group as regards social status and prestige, with a Cambridge social status score of 67, and scores of 85 on ISEI and 73 on SIOPS. (Annex A provides descriptions of these prestige scales.) Average hourly earnings excluding overtime pay for employees were about £13.30 in spring 1991, with no difference between full-time and part-time rates of pay. However, estimated earnings for female employees are well below estimated earnings for male employees: £11.67 an hour versus £15.24 an hour (Table 9.5). Estimated earnings for female full-time employees are 73% of male earnings, close to the

TABLE 9.4. *Social class and SEG of pharmacists*   column percent

	All	Men	Women
Goldthorpe Classes			
Higher service class	82	81	83
Lower service class	12	13	10
Routine non-manual	3	1	4
Personal service	1	1	1
Small proprietors, farmers	2	3	1
Lower technicians, foremen, manual workers	1	1	1
RG Social Class			
I Professional	78	78	78
II Managerial & Technical	17	18	15
IIIN Skilled white-collar	4	3	5
All manual Classes and Not Stated	1	1	2
Socio-Economic Group (SEG)			
1 employers and managers—large establishments	4	3	4
2 employers/managers—small establishments	6	10	2
3 professionals—self-employed	26	30	22
4 professionals—employees	52	49	56
5 ancillary workers, artists, supervisors	7	4	10
All other SEGs and Not Stated	5	3	7
Base N=100%	302	158	144

Source: 1% SAR, Great Britain, residents aged 16–64 years in employment whose highest educational qualification is in pharmacy.

TABLE 9.5. *Job characteristics of pharmacists*   cell percent

	All	Men	Women
Higher qualifications held			
Two or more	51	55	48
a higher degrees	8	10	7
b first degrees	87	87	86
c below degree level	2	2	2
Other	3	1	5
Hours worked (excluding overtime and meal breaks)			
Overtime 46+	16	28	6
Full-time 37–45	58	68	50
Reduced 30–36	6	2	9
Half-time 11–29	13	2	22
Marginal 1–10	7	—	13
Travel to work patterns			
Percentage of people who work:			
at home	2	3	2
no fixed place (home-based)	18	10	26
0–2 km from home	18	20	16
30+ km from home	6	7	4
walk to work	7	6	9
Employment status			
Managers/supervisors	—	—	—
Other employees	70	64	76
Solo self-employed	14	7	21
Small firms	16	29	3
Estimated hourly earnings			
All employees	1332	1524	1167
Full-time employees (30+)	1330	1517	1114
Part-time employees (<30)	1305	~	1308
Base N=100%	277	132	145

Source: 1% SAR, Great Britain, residents aged 16–64 years in employment who report their occupation as pharmacist.

average of 72% for all full-time and part-time employees in integrated occupations in Goldthorpe's Upper Service Class (see Tables 3.6 and 3.7). In all respects, pharmacists are a typical example of an integrated occupation, with the pay gap that remains in integrated occupations.

SELF-EMPLOYMENT

Information on employee earnings is less representative than for other occupations due to the high proportion of self-employed among pharmacists. One-third of male pharmacists are self-employed: 10% are solo self-employed and another 26% have their own small firm (Table 9.2), well above the average 11% rate for small firms set up by men in integrated occupations (see Table 2.3). Among women, 16% are solo self-employed (Table 9.2), slightly above the 10% rate among women in integrated occupations generally (see Table 2.3) but the 7% running a small firm is just average for women in integrated occupations (Tables 9.2 and 2.3). Significantly higher levels of self-employment are found whether pharmacists are identified by qualifications or by occupation (Table 9.3), with most men running a small firm employing others while most women are solo self-employed. As a result, four-fifths of all small firms in pharmacy are run by men (Table 9.2), and men are more likely to achieve management positions (SEG composition in Table 9.4). Men and women are roughly equally likely to use the opportunities for the independence of self-employment, but men are far more likely to exploit the opportunities for entrepreneurial activity, serious money-making, and being a manager (Table 9.5).

OTHER CHARACTERISTICS OF PHARMACISTS

In other respects, pharmacists are typical of professional people generally. For example, men tend to be more highly qualified than women: 55% compared with 48% have two or more higher education qualifications, 10% versus 7% have a higher degree (Table 9.5).

The sex differential in working hours among pharmacists (Table 9.5) is even greater than for people in mixed occupations generally (see Table 2.3). One-quarter of men regularly work 46 hours or more a week compared to only 6% of women; only 3% of men work part-time hours compared to 35% of women (Table 9.5). In effect, virtually all male pharmacists work long full-time hours whereas only half of female pharmacists do this. Given the substantial freedom of choice that exists in the profession, these patterns of work clearly reflect personal choices and preferences and imply quite different levels of commitment to paid work.

Homework is effectively not an option for pharmacists. However, one-quarter of women pharmacists work from home as a base and 16% work locally. Men are just as likely to work locally, 20%, but far fewer work from home as a base, 10% (Table 9.5). Women's greater emphasis on fitting paid work around domestic commitments is in evidence here.

ETHNIC MINORITIES AND WOMEN IN PHARMACY

There are few or no differences between men and women as regards personal characteristics. The only significant difference is that pharmacists include

TABLE 9.6. *Personal characteristics of pharmacists*

column percent

		All	Men	Women
Age	16–24	8	3	14
	25–34	33	32	34
	35–44	27	28	25
	45–54	21	25	16
	55–64	11	12	11
% non-white		14	17	12
% married		74	79	68
% living in family with				
	1+ dependent child	48	51	45
	non-dependent children	18	14	21
	no children	34	35	34
% in owner-occupied homes		95	97	93

Source: 1% SAR, Great Britain, residents aged 16–64 years in employment who report their occupation as pharmacist.

TABLE 9.7. *Self-employment rates by ethnic group and sex*

cell percent

		Solo S/E	Small firms	All S/E
Male pharmacists	all	7	32	39
	white	6	29	35
	non-white	10	50	60
Female pharmacists	all	23	4	27
	white	24	5	29
	non-white	9	—	9

Source: 1% SAR, Great Britain, residents aged 16–64 years in employment who report their occupation as pharmacist.

exceptionally high proportions of ethnic minority men and women: 17% and 12% respectively (Table 9.6) compared to 6% and 5% in integrated occupations generally (see Table 2.7). Most of the ethnic minority pharmacists are of Indian descent.

Even more notable is the way sex differences in patterns of self-employment persist across ethnic groups (Table 9.7). Men are more likely to choose self-employment than are women, but half of all ethnic minority men run their own small firm while none of the ethnic minority women do so. Women are more likely to choose to remain employees; even when they choose self-employment they typically work alone, without employees, and sometimes part-time as well. This preference for subordinate employee jobs is even more pronounced among ethnic minority women, hardly any of whom are self-employed.

It seems reasonable to assume that ethnic minority men and white women confront broadly similar levels of discrimination—in obtaining promotion within organizational hierarchies or in obtaining a bank loan to start a business, for example. The dramatic difference between these two groups of pharmacists in the proportion running a small firm thus reflects fundamental differences in work orientations, entrepreneurship, and risk-taking between men and women generally (Chauvin and Ash, 1994), which are highlighted within ethnic minority groups. These conclusions are reinforced by studies of pharmacists in the USA and other European countries.

COMPARISONS WITH THE USA

Developments in the USA are remarkably similar. Here too, the profession has been characterized by rapid expansion in the post-war decades and continuing labour shortages. So there have been plenty of jobs, full-time and part-time, for women and blacks entering the profession in recent decades (Reskin and Roos, 1990: 111–27; Sokoloff, 1992: 82–9). The proportion of women working in pharmacy rose from 8% in 1960 to 12% in 1970, 24% by 1980, and 32% by 1988, making a 40% rate seem very likely for the mid-1990s. Feminization of the profession proceeded more slowly than in Britain, despite the fact that the biggest expansion in employment was in the employee jobs in hospitals and chain store pharmacies that women prefer. The profession ranks very high in socio-economic status, only slightly lower than lawyers and physicians (Sokoloff, 1992: 26–8).

One main difference from Britain is that the expansion of chain store pharmacies in large shopping malls in the USA entailed the decline of independent retail pharmacies which had always been dominated by men. In 1956, 90% of pharmacists worked in community retail pharmacies, and half of them owned their shop, alone or with a partner. By 1970 only 22% of pharmacists were self-employed and this fell again to 10% by 1980 (6.5% of women and 12% of men). Reduced opportunities for entrepreneurial independence and upward social mobility through business ownership led to fewer men entering the profession from the late 1970s onwards, at a time when women were encouraged to qualify due to labour shortages in this and other health-care professions. The indications are that feminization is a continuing process in the USA, and will eventually turn pharmacy into an occupation dominated by women, black and white, due to the restructuring of the industry, the dominance of large employers and the way information technology has routinized much of the work.

Part-time jobs are far less common in the USA than in Britain. In 1994 almost half of all working women in the UK, compared to one-quarter in the USA, classified themselves as working part-time hours (Blossfeld and Hakim, 1997*a*: 5; see also Table 5.1). An important attraction of pharmacy for women in the USA is the potential for working part-time hours and for other forms of flexibility. In 1980 one-third of women pharmacists were working less than 35 hours a week, and half were working part-time and/or part-year (Reskin and Roos, 1990: 64, 125). It appears that labour shortages again helped graduate women to tailor jobs to their personal preferences, with convenience factors often taking priority over the pay and promotion concerns that dominate men's perspective.

OCCUPATIONAL SEGREGATION, DISCRIMINATION, AND WORK ORIENTATIONS

Pharmacy is an integrated occupation, which provides a wide range of opportunities, in most Western European countries, for full-time and part-time work, for temporary jobs and permanent jobs, for jobs in research and development as well as more routine work, for employee jobs in hospitals and pharmaceutical companies and for self-employment and running a small firm as a community pharmacist. The 'openness' of pharmacy as an occupation is demonstrated by its failure to close the door to women, as the medical profession did until equal opportunities legislation forced their hand, and by its now recruiting equal numbers of women and men. The openness of pharmacy as a profession is also attested to by the exceptionally high proportion of ethnic minority people working in the field. Pharmacy thus provides an excellent test of the thesis that occupational segregation is the principal cause of the pay gap and, more generally, is the key factor explaining women's lesser success in the labour market.

Pharmacy is an integrated occupation no matter what definition of integration is applied.[2] Therefore any remaining differences between men and women must be explained either by continuing discrimination within and around the profession or else by sex differentials in sex-role preferences and work orientations. The discrimination thesis seems to be comprehensively contradicted by all the evidence on ethnic minority groups in pharmacy, in Britain and the USA. There are disproportionately high numbers of ethnic minority men and women working in pharmacy, and ethnic minority men in

[2] As noted in Ch. 1, integrated occupations can be defined as those with 25%–55% female workers (40% ±15%) or as those with 30%–70% female workers (50% ±20%). On either definition, pharmacy became an integrated occupation by 1991, in Britain and the USA and, it appears, in many European countries. For example women's share of medical doctor and pharmacist jobs (grouped together) rose from 37% in 1977 to 42% in 1990 in West Germany, and from 30% in 1980 to 53% in 1991 in Spain (Rubery and Fagan, 1993: 19).

particular are attracted by the opportunities for combining entrepreneurial activity with a respectable profession in the form of a community pharmacy business in Britain. If discrimination is not a key factor, then the main explanation for continuing differences between men and women must be the attitudinal factors that are so often left out of the picture in labour market analysis. This conclusion is reinforced by the huge sex differentials within both white and ethnic minority groups in pharmacy.

In the context of a profession offering relatively unconstrained choice and a high demand for labour, women consistently choose part-time jobs and employee jobs while men consistently choose full-time jobs and self-employment in their own pharmacy business, not only in Britain but also in France (Crompton and Sanderson, 1990: 65–88; Crompton and Le Feuvre, 1996). Ethnic minority men in Britain are ten times more likely to establish their own pharmacy business than are white women. Even in France, where pronatalist policies support the working mother and women are more likely to work continuously if they work at all after childbirth, it is men who are most likely to be owners and partners in community pharmacy businesses while women are most likely to remain employees (Crompton and Le Feuvre, 1996: 433). The fact that institutional differences between France and Britain make no difference at all to employment patterns among women pharmacists in the two countries shows that integrated occupations reveal most clearly the impact of personal choice and sex differences in work orientations.

Highly qualified women do not necessarily adopt the same work orientations as men. They do not automatically discard 'traditional' sex-role preferences that define breadwinning as a man's responsibility and homemaking as a woman's responsibility. Highly educated women are just *less likely* to hold traditional sex-role preferences than women with secondary school qualifications or no qualifications. There is plenty of evidence from national surveys that a minority of highly qualified women continue to hold very traditional attitudes to a woman's role in the home and family and a majority hold ambivalent attitudes, which have a significant impact on their workrates (Hakim, 1996*b*: 185–6). One study found that around one-quarter of women working full-time in Service Class occupations, but more than half of those working part-time in Service Class occupations, accepted the modern sexual division of labour that allocates *primary* responsibility for homemaking to the wife and *primary* responsibility for breadwinning to the husband (Hakim and Jacobs, 1997). Crompton's research on female pharmacists and other professionals indicates that pharmacy attracts women who accept the modern sexual division of labour rather than career-committed women. Female pharmacists (along with many other female professionals) plan their employment careers around their anticipated roles as wife and mother, and frequently give priority to their domestic responsibilities over progression in their career (Crompton and Sanderson, 1990: 81–4; Crompton and Le

Feuvre, 1996: 434–5; Crompton and Harris, 1998). In terms of Hakim's (1996*a*: 110–12) typology, most pharmacists are 'drifters' or have 'unplanned careers'. More positively, they are 'adaptives' rather than work-centred or home-centred women (Hakim, 1998). The familial orientation of female pharmacists means that in practice they are secondary earners rather than coequal earners: they put their husband's career before their own, as well as putting their children before their paid work (Crompton and Le Feuvre, 1996: 434–5). The fact that pharmacists are professionals, and highly paid, does not mean that women automatically adopt the work orientations of a primary earner and thus a commitment to working full-time, year-round, continuously throughout life, which is the employment profile of virtually all men (Hakim, 1996*a*: 132–3). Most female pharmacists anticipate intermittent and part-time employment, at best, after their children are born (Crompton and Sanderson, 1990: 83) unless they live in a state that obliges all adults to work throughout life, as in Russia and Eastern Europe (Crompton and Harris, 1998).

It is thus not surprising that marked differences remain between men and women in pharmacy, in terms of hours worked, the incidence of small firms, and employee earnings. A small business, especially one employing staff, cannot be picked up and dropped at short notice in the same way as an employee job. It requires a long-term commitment and investment of time and effort of the sort that characterizes primary earners but not secondary earners. Similarly, management jobs are rarely available part-time, even in the highly flexible pharmacy trade (Crompton and Sanderson, 1990: 80), and cannot normally be picked up and put down at short notice. The lower proportion of employers and managers among female pharmacists is explained by the lower proportion of career-committed primary earners among women, most of whom are married and rely ultimately on their husband's income. The lower estimated earnings of female pharmacists, in the context of equal pay rates for full-time and part-time work, must be explained by these invisible differences in sex-role preferences and work orientations between men and women—differences that emerge in personal interviews and case studies but not in the census data on which this study is based. Differences in work orientations lead to faster promotion for men and thus vertical job segregation *within* the profession, which again remains invisible in most occupational classifications which, like the 1990 SOC, group all grades of pharmacist together in a single category.

Similar processes are found in other integrated occupations, including non-professional occupations. The travel agency industry has never been sex-stereotyped and has always employed men and women. Training is usually provided on the job, and experience is essential for promotion. The industry provides opportunities for upward mobility and for entrepreneurial activity on a very different basis from pharmacy. A case study of the travel agency industry in the USA in the mid-1970s (Mennerick, 1975) found little or no horizontal occupational segregation but substantial vertical job segregation. Travel agencies in large cities recruited roughly equal numbers of men and women, but men predominated in management while women predominated in sales jobs. However, women managers were more common in small agencies and in retail agencies, a finding that Mennerick had difficulty in explaining. The explanation may lie in women's preference for local jobs, as noted in Chapter 7, even if these jobs are less well-paid than jobs in city centres. Men are more likely to accept longer journeys to work to achieve higher-paid management jobs in larger agencies and in wholesale travel agencies, leaving greater opportunities for women to enter management jobs in small, local, retail travel agencies.

CONCLUSIONS

Pharmacy is an integrated occupation demonstrably free of sex and race discrimination with a strong demand for labour and a huge variety of work arrangements and job opportunities. None the less there is a substantial pay gap, with female full-time earnings averaging 73% of male earnings. Pharmacy provides an excellent test of the thesis that occupational segregation remains a principal cause of the pay gap between men and women and of women's lesser achievements in the workforce. Integrated occupations like pharmacy expose and highlight the sex differentials in sex-role preferences, work orientations, job choice, and work history, and their collective impact on employment careers and earnings.

In the twenty years following the introduction of sex discrimination and equal opportunities legislation in Britain there was a dramatic increase in the proportion of women entering professional and managerial positions (Hakim, 1992a). However, an insistence on paid work being fitted around familial responsibilities and a preference for convenience factors over high pay (Hakim, 1991) mean that women will generally be concentrated in the lower grades of professional and management occupations, even in the absence of sex discrimination, while men will continue to take the lion's share of higher grade jobs. The *relative* importance and impact of sex-role preferences, discrimination, and occupational segregation require reassessment.

10

Conclusions

Research on the labour market in the late twentieth century has tended to focus on perennial problems, such as unemployment and discrimination, or on the impact of changes in information and communication technologies (Daniel, 1987; Howard, 1995), economic shocks, and major swings in government policy (Boyer, 1989; Michie, 1992). This study has focused on the impact of social changes that produce less dramatic and sometimes invisible processes of gradual change and innovation in the labour market. The long-term impact of changes in sex-role attitudes, the feminization of the workforce, the prolongation of full-time education beyond adolescence and into early adulthood, the upskilling of the workforce, and the increased weight placed on autonomy and the exercise of skill by highly educated workers—all these have been slow and continuous processes of social change rather than attention-grabbing sudden events. As Lieberson (1985: 183–5) points out, it is easy to underestimate their cumulative, long-term impact. The innovations they produce remain hidden in part because labour market statistics are churned out on a regular basis to largely predetermined formats, using fixed definitions and classifications. What we perceive is shaped by theoretical and common-sense preconceptions about what it is we are looking for. Academic discipline-based theory produces just as many blind spots as policy-oriented inquiries. Both perspectives are disabling in different ways.

OCCUPATIONAL SEGREGATION AS A STRUCTURAL FEATURE OF THE LABOUR MARKET

Research on occupational segregation has so far been dominated by the search for an ideal single-number index which could be used to measure the pace of change over time in individual countries or groups of countries (Hakim, 1993*b*, 1993*c*; Watts, 1993; J. Jacobs, 1989*a*; Siltanen, Jarman, and Blackburn, 1995). The new approach applied throughout this book was more fruitful than expected, revealing that occupational segregation is not just a useful theoretical concept but also a concrete, structural feature of the labour market. Labour market analyses using the new typology of male-dominated, female-dominated, and integrated or mixed occupations reveal fundamental differences between integrated occupations and segregated occupations, and between female-dominated occupations and other occupations. A typology developed as an essentially statistical exercise (Hakim, 1993*b*) has been shown to identify three substantively different occupational sectors in the labour market, which structure patterns of employment and the characteristics of jobs and of workers, as demonstrated in Chapters 2 to 8.

Occupational segregation is a permanent structural feature of labour markets, perhaps even more so than labour market segmentation. There is some debate about the extent of labour market segmentation in countries with high labour mobility, such as the USA. But no one disputes the universality of occupational segregation and the very slow and small decline in levels of segregation even after the implementation of sex discrimination and equal opportunities legislation. Our analysis explains why occupational segregation has become an enduring feature of the labour market which is likely to continue well into the 21st century, long after equal opportunities policies have achieved their full impact.

Our explanation takes account of the differences between primary earners and secondary earners. Primary and secondary earners have different sex-role preferences, different work orientations, and seek different things from paid work (Hakim, 1996*a*: 65–75, 1997*a*: 61–2). These differences cannot be 'read off' a person's sex or gender, so the conventional focus on sex discrimination (Blau and Ferber, 1992) becomes too simplistic. At the end of the twentieth century, the majority of women still regard themselves as secondary earners who are financially dependent on another person, or the state, and who are working to supplement but not replace this other source of income. In contrast, virtually all men are expected to be primary earners throughout their life, whether they like it or not, and to support not only themselves but also a family (Hakim, 1996*a*; Hakim and Jacobs, 1997). The polarization of working women, and a revaluation of work among men may eventually modify this scenario, but are unlikely to fundamentally change it (Hakim, 1997*a*: 58–62).

Occupational segregation has different social functions in different societies and at different time periods (Hakim, 1994), but its chief function today seems to be to provide clearly differentiated groups of occupations for primary and secondary earners. Equal opportunities laws and policies ensure that all occupations and jobs must remain formally open to all and any applicants. But this does not mean that all occupations and jobs will be equally attractive to all men and all women. In practice, primary earners will gravitate towards jobs in male-dominated and integrated occupations while secondary earners, most of whom are wives and mothers, will gravitate towards jobs in female-dominated occupations. As we have shown throughout Chapters 2 to 8, the three types of occupation differ systematically in the demands they make on workers, in the rewards they offer, and in the people they attract.

CHANGING PATTERNS OF WORKING HOURS

It is widely recognized that the current dichotomous classification of jobs as full-time or part-time is crude and uninformative, particularly in the context of changing patterns of work and working time, the long-term reduction in working hours among full-time workers, and new forms of what is called 'labour flexibility', such as annual hours contracts and on-call (zero-hours) contracts. The SARs provided the basis for exploratory analyses with a number of alternative classifications, allowing us to identify a new typology that successfully differentiates between types of part-time worker and types of part-time job. Full-time jobs are redefined as those with 30 or more hours per week and subdivided into *overtime jobs* with 46 or more hours a week on a regular basis excluding meal breaks and overtime (an average of 57 hours a week in Britain, well above the average 48 hours a week limit imposed by EU health and safety rules); *long full-time jobs* with 37–45 hours a week (38 hours a week on average in Britain); and *reduced hours jobs* with 30–36 hours a week. This latter group is identified as the source of many difficulties in cross-national comparisons, as the group shares all the characteristics of full-time jobs but has been labelled as 'part-time' in countries such as Sweden and East Germany where *any* reduction in the standard 40-hour week was regarded as unusual (Bosch *et al.*, 1994). Part-time jobs are redefined as those with less than 30 hours a week and split into two groups: *half-time jobs* with 11–29 hours a week, which in practice are concentrated around 20 hours a week on average in most countries, and *marginal jobs* with up to 10 hours a week, including one-day-a-week jobs, with an average of 7–8 hours a week in Britain. The new classification fits in with current European Commission thinking and policies, particularly in the identification of marginal workers as a distinct group which is substantively outside the workforce and can legitimately be excluded from labour law and social insurance coverage. The classification helps to make sense of otherwise seriously conflicting research findings on part-time work in Europe and the USA (Blossfeld and Hakim, 1997). It is simple enough to be self-explanatory and applied in most surveys.

On this new classification, only one-third of working women aged 16–64 years (excluding student jobs) are in part-time jobs, but 92% of all part-time workers are women, and 81% of all part-time jobs are in female-dominated occupations (Table 10.1). The new classification identifies a smaller part-time workforce, but the overlap between part-time work, secondary earners, and female-dominated occupations becomes very well defined. The composition of the workforce is much the same whether we use the classification applied throughout this book or the alternative with a 50% midpoint (Table 10.1). Only 2% of men aged 16–64 in employment (excluding student jobs) hold part-time jobs. It is only among students in full-time education that male

Conclusions

TABLE 10.1. *Composition of the workforce in Britain*   total percent

	Average weekly hours excluding breaks and overtime							
	Full-time 30+		Half-time 11–29		Marginal up to 10		Total	
	a	b	a	b	a	b	a	b
All								
Male occupations	38	39	1	1	*	*	39	40
Integrated occupations	20	24	2	3	*	1	22	28
Female occupations	25	20	11	10	3	3	39	32
All persons aged 16–64 years	83	83	14	14	4	4	100	
							N=446,139	
Men								
Male occupations	62	64	1	1	*	*	63	65
Integrated occupations	23	26	*	*	*	*	23	26
Female occupations	13	8	1	1	*	*	14	9
All men aged 16–64 years	98	98	2	2	*	*	100	
							N=248,982	
Women								
Male occupations	7	8	2	2	*	*	9	9
Integrated occupations	16	23	3	6	1	1	20	30
Female occupations	41	34	24	22	6	6	71	61
All women aged 16–64 years	64	64	29	29	7	7	100	
							N=197,157	

Notes: Percentage distributions are shown in two versions:
   a with integrated occupations defined as those 25%–55% female (40% ±15%);
   b with integrated occupations defined as those 30%–70% female (50% ±20%).

Source: 2% SAR, Great Britain, data for residents in employment aged 16–64 years, excluding student jobs.

part-time employment reaches significant levels: half (47%) of all jobs ever held by male students are part-time jobs compared to two-thirds (64%) of all jobs ever held by female students. Over half of all student jobs involve part-time work, and their inclusion in official statistics on employment produces a serious distortion. Student employment demonstrates once again that the part-time workforce consists almost exclusively of secondary earners, people who are not earning a living and rely primarily on a spouse, parent, or the state for financial support, an option so far closed to men who have left full-time education but one that remains open to adult women.

EROSION OF THE BOUNDARY BETWEEN EMPLOYMENT AND ECONOMIC INACTIVITY

As the numbers of students aged 16 and over in full-time education have expanded, so has student employment. The census SARs understate student employment, but they display how widespread it has become, involving young women and men in equal numbers. The prolongation of full-time education beyond adolescence and into early adulthood seems to require and entail student employment, to provide some measure of the financial independence and sense of adulthood that has to be held in abeyance while studies continue. Most term-time jobs are marginal jobs, illustrating the fact that marginal jobs are held by people who are substantively out of the labour market. Summer holiday jobs are more likely to be full-time jobs, and temporary jobs and student workrates shoot up in the summer months.

Some countries, such as Denmark, the Netherlands, Australia, the USA, and Canada, have much higher levels of student employment than in Britain. Most European countries have lower levels, although student employment is expanding almost everywhere. Student jobs have become a permanent feature of the labour market at the start of the 21st century, thus eroding the definitional boundary line between full-time education (and hence economic inactivity) and employment. Our review exposed the ambivalence currently displayed in labour market statistics, with student jobs sometimes excluded and sometimes included in official statistics on the workforce. At the minimum, this is confusing. Arguably, it is also misleading, because a job that involves up to ten hours a week (and only 7 hours a week on average) cannot in any sense be regarded as a 'proper job' of interest to the ordinary worker who works a 37-hour week on average (with all part-timers included) or 38 hours a week (with marginal workers excluded). More concretely, the inclusion of student jobs in labour force statistics inflates headcount employment by at least 3.5%, as noted in Chapter 6, substantially inflates turnover rates (by 11% on average but far more for part-time jobs), and may also distort other labour market indicators.

We conclude that the ILO's minimalist definition of employment as one hour's work a week has become impractical and unhelpful in the context of rising student employment and a small but significant marginal workforce. The definition of a job should revert to earlier definitions that included a minimum hours threshold, for example to exclude paid work involving no more than ten hours a week. Marginal workers could still be counted, but as a separate category rather than within headcount employment.[1]

---

[1] In the 1980s and 1990s labour statisticians came to agree that the ILO one-hour-a-week definition of a job was inappropriate and should be replaced by some higher minimum hours threshold. However, they were unable to agree a common minimum, with proposals ranging

The expansion of student jobs and the difficulties of classifying them in labour force statistics also point to the need for better conceptual frameworks for the analysis of multiple activities and statuses. This is a new development that goes well beyond student jobs and is likely to be a key feature of employment in the 21st century. Multiple activities—such as holding two or more jobs—and multiple statuses—such as being *both* a full-time student and in employment, or being full-time unemployed while holding a temporary (part-time) job—have important consequences for policy. Until now, in most Western countries, employment and social welfare policies have been designed around the assumption of a clear dividing line between full-time work and full-time unemployment, between economic activity and economic inactivity. Student jobs are of particular interest because they illustrate how both boundary lines have broken down. In the long term, only universalistic policies such as a guaranteed basic income can cope with people having multiple statuses and multiple activities. In the short term, more modest, incremental policy modifications will be needed. However, neither will be possible without adequate information on the innovations that are emerging spontaneously in the way people organize and combine their activities and incomes from different sources. Labour statistics would benefit from continuous and inventive review by specialists with substantive knowledge of labour market trends, to counteract statisticians' emphasis on continuity in methods and conceptual frameworks.

SELF-EMPLOYMENT AS AN INDICATOR OF WORK ORIENTATIONS

The rise in female self-employment was especially dramatic in Britain. But across OECD countries, women increasingly see entrepreneurial activity and self-employment as alternative avenues for employment and advancement (OECD, 1994: 125). For some women, investment in higher education qualifications provides access to self-employment as a professional, for example in law, accountancy, or medicine. For other women, self-employment provides a way round the 'glass ceiling' problem restricting careers in internal labour markets. For yet others, self-employment provides one route to achieving flexible hours, part-time hours, home-based work, increased autonomy and independence.

Self-employment also illustrates, at the aggregate level, the continuing sex differences in work orientations that are partially hidden in the employee workforce where jobs are shaped primarily by employers. The self-employed

from 8 to 16 hours a week. From 1987 onwards, Statistics Netherlands has excluded people working less than 12 hours a week from Dutch employment statistics—so far the only country to make the change.

have greater freedom to structure their jobs to their own preferences than does the average employee. All the characteristics of the male and female employee workforces are also found among the self-employed, and the sex differences are sometimes magnified—for example, in hours worked. However, the key sex difference is in self-employment rates themselves. Nationally, men remain four times more likely than women to become self-employed, whether working as solo self-employed or as the owner of a small business employing others. In the highly qualified and integrated occupation of pharmacist, the sex difference takes a different form, with men far more likely to be running a small business while women are more likely to be working as solo self-employed. Women's general propensity towards a lesser investment in employment careers is displayed again among the self-employed.

The self-employed are now dispersed across the whole occupational structure. Desire for the larger degree of autonomy and independence offered by self-employment is no longer limited to a small and dwindling petite bourgeoisie class but pervades all occupational grades, and is probably filtering through to the employee workforce at each level as well. The combination of a more highly educated workforce and an increased taste for some degree of autonomy and independence in work could change employment relationships in the near future.

CONNECTED CHOICES

Most of our analysis has relied on cross-tabulation and may be rejected by some as descriptive rather than explanatory. We would argue that our approach comes closer to identifying genuine causal processes and explanations than the type of 'variable sociology' promoted by regression analysis, for example in identifying the role of home-ownership in tying women into long-term paid employment. As Lieberson (1985: 155), Esser (1996), and Hedström and Swedberg (1996) point out, multivariate analysis, and similar methodologies that focus on variables, readily use the language of explanation but rarely go beyond description. Esser argues that variable-centred sociology is *'not explanatory*, is *incomplete* and in a specific way is *meaningless'* (Esser, 1996: 159, emphasis in the original). He argues further that this type of analysis produces 'facile', 'superficial', and 'mechanistic pseudo-explanations' that 'do not in fact have anything to say about causal processes . . . processual interdependencies or . . . the subjectively sensible decisions taken by actors' (Esser, 1996). Lieberson's arguments about (unmeasured) selectivity, asymmetrical causal processes, and the misapplication of controls constitute the most compelling arguments against the now routine use of regression analysis in social science. He points out that the multivariate analyses currently fashionable in sociology would never lead to the discovery of gravity or other fundamental causes (Lieberson, 1985: 90–103). Multi-variate analysis cannot distinguish between basic and superficial causes, frequently clouds the picture with non-essential details about variation in basic causal processes, and the addition of controls can be counter-productive and produce misleading results (Lieberson, 1985: 120–51, 185, 189, 194, 207, 211). He points out that the initial zero-order association may often be the closest approximation to the true association, and argues for the principle of parsimony in identifying causes and explanations for empirical research results (Lieberson, 1985: 42, 196–7).

Regression analysis of labour market datasets can mislead because it implies that the impact of each variable can be separated from the impact of all other variables, that the impact of economic and social factors can be studied outside the causal process in which they are located. The implicit underlying assumption is that causal sequences and selectivity are irrelevant, that patterns of association are random rather than selective, that all possible combinations of occupations, job types, and work arrangements can be found in the real world, so that we can meaningfully isolate the impact of one factor—such as part-time hours—net of all other factors. This assumption is false. Most occupations do not come in an infinite variety of types. The census SARs are large enough to reveal some dominant linkages and the connected choices that ensue from them.

With occupational segregation structuring the labour market, aspects of employment that are often studied separately are in fact interconnected. As noted throughout Chapters 2 to 8, hours of work, labour turnover, workplace location, travel to work patterns, occupational grade, and earnings are all linked in the distinctive profiles of male, female, and integrated occupations. It follows that occupational choice entails a set of linked employment arrangements and options. Choices in the labour market are always *connected choices*.

Only 17% of all jobs are part-time (with less than 30 hours a week). But 43% of all women in female-dominated occupations are working part-time hours. Only one-quarter (27%) of all jobs are local, in the sense of being located within 2 km of the worker's home address. However, half (45%) of all part-time jobs are local jobs. Only 29% of all local jobs are part-time jobs, but 47% of all local jobs held by women are part-time, almost twice as many as the 28% share of women's jobs in wider labour markets. One-third (36%) of female occupations are part-time compared to only 9% of integrated occupations and 3% of male occupations. However, 54% of women in female occupations in *local* labour markets are working part-time hours, almost twice as many as the 33% part-time share of women's jobs in wider labour markets.

In practice, choosing a female occupation normally gives access to part-time jobs and to local jobs, whereas these options are rarely available in male and integrated occupations. In practice, choosing a part-time job and a local job typically entails working in a female-dominated occupation. These choices are connected choices; they overlap and link together in the way labour markets are structured and in the workers they recruit. In general, male and integrated occupations mainly recruit primary earners, while female occupations mainly recruit secondary earners. As the female work-force polarizes (Rubery, 1988: 44, 145, 159, 268, 278; Humphries and Rubery, 1992; Berger, Steinmüller, and Sopp, 1993; Fagan and Rubery, 1996; Hakim, 1996a), these distinctions are becoming more pronounced over time. The difference in average earnings between full-time and part-time jobs thus reflects and includes a number of connected choices in occupation and location, a number of connected factors such as educational qualifications, labour turnover, and job tenure, and unmeasured differences in work orientations between full-time and part-time workers. Main (1988b) also noted close links between part-time work, discontinuous work histories, and low levels of educational qualifications among women, with a joint impact on earnings; he admitted that regression analysis could not really identify the causal processes involved. The lower wages of part-time jobs reflect a complex combination of differences from full-time jobs, thus denying the simplistic conclusion of general or universal employer discrimination against part-time workers so often resorted to in feminist studies.

Feminists argue that all occupations could potentially be redesigned on a part-time basis, or to suit other preferences, that the connections observed are coincidental rather than necessary. It is undoubtedly true that many current features of occupations are gratuitous additions that are not essential to the task in question, with men contributing most of these gratuitous features which serve to define their work as essentially masculine in nature. Excessive hours of overtime, to prove one's dedication and commitment to the job, is the most obvious example of a job characteristic that is not necessary and may even be counter-productive. Many occupations that are currently organized exclusively on a full-time basis, and/or invariably entail long hours of overtime, could in fact be organized so as to permit part-time hours and/or to eliminate excessive and regular overtime hours. The Japanese model of the company man who only goes home to sleep is neither civilized nor necessary. Part-time work and reduced hours work could be extended to a wider range of jobs. Homework and telework are important innovations because they offer the potential of simultaneously solving the connected problems of work hours and work location rigidities while people remain in the same job and occupation.

However, there are limits to the potential for work reorganization, especially within senior and highly qualified grades of work. The job of President of the USA, or of any other nation state, is never going to be part-time. Similarly, senior management jobs in any organization will always require full-time work if they are at all central to the organization's activities. Part-time work at senior levels is only feasible for tasks or responsibilities that are peripheral rather than central, that arise periodically rather than on a continuous basis. The concentration of part-time jobs in lower grades of work is not due to accident or prejudice but to the genuine practical feasibility of reorganizing the work into discrete blocks of time. Work that requires a 'critical mass' to be seriously productive, at the level of the individual or the team, is less open to reorganization. One example is research. Great discoveries will rarely be made by part-time researchers. The common feature of Darwin, Einstein, Marx, and Marie Curie is that they never stopped working or thinking about their work. Certain types of work do require a major investment: long hours and a high degree of commitment to the activity in order to achieve worthwhile results as distinct from routine or mediocre results. In some occupations, the connections are necessary.

Finally, in those occupations where part-time work is feasible and accepted, it seems likely that full-time workers will generally be more successful than part-timers, in terms of achievements and promotion, even in the absence of discrimination. The reasons for this will vary from occupation to occupation, but full-time workers will generally have an edge over people working half-time hours. Even in the absence of discrimination, we can expect secondary earners to be concentrated in part-time jobs and in lower grades of work, while primary earners are concentrated in full-time jobs and achieve the greater share of promotions into the top jobs.

EQUAL OPPORTUNITIES, WORK ORIENTATIONS, AND LABOUR MARKET OUTCOMES

The academic focus on using single number indices of occupational segregation to monitor trends over time has obscured from view the emergence of a qualitatively new sector of integrated occupations sitting on the boundary line between male-dominated and female-dominated occupations. Integrated occupations recruit men and women proportionally to their numbers in the whole workforce. In Britain, they are the smallest group of occupations: one-fifth of 371 occupations listed in the 1990 SOC and one-fifth of the workforce on the definition used in this study (see Table 1.1). On other definitions, and with other datasets, integrated occupations can be a small or substantial element in the workforce (see Table 1.4). One of the key conclusions of this study is that male-dominated and female-dominated occupations have a great deal in common, contrary to the assumptions of patriarchy theorists and policy-makers. It is integrated occupations that are distinctive. Integrated occupations emerge as the most highly qualified, with a large share of Service Class occupations and very few jobs in the lowest social classes and occupational grades. They also have high proportions of self-employed people. Certificated skills and expertise create a uniquely egalitarian and open labour market in the integrated sector, overcoming the need to rely on sex stereotyping and statistical discrimination to allocate people to jobs. In Britain it is integrated occupations that have the highest average earnings and also the highest pay gap, in contrast with the USA where male-dominated occupations have the highest earnings and the highest pay gap. The pay gap for full-time employees is significantly lower within sex-segregated occupations and differs little between male-dominated and female-dominated occupations in each social class in Britain. Unmeasured vertical segregation and the pay gap are greatest in managerial grades rather than in professional grades, suggesting that comparative studies of these senior grades would be the most fruitful area for further research.

The case study of pharmacists in Chapter 9 demonstrates how and why the pay gap between men and women continues in integrated occupations, in the absence of sex and race discrimination and in the context of a strong demand for labour. Highly educated professional women do not necessarily adopt career-centred work orientations similar to those of male professionals, and if they do, these do not always last beyond the birth of children. Many women privately retain so-called 'traditional' sex-role attitudes and actively choose to organize any paid work around their role as wife and mother. Workers who give priority to familial responsibilities will inevitably prefer jobs offering convenience factors over jobs offering high pay and promotion prospects, and they are unlikely to seek management positions which often do not have well-defined limits to responsibilities and working hours. Many female pharmacists drop out of the labour market completely while their children are young and return to temporary and part-time jobs later on. Sex differences in work orientations do not imply lesser professionalism or productivity in the job. Sex differences in work orientations identify the different place of employment in the lives and priorities of men and women which can lead to vertical segregation within occupations and thus a continuing pay gap.

These results undermine a number of theories that have held sway in academic circles and that underpin many of the policies of the Equal Opportunities Commission in Britain and the European Commission in Brussels. Our findings discredit the argument from patriarchy theory that occupational segregation is essential to the maintenance of male power and dominance (Hartmann, 1976). The results undermine the widely held theory that occupational segregation is the crucial factor explaining the sex differential in earnings, so that the key to eliminating the pay gap is to break down barriers restricting women's access to male-dominated occupations. They also cast doubt on the argument that a principal cause of women's lower average earnings relative to men is the devaluation of women's work, pointing to the need for greater emphasis on equal value (comparable worth) policies. Our results show some evidence of women's jobs being devalued in that, in each RG Social Class, female-dominated occupations have lower average earnings than male-dominated occupations. But this is clearly not the most important factor in explanations for the earnings difference between men and women, and USA studies that set out to prove the importance of the devaluation of women's caring work failed to find any support for the thesis (Kilbourne *et al.*, 1994). More important, close inspection of the list of female-dominated occupations (see Annex B) shows that by the end of the twentieth century these had become typically gender-neutral rather than feminine, and had lost their historical connection with women's domestic activities and presumed skills. As the social functions of occupational segregation change, so does the work done in each sector. It may well be that caring work remains undervalued today, as compared with equivalent male jobs. However, there is no evidence that this is the main source of the undervaluation of women's work, and of women's exploitation more generally (Bubek, 1995). Women's market work now includes very little caring work and, with declining birthrates, caring work is no longer the principal component of domestic work either (Hakim, 1996*a*: 46–53), even if it can be the most disruptive element.

The patriarchy thesis that occupational segregation is essential to maintaining earning differences between men and women assumes that three separate forms of segregation are inextricably linked. It can be useful to distinguish between economic segregation, social segregation, and physical segregation. Economic segregation refers to structures and policies that maintain unequal pay for men and women. Social segregation refers to the custom of having separate occupations and other activities for men and women. Physical segregation refers to the custom of having separate workplaces, schools, hospitals, and other public establishments for men and women. The patriarchy thesis effectively argues that social segregation is both necessary and sufficient to achieve economic segregation. In practice, the historical record shows that the pay gap was maintained directly by employers and trade unions over a century of huge changes in the occupational structure and the pattern of occupational segregation (Hakim, 1994, 1996*a*: 176). The case study of pharmacy in Chapter 9 also shows that substantial sex differences in earnings persist in integrated occupations with a high demand for labour. We conclude that any links between social and economic segregation, between occupational segregation and the pay gap, are coincidental rather than causal.

One popular version of the patriarchy thesis is the idea that equality of access to highly paid occupations will produce equality of incomes for men and women. At its simplest, this popular variant presents men as monopolizing access to a hidden treasure which women believe they should share. It is reflected in European Commission thinking as well as in popular feminist writing (Hoskyns, 1985, 1996). In reality, equality of opportunity does *not* automatically produce equality of outcomes because of the *ceteris paribus* assumption. In real life, all other factors are not equal. The argument also fails to notice that many people in male-dominated occupations are not especially well paid but achieve high earnings by working long hours or accepting unattractive working conditions which most women will not tolerate.

It is hard to overstate the significance of these conclusions for employment policy. The purpose of equal opportunities and sex discrimination legislation is to create a level playing field, to ensure fair competition for unequal prizes. There is good evidence that sex discrimination may continue to operate, invisibly and unconsciously, even in the most well-intentioned organizations (Hakim, 1996a: 184). But it does not follow that all differences between women and men in employment can immediately be attributed to sex discrimination. Yet this is, in practice, the assumption underlying the European Commission's (1994d, 1997) policy proposals for the 21st century, in particular the decision to treat the elimination of occupational segregation as a main policy objective, the decision to shift the burden of proof to employers in sex discrimination cases once a worker has demonstrated a prima-facie case by showing that (small) sex differences in outcomes are present, and the individualization of rights and benefits based on the assumption that each individual worker is (or should be) self-supporting and independent.

The European Commission has very little scope for intervention in the European labour market. It makes the most of those competencies it does have, in particular by seeking to enlarge its role in the application of Article 119 of the Treaty of Rome on equal pay. The Commission has now decided that its role as guardian of the Treaty, in particular the implementation of Article 119 on equal pay for equal work and equal opportunities for men and women, requires the desegregation of the labour market as a principal policy objective (European Commission, 1996: 8, 26, 1997: 27–41).[2] Our research

[2] In the fine print of the Commission's 1994 White Paper the policy objective is specified as *vertical desegregation*, that is, opening all levels of seniority to women. This principle is already covered by the Equal Treatment Directive of 1976 which laid down the principle of non-discrimination as regards access to employment and promotion, *inter alia*, so an additional Directive is not necessary. Furthermore, the Commission's policy objective is always described under the much broader heading of 'desegregating the labour market', including horizontal desegregation, and women are described as the 'victims' of segregation of the labour market as well as pay discrimination (European Commission, 1994c: 59, 1994d: 42, 1996: 8, 26, 1997: 27–41). This wider objective of outlawing all forms of occupational segregation is consistent with other Commission policies and funded programmes, in particular their efforts to legitimize and promote positive discrimination in favour of women in selection processes for male-dominated occupations (European Commission, 1997: 27), a policy that provokes a good deal of criticism (Addison and Siebert, 1993: 28). This objective became visible in the late 1990s when the Commission attempted to neutralize the European Court of Justice's ruling in the *Kalanke* case that positive discrimination is unlawful. The primary purpose of positive

results suggest that outlawing occupational segregation will not have any significant effect on the sex differential in earnings. The policy is also contradicted by the results of the Commission's own research, which concluded that desegregation is neither a practical nor appropriate objective (Rubery and Fagan, 1993: 121). East Germany (prior to unification) provides a strategic case here. Attempts to desegregate occupations in East Germany were generally unsuccessful and women often reverted to female-dominated white-collar jobs, even though these were less well paid. As a result, women's average earnings remained only 75% of male earnings despite high levels of qualification (Rubery and Fagan, 1993: 9–10).

Occupational segregation is universal, and has varied relatively little over time and across societies. There are substantial differences between countries, and times, in the *pattern* of occupational segregation, which indicate that the sexual division of paid labour can be organized and reorganized to serve a range of different purposes. It carries advantages for women as well as for men. Occupational segregation protects women's employment opportunities, by giving women priority in certain jobs, even in recession. The European Commission is right to argue that the principle of equality of *access* to all occupations must be guaranteed. But the Commission's argument that occupational segregation is invariably disadvantageous to women and is the principal cause of low pay, atypical work, insecure jobs, and limited career possibilities (European Commission, 1996: 26) is simply unfounded.

In sum, occupational segregation is not now the main cause of the pay gap, and probably never was. We must now reassess the relative importance of sex discrimination in promotion patterns and in access to higher grade jobs and sex differences in work orientations and job preferences as explanations for the sex differential in earnings. As President Kennedy pointed out, the great enemy of truth is very often not the lie, deliberate, contrived, and dishonest,

---

discrimination in favour of women is of course to desegregate occupations as a worthwhile objective in its own right. In the *Kalanke* case there was positive discrimination in favour of a woman in preference to an equally well-qualified man for posts where women were under-represented, in accordance with the provisions of laws governing the appointment of officials in particular German *Länder*. The ECJ ruled that positive discrimination is contrary to EU law. The Commission was openly reluctant to accept this ruling and defiantly sought to neutralize it through a series of reviews of its implications which continued to argue the case for positive action in favour of women, effectively rewording the ECJ's decision so as to negate its impact. (In November 1997, the ECJ ruled that the similar *Marschall* v. *Land Nordrhein-Westfalen* case was an example of affirmative action, which is lawful, rather than positive discrimination, which is unlawful.) The Commission's emphasis on desegregating the labour market from the mid-1990s onwards is all the more remarkable because the topic of occupational segregation attracted virtually no attention at all in the 1980s, with only brief mentions in reports on women's access to jobs (European Commission, 1989: 87; 1990: 92), and because it refuses to take account of the Commission's own research results (Rubery and Fagan, 1993; Hakim, 1996*a*: 92–4).

but the myth, persistent, persuasive, and unrealistic. In attacking occupational segregation as the main source of sex inequality in the labour market, we have perhaps been tilting at windmills, like Don Quixote.

LOOKING AHEAD

There is no doubt that technological developments, particularly in IT, are having the greatest impact on employment, changing the substantive content and organization of market work. Social change has a less remarkable and more diffuse impact on the labour market, altering the social composition of labour supply, the commitment people bring to work and their expectations from it. However, the emergence of a substantial workforce of secondary earners could have major long-term implications.

Reliable methods of contraception and improved standards of health have enabled women to control and plan their childbearing and have led to a massive fall in fertility levels over the twentieth century. An average of two children per couple in rich modern societies instead of up to 12, or even 16 as in the past, has freed women to participate in the labour market or to do other things. The women's movement has promoted aspirations to self-realization beyond the domestic sphere and has championed the idea that dignity and equality for women require an independent wage. Statistics designed to monitor male employment give the impression that women now constitute almost half the workforce—in Britain, the USA, and many other countries. On a headcount basis this is true, but also misleading. In the majority of cases, women's involvement in market work is different in volume, nature, and pattern from men's lifetime full-time permanent employment histories. In addition, the extension of education beyond adolescence into early adulthood for half or more of young people, instead of a tiny élite, is the catalyst for the new phenomenon of student employment. The growth of early retirement schemes has created a substantial minority group of people aged 50 and over whose income consists of an employer's occupational pension, often supplemented by temporary, casual, or part-time jobs, as an employee or in self-employment.

In these three groups, paid work is a secondary activity or status to some other, primary status—as homemaker and mother, student, or retiree. In all these groups, employment is not the central focus of life, not the main source of income, and is probably not the main source of personal identity. The work they do may potentially be regarded as more than 'just a job', in part because secondary earners can afford to choose work they find interesting, but these secondary earners cannot be assumed to be seeking long-term careers or a 'job for life' in the same way as primary earners. Their commitment to and involvement in market work differs subtly but substantively.

One consequence is that a great proliferation of types of job and a greater diversity of working hours are acceptable to these groups of (potential) work-ers: half-time and marginal jobs, part-time or full-time self-employment, temporary and casual jobs. These innovations emerged more quickly in the unregulated British labour market than in the highly regulated labour markets of Germany and France, for example. However, the expansion of 'atypical' and 'non-standard' jobs is gradually affecting labour markets in all rich modern societies. This is the sort of visible change that trade unions readily notice and respond to. The other, less visible change is the reorgani-zation of occupational segregation to create a somewhat separate and dis-tinctive labour market for secondary workers. Because women constitute the majority of secondary workers, these occupations now employ more women than men, but they are otherwise gender-neutral occupations.

Labour market analysts, labour statisticians, and policy-makers must all adjust their theoretical perspectives, conceptual frameworks, and policies to take account of this fundamental social change which has long-term conse-quences for the labour market.

ANNEX A

Labour Market Data in the 1991 Census
1% and 2% SARs

A good introduction to the labour market data in the SARs is provided by the published census 100% and 10% statistics in the reports on *Economic Activity*, on *Qualified Manpower*, and on *Workplace and Transport to Work*. However, the data contained in the SARs goes beyond these statistics in two ways. First, the Census Microdata Unit (CMU) at Manchester University actively seeks to enhance the value of the datasets by adding extra variables from other sources and by adding new derived variables of interest to academic social scientists. Second, the coding of variables in the SARs is full enough to allow researchers to identify and utilize additional information which is not used at all in the published census reports (such as retrospective employment data) or is used only minimally (such as information on student jobs). The first type of information is described in CMU's documentation for the SARs. The second type of information is by definition 'hidden' within the SAR files and has to be extracted by the researcher's analytical work. Several chapters of this book present analyses of the most important hidden labour market data in the SARs: retrospective employment data; concurrent and previous jobs of students in full-time education who are classified as economically inactive; jobs held by people retired on occupational pensions; and people who genuinely work at home (excluding people who live at work or have live-in jobs, who also coded themselves as homeworkers). This Annex describes this additional labour market data available in the SARs but not reported on or used in the official census publications.

Earnings estimates

The British census has never included any questions on income or earnings. Earnings estimates are the most important information added into the SAR files by CMU. Earnings estimates are taken from the 1991 New Earnings Survey (NES) and refer to average hourly earnings in pence excluding any overtime pay. Instead of assigning each employee the average hourly earnings for their occupation, NES mean earnings data were broken down by age, sex, hours worked, and region, using the following breakpoints:

- sex: male, female
- age: 16–19, 20–29, 30–49, 50+
- hours worked: full-time, part-time
- occupation: one of 73 occupation groups in the 1991 SOC
- region: London and the South-east, rest of Great Britain.

The earnings data in the SARs are thus fairly close estimates of the earnings of someone in the relevant occupation and in the particular group defined by age, sex, hours worked, and the region they are in. Because the NES does not provide information on the earnings of self-employed people, no earnings estimates were added to the records of the self-employed in the SARs. The NES also excludes workers (typically part-time workers) with earnings below the threshold at which social insurance contributions become payable, so the NES earnings estimates for part-time workers in the SARs may be on the high side. (In fact, there was little evidence of this in our analyses, possibly because the problem affects weekly earnings rather more than hourly earnings.) The NES earnings estimates were also added to the records of people not currently in employment, using information on occupation and whether working part-time or full-time in their last job, plus age, sex, and region as reported in the 1991 Census. Students with a current or previous job were also assigned NES earnings estimates, but all of these cases are classified as people not currently in work in the SAR files. The NES earnings data for people not currently in work, including students in full-time education with work experience, are contained in a separate variable (NESNOTWK) from the data for people in work (NESSCORE), which is helpful for users. Two other variables give the number in the sample and the Standard Error for the mean earnings.

The fact that earnings are imputed rather than reported directly by respondents, and the way they are imputed, has to be taken into account in the interpretations placed on the data, and can even be an advantage for certain applications. In practice, the estimates report the average earnings someone in that type of job, and in the relevant region and age group, can expect to earn. This is particularly helpful with regard to previous jobs: the estimates report the earnings that people in the given region and age group could expect to get if they had been employed in spring 1991 in the same job as they had last held.

In addition to data imported from other government sources, the SARs contain derived variables used by academic social scientists. The four most important are Goldthorpe's class schema, and three continuous measures of occupational status and occupational prestige: the Cambridge occupational status scale, the International Socio-Economic Index (ISEI) of occupational status, and the Standard International Occupational Prestige Scale (SIOPS), all of which are based on either the 1990 SOC or ISCO88.

1990 Standard Occupational Classification (SOC)

The occupational classification used in the population census is always the most detailed classification employed in statistical surveys and research. There is a tradition in Britain of completely revising the occupational classification in time for each decennial census, with the new classification typically published the year beforehand, in 1970 and 1980 for example. In the 1980s it was agreed that a new common classification should be developed, of a kind that could be used by all government offices, and that could be updated between censuses rather than replaced wholesale, thus improving continuity in statistics (Thomas and Elias, 1989). The new Standard Occupational Classification was published in 1990 as the census classification but is intended to have wider application as well. For this reason, it does not require information on employment status (as in the 1970 and 1980 classifications) and is limited to a classification of jobs, defined as a set of employment tasks. The new SOC aimed to distinguish between and rank jobs in terms of the types and levels of skill required, work experience, qualifications, and training usually required to do the job. The SOC contains a more explicit ranking of occupations by skill than in previous census classifications. The classification is hierarchical, offering three levels of aggregation suitable for different analytic purposes: 371 occupation units, 77 Minor Groups, and 9 Major Groups, with an additional code in each case for unclassifiable cases. By using information on employment status, collected separately, the conventional socio-economic classifications, the RG Social Class and Socio-Economic Groups, are derived from SOC coding (OPCS, 1990).

The SOC also provides the basis, in conjunction with information on employment status, for updated versions of other socio-economic classifications employed by academic social scientists, such as Goldthorpe's class schema and the Cambridge scale of social status.

The SOC was designed to achieve compatibility with ISCO88 (see below) and the SOC unit groups can be aggregated to ISCO88 categories.

The SARs employ slightly altered versions of the 77 Minor Groups and 371 occupation units in the 1990 SOC, and this affects the assignment of occupations to the male-dominated, female-dominated, or mixed category, according to the % Female in each. In the 2% SAR, four small occupations are grouped with another one, as follows (using SOC occupation codes followed by the 2% SAR code in brackets):

- librarians are grouped with professionals nec—27 and 29 (17)
- ship officers are grouped with associate professionals—33 and 39 (21)
- legal service jobs are grouped with business professionals—35 and 36 (23)
- travel attendants are grouped with protective service jobs—63 and 69 (47).

In these cases the merged group was classified according to the sex-ratio of the largest, dominant group. This had the same effect as classifying them according to the % Female in the combined group, as the average was in practice determined by the dominant group. In the 1% SAR 23 small occupations were merged into 10 categories by combining adjacent pairs or, in two cases, by combining 3 or 4 occupations. In these cases the % Female was recalculated for the merged group in order to assign the group to the male, female, or mixed occupation categories. This usually meant that the merged groups were classified by the largest, dominant occupation. The combined occupation units are as follows (using SOC occupation codes followed by the 1% SAR code in brackets):

100 and 101 (001); 150 and 151 (23); 152, 153, 154, and 155 (24); 240 and 241 (66); 290 and 291 (77); 311 and 313 (87); 384, 385, and 387 (115); 391 and 392 (118); 702 and 703 (250); 920 and 921 (335).

The Registrar-General's Social Class and Socio-Economic Groups (SEG)

Social Class is the oldest classification of social stratification, developed in the early twentieth century by the Registrar-General's Census Office for use in the population census and in epidemiological studies (Szreter, 1984). The classification has changed and developed over the century. The most widely used social classification within government, Social Class has long been used for studies of mortality and fertility patterns, and is currently used more widely in studies of health and health service usage, housing, education, and employment. From 1921 to 1971 Social Class was described as a ranking of occupations according to their standing within the community. In response to the accusation that no empirical evidence on social status rankings had been collected, the classification was instead described in 1980 as presenting a ranking of occupations by occupational skill or grade. The validity of these interpretations is supported by the SAR analyses presented in this volume. Whether Social Class is seen as ranks within a social hierarchy or as a ranking of occupational grades, the five Social Classes form a clear hierarchy in terms of average earnings—for all employees, for full-time employees, and for part-time employees (see Tables 3.5 and 3.7).

Despite its proven utility and robust multi-purpose character, the RG Social Class classification has never been popular with academic social scientists and has been regularly criticized for not being based on any single body of social theory (Marsh, 1986; Marshall, 1988: 146, 149). Some social scientists prefer to use the Socio-Economic Group (SEG) classification which aims to group people whose social, cultural, and recreational standards and behaviour are similar. This was introduced in the 1951 Census, was extensively amended in 1961, was amended again in 1981 to offer comparability with other EU censuses and often provides the basis for international comparisons (Hakim, 1982: 179). By the early 1990s, after alternative social classifications had been developed and applied in academic research, the ONS requested the ESRC to undertake a review of Social Class and SEG and make recommendations for the 2001 Census. The Goldthorpe class schema and the Cambridge Scale are the two main potential alternatives, both widely used in academic (but not government) research.

Goldthorpe's class schema

The Goldthorpe class schema was originally developed as a seven-category schema which was specifically British. It was subsequently developed into an international class schema and the number of categories extended to 11, although these are often grouped into just three classes. The Goldthorpe class categories distinguish positions in the labour market and also reflect skill level and sectoral differences. Their primary use to date has been in analyses of intergenerational social mobility as measured by occupational mobility (Marshall *et al.*, 1988). The most recent version of the class schema can be coded from the 1990 Standard Occupational Classification (Goldthorpe and Heath, 1992) and this version is applied to the SARs.

The class schema developed by Goldthorpe over many years is described most fully in Erikson and Goldthorpe's *Constant Flux* (1993), a study that applies the schema to analyses of social mobility in ten nations in the early 1970s. The schema had its origins in, but differs from, the Hope–Goldthorpe scale of the general desirability of occupations. The aim of the Hope–Goldthorpe scale was to 'combine occupational categories whose members would appear, in the light of the available evidence, to be typically comparable, on the one hand, in terms of their sources and levels of income and other conditions of employment, in their degree of economic security and in their chances of economic advancement; and, on the other hand, in their location within the systems of authority and control governing the processes of production in which they are engaged' or broadly similar market and work situations (Goldthorpe, 1987: 40, 255). Goldthorpe and Hope noted that the H–G scale could be used as measuring occupational prestige, that is, as tapping some underlying structure of social relations of deference, acceptance, and derogation, or as a proxy for socio-economic status, but they argued for an alternative interpretation of the scale as measuring the general social desirability and social standing of occupations (Goldthorpe and Hope, 1974: 132; Goldthorpe, 1987: 43). The scores were combined to produce various social class scales, more or less disaggregated or aggregated.

The 1990 Goldthorpe class schema aims to differentiate positions within labour markets and production units in terms of the employment relations that they entail, and starts by separating employers, the self-employed, and employees. Like the RG Social Class, it does not rest on any specific survey or collection of evidence. It was not constructed around any single hierarchical principle from which a regular ordering of the classes could be derived. However, when collapsed into just three broad classes, the classification does form a hierarchical scale of Service Class, Intermediate Class, and Working Class, ranked in terms of their prestige, socio-economic status, and general desirability, and reflecting differences in levels of job rewards and job-entry requirements. This ranking is reflected in the Hope–Goldthorpe scores and in scores on other scales of occupational prestige, socio-economic status, and desirability of occupations for each of the three or seven classes in the schema (Goldthorpe, 1987: 43; Erikson and Goldthorpe, 1993: 44–5). An application of the Goldthorpe schema to Marshall's 1984 survey of employment conditions confirms its validity in relation to women's occupations just as much as for men's occupations, and also confirms that the classes are *not* ranked in terms of average earnings (Evans, 1996) as we too found (see Table 3.5). However, the class schema has been criticized by Prandy and Blackburn (1997), who point out that there are in fact no meaningful boundaries between classes or sharp clustering of occupational groups.

The Hope–Goldthorpe scale (Goldthorpe and Hope, 1974) was constructed to have a minimum value close to zero, in practice 5, and a maximum value close to 100, in practice 95, with a median of 51. When applied to the 1972 Oxford National Survey of Occupational Mobility, a national survey of employed men, the H–G scale had a minimum value of 18 and a maximum value of 82, a median of 40 and a mean value of 45 with a standard deviation of 15. These values offer the best indication of the scale's range in practice. Applying the H–G scores to the 1990 Goldthorpe class schema gives an average score of 63 for the Service Class, 39 for the Routine Non-Manual Class, 39–47 for small proprietors and farmers, 40 for skilled manual workers and technicians, 29–31 for unskilled workers and agricultural labourers, with similar scores on SIOPS (Erikson and Goldthorpe, 1993: 45).

The Cambridge scale of social status

The development of the Cambridge Scale is described in *Social Stratification and Occupations* (Stewart, Prandy, and Blackburn, 1980). Revised over the years, the new version is described by Prandy (1990), who shows that it compares favourably with the RG Social Class and the H–G scale in a variety of applications. The Cambridge Scale provides a continuous measure of social stratification and social inequality that does not refer exclusively to a person's own occupation—a feature that produces slightly different scores for men and women. The scale differs from other measures in using information on the occupations of friends and marriage partners, thus tapping the social relationships and lifestyle associated with particular labour market positions. It also differs in being used always as a continuous measure rather than being collapsed into social class groups. Prandy describes the CS as a measure of generalized advantage and lifestyle which determines patterns of social interaction. Prandy and Blackburn (1997) show that it performs better than categorical classifications, such as Goldthorpe's class schema, in predicting attendance at university.

Despite these differences in the conceptual basis and method of construction, the scale does not differ greatly from others in the results obtained in empirical applications. The original scale correlated 0.88 with the Hope–Goldthorpe scale, and the revised scale produces results that are very close parallels to those obtained with the other measures described above. One unique feature is that the scale is compiled separately for women's occupations, taking account of the fact that women are concentrated in fewer occupations, have different occupational histories, and different marriage patterns. The argument is that a female clerical worker or secretary does not have the same social status as a male clerical worker or secretary; in particular, the female secretary is far more likely to be married to someone in a higher status occupation and thus have quite different patterns of social relationships and lifestyle. As a result, Cambridge Scale scores for women tend to be slightly higher, on average, than for men in the same occupation. However, the Hope–Goldthorpe scale also produces higher average scores for women than for men, due to the strange convention that treats all white-collar jobs as having higher status than blue-collar jobs: the low-paid and relatively unskilled (female) shop assistant who sells a table is treated as having higher social status than the (male) skilled carpenter who makes the table. Clearly stated differences in the theoretical rationales for academic social stratification classifications do not, in practice, produce results that differ greatly between them or that differ greatly from the RG Social Class and SEG.

ISCO88

The International Labour Office (ILO) created the International Standard Classification of Occupations (ISCO) in 1958; updated it in 1968 to create ISCO68; then updated it again, more thoroughly, in 1988 to create ISCO88 (ILO, 1990). The classification is widely used in cross-national comparative research and it serves as a guideline for national occupational classifications in some countries. Ganzeboom and Treiman (1996) show how to derive occupational status classifications from it, including Goldthorpe's class schema.

ISEI

The International Socio-Economic Index (ISEI) of occupational status was constructed as a by-product of a cross-national comparative study of status attainment (Ganzeboom, de Graaf, and Treiman, 1992; Ganzeboom and Treiman, 1996). Ganzeboom *et al.* (1992) define the socio-economic indicator as the intervening variable between education and income that maximizes the *indirect* effect of education on income and minimizes the *direct* effect. In essence, the occupational status indicator consists of the weighted sum of mean education and mean income for each occupational group, taking into account the influence of age. Originally constructed with the 1968 version of ISCO, the variable was updated to the 1988 ISCO. Like Goldthorpe's class schema, it employs information on self-employment and supervisory status as well as detailed occupation codes.

The original version of ISEI was constructed from 31 datasets covering 16 nations in the 1970s (more precisely, various years over 1968–82). The 16 nations for which data was used included Brazil, India, the Philippines, Taiwan, Japan, the USA, the Netherlands, Great Britain, West Germany, the Irish Republic, Finland, Italy, Hungary, and Switzerland. The ISEI is thus said to be equally applicable in developing countries and in industrial economies. Like many other studies of this nature, the analysis was limited to data for men of working age (21–64 years) because the datasets did not cover women, and in many cases the analysis was further restricted to men working full-time. ISEI scores for female-dominated occupations are estimated from data for men in these occupations. The original ISEI variable provided occupational status scores for 271 occupational groups. The revised version provides scores for some 400 occupation units (390 occupation units in ISCO88 plus some additional categories). However, the number of independent unit groups for which an ISEI score was derived was somewhat smaller than in the original version: 209 instead of 271, reflecting the higher degree of aggregation in ISCO88 (Ganzeboom and Treiman, 1996).

SIOPS

The Standard International Occupational Prestige Scale (SIOPS) created by Treiman (1977) was also originally constructed with reference to ISCO68 and then updated to refer to ISCO88. In essence, SIOPS integrated the numerous national occupational prestige scales available in the 1970s into an international prestige scale linked to ISCO. The procedure used by Treiman was to match occupational titles from national and local prestige studies conducted in 60 countries to the three-digit version of ISCO68. He then added a fourth digit to accommodate distinctions that were found cross-nationally in prestige scales but not in ISCO68. The SIOPS scale was generated by averaging the national prestige scores, appropriately rescaled to a common metric.

Although occupational status (socio-economic status) and occupational prestige are correlated, they differ in some key respects. Prestige is the approval and respect members of society give to incumbents of occupations as rewards for their valuable services to society (Treiman, 1977: 16–22) and prestige scores usually have their source in interview surveys or other first-hand studies providing information on popular prestige rankings of occupations. In most prestige studies, farmers come out with a grading somewhere in the middle. Since farmers tend to have both low money income and low education, they consistently appear at the low end of socio-economic index scales. Certain other occupations also attract discrepant scores on the two types of scale, so that occupational status and occupational prestige scales remain distinctively different, albeit associated.

The original ISEI and SIOPS scales have been updated to refer to ISCO88 instead of ISCO68 (Ganzeboom and Treiman, 1996), but the research evidence for the 1970s on which the scales rely has not been updated. Thus Treiman did not employ any new prestige studies for the 1980s or 1990s to reassess the prestige ranking of occupations twenty years after the first exercise. Similarly Ganzeboom still used the original database of studies for 1968–82 to produce the ISCO88 update of ISEI. So in some respects the updated versions of ISEI and SIOPS are substantively unchanged, and potentially dated.

Occupational segregation variables

Three versions of the occupational segregation variable were added to the SARs as a result of this research project. All are created on the same basis and from the same 1991 Census source, differing only in the sex ratio used to define the midpoint in the classification and the width of the middle band of integrated occupations. The source for all three versions of the occupational classification variable is table 4 of the 1991 Census *Economic Activity* report (OPCS and GROS, 1994*a*). Statistics for all in employment were used to compile sex ratios for all occupations (see Annex B) and occupations were then grouped into three bands. The three versions are:

JobSeg1	Male occupations	<25% female
	Mixed occupations	25%–55% female (40% ± 15%)
	Female occupations	>55% female
JobSeg2	Male occupations	<30% female
	Mixed occupations	30%–70% female (50% ± 20%)
	Female occupations	>70% female
JobSeg3	Male occupations	<15% female
	Mixed occupations	15%–45% female (30% ± 15%)
	Female occupations	>45% female.

In 1991 the British workforce was 44% female, so 40% was used as the midpoint for JobSeg1. This variable is appropriate for the widest range of applications. Some researchers prefer to use a single unvarying midpoint of 50% for all analyses of occupational segregation. The problem with this option is that women have never constituted 50% of the workforce on a headcount basis, let alone on the basis of full-time equivalent data, and the distribution of the workforce around this artificial midpoint will invariably be unbalanced. In 1991 the full-time workforce was 32% female, so 30% was used as the midpoint for JobSeg3. This is the appropriate variable for analyses focused on the full-time workforce, or for analyses of long-term trends covering the nineteenth century as well as the twentieth century.

Multiple statuses and double coding in the census

Fig. 3 shows the economic activity question used in the 1991 Census. The question used in 1991 was very similar to the questions used in the 1981 Census and the 1971 Census, which invited people to tick all appropriate boxes. The questions being developed for the 2001 Census are very different, with one question asking only about any paid work in the last week and another question, somewhat later on the form, asking people to tick Yes or No for *each one* of a list of other activities that might apply to them, including unemployment, being a student in full-time education, retired, or looking after the home or family.

To the extent that multiple statuses on the economic activity question were all coded for 1971, 1981, and 1991, it could be argued that double coding has been applied for some time in the population census. In practice, however, the multiple codes were only used to identify the one 'correct' status that overrode all others, and people were then classified by this one status in all statistical tables and other outputs. The SARs opened up the possibility of treating multiple status codes as substantive information in its own right. The Census Offices have already started to do this in their own analyses. The 1991 Census was the first to identify working students within tables in the *Economic Activity* volume. Prior to that students were classified exclusively among the economically inactive. A degree of uncertainty about the appropriate classification of student jobs is evident in their inconsistent treatment in statistical analyses. Working students are sometimes included within statistics on the economically active (as in tables 1 and 2 of the *Economic Activity* report) and sometimes listed as a separate category that is excluded from statistics on the economically active (as in table 4 on the occupational structure and table 8 on the industrial structure). In other tables, the treatment of student jobs is left unclear.

Self-employment status coding

As noted in Chapter 8, the 10% sample editing procedure excluded from the count of the self-employed all those who reported working within their own incorporated company, who are thus employees for tax and social security purposes (OPCS and GROS, 1994*a*: 8). This editing procedure reduces the self-employment count by 5% overall (see Table 8.1), almost 10% for the self-employed with employees and 3% for the self-employed without employees.

All the SARs data is taken from the edited 10% sample, so that almost all the larger employers, who are most likely to be incorporated, are already removed from the self-employment count and reclassified as employees. None the less there are two variables in the 1% SAR that identify the self-employed and they yield discrepant

Answers to the remaining questions are not required for any person under 16 years of age (born after 21st April 1975)

13	**Whether working, retired, looking after the home etc last week**	Was working for an employer full time (more than 30 hours a week) ☐ 1	Was working for an employer full time (more than 30 hours a week) ☐ 1

Which of these things was the person doing last week?

Please read carefully right through the list and tick all the descriptions that apply.

Casual or temporary work should be counted at boxes 1, 2, 3 or 4. Also tick boxes 1, 2, 3 or 4 if the person had a job last week but was off sick, on holiday, temporarily laid off or on strike.

Boxes 1, 2, 3 and 4 refer to work for pay or profit but not to unpaid work except in a family business.

Working for an employer is **part time** (box 2) if the hours worked, excluding any overtime and mealbreaks, are usually 30 hours or less per week.

Include any person wanting a job but prevented from looking by holiday or temporary sickness.

Do not count training given or paid for by an employer.

Was working for an employer part time (one hour or more a week) ☐ 2   Was working for an employer part time (one hour or more a week) ☐ 2

Was self-employed, employing other people ☐ 3   Was self-employed, employing other people ☐ 3

Was self-employed, not employing other people ☐ 4   Was self-employed, not employing other people ☐ 4

Was on a government employment or training scheme ☐ 5   Was on a government employment or training scheme ☐ 5

Was waiting to start a job he/she had already accepted ☐ 6   Was waiting to start a job he/she had already accepted ☐ 6

Was unemployed and looking for a job ☐ 7   Was unemployed and looking for a job ☐ 7

Was at school or in other full time education ☐ 8   Was at school or in other full time education ☐ 8

Was unable to work because of long term sickness or disability ☐ 9   Was unable to work because of long term sickness or disability ☐ 9

Was retired from paid work ☐ 10   Was retired from paid work ☐ 10

Was looking after the home or family ☐ 11   Was looking after the home or family ☐ 11

Other ☐ *please specify*   Other ☐ *please specify*

FIG. 3. 1991 Census economic activity question

counts, which differ by 3% in the sample used for this study (residents aged 16–64 years in employment).

The 1% SAR EMPSTAT variable is based on questions 15 and 16 in the 1991 Census form, which ask for information about the occupation of a person's main job, and the nature of their employer's business or their own self-employment business (for industry coding). Because these questions refer to a person's main job and occupation, the EMPSTAT variable is the most appropriate one to use in studies of the self-employed and is used in Table 8.5. Unfortunately, the variable is not included in the 2% SAR which, because of its larger size, is the more reliable for studies of small minority groups such as the self-employed.

The classification of the self-employed used in Chapter 8 is based on the ECONPRIM variable which is available in both the 1% and 2% SARs. This variable undercounts the self-employed by 3% in the 16–64 age group. That is, 3% of the self-employed (as identified on EMPSTAT) are reclassified as employees on the ECONPRIM variable, virtually all (80%) of them self-employed without employees who also had an employee job, typically full-time (58% of cases). The ECONPRIM variable is based on the economic activity question 13 in the 1991 Census form, which allowed multiple response (see Fig. 3). Where more than one box was ticked, the coding scheme for *primary* activity gave precedence to employed categories over the self-employed categories. The self-employed who also reported an employee job, even if part-time or temporary, would thus be classified as employees rather than self-employed as their primary activity.

The Census Office states that the figures for self-employment from the two variables in the 1% SAR are 'not directly comparable'. It is not clear whether part of the explanation for the discrepancy between them is the practice of reclassifying owner-managers as employees of their own businesses, but if it is a factor it is not the main factor.

Revised classification of homeworking and home-based work

Published census 10% sample statistics and unpublished small area statistics identify as homeworkers everyone who ticked the 'mainly at home' box in the transport to work question. The analysis here splits this group into two, by identifying people with live-at-work jobs and placing them in a separate category.

Among people currently in employment aged 16–64 years in the 2% SAR, 21,784 people had ticked the 'mainly at home' box. This number was reduced to 15,407 homeworkers as follows. People in communal establishments who said they worked at home were excluded: 935 cases. People who held their residential accommodation (renting, rent free, or by lease) with a job, shop, farm, or other business and who said they worked 'at home' were excluded: 3,203 cases. People in farming occupations (SEGs 16, 17, and 18) who said they worked 'at home' were excluded: 3,113 cases. In practice there were 874 cases double counted under the housing tenure and occupational exclusions. In total 6,377 cases were reclassified as live-at-work jobs rather than as homework jobs. This reduced the homework count by 29%, exactly the same reduction as was achieved in the 1981 Census using the same procedure (Hakim, 1987*b*: 22).

It is possible that a few live-at-work jobs were not detected by the above exclusions and remain classified (incorrectly) as homeworkers. For example, the 2% SAR contains 5,303 residents aged 16–64 years working in the hotel and catering industry, of whom 1,015 (19%) state that they work 'at home'. The procedures described above led to half of this group being reclassified as having live-in jobs. This group would consist of employees provided with residential accommodation in large hotels and hotels in remote locations. The remaining half are probably all boarding-house keepers and people supplying bed-and-breakfast accommodation in their own homes, correctly classified as working at home. The limited information in census files means that there is no way of checking that all cases that should have been reclassified as live-in jobs were identified by the above procedures. However, the results of the 1993 GHS agree closely with our edited census data, suggesting that the results are valid and reliable.

The 1993 GHS showed that 90% of people aged 16+ in employment had a separate workplace; 1% had accommodation attached to their job; 5% were homeworkers (6% of women and 4% of men); and 4% worked from home as a base (6% of men and 2% of women). The GHS definition of homeworkers included people working 'in the same grounds or building as their home', so that farmers and live-in jobs were included with homeworkers rather than with people holding their accommodation with a job (OPCS, 1995: 55, 75). Taking this into account, the 1993 GHS results closely parallel our edited SAR results.

Retrospective employment data

This is the most important hidden data in the SAR files, in terms of the number of cases affected and in terms of its potential uses.

The 1991 Census very explicitly collected information on occupation, employment status (employee or self-employed), industry, and hours worked per week for everyone who had a job within the last ten years even if not currently employed as well as for people who had a job in the week before the census. Information on workplace address and the type of transport used for the daily journey to work was only collected for those currently in work. The question on any higher education qualifications held was addressed to everyone aged 18 and over, whether working or not.

It is the fact that systematic information was collected for everyone who had a job within a defined ten-year reference period—in effect, the decade between the 1981 Census and the 1991 Census—that makes the retrospective employment data a usable additional data item. The 1971 and 1981 Censuses had collected information on the most recent job of the unemployed and the retired, including occupation details, but this is a less well defined group, especially as regards the timing of the last job. The 1991 Census included a specific question asking whether a paid job had been held in the previous ten years; however, there is no code for this item in the SAR tapes. As a result it is easy to overlook the fact that occupation and related data are provided for a much wider *de facto* definition of the labour force than is suggested by the conventional definition of economic activity, which relies on a narrow one-week reference period. Although the information was not analysed and presented in the published census statistics, it is available for secondary analysis in the SARs. In practice, census analysts have a choice of two reference periods for employment data: the last week or the last ten years.

The wider reference period has a substantial impact on the data available for women, as they move in and out of the labour market far more frequently than men, in the USA as well as in Britain (Hakim, 1996c). Applying a *post hoc* rationalization, the change in question-wording helps to overcome the limitations of the one-week reference period for defining women's labour force attachment and occupational grade. A side-effect is that information on the last job was also collected for students in full-time education, many of whom take short-term jobs during the summer vacation. With the rise of what is variously termed 'flexible', non-standard', and 'atypi-cal' work (Hakim, 1987*c*, 1990*a*, 1990*b*), and the increasing discontinuity of women's employment (Main, 1988*a*; Hakim, 1996*c*), social scientists are increasingly agreed that new measures of workforce participation and of the volume of employment are needed (European Commission, 1989: 19; Clogg *et al.*, 1990; Hakim, 1993*a*: 109–14; Jonung and Persson, 1993; Zighera, 1996). The 1991 Census data collection is a step in the right direction. The new approach is developed further in the 2001 Census, with an extra question asking how long ago the last job was held, and other questions focusing on the person's last *main* job rather than the last job strictly defined for those not in employment.

The 1% and 2% SARs thus provide employment data on a much larger group than the subgroup in employment in the census reference week (the third week in April 1991). Women can be divided into three groups: those 'currently' in work; those who had a job in the last ten years but are not currently working; and women who have not done any paid work for ten years or longer. This last group includes unemployed school-leavers who have yet to obtain their first job, women who followed the home-maker career and have not worked since marriage or their first child, and people who have been retired for over ten years. Limiting an analysis to people of working age auto-matically excludes most retired people from Tables A1–A4, so that the great majority of women without a job in the last ten years (labelled 'non-working' in Tables A1–A4 to distinguish them from the other economically inactive groups) are full-time home-makers, supported either by a breadwinner partner or by state benefits. The impact of the wider reference period on men is minimal, as few men have spells out of the work-force other than unemployment, and very few have long spells out of employment.

Tables A1–A4 show how two different bases can be used for analyses of occupa-tional and related data: people in work (current jobs) or people with a job within the last ten years (current and last jobs). The fact that the two base numbers are of roughly similar magnitudes increases the chance that they may be mistaken for each other by social scientists who are not specialists in labour market analysis. However, their composition is quite different, especially for women, with implications for research results. Among people of working age, defined throughout this book as 16–64 years for simplicity, the 2% SAR identifies 517 thousand economically active, 589 thousand people with current or last job data, and 461 thousand currently in work (Tables A1–A2). Numbers are roughly halved in the 1% SAR, with data for 254 thousand economically active, 288 thousand people with current and last job data, and 227 thousand people in work (Tables A3–A4).

The figures in Tables A1–A4 are all slightly lower than in a similar earlier analysis (Hakim, 1995*a*) because the analysis here is restricted to people who are residents in Great Britain, as is conventional in labour market analyses of census data, whereas the earlier analysis included everyone present at the time of the 1991 Census, includ-ing visitors. In addition, Tables A1–A4 employ the definition of part-time work used throughout this book, that is jobs involving less than 30 hours a week, whereas the earlier analysis used the conventional British statistical definition of part-time work as jobs involving less than 31 hours a week. This change alters the balance between full-time and part-time jobs.

Tables A1–A4 show the base numbers for the analyses presented in this book, and the relative sizes of groups included and excluded from particular analyses.

TABLE A1. *Composition of the resident working-age population, 1991, 2% SAR*

	Current and last jobs			No job in last 10 years	Total: all aged 16–64
	Full-time 30+ hours	Part-time <30 hours	All[1]		
Women					
In work	125,420	71,737	202,751	0	202,751
Unemployed	8,865	2,486	12,348	5,430	17,778
Non-working	20,803	13,096	36,135	44,302	80,437
Inactive[2]	12,688	10,094	24,123	26,530	50,653
All women	167,776	97,413	275,357	76,262	351,619
Men					
In work	242,936	6,046	258,213	0	258,213
Unemployed	25,273	974	28,848	9,686	38,534
Non-working	1,368	111	1,627	1,508	3,135
Inactive[2]	19,942	3,504	24,945	22,323	47,268
All men	289,519	10,635	313,633	33,517	347,150
All Persons					
In work	368,356	77,783	460,964	0	460,964
Unemployed	34,138	3,460	41,196	15,116	56,312
Non-working	22,171	13,207	37,762	45,810	83,572
Inactive[2]	32,630	13,598	49,068	48,853	97,921
Totals	457,295	108,048	588,990	109,779	698,769

[1] Includes those not stating hours worked.
[2] Inactive people comprise students, the permanently sick, and retired.

TABLE A2. *Work experience among men and women of working age, 1991, 2% SAR*

	Women		Men		Total	
	N	%	N	%	N	%
Economically active	220,529	63	296,747	85	517,276	74
Current or last job data	275,357	78	313,633	90	588,990	84
Economically active *and* current or last job data	215,099	61	287,061	83	502,160	72
In employment[1]	202,751	58	258,213	74	460,964	66
Full-time 30+	125,420	36	242,936	70	368,356	53
Part-time <30	71,737	20	6,046	2	77,783	11
Not currently in work but had job in last 10 years[1]	72,606	21	55,420	16	128,026	18
Full-time	42,356	12	46,583	13	88,939	13
Part-time	25,676	7	4,589	1	30,265	4
No paid work in last 10 years	76,262	22	33,517	10	109,779	16
Discontinuous workers: Non-working people	80,437	23	3,135	1	83,572	12
Non-working people with a job in last 10 years	36,135	10	1,627	*	37,762	5
Base: all aged 16–64 years	351,619	100	347,150	100	698,769	100

[1] Includes people not stating hours worked.

Source: 2% SAR, Great Britain, data for residents aged 16–64 years.

Table A3. *Composition of the resident working-age population, 1991, 1% SAR*

	Current and last jobs			No job in last 10 years	Total: all aged 16–64
	Full-time 30+ hours	Part-time <30 hours	All[1]		
Women					
In work	61,282	35,698	99,776	0	99,776
Unemployed	4,406	1,202	6,152	2,624	8,776
Non-working	10,285	6,354	17,732	21,876	39,608
Inactive[2]	5,982	4,765	11,386	12,395	23,781
All women	81,958	48,019	135,046	36,895	171,941
Men					
In work	119,352	3,004	126,940	0	126,940
Unemployed	12,421	476	14,133	4,718	18,851
Non-working	492	27	595	498	1,093
Inactive[2]	9,270	1,575	11,586	9,979	21,565
All men	141,535	5,082	153,254	15,195	168,449
All Persons					
In work	180,634	38,702	226,716	0	226,716
Unemployed	16,830	1,678	20,285	7,342	27,627
Non-working	10,777	6,381	18,327	22,374	40,701
Inactive[2]	15,252	6,340	22,972	22,374	45,346
Totals	223,493	53,101	288,298	52,090	340,390

[1] Includes those not stating hours worked.
[2] Inactive people comprise students, the permanently sick, and retired.

Table A4. *Work experience among men and women of working age, 1991, 1% SAR*

	Women		Men		Total	
	N	%	N	%	N	%
Economically active	108,552	63	145,791	87	254,343	75
Current or last job data	135,046	79	153,254	91	288,298	85
Economically active *and* current or last job data	105,928	62	141,073	87	247,001	73
In employment[1]	99,776	58	126,940	75	226,716	67
Full-time	61,282	36	119,352	71	180,634	53
Part-time	35,698	21	3,004	2	38,702	11
Not currently in work but had job within last 10 years[1]	35,270	21	26,314	16	61,584	18
Full-time	20,673	12	22,183	13	42,859	13
Part-time	12,321	7	2,078	1	14,399	4
No paid work within last 10 years	36,895	21	15,195	9	52,090	15
Discontinuous workers:						
Non-working people	39,608	23	1,093	1	40,701	12
Non-working people with a job in last 10 years	17,732	10	595	*	18,327	5
Total aged 16–64 years	171,941	100	168,449	100	340,390	100

[1] Includes people not stating hours worked.

Source: 1% SAR, Great Britain, data for residents aged 16–64 years.

ANNEX B

1991 Census 10% Sample Data on Occupational Structure and Sex Ratios

TABLE B1. *Sex ratios within occupations: 371 occupational groups*

Occupation (371 groups)	Total	Men	Women	% female	% of all	% of men	% of women
All economically active	2525146	1439623	1085523	43%	100	100	100
341 Midwives	3200	14	3186	100%	0.13	0.00	0.29
450 Medical secretaries	2738	12	2726	100%	0.11	0.00	0.25
451 Legal secretaries	5000	24	4976	100%	0.20	0.00	0.46
643 Dental nurses	2856	23	2833	99%	0.11	0.00	0.26
659 Other childcare and related occupations	19211	196	19015	99%	0.76	0.01	1.75
452 Typists and word processor operators	12132	133	11999	99%	0.48	0.01	1.11
461 Receptionists/telephonists	3683	43	3640	99%	0.15	0.00	0.34
650 Nursery nurses	5925	72	5853	99%	0.23	0.01	0.54
661 Beauticians and related occupations	1530	20	1510	99%	0.06	0.00	0.14
459 Other secretaries, PAs, typists nec	62861	921	61940	99%	2.49	0.06	5.71
460 Receptionists	18374	481	17893	97%	0.73	0.03	1.65
652 Educational assistants	4248	120	4128	97%	0.17	0.01	0.38
671 Housekeepers (non-domestic)	868	26	842	97%	0.03	0.00	0.08
651 Playgroup leaders	1957	66	1891	97%	0.08	0.00	0.17
644 Care assistants and attendants	28276	1705	26571	94%	1.12	0.12	2.45
640 Assistant nurses, nursing auxiliaries	15693	967	14726	94%	0.62	0.07	1.36
553 Sewing machinists, menders, embroiderers	16219	1298	14921	92%	0.64	0.09	1.37
721 Retail cash desk and check-out operators	13737	1265	12472	91%	0.54	0.09	1.15
343 Physiotherapists	2014	189	1825	91%	0.08	0.01	0.17
349 Other health associate professionals nec	752	71	681	91%	0.03	0.00	0.06
660 Hairdressers, barbers	8345	818	7527	90%	0.33	0.06	0.69
340 Nurses	48432	4874	43558	90%	1.92	0.34	4.01
421 Library assistants/clerks	3337	355	2982	89%	0.13	0.02	0.27
670 Domestic housekeepers and related	3082	347	2735	89%	0.12	0.02	0.25

Occupation (371 groups)	Total	Men	Women	% female	% of all	% of men	% of women
953 Counterhands, catering assistants	20979	2408	18571	89%	0.83	0.17	1.71
491 Tracers, drawing office assistants	533	63	470	88%	0.02	0.00	0.04
462 Telephone operators	5754	724	5030	87%	0.23	0.05	0.46
342 Medical radiographers	1349	176	1173	87%	0.05	0.01	0.11
347 Occupational/speech therapists, therapists nec	3031	423	2608	86%	0.12	0.03	0.24
791 Window dressers, floral arrangers	2256	323	1933	86%	0.09	0.02	0.18
958 Cleaners, domestics	77860	11784	66076	85%	3.08	0.82	6.09
234 Primary and nursery school teachers	26770	4361	22409	84%	1.06	0.30	2.06
383 Clothing designers	786	136	650	83%	0.03	0.01	0.06
346 Medical technicians, dental auxiliaries	2108	370	1738	82%	0.08	0.03	0.16
430 Clerks nec	64659	12337	52322	81%	2.56	0.86	4.82
720 Sales assistants	103059	19982	83077	81%	4.08	1.39	7.65
790 Merchandisers	1805	388	1417	79%	0.07	0.03	0.13
401 Local government clerical officers	17001	3745	13256	78%	0.67	0.26	1.22
370 Matrons, houseparents	4870	1118	3752	77%	0.19	0.08	0.35
952 Kitchen porters, hands	12396	2885	9511	77%	0.49	0.20	0.88
792 Telephone sales persons	3229	752	2477	77%	0.13	0.05	0.23
641 Hospital ward assistants	2448	575	1873	77%	0.10	0.04	0.17
411 Counter clerks and cashiers	38903	9157	29746	76%	1.54	0.64	2.74
172 Hairdresser/barber shop managers/ proprietors	7242	1753	5489	76%	0.29	0.12	0.51
127 Company secretaries	6479	1608	4871	75%	0.26	0.11	0.45
813 Winders, reelers	522	132	390	75%	0.02	0.01	0.04
363 Personnel and industrial relations officers	3727	980	2747	74%	0.15	0.07	0.25
293 Social workers, probation officers	10296	2717	7579	74%	0.41	0.19	0.70
621 Waiters, waitresses	12328	3399	8929	72%	0.49	0.24	0.82
235 Special education teaching professionals	2454	681	1773	72%	0.10	0.05	0.16
371 Welfare, community and youth workers	9739	2761	6978	72%	0.39	0.19	0.64
556 Tailors and dress-makers	1526	436	1090	71%	0.06	0.03	0.10
410 Accounts and wages clerks, book-keepers etc.	62421	17973	44448	71%	2.47	1.25	4.09

Occupation (371 groups)	Total	Men	Women	% female	% of all	% of men	% of women
673 Launderers, dry cleaners, pressers	5023	1450	3573	71%	0.20	0.10	0.33
490 Computer operators, data processors etc.	16055	4793	11262	70%	0.64	0.33	1.04
270 Librarians	1547	464	1083	70%	0.06	0.03	0.10
239 Other teaching professionals nec	3329	1005	2324	70%	0.13	0.07	0.21
630 Travel and flight attendants	4442	1370	3072	69%	0.18	0.10	0.28
622 Bar staff	15671	4893	1077	69%	0.62	0.34	0.99
420 Filing, computer and other records clerks	24686	7734	16952	69%	0.98	0.54	1.56
390 Information officers	1978	626	1352	68%	0.08	0.04	0.12
400 Civil Service administrative officers	21047	6665	14382	68%	0.83	0.46	1.32
862 Packers, bottlers, canners, fillers	24719	8075	16644	67%	0.98	0.56	1.53
130 Credit controllers	3800	1246	2554	67%	0.15	0.09	0.24
344 Chiropodists	860	286	574	67%	0.03	0.02	0.05
861 Inspectors, viewers, testers, goods examiners	3918	1322	2596	66%	0.16	0.09	0.24
864 Routine laboratory testers	1688	584	1104	65%	0.07	0.04	0.10
850 Assemblers/ lineworkers (electrical)	9170	3195	5975	65%	0.36	0.22	0.55
954 Shelf fillers	2912	1049	1863	64%	0.12	0.07	0.17
392 Careers advisers	993	360	633	64%	0.04	0.03	0.06
559 Other textiles, garments and related nec	1777	683	1094	62%	0.07	0.05	0.10
191 Registrars and administrators (education)	2238	899	1339	60%	0.09	0.06	0.12
290 Psychologists	698	287	411	59%	0.03	0.02	0.04
591 Glass product/ ceramics finishers/ decorators	1312	543	769	59%	0.05	0.04	0.07
440 Stores, despatch and production control clerks	2822	1184	1638	58%	0.11	0.08	0.15
620 Chefs, cooks	23374	10017	13357	57%	0.93	0.70	1.23
619 Other security and protective service nec	2935	1261	1674	57%	0.12	0.09	0.15
562 Bookbinders and print finishers	1419	612	807	57%	0.06	0.04	0.07
177 Travel agency managers	2276	985	1291	57%	0.09	0.07	0.12
902 All other occupations in farming	3562	1558	2004	56%	0.14	0.11	0.18

Occupation (371 groups)	Total	Men	Women	% female	% of all	% of men	% of women
132 Civil Service executive officers	8205	3594	4611	56%	0.32	0.25	0.42
800 Bakery and confectionery process operatives	3149	1393	1756	56%	0.12	0.10	0.16
859 Other assemblers/ lineworkers nec	3860	1714	2146	56%	0.15	0.12	0.20
233 Secondary school teachers	30063	13516	16547	55%	1.19	0.94	1.52
730 Collector salespersons and credit agents	877	400	477	54%	0.03	0.03	0.04
551 Knitters	1894	874	1020	54%	0.08	0.06	0.09
614 Traffic wardens	543	252	291	54%	0.02	0.02	0.03
173 Hotel and accommodation managers	7511	3524	3987	53%	0.30	0.24	0.37
231 Higher and further education teachers	15040	7093	7947	53%	0.60	0.49	0.73
139 Other financial institution/office managers nec	20480	9680	10800	53%	0.81	0.67	0.99
190 Officials of trade associations	2744	1297	1447	53%	0.11	0.09	0.13
463 Radio and telegraph operators, etc.	2345	1135	1210	52%	0.09	0.08	0.11
802 Tobacco process operatives	340	165	175	51%	0.01	0.01	0.02
700 Buyers (retail trade)	952	463	489	51%	0.04	0.03	0.05
102 Local government officers (admin/ executive)	6018	2961	3057	51%	0.24	0.21	0.28
555 Shoe repairers, leather cutters	4301	2122	2179	51%	0.17	0.15	0.20
124 Personnel, training and IR managers	6920	3424	3496	51%	0.27	0.24	0.32
271 Archivists and curators	633	315	318	50%	0.03	0.02	0.03
350 Legal service and related occupations	2418	1207	1211	50%	0.10	0.08	0.11
412 Debt, rent and other cash collectors	2657	1328	1329	50%	0.11	0.09	0.12
174 Restaurant and catering managers	14612	7331	7281	50%	0.58	0.51	0.67
345 Dispensing opticians	353	182	171	48%	0.01	0.01	0.02
722 Petrol pump forecourt attendants	1260	655	605	48%	0.05	0.05	0.06
595 Horticultural trades	2231	1163	1068	48%	0.09	0.08	0.10
221 Pharmacists/ pharmacologists	2566	1362	1204	47%	0.10	0.09	0.11
557 Clothing cutters, milliners, furriers	1437	770	667	46%	0.06	0.05	0.06

Occupation (371 groups)	Total	Men	Women	% female	% of all	% of men	% of women
399 Other associate professional/technical work nec	2089	1134	955	46%	0.08	0.08	0.09
123 Advertising and public relations managers	4509	2459	2050	45%	0.18	0.17	0.19
863 Weighers, graders, sorters	1897	1068	829	44%	0.08	0.07	0.08
300 Laboratory technicians	9603	5451	4152	43%	0.38	0.38	0.38
380 Authors, writers, journalists	7935	4517	3418	43%	0.31	0.31	0.31
201 Biological scientists and biochemists	3943	2247	1696	43%	0.16	0.16	0.16
391 Vocational and industrial trainers	7011	4024	2987	43%	0.28	0.28	0.28
699 Other personal and protective service nec	6837	3937	2900	42%	0.27	0.27	0.27
809 Other food, drink, tobacco operatives nec	10909	6346	4563	42%	0.43	0.44	0.42
569 Other printing and related trades nec	6632	3914	2718	41%	0.26	0.27	0.25
175 Publicans, innkeepers and club stewards	10751	6364	4387	41%	0.43	0.44	0.40
869 Other routine process operatives nec	2825	1678	1147	41%	0.11	0.12	0.11
582 Fishmongers, poultry dressers	1741	1038	703	40%	0.07	0.07	0.06
291 Other social and behavioural scientists	282	170	112	40%	0.01	0.01	0.01
384 Actors, entertainers, stage managers, directors	5171	3118	2053	40%	0.20	0.22	0.19
812 Spinners, doublers, twisters	651	393	258	40%	0.03	0.03	0.02
959 Other occupations in sales and services nec	1060	644	416	39%	0.04	0.04	0.04
382 Industrial designers	1118	680	438	39%	0.04	0.05	0.04
232 Education officers, school inspectors	1071	656	415	39%	0.04	0.05	0.04
381 Artists, commercial artists, graphic designers	9019	5608	3411	38%	0.36	0.39	0.31
199 Other managers and administrators nec	17954	11323	6631	37%	0.71	0.79	0.61
814 Other textiles processing operatives	2377	1507	870	37%	0.09	0.10	0.08
732 Market and street traders and assistants	2803	1781	1022	36%	0.11	0.12	0.09
000 not stated, inadequately described occupations	26981	17164	9817	36%	1.07	1.19	0.90

Occupation (371 groups)	Total	Men	Women	% female	% of all	% of men	% of women
179 Managers and proprietors in services nec	75161	48147	27014	36%	2.98	3.34	2.49
222 Ophthalmic opticians	691	443	248	36%	0.03	0.03	0.02
387 Professional athletes, sports officials	2336	1507	829	35%	0.09	0.10	0.08
362 Taxation experts	1626	1050	576	35%	0.06	0.07	0.05
841 Press stamping/ automatic machine operatives	2746	1777	969	35%	0.11	0.12	0.09
719 Other sales representatives nec	12386	8121	4265	34%	0.49	0.56	0.39
169 Other managers in farming, fishing, forestry nec	1497	999	498	33%	0.06	0.07	0.05
176 Entertainment and sports managers	4698	3149	1549	33%	0.19	0.22	0.14
701 Buyers and purchasing officers	4492	3064	1428	32%	0.18	0.21	0.13
220 Medical practitioners	9544	6589	2955	31%	0.38	0.46	0.27
550 Weavers	1000	691	309	31%	0.04	0.05	0.03
209 Other natural scientists nec	3486	2433	1053	30%	0.14	0.17	0.10
103 General administrators: national government	5218	3668	1550	30%	0.21	0.25	0.14
224 Veterinarians	717	509	208	29%	0.03	0.04	0.02
552 Warp preparers, bleachers, dyers, finishers	1596	1135	461	29%	0.06	0.08	0.04
121 Marketing and sales managers	34473	24525	9948	29%	1.37	1.70	0.92
242 Solicitors	7045	5024	2021	29%	0.28	0.35	0.19
851 Assemblers/ lineworkers (vehicles, metal goods)	5950	4253	1697	29%	0.24	0.30	0.16
580 Bakers, flour confectioners	4124	2948	1176	29%	0.16	0.20	0.11
899 Other plant and machine operatives nec	11101	7998	3103	28%	0.44	0.56	0.29
691 Bookmakers	1415	1028	387	27%	0.06	0.07	0.04
252 Actuaries, economists, and statisticians	1411	1037	374	27%	0.06	0.07	0.03
613 Customs and excise/ immigration officers	617	455	162	26%	0.02	0.03	0.01
223 Dental practitioners	2043	1508	535	26%	0.08	0.10	0.05
599 Other craft and related occupations nec	3141	2322	819	26%	0.12	0.16	0.08
170 Property and estate managers	5525	4146	1379	25%	0.22	0.29	0.13

Occupation (371 groups)	Total	Men	Women	% female	% of all	% of men	% of women
361 Underwriters, claim assessors, brokers, etc.	14309	10813	3496	24%	0.57	0.75	0.32
518 Goldsmiths, silversmiths, precious stone workers	933	706	227	24%	0.04	0.05	0.02
230 University and polytechnic teachers	6885	5211	1674	24%	0.27	0.36	0.15
560 Originators, compositors and print preparers	3302	2502	800	24%	0.13	0.17	0.07
131 Bank, Building Society, & Post Office managers	12869	9788	3081	24%	0.51	0.68	0.28
672 Caretakers	7743	5917	1826	24%	0.31	0.41	0.17
240 Judges and officers of the Court	246	188	58	24%	0.01	0.01	0.01
825 Plastics process operatives, moulders	6312	4833	1479	23%	0.25	0.34	0.14
348 Environmental health officers	874	670	204	23%	0.03	0.05	0.02
875 Bus conductors	242	186	56	23%	0.01	0.01	0.01
563 Screen printers	995	766	229	23%	0.04	0.05	0.02
385 Musicians	2096	1616	480	23%	0.08	0.11	0.04
941 Messengers, couriers	3812	2959	853	22%	0.15	0.21	0.08
900 Farm workers	11087	8608	2479	22%	0.44	0.60	0.23
251 Management accountants	1062	827	235	22%	0.04	0.06	0.02
141 Stores controllers	5196	4049	1147	22%	0.21	0.28	0.11
261 Town planners	839	656	183	22%	0.03	0.05	0.02
811 Preparatory fibre processors	397	311	86	22%	0.02	0.02	0.01
250 Chartered and certified accountants	10589	8322	2267	21%	0.42	0.58	0.21
320 Computer analyst/ programmers	14530	11489	3041	21%	0.58	0.80	0.28
120 Treasurers and company financial managers	7197	5692	1505	21%	0.29	0.40	0.14
241 Barristers and advocates	936	742	194	21%	0.04	0.05	0.02
860 Inspectors, viewers, and testers	9659	7661	1998	21%	0.38	0.53	0.18
309 Other scientific technicians nec	11520	9154	2366	21%	0.46	0.64	0.22
590 Glass product and ceramics makers	4222	3361	861	20%	0.17	0.23	0.08
579 Other woodworking trades nec	1348	1078	270	20%	0.05	0.07	0.02
642 Ambulance staff	2195	1764	431	20%	0.09	0.12	0.04
364 Organization and methods officers	1756	1419	337	19%	0.07	0.10	0.03

Occupation (371 groups)	Total	Men	Women	% female	% of all	% of men	% of women
919 Other labourers in making and processing nec	7593	6146	1447	19%	0.30	0.43	0.13
126 Computer systems/ data processing managers	6628	5397	1231	19%	0.26	0.37	0.11
810 Tannery production operatives	424	346	78	18%	0.02	0.02	0.01
253 Management consultants, business analysts	3552	2903	649	18%	0.14	0.20	0.06
386 Photographers, camera, sound, video operators	3964	3244	720	18%	0.16	0.23	0.07
710 Technical and wholesale sales representatives	25540	21046	4494	18%	1.01	1.46	0.41
702 Importers and exporters	740	611	129	17%	0.03	0.04	0.01
891 Printing machine minders and assistants	4668	3855	813	17%	0.18	0.27	0.07
520 Production fitters (electrical/electronic)	1979	1638	341	17%	0.08	0.11	0.03
824 Rubber process operatives, moulders	2380	1976	404	17%	0.09	0.14	0.04
200 Chemists	2612	2187	425	16%	0.10	0.15	0.04
690 Undertakers	539	452	87	16%	0.02	0.03	0.01
122 Purchasing managers	1634	1372	262	16%	0.06	0.10	0.02
330 Air traffic planners and controllers	346	291	55	16%	0.01	0.02	0.01
592 Dental technicians	816	687	129	16%	0.03	0.05	0.01
840 Machine tool operatives (inc. CNC)	17209	14519	2690	16%	0.68	1.01	0.25
801 Brewery and vinery process operatives	864	730	134	16%	0.03	0.05	0.01
303 Architectural and town planning technicians	2018	1714	304	15%	0.08	0.12	0.03
821 Paper, wood, and related process operatives	1978	1682	296	15%	0.08	0.12	0.03
396 Occupational hygienists and safety officers	1205	1025	180	15%	0.05	0.07	0.02
441 Storekeepers and warehousemen/women	31608	26952	4656	15%	1.25	1.87	0.43
843 Metal dressing operatives	815	695	120	15%	0.03	0.05	0.01
554 Coach trimmers, upholsterers	2349	2007	342	15%	0.09	0.14	0.03
395 Other statutory and similar inspectors nec	512	438	74	14%	0.02	0.03	0.01

Occupation (371 groups)	Total	Men	Women	% female	% of all	% of men	% of women
100 General administrators: national government (G51)	479	410	69	14%	0.02	0.03	0.01
393 Driving instructors (excluding HGV)	2566	2197	369	14%	0.10	0.15	0.03
601 NCOs and other ranks, foreign armed forces	1635	1404	231	14%	0.06	0.10	0.02
703 Air commodity and ship brokers	1630	1402	228	14%	0.06	0.10	0.02
160 Farm owners and managers, horticulturalists	20015	17246	2769	14%	0.79	1.20	0.26
394 Inspectors of factories, utilities, and related	711	613	98	14%	0.03	0.04	0.01
940 Postal workers, mail sorters	15590	13446	2144	14%	0.62	0.93	0.20
125 Organization and methods managers	127	110	17	13%	0.01	0.01	0.00
214 Software engineers	5857	5083	774	13%	0.23	0.35	0.07
820 Chemical, gas, and petroleum process operatives	7008	6082	926	13%	0.28	0.42	0.09
561 Printers	4284	3733	551	13%	0.17	0.26	0.05
292 Clergy	3411	2975	436	13%	0.14	0.21	0.04
202 Physicists, geologists, and meteorologists	1446	1265	181	13%	0.06	0.09	0.02
912 Labourers in engineering and allied trades	6337	5570	767	12%	0.25	0.39	0.07
140 Transport managers	5948	5229	719	12%	0.24	0.36	0.07
610 Police officers (sergeant and below)	13524	11897	1627	12%	0.54	0.83	0.15
999 All others in miscellaneous occupations nec	657	578	79	12%	0.03	0.04	0.01
110 Production, works, and maintenance managers	46398	40842	5556	12%	1.84	2.84	0.51
593 Musical instrument makers, piano tuners	414	365	49	12%	0.02	0.03	0.00
171 Garage managers and proprietors	3301	2911	390	12%	0.13	0.20	0.04
889 Other transport and machinery operatives nec	3759	3332	427	11%	0.15	0.23	0.04
260 Architects	3434	3049	385	11%	0.14	0.21	0.04
304 Building and civil engineering technicians	872	778	94	11%	0.03	0.05	0.01
101 General managers: large companies	319	285	34	11%	0.01	0.02	0.00
822 Cutting and slitting machine operatives	686	614	72	10%	0.03	0.04	0.01

Occupation (371 groups)	Total	Men	Women	% female	% of all	% of men	% of women
178 Managers/proprietors—butchers/fishmongers	2866	2577	289	10%	0.11	0.18	0.03
310 Draughtspersons	6873	6190	683	10%	0.27	0.43	0.06
360 Estimators, valuers	3510	3166	344	10%	0.14	0.22	0.03
113 Managers in mining and energy industries	2042	1845	197	10%	0.08	0.13	0.02
154 Prison officers (principal and above)	185	168	17	9%	0.01	0.01	0.00
631 Railway station staff	1396	1268	128	9%	0.06	0.09	0.01
151 Officers in foreign armed forces	277	252	25	9%	0.01	0.02	0.00
897 Woodworking machine operatives	4119	3748	371	9%	0.16	0.26	0.03
530 Smiths and forge workers	1106	1014	92	8%	0.04	0.07	0.01
615 Security guards and related occupations	12707	11658	1049	8%	0.50	0.81	0.10
218 Planning and quality control engineers	6089	5590	499	8%	0.24	0.39	0.05
517 Precision instrument makers/repairers	3601	3306	295	8%	0.14	0.23	0.03
829 Other chemicals, paper, plastics operatives nec	1446	1330	116	8%	0.06	0.09	0.01
142 Managers in warehousing and related	4652	4281	371	8%	0.18	0.30	0.03
990 All other labourers and related	9940	9166	774	8%	0.39	0.64	0.07
612 Prison service officers (below principal)	2257	2084	173	8%	0.09	0.14	0.02
581 Butchers, meat cutters	4754	4392	362	8%	0.19	0.31	0.03
731 Roundsmen/women and van salespersons	4817	4451	366	8%	0.19	0.31	0.03
219 Other engineers and technologists nec	5570	5160	410	7%	0.22	0.36	0.04
842 Metal polishers	791	733	58	7%	0.03	0.05	0.01
839 Other metal making operatives nec	1625	1507	118	7%	0.06	0.10	0.01
215 Chemical engineers	420	390	30	7%	0.02	0.03	0.00
600 NCOs and other ranks, UK armed forces	15824	14697	1127	7%	0.63	1.02	0.10
511 Boring and drilling machine setters	879	817	62	7%	0.03	0.06	0.01
733 Scrap dealers, scrap metal merchants	573	533	40	7%	0.02	0.04	0.00
871 Road transport depot inspectors	487	454	33	7%	0.02	0.03	0.00
531 Moulders, core makers, die casters	1437	1348	89	6%	0.06	0.09	0.01
571 Cabinet makers	2981	2797	184	6%	0.12	0.19	0.02

Occupation (371 groups)	Total	Men	Women	% female	% of all	% of men	% of women
834 Electroplaters, galvanizers, colour coaters	842	791	51	6%	0.03	0.05	0.00
894 Oilers, greasers, lubricators	351	330	21	6%	0.01	0.02	0.00
155 Customs and excise/ immigration officers	67	63	4	6%	0.00	0.00	0.00
526 Computer engineers, installation & maintenance	2090	1968	122	6%	0.08	0.14	0.01
150 Officers in UK armed forces	3165	2983	182	6%	0.13	0.21	0.02
873 Bus and coach drivers	9643	9093	550	6%	0.38	0.63	0.05
111 Managers in building and contracting	14722	13883	839	6%	0.58	0.96	0.08
537 Welding trades	11719	11052	667	6%	0.46	0.77	0.06
955 Lift and car park attendants	776	732	44	6%	0.03	0.05	0.00
831 Metal drawers	354	334	20	6%	0.01	0.02	0.00
331 Aircraft flight deck officers	1077	1018	59	5%	0.04	0.07	0.01
874 Taxi, cab drivers and chauffeurs	12863	12180	683	5%	0.51	0.85	0.06
262 Building, land, mining, general surveyors	5767	5467	300	5%	0.23	0.38	0.03
572 Case and box makers	580	552	28	5%	0.02	0.04	0.00
870 Bus inspectors	292	278	14	5%	0.01	0.02	0.00
826 Synthetic fibre makers	214	204	10	5%	0.01	0.01	0.00
594 Gardeners, groundsmen/ groundswomen	13198	12588	610	5%	0.52	0.87	0.06
312 Quantity surveyors	3845	3670	175	5%	0.15	0.25	0.02
302 Electrical/electronic technicians	2153	2057	96	4%	0.09	0.14	0.01
872 Drivers of road goods vehicles	51041	48806	2235	4%	2.02	3.39	0.21
313 Marine insurance and other surveyors	436	417	19	4%	0.02	0.03	0.00
883 Rail signal operatives and crossing keepers	641	614	27	4%	0.03	0.04	0.00
301 Engineering technicians	4173	3999	174	4%	0.17	0.28	0.02
311 Building inspectors	480	461	19	4%	0.02	0.03	0.00
892 Water and sewerage plant attendants	1376	1327	49	4%	0.05	0.09	0.00
913 Mates to metal/ electrical and related fitters	2639	2546	93	4%	0.10	0.18	0.01
217 Process and production engineers	2042	1971	71	3%	0.08	0.14	0.01

Occupation (371 groups)	Total	Men	Women	% female	% of all	% of men	% of women
832 Rollers	234	226	8	3%	0.01	0.02	0.00
540 Motor mechanics, auto engineers	21055	20337	718	3%	0.83	1.41	0.07
950 Hospital porters	1842	1781	61	3%	0.07	0.12	0.01
529 Other electrical/ electronic trades nec	5056	4889	167	3%	0.20	0.34	0.02
881 Rail transport inspectors, supervisors	1532	1483	49	3%	0.06	0.10	0.00
844 Shot blasters	441	427	14	3%	0.02	0.03	0.00
931 Goods porters	6897	6679	218	3%	0.27	0.46	0.02
573 Pattern makers (moulds)	579	561	18	3%	0.02	0.04	0.00
523 Telephone fitters	7657	7439	218	3%	0.30	0.52	0.02
596 Coach painters, other spray painters	4125	4008	117	3%	0.16	0.28	0.01
823 Glass and ceramics furnace operatives	522	508	14	3%	0.02	0.04	0.00
211 Mechanical engineers	6335	6166	169	3%	0.25	0.43	0.02
213 Electronic engineers	1725	1679	46	3%	0.07	0.12	0.00
152 Police officers (inspector and above)	1164	1133	31	3%	0.05	0.08	0.00
507 Painters and decorators	19869	19344	525	3%	0.79	1.34	0.05
951 Hotel porters	1287	1255	32	2%	0.05	0.09	0.00
930 Stevedores, dockers	1167	1138	29	2%	0.05	0.08	0.00
598 Office machinery mechanics	332	324	8	2%	0.01	0.02	0.00
216 Design and development engineers	6864	6703	161	2%	0.27	0.47	0.01
904 Forestry workers	1511	1476	35	2%	0.06	0.10	0.00
957 Road sweepers	1081	1056	25	2%	0.04	0.07	0.00
896 Construction and related operatives	10969	10719	250	2%	0.43	0.74	0.02
833 Annealers, hardeners, temperers	397	388	9	2%	0.02	0.03	0.00
893 Electrical energy boiler and related operatives	1993	1948	45	2%	0.08	0.14	0.00
519 Other machine tool setters nec	5007	4894	113	2%	0.20	0.34	0.01
920 Mates to woodworking trades workers	179	175	4	2%	0.01	0.01	0.00
901 Agricultural machinery drivers	1084	1060	24	2%	0.04	0.07	0.00
210 Civil, structural, municipal, mining engineers	6234	6099	135	2%	0.25	0.42	0.01
934 Driver's mates	377	369	8	2%	0.01	0.03	0.00
880 Seafarers (merchant navy)/barge operatives	1445	1416	29	2%	0.06	0.10	0.00
503 Glaziers	1591	1560	31	2%	0.06	0.11	0.00

Occupation (371 groups)	Total	Men	Women	% female	% of all	% of men	% of women
522 Electrical engineers (not professional)	2327	2282	45	2%	0.09	0.16	0.00
525 Radio, TV, and video engineers	2161	2120	41	2%	0.09	0.15	0.00
933 Refuse and salvage collectors	2149	2109	40	2%	0.09·	0.15	0.00
524 Cable jointers, lines repairers	1488	1461	27	2%	0.06	0.10	0.00
153 Fire service officers (station officers & above)	848	833	15	2%	0.03	0.06	0.00
911 Labourers in foundries	1005	988	17	2%	0.04	0.07	0.00
884 Shunters and points operatives	360	354	6	2%	0.01	0.02	0.00
534 Metal plate workers, shipwrights, riveters	3060	3011	49	2%	0.12	0.21	0.00
956 Window cleaners	2576	2536	40	2%	0.10	0.18	0.00
212 Electrical engineers	3035	2988	47	2%	0.12	0.21	0.00
533 Sheet metal workers	4290	4224	66	2%	0.17	0.29	0.01
516 Metal working production and maintenance	42237	41605	632	1%	1.67	2.89	0.06
903 Fishing and related workers	1272	1253	19	1%	0.05	0.09	0.00
515 Tool makers, tool fitters, and markers-out	4801	4731	70	1%	0.19	0.33	0.01
512 Grinding machine setters	1353	1334	19	1%	0.05	0.09	0.00
898 Mine (excluding coal) and quarry workers	1904	1878	26	1%	0.08	0.13	0.00
887 Fork lift and mechanical truck drivers	9350	9225	125	1%	0.37	0.64	0.01
521 Electricians, electrical maintenance fitters	24811	24490	321	1%	0.98	1.70	0.03
882 Rail engine drivers and assistants	2195	2167	28	1%	0.09	0.15	0.00
509 Other construction trades nec	4622	4566	56	1%	0.18	0.32	0.01
532 Plumbers, heating engineers	17258	17055	203	1%	0.68	1.18	0.02
513 Milling machine setters and setter-operators	1062	1050	12	1%	0.04	0.07	0.00
895 Mains and service pipe layers	1811	1792	19	1%	0.07	0.12	0.00
504 Builders, building contractors	16004	15838	166	1%	0.63	1.10	0.02
923 Road construction and maintenance workers	2623	2596	27	1%	0.10	0.18	0.00

Occupation (371 groups)	Total	Men	Women	% female	% of all	% of men	% of women
332 Ship and hovercraft officers	1752	1734	18	1%	0.07	0.12	0.00
830 Furnace operatives (metal)	786	778	8	1%	0.03	0.05	0.00
544 Tyre and exhaust fitters	1280	1268	12	1%	0.05	0.09	0.00
506 Floorers, floor coverers, tilers	3396	3365	31	1%	0.13	0.23	0.00
541 Coach and vehicle body builders	1540	1526	14	1%	0.06	0.11	0.00
885 Mechanical plant drivers and operatives	4808	4767	41	1%	0.19	0.33	0.00
929 Other building/civil engineering labourers nec	20819	20646	173	1%	0.82	1.43	0.02
570 Carpenters and joiners	30940	30688	252	1%	1.23	2.13	0.02
611 Fire service officers	3752	3722	30	1%	0.15	0.26	0.00
922 Rail construction and maintenance workers	1436	1425	11	1%	0.06	0.10	0.00
910 Coal mine labourers	2093	2077	16	1%	0.08	0.14	0.00
921 Mates to building trades workers	1578	1566	12	1%	0.06	0.11	0.00
535 Steel erectors	1859	1845	14	1%	0.07	0.13	0.00
501 Roofers, slaters, tilers, sheeters	5476	5435	41	1%	0.22	0.38	0.00
514 Press setters and setter-operators	436	433	3	1%	0.02	0.03	0.00
536 Barbenders, steel fixers	729	724	5	1%	0.03	0.05	0.00
500 Bricklayers, masons	12467	12393	74	1%	0.49	0.86	0.01
886 Crane drivers	2453	2439	14	1%	0.10	0.17	0.00
510 Centre, capstan, turret, and lathe setters	2655	2640	15	1%	0.11	0.18	0.00
543 Auto electricians	926	921	5	1%	0.04	0.06	0.00
505 Scaffolders, stagers, steeplejacks	3160	3143	17	1%	0.13	0.22	0.00
502 Plasterers	4945	4923	22	*%	0.20	0.34	0.00
890 Washers, screeners, and crushers in mines	242	241	1	*%	0.01	0.02	0.00
542 Vehicle body repairers, panel beaters	2971	2959	12	*%	0.12	0.21	0.00
924 Paviors, kerb layers	555	553	2	*%	0.02	0.04	0.00
932 Slingers	356	355	1	*%	0.01	0.02	0.00
597 Face trained coalmining workers	2589	2584	5	*%	0.10	0.18	0.00
112 Clerks of works	824	824	0	0%	0.03	0.06	0.00

* Less than 0.5%.   nec Not elsewhere classified.

Source: 1991 Census 10% sample, Great Britain, economically active population aged 161 as reported in table 4 in OPCS and GROS (1994a), *1991 Census—Economic Activity* report.

TABLE B2. *Sex ratios within occupations: 78 occupational groups*

Occupation (78 groups)	Total	Men	Women	% female	% of all	% of men	% of women
All economically active	2525146	1439623	1085523	43%	100	100	100
45 Secretaries, PAs, typists, WP operators	82731	1090	81641	99%	3.28	0.08	7.52
65 Childcare & related occupations	31341	454	30887	99%	1.24	0.03	2.85
46 Receptionists, telephonists, & related	30156	2383	27773	92%	1.19	0.17	2.56
66 Hairdressers, beauticians, & related	9875	838	9037	92%	0.39	0.06	0.83
64 Health & related occupations	51468	5034	46434	90%	2.04	0.35	4.28
34 Health associate professionals	62973	7255	55718	88%	2.49	0.50	5.13
72 Sales assistants, check-out operators	118056	21902	96154	81%	4.68	1.52	8.86
43 Clerks nec	64659	12337	52322	81%	2.56	0.86	4.82
79 Sales occupations nec	7290	1463	5827	80%	0.29	0.10	0.54
95 Other occups in sales & services	122769	26130	96639	79%	4.86	1.82	8.90
37 Social welfare associate professionals	14609	3879	10730	73%	0.58	0.27	0.99
40 Admin/clerical officers & assistants in government	38048	10410	27638	73%	1.51	0.72	2.55
41 Numerical clerks & cashiers	103981	28458	75523	73%	4.12	1.98	6.96
42 Filing & records clerks	28023	8089	19934	71%	1.11	0.56	1.84
49 Clerical & secretarial occupations nec	16588	4856	11732	71%	0.66	0.34	1.08
55 Textiles, garments, & related trades	32099	10016	22083	69%	1.27	0.70	2.03
62 Catering occupations	51373	18309	33064	64%	2.03	1.27	3.05
27 Librarians & related professionals	2180	779	1401	64%	0.09	0.05	0.13
23 Teaching professionals	85612	32523	53089	62%	3.39	2.26	4.89
29 Professional occupations nec	14687	6149	8538	58%	0.58	0.43	0.79
63 Travel attendants & related	5838	2638	3200	55%	0.23	0.18	0.29
86 Other routine process operatives	44706	20388	24318	54%	1.77	1.42	2.24
67 Domestic staff & related	16716	7740	8976	54%	0.66	0.54	0.83
85 Assemblers, lineworkers	18980	9162	9818	52%	0.75	0.64	0.90
35 Legal associate professionals	2418	1207	1211	50%	0.10	0.08	0.11
13 Financial institution/ office managers, EOs	45354	24308	21046	46%	1.80	1.69	1.94

Occupation (78 groups)	Total	Men	Women	% female	% of all	% of men	% of women
80 Food, drink, tobacco process operatives	15262	8634	6628	43%	0.60	0.60	0.61
19 Managers & administrators nec	22936	13519	9417	41%	0.91	0.94	0.87
17 Managers & proprietors, service industries	133943	80887	53056	40%	5.30	5.62	4.89
10 Managers/ administrators, government/large organizations	12034	7324	4710	39%	0.48	0.51	0.43
39 Associate professional/ technical jobs nec	17065	10417	6648	39%	0.68	0.72	0.61
81 Textiles & tannery process operatives	4371	2689	1682	38%	0.17	0.19	0.15
69 Personal & protective service occups nec	8791	5417	3374	38%	0.35	0.38	0.31
38 Literary, artistic, sports professionals	32425	20426	11999	37%	1.28	1.42	1.11
00 Not stated, inadequately described	26981	17164	9817	36%	1.07	1.19	0.90
12 Specialist managers	67967	44587	23380	34%	2.69	3.10	2.15
22 Health professionals	15561	10411	5150	33%	0.62	0.72	0.47
56 Printing & related trades	16632	11527	5105	31%	0.66	0.80	0.47
36 Business/financial associate professionals	24928	17428	7500	30%	0.99	1.21	0.69
20 Natural scientists	11487	8132	3355	29%	0.45	0.56	0.31
70 Buyers, brokers, related agents	7814	5540	2274	29%	0.31	0.38	0.21
24 Legal professionals	8227	5954	2273	28%	0.33	0.41	0.21
90 Other occups in agriculture and related	18516	13955	4561	25%	0.73	0.97	0.42
30 Scientific technicians	30339	23153	7186	24%	1.20	1.61	0.66
71 Sales representatives	37926	29167	8759	23%	1.50	2.03	0.81
25 Business & financial professionals	16614	13089	3525	21%	0.66	0.91	0.32
58 Food preparation trades	10619	8378	2241	21%	0.42	0.58	0.21
73 Mobile, market, door-to-door salespersons & agents	9070	7165	1905	21%	0.36	0.50	0.18
32 Computer analysts, programmers	14530	11489	3041	21%	0.58	0.80	0.28
44 Stores & despatch clerks, storekeepers	34430	28136	6294	18%	1.36	1.95	0.58
84 Metal working process operatives	22002	18151	3851	18%	0.87	1.26	0.35
82 Chemicals, paper, plastics & related process operatives	20546	17229	3317	16%	0.81	1.20	0.31

Occupation (78 groups)	Total	Men	Women	% female	% of all	% of men	% of women
94 Other occups in communication	19402	16405	2997	15%	0.77	1.14	0.28
16 Managers in farming, hort, forestry, fishing	21512	18245	3267	15%	0.85	1.27	0.30
14 Managers in transport & storing	15796	13559	2237	14%	0.63	0.94	0.21
61 Security & protective service occups	36335	31329	5006	14%	1.44	2.18	0.46
59 Other craft & related occupations nec	32380	27945	4435	14%	1.28	1.94	0.41
89 Plant & machine operatives nec	38534	33836	4698	12%	1.53	2.35	0.43
91 Other occups in mining & manufacturing	19667	17327	2340	12%	0.78	1.20	0.22
11 Production managers in manuf, construction, mining, & energy	63986	57394	6592	10%	2.53	3.99	0.61
26 Architects, town planners, surveyors	10040	9172	868	9%	0.40	0.64	0.08
99 Other occups nec	10597	9744	853	8%	0.42	0.68	0.08
60 NCOs & other ranks, armed forces	17459	16101	1358	8%	0.69	1.12	0.13
31 Draughtpersons, quantity & other surveyors	11634	10738	896	8%	0.46	0.75	0.08
21 Engineers & technologists	44171	41829	2342	5%	1.75	2.91	0.22
83 Metal making & treating process operatives	4238	4024	214	5%	0.17	0.28	0.02
15 Protective service officers	5706	5432	274	5%	0.23	0.38	0.03
87 Road transport operatives	74568	70997	3571	5%	2.95	4.93	0.33
33 Ship/aircraft officers, air traffic controllers	3175	3043	132	4%	0.13	0.21	0.01
53 Metal forming, welding, & related trades	41458	40273	1185	3%	1.64	2.80	0.11
88 Other transport & machinery operatives	26543	25797	746	3%	1.05	1.79	0.07
54 Vehicle trades	27772	27011	761	3%	1.10	1.88	0.07
93 Other occups in transport	10946	10650	296	3%	0.43	0.74	0.03
52 Electrical/electronic trades	47569	46287	1282	3%	1.88	3.22	0.12
51 Metal machining/fitting, instrument making	62964	61516	1448	2%	2.49	4.27	0.13
57 Woodworking trades	36428	35676	752	2%	1.44	2.48	0.07
50 Construction trades	71530	70567	963	1%	2.83	4.90	0.09
92 Other occups in construction	27190	26961	229	1%	1.08	1.87	0.02

Source: 1991 Census 10% sample, Great Britain, economically active population aged 16↑, reported in table 4 in OPCS and GROS (1994*a*), *1991 Census—Economic Activity* report.

TABLE B3. *Sex ratios within occupations: 10 major groups*

Occupation (11 groups)	Total	Men	Women	% female	% of all	% of men	% of women
1a Corporate managers and administrators	233779	166123	67656	29%	9.26	11.54	6.23
1b Managers/proprietors in agriculture & services	155455	99132	56323	36%	6.16	6.89	5.19
2 Professional occupations	208579	128038	80541	38%	8.26	8.89	7.42
3 Associate technical/ professional occupations	214096	109035	105061	49%	8.48	7.57	9.68
4 Clerical and secretarial	398616	95759	302857	76%	15.79	6.65	27.90
5 Craft and related	379451	339196	40255	11%	15.03	23.56	3.71
6 Personal and protective service	229196	87860	141336	62%	9.08	6.10	13.02
7 Sales occupations	180156	65237	114919	64%	7.13	4.53	10.59
8 Plant and machine operatives	269750	210907	58843	22%	10.68	14.65	5.42
9 Other occupations	229087	121172	107915	47%	9.07	8.42	9.94
Not stated and inadequately described	26981	17164	9817	36%	1.07	1.19	0.90

Source: 1991 Census 10% sample, Great Britain, economically active population aged 161 , reported in table 4 in OPCS and GROS (1994*a*), *1991 Census—Economic Activity* report.

ANNEX C

The International Standard Classification of Occupations (ISCO88): Occupational Sex Ratios and Part-Time Workrates by Type of Occupation

ISCO88 as applied to the 1% SAR		Male occupations <25% F	Mixed occupations 25%–55% F	Female occupations >25% F	Total
All in employment	N	93055	38625	92441	224121
	% F	9%	39%	82%	44%
	% PT	3%	9%	36%	18%
111 Legislators and senior officials	N	72	594	—	666
	% F	17%	47%	—	44%
	% PT	0%	8%	—	7%
114 Senior officials—special interest organizations	N	—	240	—	240
	% F	—	53%	—	53%
	% PT	—	14%	—	14%
122 Department managers in enterprises with 25+ employees	N	4404	1884	135	6423
	% F	14%	38%	57%	22%
	% PT	1%	3%	9%	2%
123 Other department managers in enterprises with 25+ employees	N	1463	6253	1295	9011
	% F	19%	40%	74%	41%
	% PT	2%	6%	21%	7%
131 General managers of small enterprises	N	5656	10180	771	16607
	% F	12%	39%	74%	31%
	% PT	2%	7%	20%	6%
211 Physicists, chemists, and related professionals	N	369	311	—	680
	% F	16%	34%	—	24%
	% PT	2%	5%	—	3%
212 Mathematicians, statisticians, etc.	N	—	144	—	144
	% F	—	28%	—	28%
	% PT	—	4%	—	4%
213 Computing professionals	N	2012	—	—	2012
	% F	19%	—	—	19%
	% PT	3%	—	—	3%
214 Architects, engineers, etc.	N	5168	—	—	5168
	% F	5%	—	—	5%
	% PT	2%	—	—	2%
221 Life sciences professionals (biologists, etc.)	N	—	344	—	344
	% F	—	47%	—	47%
	% PT	—	8%	—	8%
222 Health professionals	N	—	1395	—	1395
	% F	—	33%	—	33%
	% PT	—	11%	—	11%

ISCO88 as applied to the 1% SAR		Male occupations <25% F	Mixed occupations 25%–55% F	Female occupations >25% F	Total
223 Nurses and midwives	N	—	—	4857	4857
	% F	—	—	91%	91%
	% PT	—	—	29%	29%
231 Higher education teachers	N	660	1486	—	2146
	% F	20%	52%	—	42%
	% PT	11%	34%	—	27%
232 Secondary education teachers	N	—	—	2901	2901
	% F	—	—	55%	55%
	% PT	—	—	19%	19%
233 Primary and pre-primary teachers	N	—	—	2547	2547
	% F	—	—	83%	83%
	% PT	—	—	21%	21%
234 Special education teachers	N	—	—	252	252
	% F	—	—	70%	70%
	% PT	—	—	13%	13%
235 Other teachers	N	—	849	275	1124
	% F	—	47%	78%	54%
	% PT	—	9%	57%	20%
241 Business professionals (accountants, etc.)	N	1473	—	—	1473
	% F	21%	—	—	21%
	% PT	4%	—	—	4%
242 Legal professionals	N	105	711	—	816
	% F	19%	30%	—	28%
	% PT	3%	3%	—	3%
243 Archivists, librarians	N	—	70	299	369
	% F	—	59%	71%	68%
	% PT	—	17%	25%	23%
244 Social science professionals (economists, etc.)	N	—	—	1090	1090
	% F	—	—	72%	72%
	% PT	—	—	17%	17%
245 Writers, creative and performing artists	N	—	1576	—	1576
	% F	—	39%	—	39%
	% PT	—	21%	—	21%
246 Religious professionals	N	—	325	—	325
	% F	—	13%	—	13%
	% PT	—	6%	—	6%
247 Public service administrators	N	—	480	823	1303
	% F	—	29%	54%	45%
	% PT	—	3%	7%	5%
311 Physical & engineering science technicians	N	2563	893	—	3456
	% F	12%	41%	—	20%
	% PT	3%	9%	—	4%
313 Optical and electronic equipment operators	N	349	205	120	674
	% F	16%	55%	88%	41%
	% PT	9%	12%	29%	14%
314 Ship and aircraft controllers and technicians	N	282	—	—	282
	% F	3%	—	—	3%
	% PT	3%	—	—	3%

ISCO88 as applied to the 1% SAR		Male occupations <25% F	Mixed occupations 25%–55% F	Female occupations >25% F	Total
315 Safety and quality inspectors	N	335	—	—	335
	% F	12%	—	—	12%
	% PT	2%	—	—	2%
322 Modern health associates (opticians, physiotherapists, etc.)	N	87	87	853	1027
	% F	14%	48%	86%	77%
	% PT	5%	12%	35%	31%
323 Nursing & midwifery assistants	N	—	—	1431	1431
	% F	—	—	95%	95%
	% PT	—	—	42%	42%
332 Pre-primary education assistants	N	—	—	586	586
	% F	—	—	100%	100%
	% PT	—	—	28%	28%
334 Other teaching assistants	N	223	—	—	223
	% F	12%	—	—	12%
	% PT	22%	—	—	22%
341 Finance & sales associates	N	4604	1634	192	6430
	% F	20%	37%	59%	25%
	% PT	5%	11%	7%	6%
342 Business services agents and brokers	N	207	—	—	207
	% F	20%	—	—	20%
	% PT	5%	—	—	5%
343 Administrative associates	N	—	428	—	428
	% F	—	46%	—	46%
	% PT	—	8%	—	8%
344 Customs, tax, etc. associates	N	—	212	—	212
	% F	—	33%	—	33%
	% PT	—	4%	—	4%
345 Police inspectors and detectives	N	211	—	—	211
	% F	3%	—	—	3%
	% PT	0%	—	—	0%
346 Social work assistants	N	—	—	1342	1342
	% F	—	—	74%	74%
	% PT	—	—	25%	25%
347 Artistic, entertainment, & sports workers	N	—	940	476	1416
	% F	—	37%	84%	53%
	% PT	—	10%	38%	19%
411 Secretaries & keyboard clerks	N	—	—	9208	9208
	% F	—	—	94%	94%
	% PT	—	—	25%	25%
412 Numerical clerks	N	—	—	5834	5834
	% F	—	—	72%	72%
	% PT	—	—	18%	18%
413 Material-recording & transport clerks	N	2731	—	235	2966
	% F	15%	—	61%	19%
	% PT	6%	—	14%	7%
414 Library, mail etc. clerks	N	1456	—	2610	4066
	% F	15%	—	70%	51%
	% PT	9%	—	29%	22%

ISCO88 as applied to the 1% SAR		Male occupations <25% F	Mixed occupations 25%–55% F	Female occupations >25% F	Total
419 Other office clerks	N	—	—	9572	9572
	% F	—	—	79%	79%
	% PT	—	—	22%	22%
421 Cashiers, tellers clerks	N	—	359	4871	5230
	% F	—	44%	81%	78%
	% PT	—	21%	32%	32%
422 Client information clerks	N	—	—	2543	2543
	% F	—	—	96%	96%
	% PT	—	—	40%	40%
511 Travel attendants etc.	N	291	—	359	650
	% F	9%	—	69%	42%
	% PT	2%	—	39%	21%
512 Housekeeping and restaurant services workers	N	—	—	6391	6391
	% F	—	—	76%	76%
	% PT	—	—	46%	46%
513 Personal care workers	N	220	—	5573	5793
	% F	19%	—	96%	93%
	% PT	10%	—	61%	59%
514 Other personal services workers	N	48	—	883	931
	% F	13%	—	93%	89%
	% PT	2%	—	23%	22%
516 Protective services workers	N	2892	53	247	3192
	% F	9%	51%	62%	13%
	% PT	2%	0%	59%	6%
522 Shop salespersons	N	58	367	8980	9405
	% F	7%	44%	83%	81%
	% PT	6%	29%	57%	56%
611 Market gardeners, crop growers	N	1109	172	—	1281
	% F	4%	45%	—	10%
	% PT	8%	27%	—	10%
613 Market-oriented animal producers workers	N	946	—	—	946
	% F	13%	—	—	13%
	% PT	4%	—	—	4%
614 Forestry etc. workers	N	135	—	—	135
	% F	1%	—	—	1%
	% PT	2%	—	—	2%
615 Fishery workers	N	107	—	—	107
	% F	1%	—	—	1%
	% PT	2%	—	—	2%
711 Miners, stonecutters, carvers	N	341	—	—	341
	% F	1%	—	—	1%
	% PT	0%	—	—	0%
712 Builders, carpenters, etc.	N	6636	—	—	6636
	% F	1%	—	—	1%
	% PT	2%	—	—	2%
713 Building finishers	N	4027	—	—	4027
	% F	1%	—	—	1%
	% PT	2%	—	—	2%

ISCO88 as applied to the 1% SAR		Male occupations <25% F	Mixed occupations 25%–55% F	Female occupations >25% F	Total
714 Painters	N	1960	—	—	1960
	% F	2%	—	—	2%
	% PT	2%	—	—	2%
721 Metal moulders	N	2316	—	—	2316
	% F	3%	—	—	3%
	% PT	1%	—	—	1%
722 Blacksmiths, tool makers	N	1649	—	—	1649
	% F	3%	—	—	3%
	% PT	1%	—	—	1%
723 Machinery mechanic, fitters	N	5979	—	—	5979
	% F	2%	—	—	2%
	% PT	1%	—	—	1%
724 Electrical & electronic mechanics	N	3503	—	—	3503
	% F	3%	—	—	3%
	% PT	1%	—	—	1%
731 Precision workers	N	542	—	—	542
	% F	13%	—	—	13%
	% PT	4%	—	—	4%
732 Potters, glassmakers	N	357	—	113	470
	% F	25%	—	59%	33%
	% PT	5%	—	12%	7%
733 Handicraft workers	N	—	263	—	263
	% F	—	27%	—	27%
	% PT	—	7%	—	7%
734 Printing etc. workers	N	859	623	109	1591
	% F	19%	40%	61%	30%
	% PT	4%	8%	15%	6%
741 Food processing workers	N	367	684	—	1051
	% F	10%	34%	—	25%
	% PT	5%	9%	—	7%
742 Wood treaters	N	460	—	—	460
	% F	10%	—	—	10%
	% PT	3%	—	—	3%
743 Textile, garment workers	N	221	395	1738	2354
	% F	15%	44%	88%	73%
	% PT	2%	6%	16%	13%
744 Pelt, leather, shoemaking workers	N	—	372	—	372
	% F	—	54%	—	54%
	% PT	—	8%	—	8%
811 Mining & mineral processing plant operators	N	19	—	—	19
	% F	5%	—	—	5%
	% PT	0%	—	—	0%
812 Metal processing plant operators	N	326	—	—	326
	% F	4%	—	—	4%
	% PT	1%	—	—	1%
813 Glass, ceramics plant operators	N	44	—	—	44
	% F	2%	—	—	2%
	% PT	0%	—	—	0%

ISCO88 as applied to the 1% SAR		Male occupations <25% F	Mixed occupations 25%–55% F	Female occupations >25% F	Total
814 Wood processing plant operators	N	153	—	—	153
	% F	16%	—	—	16%
	% PT	1%	—	—	1%
815 Chemical processing plant operators	N	730	—	—	730
	% F	12%	—	—	12%
	% PT	2%	—	—	2%
816 Power production plant operators	N	1414	—	—	1414
	% F	28%	—	—	28%
	% PT	11%	—	—	11%
821 Metal & mineral machine operators	N	1506	1235	—	2741
	% F	15%	28%	—	21%
	% PT	2%	5%	—	3%
822 Chemical product machine operators	N	159	—	150	309
	% F	7%	—	73%	39%
	% PT	3%	—	23%	13%
823 Rubber & plastics machine operators	N	756	—	—	756
	% F	22%	—	—	22%
	% PT	5%	—	—	5%
824 Wood products machine operators	N	329	—	—	329
	% F	6%	—	—	6%
	% PT	2%	—	—	2%
825 Printing & binding machine operators	N	448	—	—	448
	% F	16%	—	—	16%
	% PT	4%	—	—	4%
826 Textile, fur machine operators	N	106	404	385	895
	% F	12%	36%	65%	46%
	% PT	1%	6%	12%	8%
827 Food etc. production machine operators	N	61	974	268	1303
	% F	12%	41%	56%	43%
	% PT	2%	14%	24%	15%
828 Assemblers	N	891	544	1140	2575
	% F	20%	30%	63%	41%
	% PT	3%	3%	11%	7%
831 Locomotive engine drivers	N	331	—	—	331
	% F	2%	—	—	2%
	% PT	1%	—	—	1%
832 Motor vehicle drivers	N	6493	—	—	6493
	% F	4%	—	—	4%
	% PT	4%	—	—	4%
833 Agricultural plant etc. operators	N	1853	—	—	1853
	% F	3%	—	—	3%
	% PT	2%	—	—	2%
834 Ships decks crews etc.	N	129	—	—	129
	% F	2%	—	—	2%
	% PT	2%	—	—	2%
911 Street vendors	N	433	65	301	799
	% F	6%	59%	78%	37%
	% PT	5%	45%	24%	16%

ISCO88 as applied to the 1% SAR		Male occupations <25% F	Mixed occupations 25%–55% F	Female occupations >25% F	Total
913 Domestic etc. helpers,	N	156	—	8331	8487
cleaners, launderers	% F	4%	—	87%	85%
	% PT	3%	—	73%	72%
914 Building caretakers,	N	916	—	—	916
window cleaners	% F	19%	—	—	19%
	% PT	18%	—	—	18%
915 Messengers, porters etc.	N	408	633	—	1041
	% F	20%	44%	—	34%
	% PT	18%	28%	—	24%
916 Garbage collectors etc.	N	290	—	—	290
	% F	3%	—	—	3%
	% PT	3%	—	—	3%
921 Agricultural, fishery	N	972	—	313	1285
labourers	% F	23%	—	58%	31%
	% PT	9%	—	20%	12%
931 Mining, construction etc.	N	2064	—	—	2064
workers	% F	1%	—	—	1%
	% PT	1%	—	—	1%
932 Manufacturing labourers	N	1942	241	2042	4225
	% F	13%	42%	69%	42%
	% PT	5%	8%	22%	13%
933 Transport labourers	N	673	—	—	673
	% F	2%	—	—	2%
	% PT	4%	—	—	4%

Source: 1% SAR, Great Britain, data for residents in employment aged 16–64 years.

Bibliography

Addison, J.T., and Siebert, W.S. (1993), *Social Engineering in the European Community: The Social Charter, Maastricht and Beyond*, London: Institute of Economic Affairs.

Allen, S., and Wolkowitz, C. (1987), *Homeworking: Myths and Realities*, London: Macmillan.

Anderson, M., Bechhofer, F., and Kendrick, S. (1994), 'Individual and household strategies', in M. Anderson, F. Bechhofer, and J. Gershuny (eds.), *The Social and Political Economy of the Household*, Oxford: Oxford University Press, 19–67.

Andrews, H.F. (1978), 'Journey to work considerations in the labour force participation of married women', *Regional Studies*, 12: 11–20.

Applebaum, E. (1987), 'Restructuring work: temporary, part-time and at-home employment', in H. I. Hartmann (ed.), *Computer Chips and Paper Clips: Technology and Women's Employment: Case Studies and Policy Perspectives*, Washington: National Academy Press, 268–310.

Arrow, K.J. (1973), 'The theory of discrimination', in O. Ashenfelter and A. Rees (eds.), *Discrimination in Labour Markets*, Princeton: Princeton University Press, 3–33.

Bannock, G., and Stanworth, J. (1990), *The Making of Entrepreneurs*, London: Small Business Research Trust.

Beatson, M. (1995), *Labour Market Flexibility*, Research Series No. 48; London: Employment Department.

Becker, G.S. (1975), *Human Capital*, 2nd edn., Chicago: University of Chicago Press.

—— (1985), 'Human capital, effort and the sexual division of labour', *Journal of Labor Economics*, 3: S33–S58.

—— (1981, 1991), *A Treatise on the Family*, Cambridge, Mass.: Harvard University Press.

Beechey, V., and Perkins, T. (1987), *A Matter of Hours: Women, Part-Time Work and the Labour Market*, Cambridge: Polity Press/Blackwell.

Berger, P.A., Steinmüller, P., and Sopp, P. (1993), 'Differentiation of life-courses? Changing patterns of labour-market sequences in West Germany', *European Sociological Review*, 9: 43–65.

Berk, R. (1983), 'An introduction to sample selection bias in sociological data', *American Sociological Review*, 48: 386–98.

Bevan, J., *et al.* (1988), *Barriers to Business Start-Up: A Study of the Flow into and out of Self-Employment*, Research Paper No. 71; London: Department of Employment.

Bielby, W.T., and Baron, J.N. (1984), 'A woman's place is with other women: sex segregation within organisations', in B. F. Reskin (ed.), *Sex Segregation in the Workplace: Trends, Explanations, Remedies*, Washington: National Academy Press, 27–55.

Blackburn, R.M., Siltanen, J., and Jarman, J. (1995), 'The measurement of occupational gender segregation: current problems and a new approach', *Journal of the Royal Statistical Society*, Series A, 158: 319–31.

Blanpain, R., and Rojot, J. (1997) (eds.), *Legal and Contractual Limitations to Working Time in the European Union*, 2nd edn., Leuven: Peeters for OOPEC.

Blau, D.M. (1987), 'A time series analysis of self-employment in the United States', *Journal of Political Economy*, 95: 445–6.

Blau, F.D., and Ferber, M.A. (1992), *The Economics of Women, Men and Work*, 2nd edn., Englewood Cliffs, NJ: Prentice-Hall.

Blaxall, M., and Reagan, B. (1976) (eds.), *Women and the Workplace: The Implications of Occupational Segregation*, Chicago and London: University of Chicago Press.

Blossfeld, H.-P. (1987), 'Labour market entry and the sexual segregation of careers in the Federal Republic of Germany', *American Journal of Sociology*, 93: 89–118.

—— (1997), 'Conclusions', in *Between Equalisation and Marginalisation: Women Working Part-Time in Europe and the USA*, Oxford: Oxford University Press.

—— and Hakim, C. (1997) (eds.), *Between Equalization and Marginalization: Women Working Part-time in Europe and the USA*, Oxford: Oxford University Press.

Bone, M., *et al.* (1992), *Retirement and Retirement Plans*, London: HMSO.

Boris, E., and Daniels, C.R. (1989) (eds.), *Homework: Historical and Contemporary Perspectives on Paid Labor at Home*, Urbana and Chicago: University of Illinois Press.

Bosch, G., Dawkins, P., and Michon, F. (1994) (eds.), *Times are Changing: Working Time in 14 Industrialised Countries*, Geneva: International Institute for Labour Studies.

Boyer, R. (1989) (ed.), *The Search for Labour Market Flexibility: The European Economies in Transition*, Oxford: Oxford University Press.

Bradley, H. (1989), *Men's Work, Women's Work: A Sociological History of the Sexual Division of Labour in Employment*, Cambridge: Polity Press.

Breakwell, G.M., and Weinberger, B. (1987), *Young Women in Gender Atypical Jobs: The Case of Trainee Technicians in the Engineering Industry*, Research Paper No. 49; London: Department of Employment.

Brown, C. (1984), *Black and White Britain: The Third PSI Survey*, London: Heinemann for the Policy Studies Institute.

Bruegel, I. (1994), 'Labour market prospects for women from ethnic minorities' in R. Lindley (ed.), *Labour Market Structures and Prospects for Women*, Manchester: EOC, 54–71.

—— and Hegewisch, A. (1994), 'Flexibilization and part-time work in Europe', in P. Brown and R. Crompton (eds.), *Economic Restructuring and Social Exclusion*, London: UCL Press, 33–57.

Bryson. A., and White, M. (1996a), *From Unemployment to Self-Employment*, London: Policy Studies Institute.

—— —— (1996b), *Moving In and Out of Self-Employment*, London: Policy Studies Institute.

Bubek, D. (1995), *Gender, Care and Justice*, Oxford: Clarendon Press.

Büchtemann, C.F., and Quack, S. (1989), 'Bridges or traps? Non-standard employment in the Federal Republic of Germany', in G. Rodgers and J. Rodgers (eds.), *Precarious Jobs in Labour Market Regulation*, Geneva: ILO, 109–48.

Burchell, B., and Rubery, J. (1994), 'Divided women: labour market segmentation and gender segregation', in A. M. Scott (ed.), *Gender Segregation and Social Change*, Oxford: Oxford University Press, 80–120.

Burgess, S., and Rees, H. (1996), 'Job tenure in Britain 1975–1992', *Economic Journal*, 106: 334–44.

Cain, G.G. (1986), 'The economic analysis of labour market discrimination: a survey', in O. Ashenfelter and R. Layard (eds.), *Handbook of Labor Economics*, Amsterdam: North Holland, 693–785.

Carter, S., and Cannon, T. (1988*a*), 'Women in business', *Employment Gazette*, 97: 565–71.

—— —— (1988*b*), *Female Entrepreneurs*, Research Paper No. 65; London: Department of Employment.

Charles, M., and Grusky, D.B. (1995), 'Models for describing the underlying structure of sex segregation', *American Journal of Sociology*, 100: 931–71.

Chauvin, K.W., and Ash, R.A. (1994), 'Gender earnings differentials in total pay, base pay and contingent pay', *Industrial and Labor Relations Review*, 47: 634–49.

Chiplin, B., and Sloane, P.J. (1974), 'Sexual discrimination in the labour market', *British Journal of Industrial Relations*, 12: 371–402.

Clark, A.E. (1996), 'Job satisfaction in Britain', *British Journal of Industrial Relations*, 34: 189–217.

Clogg, C.C., Eliason, S.R., and Wahl, R.J. (1990), 'Labour market experiences and labor-force outcomes', *American Journal of Sociology*, 95: 1536–76.

Cockburn, C. (1983), *Brothers: Male Dominance and Technological Change*, London: Pluto Press.

—— (1996), *Strategies for Gender Democracy: Women and the European Social Dialogue*, Supplement 4/95, *Social Europe*, Luxembourg: OOPEC.

Cohn, S. (1985), *The Process of Occupational Sex-Typing: The Feminisation of Clerical Work in Great Britain*, Philadelphia: Temple University Press.

Connor, H., LaValle, I., Tackey, N., and Perryman, S. (1996), *Ethnic Minority Graduates: Differences by Degrees*, Institute for Employment Studies Report No. 309; Brighton: University of Sussex.

Corcoran, M., Duncan, G.J., and Ponza, M. (1984), 'Work experience, job segregation and wages', in B. F. Reskin (ed.), *Sex Segregation in the Workplace: Trends, Explanations, Remedies*, Washington: National Academy Press, 171–91.

Corti, L., Laurie, H., and Dex, S. (1995), *Highly Qualified Women*, Research Series No. 50; London: Department of Employment.

Cragg, A., and Dawson, T. (1981), *Qualitative Research Among Homeworkers*, Research Paper No. 21; London: Department of Employment.

Craig, C., and Wilkinson, F. (1985), *Pay and Employment in Four Retail Trades*, Research Paper No. 51; London: Department of Employment.

Crompton, R., and Harris, F. (1998), 'Explaining women's employment patterns: orientations to work revisited', *British Journal of Sociology*, 49: 148–70.

—— and Le Feuvre, N. (1996), 'Paid employment and the changing system of gender relations: a cross-national comparison', *Sociology*, 30: 427–45.

294 *Bibliography*

Crompton, R., and Sanderson, K. (1990), *Gendered Jobs and Social Change*, London: Routledge/Unwin-Hyman.

—— Gallie, D., and Purcell, K. (1996), *Changing Forms of Employment: Organisations, Skills and Gender*, London and New York: Routledge.

Cunningham, J.S., and Zalokar, N. (1992), 'The economic progress of black women 1940–1980: occupational distribution and relative wages', *Industrial and Labor Relations Review*, 45: 540–55.

Curran, J. (1986), *Bolton Fifteen Years On: A Review and Analysis of Small Business Research in Britain 1971–1986*, London: Small Business Research Trust.

—— and Burrows, R. (1986), 'The sociology of petit capitalism: a trend report', *Sociology*, 20: 265–79.

—— —— (1987), 'The social analysis of small business: some emerging themes' in R. Goffee and R. Scase (eds.), *Entrepreneurship in Europe*, London: Croom Helm, 164–91.

—— —— (1988), *Enterprise in Britain: A National Profile of Small Business Owners and the Self-Employed*, London: Small Business Research Trust.

—— Stanworth, J., and Watkins, D. (1986) (eds.), *The Survival of the Small Firm*, Aldershot: Gower.

Curtice, J. (1993), 'Satisfying work—if you can get it', in R. Jowell (ed.), *International Social Attitudes: the 10th BSA Report*, Aldershot, Hants: Gower, 103–21.

Dahrendorf, R., Kohler, E., and Piotet, F. (1986), *New Forms of Work and Activity*, Dublin: European Foundation for the Improvement of Living and Working Conditions.

Dale, A. (1986), 'Social class and the self-employed', *Sociology*, 20: 430–4.

—— and Glover, J. (1990), *An Analysis of Women's Employment Patterns in the UK, France and the USA*, Research Paper No. 75; London: Department of Employment.

Dale, I. and Kerr, J. (1995), 'Small and medium-sized enterprises: their numbers and importance to employment', *Labour Market Trends*, 103: 461–5.

Daly, M. (1991), 'The 1980s—a decade of growth in enterprise: self-employment data from the Labour Force Survey', *Employment Gazette*, 99: 109–34.

Daniel, W.W. (1987), *Workplace Industrial Relations and Technical Change*, London: Frances Pinter and the Policy Studies Institute.

Darian, J.C. (1975), 'Convenience of work and the job constraint of children', *Demography*, 12: 245–58.

Davidoff, L. (1979), 'The separation of home and work? Landladies and lodgers in nineteenth and twentieth century England', in S. Burman (ed.), *Fit Work for Women*, London: Croom Helm, 64–97.

De Grip, A., Hoevenberg, J., and Willems, E. (1997), 'Atypical employment in the European Union', *International Labour Review*, 136: 49–71.

Department of Employment (1991), *New Earnings Survey 1991*, 4 vols., London: HMSO.

Department of Transport (1988), *National Travel Survey: 1985/86 Report—Part 1: An Analysis of Personal Travel*, London: HMSO.

—— (1993), *National Travel Survey 1989/91*, London: HMSO.

—— (1995), *National Travel Survey 1992/94*, London: HMSO.

Dex, S. (1987), *Women's Occupational Mobility: A Lifetime Perspective*, London: Macmillan.
—— (1988), *Women's Attitudes Towards Work*, London: Macmillan.
—— (1990), 'Women and class analysis' in J. Clark, C. Modgil and S. Modgil (eds.), *John H. Goldthorpe: Consensus and Controversy*, London: Falmer Press, 117–56.
—— and McCulloch, A. (1995), *Flexible Employment in Britain: A Statistical Analysis*, Manchester: Equal Opportunities Commission.
Di Martino, V., and Wirth, L. (1990), 'Telework: a new way of working and living', *International Labour Review*, 129: 529–54.
Drake, C.D. (1968), 'Wage slave or entrepreneur?', *Modern Law Review*, 31: 408–23.
Duffy, A., and Pupo, N. (1992), *Part-Time Paradox: Connecting Gender, Work and Family*, Toronto: McClelland & Stewart.
Duncan, A., Giles, C., and Webb, S. (1995), *The Impact of Subsidising Childcare*, Manchester: EOC.
Dustmann, C., Micklewright, J., Rajah, N., and Smith, S. (1996), 'Earning and learning: educational policy and the growth of part-time work by full-time pupils', *Fiscal Studies*, 17: 79–103.
Eardley, T., and Corden, A. (1996), *Low Income Self-Employment*, Aldershot: Avebury.
Edgeworth, F.Y. (1922), 'Equal pay to men and women for equal work', *Economic Journal*, 32: 431–57.
Ehrenberg, R.G., and Sherman, D.R. (1987), 'Employment while in college, academic achievement and post-college outcomes: a summary of results', *Journal of Human Resources*, 22: 1–23.
Elias, P., and Main, B. (1982), *Women's Working Lives: Evidence from the National Training Survey*, University of Warwick: Institute for Employment Research.
England, P. (1984), 'Wage appreciation and depreciation: a test of neoclassical economic explanations of occupational sex segregation', *Social Forces*, 62: 726–49.
Erikson, R., and Goldthorpe, J.H. (1993), *The Constant Flux: A Study of Class Mobility in Industrial Societies*, Oxford: Clarendon Press.
Esser, H. (1996), 'What is wrong with variable sociology?' *European Sociological Review*, 12: 159–66.
European Commission (1989), *Employment in Europe 1989*, Luxembourg: OOPEC.
—— (1990), *Employment in Europe 1990*, Luxembourg: OOPEC.
—— (1991), *Lifestyles in the European Community: Family and Employment Within the Twelve*, Special Report on Eurobarometer No. 34; Brussels: Directorate General for Employment, Industrial Relations and Social Affairs.
—— (1993), *Employment in Europe 1993*, Luxembourg: OOPEC.
—— (1994*a*), 'Changes in working time', *Employment in Europe 1994*, Luxembourg: OOPEC, 103–27.
—— (1994*b*), 'Mobility, labour turnover and labour market flexibility', *Employment in Europe 1994*, Luxembourg: OOPEC, 83–101.
—— (1994*c*), Directorate-General for Employment, Industrial Relations and Social Affairs, *Two Years of Community Social Policy: July 1993–June 1995*, *Social Europe*, 3/94, Luxembourg: OOPEC.
—— (1994*d*), *European Social Policy: A Way Forward for the Union—A White Paper*, Luxembourg: OOPEC.

European Commission (1995*a*), *Employment in Europe 1995*, Luxembourg: OOPEC.
—— (1995*b*), *Social Protection in Europe*, Luxembourg: OOPEC.
—— (1995*c*), DGV, *Flexibility and Work Organisation, Social Europe*, Supplement 1/95, Luxembourg: OOPEC.
—— (1995*d*), DGV, *Homeworking in the European Union, Social Europe*, Supplement 2/95, Luxembourg: OOPEC.
—— (1995*e*), DGV, *Follow-Up to the White Paper: Teleworking and the Informal Sector, Social Europe*, Supplement 3/95, Luxembourg: OOPEC.
—— (1996), *Employment in Europe 1996*, Luxembourg: OOPEC.
—— (1997), Employment and Social Affairs Unit, *Equal Opportunities for Women and Men in the European Union 1996*, Luxembourg: OOPEC.
Evans, D.S., and Leighton, L.S. (1987), *Self-Employment Selection and Earnings over the Life Cycle*, Research report to the US Small Business Administration.
Evans, G. (1996), 'Putting men and women into classes: an assessment of the cross-sex validity of the Goldthorpe class schema', *Sociology*, 30: 209–34.
Fagan, C., and Rubery, J. (1996), 'The salience of the part-time divide in the European Union', *European Sociological Review*, 12: 227–50.
Feinberg, W.E. (1984), 'At a snail's pace: time to equality in simple models of affirmative action programs', *American Journal of Sociology*, 90: 168–81.
—— (1985), 'Are affirmative action and economic growth alternative paths to racial equality?', *American Sociological Review*, 50: 561–71.
Felstead, A. (1996), 'Homeworking in Britain: the national picture in the mid-1990s', *Industrial Relations Journal*, 27: 225–38.
—— and Jewson, N. (1995), 'Working at home: estimates from the 1991 Census', *Employment Gazette*, March, 95–9.
—— —— (1997), 'Researching a problematic concept: homeworkers in Britain', *Work, Employment and Society*, 11: 327–46.
—— —— and Goodwin, J. (1996), 'Homeworkers in Britain', *Research Studies RS1P*, London: HMSO.
Fielding, A.J. (1992), 'Migration and social mobility: South East England as an escalator region', *Regional Studies*, 26: 1–15.
—— and Halford, S. (1993), 'Geographies of opportunity: a regional analysis of gender-specific social and spatial mobilities in England and Wales 1971–81', *Environment and Planning A*, 25: 1421–40.
Finch, J. (1983), *Married to the Job: Wives' Incorporation in Men's Work*, London: Allen & Unwin.
Fine, B. (1992), *Women's Employment and the Capitalist Family*, London and New York: Routledge.
Fiorentine, R. (1987), 'Men, women and the premed persistence gap: a normative alternatives approach', *American Journal of Sociology*, 92: 1118–39.
Forrest, R., Murie, A., and Williams, P. (1990), *Home Ownership: Differentiation and Fragmentation*, London: Routledge/Unwin Hyman.
Gallie, D., and Vogler, C. (1994), 'Labour market deprivation, welfare and collectivism' in D. Gallie, C. Marsh, and C. Vogler (eds.), *Social Change and the Experience of Unemployment*, Oxford: Oxford University Press, 299–336.
Ganzeboom, H.B.G., de Graaf, P.M., and Treiman, D.J. (1992), 'A standard inter-

national socio-economic index of occupational status', *Social Science Research*, 21: 1–56.

—— and Treiman, D.J. (1996), 'Internationally comparable measures of occupational status for the 1988 International Standard Classification of Occupations', *Social Science Research*, 25: 201–39.

Gladstone, A. (1992) (ed.), *Labour Relations in a Changing Environment*, Berlin and New York: Walter de Gruyter.

Goldberg, P. (1968), 'Are women prejudiced against women?', *Trans-Action*, 5: 28–30.

Goldberg, S. (1993), *Why Men Rule: A Theory of Male Dominance*, Chicago: Open Court.

Goldin, C. (1990), *Understanding the Gender Gap*, New York and Oxford: Oxford University Press.

Goldthorpe, J.H. (1984), 'The end of convergence: corporatist and dualist tendencies in modern western societies', in J. H. Goldthorpe (ed.), *Order and Conflict in Contemporary Capitalism: Studies in the Political Economy of Western European Nations*, Oxford: Clarendon Press, 315–43; repr. in R. Roberts, R. Finnegan, and D. Gallie (eds.), *New Approaches to Economic Life*, 1985, Manchester University Press, 124–53.

—— with Lewellyn, C., and Payne, C. (1987), *Social Mobility and Class Structure in Modern Britain*, 2nd edn., Oxford: Clarendon Press.

—— and Heath, A. (1992), *Revised Class Schema 1992*, Working Paper No. 13; London: JUSST.

—— and Hope, K. (1974), *The Social Grading of Occupations: A New Approach and Scale*, Oxford: Clarendon Press.

Granger, B., Stanworth, J., and Stanworth, C. (1995), 'Self-employment career dynamics: the case of "unemployment push" in UK book publishing', *Work, Employment and Society*, 9: 499–516.

Green, A.E., Coombes, M.G., and Owen, D.W. (1986), 'Gender-specific local labour market areas in England and Wales', *Geoforum*, 17: 339–51.

Gregg, P., and Wadsworth, J. (1995), 'A short history of labour turnover, job tenure and job security, 1975–93', *Oxford Review of Economic Policy*, 11: 73–90.

Gregory, M.B., and Thomson, A.W.J. (1990) (eds.), *A Portrait of Pay 1970–1982: An Analysis of the New Earnings Survey*, Oxford: Clarendon Press.

Griliches, Z. (1980), 'Schooling interruption, work while in school and the returns from schooling', *Scandinavian Journal of Economics*, 82: 291–303.

Gross, E. (1968), 'Plus ça change . . .? The sexual structure of occupations over time', *Social Problems*, 16: 198–208.

Haber, S.E., Lamas, E.J., and Lichtenstein, J.H. (1987), 'On their own: the self-employed and others in private business', *Monthly Labor Review*, 110/5: 17–23.

Hakim, C. (1979), *Occupational Segregation: A Comparative Study of the Degree and Pattern of the Differentiation between Men and Women's Work in Britain, the United States and Other Countries*, Research Paper No. 9; London: Department of Employment.

—— (1980), 'Census reports as documentary evidence: the census commentaries 1801–1951', *Sociological Review*, 28: 551–80.

—— (1981), 'Job segregation: trends in the 1970s', *Employment Gazette*, 89: 521–9.

Hakim, C. (1982), *Secondary Analysis in Social Research: A Guide to Data Sources and Methods with Examples*, London: Routledge/Allen & Unwin.

—— (1984), 'Homework and outwork: national estimates from two surveys', *Employment Gazette*, 92: 7–12.

—— (1985), *Employers' Use of Outwork: A Study using the 1980 Workplace Industrial Relations Survey and the 1981 National Survey of Homeworking*, Research Paper No. 44; London: Department of Employment.

—— (1987a), *Research Design: Strategies and Choices in the Design of Social Research*, London: Routledge/Allen & Unwin.

—— (1987b), *Home-Based Work in Britain: A Report on the 1981 National Home-working Survey and the DE Research Programme on Homework*, Research Paper No. 60; London: Department of Employment.

—— (1987c), 'Trends in the flexible workforce', *Employment Gazette*, 95: 549–60.

—— (1988a), 'Homeworking in Britain', in R. Pahl (ed.), *On Work: Historical, Comparative and Theoretical Approaches*, Oxford: Blackwell, 609–32.

—— (1988b), 'Self-employment in Britain: recent trends and current issues', *Work, Employment and Society*, 2: 421–50.

—— (1989a), 'Employment rights: a comparison of part-time and full-time employees', *Industrial Law Journal*, 18: 69–83.

—— (1989b), 'Workforce restructuring, social insurance coverage and the black economy', *Journal of Social Policy*, 18: 471–503.

—— (1989c), 'Identifying fast growth small firms', *Employment Gazette*, 97: 29–41.

—— (1989d), 'New recruits to self-employment in the 1980s', *Employment Gazette*, 97: 286–97.

—— (1990a), 'Workforce restructuring in Europe in the 1980s', *International Journal of Comparative Labour Law and Industrial Relations*, 5: 167–203.

—— (1990b), 'Core and periphery in employers' workforce strategies: evidence from the 1987 ELUS survey', *Work, Employment and Society*, 4: 157–88. .

—— (1991), 'Grateful slaves and self-made women: fact and fantasy in women's work orientations', *European Sociological Review*, 7: 101–21.

—— (1992a), 'Explaining trends in occupational segregation: the measurement, causes and consequences of the sexual division of labour', *European Sociological Review*, 8: 127–52. .

—— (1992b), 'Unemployment, marginal work and the black economy,' in E. McLaughlin (ed.), *Understanding Unemployment: New Perspectives on Active Labour Market Policies*, London: Routledge, 144–59.

—— (1993a), 'The myth of rising female employment', *Work, Employment and Society*, 7: 97–120.

—— (1993b), 'Segregated and integrated occupations: a new approach to analysing social change', *European Sociological Review*, 9: 289–314.

—— (1993c), 'Refocusing research on occupational segregation: reply to Watts', *European Sociological Review*, 9: 321–4.

—— (1994), 'A century of change in occupational segregation 1891–1991', *Journal of Historical Sociology*, 7: 435–54.

—— (1995a), '1991 Census SARs: opportunities and pitfalls in the labour market data', *Work, Employment and Society*, 9: 569–82.

—— (1995*b*), 'Five feminist myths about women's employment', *British Journal of Sociology*, 46: 429–55.

—— (1996*a*), *Key Issues in Women's Work: Female Heterogeneity and the Polarisation of Women's Employment*, London: Athlone Press.

—— (1996*b*), 'The sexual division of labour and women's heterogeneity', *British Journal of Sociology*, 47: 178–88.

—— (1996*c*), 'Labour mobility and employment stability: rhetoric and reality on the sex differential in labour market behaviour', *European Sociological Review*, 12: 1–31.

—— (1996*d*), 'Theoretical and measurement issues in the analysis of occupational segregation', in P. Beckmann (ed.), *Gender Specific Occupational Segregation, Beiträge zur Arbeitsmarkt- und Berufsforschung* (Monographs on Employment Research), No. 188; Nuremberg: Institute for Employment Research of the Federal Employment Services (IAB), 67–88.

—— (1997*a*), 'A sociological perspective on part-time work', in H.-P. Blossfeld and C. Hakim (eds.), *Between Equalization and Marginalization: Women Part-Time Workers in Europe and the USA*, Oxford: Oxford University Press, 22–70.

—— (1997*b*), 'Diversity and choice in the sexual contract: models for the 21st century', in G. Dench (ed.), *Rewriting the Sexual Contract*, London: Institute of Community Studies, 165–79.

—— (1998), 'Developing a sociology for the the 21st century: Preference Theory', *British Journal of Sociology*, 49: 171–6.

—— and Dennis, R. (1982), *Homeworking in Wages Council Industries: A Study based on Wages Inspectorate Records of Pay and Earnings*, Research Paper No. 37; London: Department of Employment.

—— and Jacobs, S. (1997), *Sex-Role Preferences and Work Histories: Is There a Link?*, Working Paper No. 12; London School of Economics Department of Sociology.

Handy, C. (1984), *The Future of Work*, Oxford: Basil Blackwell.

—— (1994), *The Empty Raincoat*, London: Hutchinson.

Hartmann, H. (1976), 'Capitalism, patriarchy and job segregation by sex', in M. Blaxall and B. Reagan (eds.), *Women and the Workplace: The Implications of Occupational Segregation*, Chicago and London: University of Chicago Press, 137–69.

—— Kraut, R.E., and Tilly, L.A. (1986) (eds.), *Computer Chips and Paper Clips: Technology and Women's Employment*, Washington: National Academy Press.

Hedström, P., and Swedberg, R. (1996), 'Rational choice, empirical research and the sociological tradition', *European Sociological Review*, 12: 127–46.

Hepple, B.A. (1986), 'Restructuring employment rights', *Industrial Law Journal*, 15: 69–83.

—— (1990), *Working Time*, London: Institute of Public Policy Research.

—— and Hakim, C. (1997), 'Working time in the United Kingdom', in R. Blanpain and J. Rojot (eds.), *Legal and Contractual Limitations to Working Time in the European Community Member States*, 2nd edn., Leuven: Peeters, 659–93.

Hochschild, A. (1990), *The Second Shift: Working Parents and the Revolution at Home*, London: Piatkus.

Hofstede, G. (1980, 1994), *Culture's Consequences: International Differences in Work-Related Values*, Beverly Hills and New York: Sage.

Hofstede, G. (1991), *Cultures and Organisations*, London: HarperCollins.

Hogarth, T., Elias, P., and Ford, J. (1996), *Mortgages, Families and Jobs: An Exploration of the Growth in Home Ownership in the 1980s*, Coventry: University of Warwick Institute for Employment Research.

Holmans, A.F. (1993), 'The changing employment circumstances of Council tenants' and 'Sales of houses and flats by local authorities to sitting tenants', in Department of Environment, *Housing in England: Housing Trailers to the 1988 and 1991 Labour Force Surveys*, London: HMSO, 78–109.

Hörning, K.H., Gerhard, A., and Michailow, M. (1995), *Time Pioneers: Flexible Working Time and New Lifestyles*, Cambridge: Polity Press.

Hoskyns, C. (1985), 'Women's equality and the European Community', *Feminist Review*, No. 20: 71–88.

—— (1996), *Integrating Gender: Women, Law and Politics in the European Union*, London: Verso.

Howard, A. (1995) (ed.), *The Changing Nature of Work*, San Francisco: Jossey-Bass.

Huet, M., Marchand, O., and Salais, R. (1982), 'The concentration of female employment: the example of France', research report to the OECD.

Humphries, J. (1987), 'The most free from objection . . . the sexual division of labour and women's work in nineteenth-century England', *Journal of Economic History*, 47: 929–49.

—— and Rubery, J. (1992), 'The legacy for women's employment: integration, differentiation and polarisation', in J. Michie (ed.), *The Economic Legacy of Thatcherism*, London: Academic Press, 236–357.

Hutson, S., and Cheung, W.-Y. (1992), 'Saturday jobs: sixth-formers in the labour market and in the family', in C. Marsh and S. Arber (eds.), *Families and Households: Divisions and Change*, Basingstoke: Macmillan, 45–62.

Huws, U. (1984), 'New technology homeworkers', *Employment Gazette*, 92: 13–17.

—— (1994), *Home Truths: Key Results from a National Survey of Homeworkers*, Leeds: National Group on Homeworking.

ILO (1989), *Conditions of Work Digest: Vol. 8, No. 1: Part-Time Work*, Geneva: International Labour Office.

—— (1990), *International Standard Classification of Occupations—ISCO88* , Geneva: ILO.

Jacobs, J.A. (1989a), 'Long-term trends in occupational segregation by sex', *American Journal of Sociology*, 95: 160–73.

—— (1989b), *Revolving Doors: Sex Segregation and Women's Careers*, Stanford: Stanford University Press.

—— (1993), 'Men in female-dominated fields: trends and turnover', in C. L. Williams (ed.), *Doing Women's Work: Men in Nontraditional Occupations*, London: Sage, 49–63.

Jacobs, S.C. (1995), 'Changing patterns of sex segregated occupations throughout the life-course', *European Sociological Review*, 11: 157–71.

James, D.R., and Taeuber, K.E. (1985), 'Measures of segregation', in N. B. Tuma (ed.), *Sociological Methodology*, San Francisco and London: Jossey-Bass, 1–32.

Jenson, J., Hagen, E., and Reddy, C. (1988) (eds.), *Feminisation of the Labour Force: Paradoxes and Promises*, New York: Oxford University Press.

Jonung, C., and Persson, I. (1993), 'Women and market work: the misleading tale of participation rates in international comparisons', *Work, Employment and Society*, 7: 259–74.

Joshi, H., and Davies, H. (1996), 'Financial dependency on men: have women born in 1958 broken free?', *Policy Studies*, 17: 35–54.

Kauppinen-Toropainen, K., and Lammi, J. (1993), 'Men in female-dominated occupations: a cross-cultural comparison' in C. L. Williams (ed.), *Doing Women's Work: Men in Nontraditional Occupations*, London: Sage, 91–112.

Kay, H. (1984), 'Is childminding real work?', *Employment Gazette*, 92: 483–6.

Kilbourne, B.S., England, P., Farkas, G., Beron, K., and Weir, D. (1994), 'Returns to skill, compensating differentials and gender bias: effects of occupational characteristics on the wages of white women and men', *American Journal of Sociology*, 100: 689–719.

King, M.C. (1992), 'Occupational segregation by race and sex, 1940–88', *Monthly Labor Review*, 115/4: 30–7.

Kohn, M.L., and Schooler, C. (1983), *Work and Personality*, Norwood, N.J.: Ablex.

—— Slomczynski, K.M., and Schoenbach, C. (1990), *Social Structure and Self-Direction*, Oxford: Blackwell.

Kovalainen, A. (1993), *At the Margins of the Economy: Women's Self-Employment in Finland 1960–1990*, Aldershot: Avebury Press.

Kravaritou-Manitakis, Y. (1988), *New Forms of Work: Labour Law and Social Security Aspects in the European Community*, Luxembourg: OOPEC for the European Foundation for the Improvement of Living and Working Conditions.

Lampard, R. (1994), 'Comment on Blackburn, Jarman and Siltanen: marginal matching and the Gini Coefficient', *Work, Employment and Society*, 8: 407–11.

Lane, C. (1989), 'From welfare capitalism to market capitalism: a comparative review of trends towards employment flexibility in the labour markets of three major European societies', *Sociology*, 23: 583–610.

La Valle, I., Connor, H., and Jagger, N. (1996), *The IES Annual Graduate Review 1996–97*, Brighton: University of Sussex Institute of Employment Studies.

Leighton, P. (1983), *Contractual Arrangements in Selected Industries: A Study of Employment Relationships in Industries with Outwork*, Research Paper No. 39; London: Department of Employment.

Lewenhak, S. (1977), *Women and Trade Unions*, London: Earnest Benn Ltd.

Lewis, J. (1984), *Women in England 1870–1950*, Sussex: Wheatsheaf Books.

—— Stanworth, J., and Gibb, A. (1984) (eds.), *Success and Failure in Small Business*, Aldershot: Gower.

Lieberson, S. (1985), *Making it Count: The Improvement of Social Research and Theory*, Berkeley and London: University of California Press.

Light, A., and Ureta, M. (1992), 'Panel estimates of male and female job turnover behaviour: can female nonquitters be identified?', *Journal of Labor Economics*, 10: 156–81.

Lindblom, C.E., and Cohen, D.K. (1979), *Useable Knowledge: Social Science and Problem Solving*, New Haven and London: Yale University Press.

Linder, M. (1989*a*), *The Employment Relationship in Anglo-American Law: A Historical Perspective*, Westport, Conn.: Greenwood.

—— (1989*b*), 'What is an employee? Why it does, but should not, matter', *Law and Inequality*, 7: 155–87.

Linder, M. (1992), *Farewell to the Self-Employed: Deconstructing a Socioeconomic and Legal Solipsism*, New York and London: Greenwood Press.

—— and Houghton, J. (1990), 'Self-employment and the petty bourgeoisie: Comment on Steinmetz and Wright', with Reply by Steinmetz and Wright, *American Journal of Sociology*, 96: 727–35.

Loutfi, M.F. (1992), 'An overview of self-employment in Europe: nature, trends and policy issues', in P. Leighton and A. Felstead (eds.), *The New Entrepreneurs: Self-Employment and Small Business in Europe*, London: Kogan Page, 41–68.

Lucas, R., and Ralston, L. (1997), 'Youth, gender and part-time employment: A preliminary appraisal of student employment', *Employee Relations*, 19: 51–66.

Lui, T.-L. (1994), *Waged Work at Home: The Social Organisation of Industrial Outwork in Hong Kong*, Aldershot: Avebury.

Macran, S., Joshi, H., and Dex, S. (1996), 'Employment after childbearing: A survival analysis', *Work, Employment and Society*, 10: 273–96.

McCrone, D. (1994), 'Getting by and making out in Kirkaldy', in M. Anderson, F. Bechhofer, and J. Gershuny (eds.), *The Social and Political Economy of the Household*, Oxford: Oxford University Press, 68–99.

McRae, S. (1990), 'Women and class analysis', in J. Clark, C. Modgil, and S. Modgil (eds.), *John H. Goldthorpe: Consensus and Controversy*, London: Falmer Press, 117–56.

—— (1991), *Maternity Rights in Britain*, London: Policy Studies Institute. .

—— (1993), 'Returning to work after childbirth: opportunities and inequalities', *European Sociological Review*, 9: 125–38.

—— (1995), *Part-Time Work in the European Union: The Gender Dimension*, Dublin: European Foundation for the Improvement of Living and Working Conditions.

—— Devine, F., and Lakey, J. (1991), *Women into Engineering and Science*, London: Policy Studies Institute.

Madden, J.F. (1981), 'Why women work closer to home', *Urban Studies*, 18: 181–94.

Main, B. (1988*a*), 'The lifetime attachment of women to the labour market', in A. Hunt (ed.), *Women and Paid Work*, London: Macmillan, 23–51.

—— (1988*b*), 'Women's hourly earnings: the influence of work histories on rates of pay', in A. Hunt (ed.), *Women and Paid Work*, London: Macmillan, 105–22.

Marsh, C. (1986), 'Social class and occupation', in R. G. Burgess (ed.), *Key Variables in Social Investigation*, London: Routledge.

Marshall, G. (1988), 'Classes in Britain: marxist and official', *European Sociological Review*, 4: 141–54.

—— Rose, D., Newby, H., and Vogler, C. (1988, 1991), *Social Class in Modern Britain*, London: Hutchinson.

—— *et al.* (1995), 'Class, gender and the asymmetry hypothesis', *European Sociological review*, 11: 1–15.

Martin, J., and Roberts, C. (1984), *Women and Employment: A Lifetime Perspective*, London: HMSO for the Department of Employment.

Matthaei, J.A. (1982), *An Economic History of Women in America: Women's work, the sexual division of labour and the development of capitalism*, New York: Schocken/Brighton: Harvester.

Mayhew, K., and Rosewell, B. (1978), 'Immigrants and occupational crowding in Great Britain', *Oxford Bulletin of Economics and Statistics*, 40: 223–48.

Meager, N. (1991), *Self-Employment in the UK*, Brighton: University of Sussex Institute of Manpower Studies.

—— (1992), 'The fall and rise of self-employment (again): A comment on Bögenhold and Staber', *Work, Employment and Society*, 6: 127–34.

—— Court, G., and Moralee, J. (1994), *Self-Employment and the Distribution of Income*, Report No. 270; Brighton: University of Sussex Institute of Manpower Studies.

Mennerick, L.A. (1975), 'Organisational structuring of sex roles in a nonstereotyped industry', *Administrative Science Quarterly*, 20: 570–86.

Meulders, D., Plasman, R., and Vander Stricht, V. (1993), *The Position of Women on the Labour Market in the EC*, Aldershot: Dartmouth Publishing.

—— Plasman, O., and Plasman, R. (1994), *Atypical Employment in the EC*, Aldershot: Dartmouth Publishing.

Meyer, R.H., and Wise, D.A. (1984), 'The transition from school to work: the experience of blacks and whites', *Research in Labor Economics*, 6: 123–76.

Michael, R.T., and Tuma, N.B. (1984), 'Youth employment: does life begin at 16?', *Journal of Labor Economics*, 2: 464–76.

Michie, J. (1992) (ed.), *The Economic Legacy of Thatcherism*, London: Academic Press.

Micklewright, J., Rajah, N., and Smith, S. (1994), 'Labouring and learning: part-time work and full-time education', *National Institute Economic Review*, 148, 73–87.

Milkman, R. (1987), *Gender at Work: The Dynamics of Job Segregation by Sex During World War II*, Urbana and Chicago: University of Illinois Press.

Mincer, J. (1985), 'Intercountry comparisons of labor force trends and of related developments: An overview', *Journal of Labor Economics*, 3: S1–S32.

Morokvasic, M., Phizacklea, A., and Rudolf, H. (1986), 'Small firms and minority groups: contradictory trends in the French, German and British clothing industry', *International Sociology*, 1: 397–420.

Murphy, M.J. (1985), 'Marital breakdown and socio-economic status: a reappraisal of the evidence from recent British sources', *British Journal of Sociology*, 36: 81–92.

Nätti, J. (1993), 'Temporary employment in the Nordic countries: A trap or a bridge?', *Work, Employment and Society*, 7: 451–64.

—— (1995), 'Part-time work in the Nordic countries: A trap for women?', *Labour*, 9: 343–57.

Naylor, K. (1994), 'Part-time working in Great Britain—an historical analysis', *Employment Gazette*, 102: 473–84.

Nerb, G. (1986), 'Employment problems: views of businessmen and the workforce—Results of an employee and employer survey on labour market issues in the Member States', *European Economy*, 27: 5–110.

Neubourg, C. de (1985), 'Part-time work: An international quantitative comparison', *International Labour Review*, 124: 559–76.

NUS (1996), *Students at Work, A Report on the Economic Conditions of Students in Employment*, London: National Union of Students and GMB.

Oakley, A. (1974, 1985), *The Sociology of Housework*, Oxford: Blackwell.

OECD (1980), *Women and Employment: Policies for Equal Opportunities*, Paris: OECD.

OECD (1985), *The Integration of Women into the Economy*, Paris: OECD.

—— (1986), 'Self-employment in OECD countries' in *Employment Outlook*, Paris: OECD, 43–65.

—— (1988), 'Women's activity, employment and earnings: A review of recent developments', in *Employment Outlook*, Paris: OECD, 129–71.

—— (1990), 'Involuntary part-time work as a component of underemployment', in *Employment Outlook*, Paris: OECD, 179–93.

—— (1991), 'Absence from work reported in labour force surveys', in *Employment Outlook*, Paris: OECD, 177–98.

—— (1992), 'Recent developments in self-employment', in *Employment Outlook*, Paris: OECD, 155–94.

—— (1994), *Women and Structural Change: New Perspectives*, Paris: OECD.

—— (1995), 'Recent labour market developments' and 'Supplementary measures of labour market slack: An analysis of discouraged and involuntary part-time workers', in *Employment Outlook*, Paris: OECD, 3–42 and 43–97.

—— (1996), 'Growing into work: youth and the labour market', in *Employment Outlook*, Paris: OECD, 109–59.

O'Neill, G. (1990), *Pull No More Bines: An Oral History of East London Women Hop Pickers*, London: The Women's Press.

OPCS (1970), *Classification of Occupations 1970*, London: HMSO.

—— (1980), *Classification of Occupations 1980*, London: HMSO.

—— (1983), *General Household Survey 1981*, London: HMSO.

—— (1988), *Census 1971–1981: The Longitudinal Study—England and Wales*, CEN81LS; London: HMSO.

—— (1990), *Standard Occupational Classification*, 3 vols., London: HMSO.

—— (1995), *General Household Survey 1993*, London: HMSO.

—— and GROS (1994*a*), *1991 Census—Economic Activity—Great Britain*, 2 vols., London: HMSO.

—— —— (1994*b*), *1991 Census—Workplace and Transport to Work*, 2 vols., London: HMSO.

—— —— (1994*c*), *1991 Census—Qualified Manpower*, 2 vols., London: HMSO.

O'Reilly, J., and Fagan, C. (1998) (eds.), *Part-Time Prospects: An International Comparison of Part-Time Work*, London: Routledge.

Paci, P., and Joshi, H. (1996), *Wage Differentials Between Men and Women: Evidence from Cohort Studies*, Research Series No. 71; London: Department for Education and Employment.

Parcel, T.L., and Mueller, C.W. (1983), 'Occupational differentiation, prestige and socioeconomic status', *Work and Occupations*, 10: 49–80.

Payne, M. (1995), 'Patterns of pay: results of the 1995 New Earnings Survey', *Labour Market Trends*, 103: 405–12.

Pfau-Effinger, B. (1993), 'Modernisation, culture and part-time employment: the example of Finland and West Germany', *Work, Employment and Society*, 7: 383–410.

Phelps, E.S. (1972), 'The statistical theory of racism and sexism', *American Economic Review*, 62: 659–61.

Phizacklea, A., and Wolkowitz, C. (1995), *Homeworking Women: Gender, Racism and Class at Work*, London: Sage.

Piore, M., and Sabel, C.F. (1984), *The Second Industrial Divide: Possibilities for Success*, New York: Basic Books.

Plantenga, J. (1995), 'Part-time work and equal opportunities: the case of the Netherlands', in J. Humphries and J. Rubery (eds.), *The Economics of Equal Opportunities*, Manchester: EOC, 277–90.

Polachek, S.W. (1979), 'Occupational segregation among women: theory, evidence and a prognosis', in C. B. Lloyd, E. S. Andrews, and C. L. Gilroy (eds.), *Women in the Labor Market*, New York: Columbia University Press, 137–70.

Pollert, A. (1983), *Girls, Wives, Factory Lives*, London: Macmillan.

—— (1991) (ed.), *Farewell to Flexibility*, Oxford: Blackwell.

Pott-Buter, H.A. (1993), *Facts and Fairy Tales about Female Labor, Family and Fertility*, Amsterdam: Amsterdam University Press.

Prandy, K. (1990), 'The revised Cambridge scale of occupations', *Sociology*, 24: 629–55.

—— and Blackburn, R.M. (1997), 'Putting men and women into classes: But is that where they belong? A comment on Evans', *Sociology*, 31: 143–52.

Pringle, R. (1988, 1989), *Secretaries Talk: Sexuality, Power and Work*, London and New York: Verso.

Rainbird, H. (1991), 'The self-employed: small entrepreneurs or disguised wage labourers?', in A. Pollert (ed.), *Farewell to Flexibility*, Oxford: Blackwell, 200–14.

Reskin, B.F. (1984) (ed.), *Sex Segregation in the Workplace: Trends, Explanations, Remedies*, Washington: National Academy Press.

—— (1988), 'Bringing the men back in: sex differentiation and the devaluation of women's work', *Gender and Society*, 2: 58–81.

—— and Hartmann, H.I. (1986), *Women's Work, Men's Work: Sex Segregation on the Job*, Washington: National Academy of Sciences.

—— and Padavic, I. (1994), *Women and Men at Work*, Thousand Oaks, Calif.: Pine Forge.

—— and Roos, P.A. (1990), *Job Queues, Gender Queues: Explaining Women's Inroads into Male Occupations*, Philadelphia: Temple University Press.

Rexroat, C. (1992), 'Changes in the employment continuity of succeeding cohorts of young women', *Work and Occupations*, 19: 18–34.

Riemer, J.W. (1982) (ed.), *Nontraditional Occupations*, special issue of *Work and Occupations*, 9: 267–407.

Roberts, K., Dench, S., and Richardson, D. (1987), *The Changing Structure of Youth Labour Markets*, Research Paper No. 59; London: Department of Employment.

Rodgers, G., and Rodgers, J. (1989), *Precarious Jobs in Labour Market Regulation*, Geneva: ILO.

Rose, D., and Marshall, G. (1986), 'Constructing the (W)right classes', *Sociology*, 20: 440–55.

Rosenfeld, R. (1983), 'Sex segregation and sectors', *American Sociological Review*, 48: 637–56.

—— (1984), 'Job changing and occupational sex segregation: sex and race comparisons', in B. F. Reskin (ed.), *Sex Segregation in the Workplace*, Washington: National Academy Press, 56–86.

—— and Birkelund, G.E. (1995), 'Women's part-time work: A cross-national comparison', *European Sociological Review*, 11: 111–34.

Rosenfeld, R. and Spenner, K.I. (1992), 'Occupational segregation and women's early career job shifts', *Work and Occupations*, 19: 424–49; repr. in J. A. Jacobs (ed.), *Gender Inequality at Work*, 1995, London: Sage, 231–58.

Routh, G. (1965, 1980), *Occupation and Pay in Great Britain 1906–79*, London: Macmillan.

—— (1987), *Occupations of the People of Great Britain 1801–1981*, London: Macmillan.

Rubenstein, M. (1996), *Discrimination: A Guide to the Relevant Case Law on Race and Sex Discrimination and Equal Pay*, 9th edn., London: Industrial Relations Services.

Rubery, J. (1988) (ed.), *Women and Recession*, London and New York: Routledge.

—— (1989), 'Precarious forms of work in the United Kingdom', in G. Rodgers and J. Rodgers (eds.), *Precarious Jobs in Labour Market Regulation*, Geneva: ILO, 49–74.

—— and Fagan, C. (1993), *Occupational Segregation of Women and Men in the European Community*, *Social Europe*, Supplement 3/93, Luxembourg: OOPEC.

—— Horrell, S., and Burchell, B. (1994), 'Part-time work and gender inequality in the labour market', in A. M. Scott (ed.), *Gender Segregation and Social Change*, Oxford: Oxford University Press, 205–34.

—— and Tarling, R. (1988), 'Women's employment in declining Britain' in J. Rubery (ed.), *Women and Recession*, London: Routledge, 100–32.

Rytina, N. (1981), 'Occupational segregation and earnings differences by sex', *Monthly Labor Review*, 104/1: 49–53.

—— and Bianchi, S.M. (1984), 'Occupational reclassification and changes in distribution by gender', *Monthly Labor Review*, 107/3: 11–17.

Sainsbury, D. (1996), *Gender, Equality and Welfare States*, Cambridge: Cambridge University Press.

Sandell, S., and Shapiro, D. (1980), 'Work expectations, human capital accumulation and the wages of young women', *Journal of Human Resources*, 15: 335–53.

Saunders, P. (1990), *A Nation of Homeowners*, London: Routledge/UnwinHyman.

Scase, R., and Goffee, R. (1980), *The Real World of the Small Business Owner*, London: Croom Helm.

—— —— (1981), 'Traditional petty bourgeois attitudes: The case of self-employed craftsmen', *Sociological Review*, 29: 729–47.

—— —— (1982), *The Entrepreneurial Middle Class*, London: Croom Helm.

Schneider de Villegas, G. (1990), 'Homework: a case for social protection', *International Labour Review*, 129: 423–39.

Schoer, K. (1987), 'Part-time employment: Britain and West Germany', *Cambridge Journal of Economics*, 11: 83–94.

Schumpeter, J.A. (1934), *The Theory of Economic Development*, Cambridge, Mass.: Harvard University Press.

Scott, A.M. (1994) (ed.), *Gender Segregation and Social Change*, Oxford: Oxford University Press.

—— and Burchell, B. (1994), 'And never the twain shall meet? Gender segregation and work histories', in A. M. Scott (ed.), *Gender Segregation and Social Change*, Oxford: Oxford University Press, 121–56.

Scott, R.A., and Shore, A.R. (1979), *Why Sociology Does Not Apply: A Study of the Use of Sociology in Public Policy*, New York and Oxford: Elsevier.

Sengenberger, W., Loveman, G.W., and Piore, M.J. (1990), *The Re-emergence of Small Enterprises: Industrial Restructuring in Industrialised Countries*, Geneva: ILO.

Shamir, B., and Salomon, I. (1985), 'Work-at-home and the quality of working life', *Academy of Management Review*, 10: 455–64.

Sieling, M.S. (1984), 'Staffing patterns prominent in female-male earnings gap', *Monthly Labor Review*, 107/6: 29–33.

Siltanen, J., Jarman, J., and Blackburn, R.M. (1995), *Gender Inequality in the Labour Market: Occupational Concentration and Segregation*, Geneva: ILO.

Simpson, I.H., *et al.* (1982), 'Occupational recruitment, retention and labor force cohort representation', *American Journal of Sociology*, 87: 1287–313.

Sloane, P.J. (1990), 'Sex differentials: structure, stability and change', in M. B. Gregory and A.W. J. Thomson (eds.), *A Portrait of Pay, 1970–1982: An Analysis of the New Earnings Survey*, Oxford: Clarendon Press, 125–71.

—— (1994), 'The gender wage differential', in A. M. Scott (ed.), *Gender Segregation and Social Change*, Oxford: Oxford University Press, 157–204.

Sly, F. (1993), 'Economic activity of 16 and 17 year olds', *Employment Gazette*, 101: 307–12.

—— (1994*a*), 'Economic activity results from the 1991 Labour Force Survey and the Census of Population', *Employment Gazette*, 102: 87–96.

—— (1994*b*), 'The educational and labour market status of 16 and 17 year olds', *Employment Gazette*, 102: 329–34.

—— Price, A., and Risdon, A. (1997), 'Women in the labour market: results from the Spring 1996 Labour Force Survey', *Labour Market Trends*, 105: 99–120.

Sokoloff, N.J. (1992), *Black Women and White Women in the Professions: Occupational Segregation by Race and Gender 1960–1980*, New York and London: Routledge.

Sommers, D., and Eck, A. (1977), 'Occupational mobility in the American labour force', *Monthly Labor Review*, 100/1: 3–19.

Spaeth, J.L. (1979), 'Vertical differentiation among occupations', *American Sociological Review*, 44: 746–62.

Spence, A. (1992), 'Patterns of pay: results of the 1992 New Earnings Survey', *Employment Gazette*, 100: 579–91.

Staber, U., and Bögenhold, D. (1991), 'The decline and rise of self-employment', *Work, Employment and Society*, 5: 223–39.

—— —— (1993), 'Self-employment dynamics: A reply to Meager', *Work, Employment and Society*, 7: 465–72.

Stanworth, C., and Stanworth, J. (1995), 'The self-employed without employees: autonomous or atypical?', *Industrial Relations Journal*, 26: 221–9.

—— —— (1997), 'Managing an externalised workforce: freelance labour-use in the UK book publishing industry', *Industrial Relations Journal*, 28: 43–55.

Stanworth, J., and Curran, J. (1976), 'Growth and the small firm—an alternative view', *Journal of Management Studies*, 13: 95–110; repr. in J. Curran, J. Stanworth, D. Watkins (eds.), *The Survival of the Small Firm: Employment, Growth, Technology and Politics*, 1986, Aldershot: Gower, 81–99.

—— Westrip, A., and Watkins, D. (1982) (eds.), *Perspectives on a Decade of Small Business Research: Bolton Ten Years On*, Aldershot: Gower.

Steinmetz, G., and Wright, E.O. (1989), 'The fall and rise of the petty bourgeoisie: Changing patterns of self-employment in the postwar United States', *American Journal of Sociology*, 94: 973–1018.

—— —— (1990), 'Reply to Linder and Houghton', *American Journal of Sociology*, 96: 736–40.

Stewart, A., Prandy, K., and Blackburn, R.M. (1980), *Social Stratification and Occupations*, London: Macmillan.

Stewart, M.B. (1983), 'Racial discrimination and occupational attainment in Britain', *Economic Journal*, No. 371, 93: 521–41.

Storey, D.J. (1994), *Understanding the Small Business Sector*, London and New York: Routledge.

Streeck, W. (1987), 'The uncertainties of management in the management of uncertainty: employers, labor relations and industrial adjustment in the 1980s', *Work, Employment and Society*, 1: 281–308.

Strober, M.H. (1984), 'Towards a general theory of occupational segregation: the case of public school teaching' in B. F. Reskin (ed.), *Sex Segregation in the Workplace: Trends, Explanations, Remedies*, Washington: National Academy Press, 144–56.

Strom, S.H. (1989), 'Light manufacturing: the feminisation of American office work, 1900–1930', *Industrial Labor Relations Review*, 43: 53–71.

Suter, L.E., and Miller, H.P. (1973), 'Income differences between men and career women', *American Journal of Sociology*, 78: 962–74.

Szreter, S.R.S. (1984), 'The genesis of the Registrar General's social classification of occupations', *British Journal of Sociology*, 35: 522–46.

Thomas, J.J. (1992), *Informal Economic Activity*, London and New York: Harvester Wheatsheaf.

Thomas, R., and Elias, P. (1989), 'Development of the Standard Occupational Classification', *Population Trends*, 55: 16–21.

Thompson, E.J. (1995), 'The 1991 Census of Population in England and Wales', with discussion, *Journal of the Royal Statistical Society*, Series A, 158: 203–40.

Thomson, K. (1995), 'Working mothers: choice or circumstance?', in R. Jowell *et al.* (eds.), *British Social Attitudes—the 12th Report*, Aldershot, Hants: Dartmouth, 61–91.

Thurow, L. (1969), *Poverty and Discrimination*, Washington: Brookings Institution.

Tilly, C. (1991), 'Reasons for the continuing growth of part-time employment', *Monthly Labor Review*, 114/3: 10–18.

Tomaskovic-Devey, D. (1993), *Gender and Racial Inequality at Work: The Sources and Consequences of Job Segregation*, Ithaca, NY: ILR Press.

Treiman, D.J. (1977), *Occupational Prestige in Comparative Perspective*, New York: Academic Press.

—— (1985), 'The work histories of women and men: What we know and what we need to find out', in A. S. Rossi (ed.), *Gender and the Life Course*, New York: Aldine, 213–31.

van Doorne-Huiskes, A., van Hoof, J., and Roelofs, E. (1995) (eds.), *Women and the European Labour Markets*, London: Paul Chapman.

Varesi, A., and Villa, P. (1986), *Homeworking in Italy, France and the United Kingdom, Final Report*, Brussels: European Commission.

Vogler, C. (1994), 'Segregation, sexism and labour supply', in A. M. Scott (ed.), *Gender Segregation and Social Change*, Oxford: Oxford University Press, 39–79.

Wagner, D.G., Ford, R.S., and Ford, T.W. (1986), 'Can gender inequalities be reduced?', *American Sociological Review*, 51: 47–61.

Waite, L.J., and Berryman, S.E. (1986), 'Job stability among young women: A comparison of traditional and non-traditional occupations', *American Journal of Sociology*, 92: 568–95.

Walby, S. (1986), *Patriarchy at Work*, Cambridge: Polity Press.

—— (1990), *Theorising Patriarchy*, Oxford: Blackwell.

Wareing, A. (1992), 'Working arrangements and patterns of working hours in Britain', *Employment Gazette*, 100: 88–100.

Warr, P. (1982), 'A national study of non-financial employment commitment', *Journal of Occupational Psychology*, 55: 297–312.

Watkins, D., Stanworth, J., and Westrip, A. (1982) (eds.), *Stimulating Small Firms*, Aldershot: Gower.

—— and Watkins, J. (1982), 'The female entrepreneur—American experience and its implications for the UK', in J. Stanworth *et al.* (eds.), *Perspectives on a Decade of Small Business*, Aldershot: Gower.

—— —— (1984), 'The female entrepreneur, her background and determinants of business choice: some British data', *International Small Business Journal*, 2: 21–31.

Watson, G. (1992), 'Hours of work in Great Britain and Europe: evidence from the UK and European Labour Force Surveys', *Employment Gazette*, 100: 539–57.

—— (1994), 'The flexible workforce and patterns of working hours in the UK', *Employment Gazette*, 102: 239–47.

Watts, M. (1993), 'Explaining trends in occupational segregation: some comments', *European Sociological Review*, 9: 315–19.

—— (1994), 'A critique of marginal matching', *Work, Employment and Society*, 8: 421–31.

—— (forthcoming), 'Measurement of occupational gender segregation: some comments', *Journal of the Royal Statistical Society*, Series A.

—— and Rich, J. (1992), 'Occupational sex segregation in the UK 1979–89: the role of part-time employment', *International Review of Applied Economics*, 6: 286–308.

Wedderburn, A. (1995) (ed.), *Part-Time Work*, Bulletin of European Studies on Time No. 8; Dublin: European Foundation.

Wharton, A.S., and Baron, J.N. (1987), 'So happy together? The impact of gender segregation on men at work', *American Sociological Review*, 52: 574–87.

Wickham, J. (1997), 'Part-time work in Ireland and Europe: who wants what where?', *Work, Employment and Society*, 11: 133–51.

Willborn, S.L. (1989), *A Secretary and a Cook: Challenging Women's Wages in the Courts of the United States and Great Britain*, Ithaca, NY: ILR Press.

Williams, C.L. (1993) (ed.), *Doing Women's Work: Men in Nontraditional Occupations*, London: Sage.

Williams, G. (1976), 'Trends in occupational differentiation by sex', *Sociology of Work and Occupations*, 3: 38–62.

Wright, E.O. (1985), *Classes*, London: Verso.

—— Baxter, J., and Birkelund, G.E. (1995), 'The gender gap in workplace authority: a cross-national study', *American Sociological Review*, 60: 407–35.

Zabalza, A., and Tzannatos, Z. (1988), 'Reply to comments on the effects of Britain's anti-discrimination legislation on relative pay and employment', *Economic Journal*, 98: 839–43.

Zighera, J. (1996), 'How to measure and compare female activity in the European Union', in P. Beckmann (ed.), *Gender Specific Occupational Segregation, Beiträge zur Arbeitsmarkt- und Berufsforschung* (Monographs on Employment Research), No. 188, Nuremberg: Institute for Employment Research of the Federal Employment Services (IAB), 89–105.

AUTHOR INDEX

SUBJECT INDEX